The Peace of Nicias and
the Sicilian Expedition

The Peace of Nicias and the Sicilian Expedition

DONALD KAGAN

Cornell University Press

ITHACA AND LONDON

First published 1981 by Cornell University Press.
Fourth printing 1992.
First printing, Cornell Paperbacks, 1991.
Third printing 1996.

International Standard Book Number 0-8014-1367-2 (cloth)
International Standard Book Number 0-8014-9940-2 (paper)
Library of Congress Catalog Card Number 81-3150
Printed in the United States of America
*Librarians: Library of Congress cataloging information
appears on the last page of the book.*

⊗ The paper in this book meets the minimum requirements of the American
National Standard for Information Sciences—Permanence of Paper for Printed
Library Materials, ANSI Z39.48-1984.

For my son Fred

Preface

This book is the third volume of a projected history of the Peloponnesian War, which I will complete with a fourth volume carrying the story down to the surrender of Athens in 404 B.C. The present book deals with the period from the Peace of Nicias in 421 to the destruction of the Athenian expedition against Sicily in 413. Although the period is generally divided into two parts, as it is in this book, I believe that it demonstrates a basic unity; its tale is of the failure of an unsatisfactory peace. The Sicilian expedition, though not the inevitable result of the inadequacies of the peace, arose from those shortcomings. I believe that the period is further unified by its central character, Nicias, whose policy dominated its first part, whose leadership dominated the second, and whose personality, talents, and flaws were so important for the shape and outcome of both. My purpose in this volume, as in the earlier ones, is to illuminate the course of events by examining the ancient accounts critically in order to reveal, especially, the close relationship between domestic politics and foreign policy.

For the reasons given in my preface to *The Archidamian War*, I have continued to follow Thucydides' annalistic organization. I again treat later, non-Thucydidean sources such as Plutarch and Diodorus with respect if not, I hope, with gullibility. This practice has drawn some criticism, but my work persuades me more than ever that the ancients knew more about the fifth century than Thucydides chose, or was able, to tell us, and that careful use of other sources can increase our understanding.

I also continue to treat the speeches in Thucydides as honest attempts to produce some semblance of the arguments made in speeches that were actually given, whatever they may be in addition. I have lately tried to justify this practice in an article called "The Speeches in Thucydides and the Mytilene Debate" (*Yale Classical Studies* 24 [1975], 71–94). Further arguments in defense of both practices are found at appropriate places in this volume.

Again I must acknowledge my obvious debt to the fundamental work of Georg Busolt. In this volume more than in the earlier ones I have benefited much from the perceptive and pioneering work of George Grote. There are many scholars of our own time to whom I owe important debts; among them I must give special mention to Antony Andrewes and K. J. Dover, whose work on the fourth volume of A. W. Gomme's commentary on Thucydides is an indispensable aid to historians, and to Russell Meiggs and David Lewis for their edition of the Greek inscriptions.

I am grateful to Heinrich von Staden, Paul Rahe, Barry Strauss, and Alvin Bernstein for their criticism of parts or all of the manuscript. I am also indebted to the A. Whitney Griswold Fund of Yale University for defraying the cost of typing.

Donald Kagan

New Haven, Connecticut

Contents

Maps

Abbreviations and Short Titles

AHR	*American Historical Review*
AJA	*American Journal of Archaeology*
AJP	*American Journal of Philology*
ASI	E. Badian, ed., *Ancient Society and Institutions*
ATL	B. D. Meritt, H. T. Wade-Gery, and M. F. McGregor, *The Athenian Tribute Lists*
BCH	*Bulletin de correspondance hellénique*
Beloch, *AP*	K. J. Beloch, *Die Attische Politik seit Perikles*
Beloch, *GG²*	K. J. Beloch, *Griechische Geschichte*, 2d ed.
BICS	*Bulletin of the Institute of Classical Studies of the University of London*
BSA	*Proceedings of the British School at Athens*
Busolt, *Forsch.*	G. Busolt, *Forschungen zur Griechischen Geschichte*
Busolt, *GG*	G. Busolt, *Griechische Geschichte*
Busolt and Swoboda, *GS*	Georg Busolt and Heinrich Swoboda, *Griechische Staatskunde*
CAH	*Cambridge Ancient History*
CP	*Classical Philology*
CQ	*Classical Quarterly*
CR	*Classical Review*
Davies, *APF*	J. K. Davies, *Athenian Propertied Families*
FGrH	F. Jacoby, *Die Fragmente der griechischen Historiker*
Fornara, *Generals*	C. Fornara, *The Athenian Board of Generals*
Freeman, *History of Sicily*	E. A. Freeman, *A History of Sicily*
GHI	R. Meiggs and D. Lewis, *A Selection of Greek Historical Inscriptions*

Gilbert, *Beiträge*	G. Gilbert, *Beiträge zur innern geschichte Athens*
Gomme, *Essays*	A. W. Gomme, *Essays in Greek History and Literature*
Gomme, *More Essays*	A. W. Gomme, *More Essays in Greek History and Literature*
GRBS	*Greek, Roman, and Byzantine Studies*
Green, *Armada*	P. Green, *Armada from Athens*
Grote	George Grote, *A History of Greece*
HCT	A. W. Gomme, A. Andrewes, and K. J. Dover, *A Historical Commentary on Thucydides*
Hatzfeld, *Alcibiade*	J. Hatzfeld, *Alcibiade: Etude sur l'histoire d'Athènes à la fin du Ve siècle*
Henderson, *Great War*	B. W. Henderson, *The Great War between Athens and Sparta*
Hignett, *HAC*	C. Hignett, *A History of the Athenian Constitution*
HSCP	*Harvard Studies in Classical Philology*
IG	*Inscriptiones Graecae*
JHS	*Journal of Hellenic Studies*
Kagan, *Outbreak*	D. Kagan, *The Outbreak of the Peloponnesian War*
Kagan, *Archidamian War*	D. Kagan, *The Archidamian War*
Meyer, *Forsch.* II	E. Meyer, *Forschungen zur alten Geschichte*, II
Meyer, *GdA*	E. Meyer, *Geschichte des Altertums*
PCPhS	*Proceedings of the Cambridge Philological Society*
PW	A. Pauly, G. Wissowa, and W. Kroll, *Realenzyklopädie der klassischen Altertumswissenschaft*
REG	*Revue des études grecques*
RIL	*Rendiconti dell' Istituto Lombardo, Classe di Lettere, Scienze morali e storiche*
Riv. Fil.	*Rivista di Filologia e di Istruzione Classica*
RSC	*Rivista di Studi Classici*
Ste. Croix, *Origins*	G. E. M. de Ste. Croix, *The Origins of the Peloponnesian War*
TAPA	*Transactions of the American Philological Association*
Tod	M. N. Tod, *A Selection of Greek Historical Inscriptions*
Westlake, *Essays*	H. D. Westlake, *Essays on the Greek Historians and Greek History*

The Peace of Nicias and the Sicilian Expedition

Part One

The Unraveling
of the Peace

In March of 421, after ten years of devastating, disruptive, and burdensome war, the Athenians and the Spartans made peace on behalf of themselves and those of their allies for whom they could speak. Weariness, the desire for peace, the desire of the Athenians to restore their financial resources, the Spartans' wish to recover their men taken prisoner at Sphacteria in 425 and to restore order and security to the Peloponnesus, the removal by death in battle of the leading advocate of war in each city—all helped to produce a treaty that most Greeks hoped would bring a true end to the great war. In fact, the peace lasted no more than eight years, for in the spring of 413, Agis, son of Archidamus, led a Peloponnesian army into Attica, ravaged the land as his father had done eighteen years earlier, and took the further step of establishing a permanent fort at Decelea.[1]

Ever since antiquity the peace has borne the name of Nicias,[2] the man who more than any other brought it into being, de-

---

[1] 7.19.1-2. All references are to Thucydides unless otherwise indicated. The precise duration of the formal peace is much debated, for Thucydides' remark in 5.25.3 that Athens and Sparta held off from invading each other's territory καὶ ἐπὶ ἓξ ἔτη μὲν καὶ δέκα μῆνας ἀπέσχοντο μὴ ἐπὶ τὴν ἑκατέρων γῆν στρατεῦσαι, cannot be squared with his account of the Athenian attack on Laconia in the summer of 414. Since Thucydides himself emphasizes that fighting continued throughout the entire period, the point is not of great importance. Modern scholars treat the entire period from the peace of 421 to the destruction of the Sicilian expedition as a unit. For a good discussion of the chronological problems see *HCT* IV, 6-9.

[2] Andoc. 3.8; Plut. *Nic.* 9.7, *Alc.* 14.2.

fended it, and worked to maintain it. Although the years 421–413 easily fall into two phases, before and after the Athenians launched their invasion of Sicily, the entire period is given unity by the central role played in it by Nicias. Relations between Greek states and between Athenian factions were volatile in these years, but Athens remained the vital and active power in the Greek system of states, and Nicias was the central figure in Athens. Stodgier, less spoken of, and less impressive than his brilliant contemporary Alcibiades, he nonetheless was more responsible than anyone else for the course of events. The death of Cleon had left Nicias without a political opponent who could match his own experience and stature. The Athenian defeats at Megara and Delium and the loss of Amphipolis and other northern cities made Nicias' repeated arguments for restraint and a negotiated peace with Sparta seem wise in retrospect. His chain of successful campaigns unblemished by defeat and his reputation for extraordinary piety further strengthened his appeal to the Athenian voters. At no time since the death of Pericles had an Athenian politician had a comparable opportunity to achieve a position of leadership and to place his own stamp on the policy of Athens. As it is natural to connect the outcome of the Archidamian War with the plans and conduct of Pericles, so it is appropriate and illuminating to see how the outcome of the Peace of Nicias, in both its phases, was, to a great extent, the product of the plans and conduct of the man most responsible for creating it and seeking to make it effective.

1. A Troubled Peace

No amount of relief and rejoicing by the Spartan and Athenian signers of the Peace of Nicias could conceal its deficiencies. The very ratification of the peace revealed its tenuous and unsatisfactory character, for the Boeotians, Eleans, and Megarians rejected the treaty and refused to swear the oaths.[1] Nor did Sparta's recently acquired allies in Amphipolis and the rest of the Thraceward region accept the peace, which required them once again to submit to the unwelcome rule of Athens.[2] The Spartans and Athenians drew lots to see who should take the first step in carrying out the treaty, and the Spartans lost. An ancient story says that Nicias used his great personal wealth to assure the outcome, but if the story is true he wasted his money.[3] The Spartans, to be sure, returned such Athenian prisoners as they held and sent an embassy to Clearidas, their governor in Amphipolis, ordering him to surrender Amphipolis and force the other cities of the neighborhood to accept the peace treaty (see Map 1). Sparta's allies in Thrace refused the demand and, even worse, Clearidas did the same. In defense of his refusal, Clearidas pointed to the Amphipolitans' unwillingness to yield and his own inability to force them, but, in fact, he himself was unsympathetic to the order and unwilling to carry it out.[4] He hurried back to Sparta to defend himself against possible charges

[1] 5.17.2.
[2] 5.35.3.
[3] Thucydides (5.21.1) mentions no chicanery. Plutarch (*Nic.* 10.1) tells the tale, attributing it to Theophrastus.
[4] 5.21.1-2. Thucydides says Clearidas refused the order "to please the Chalcidians."

of disobedience and to see if the terms of the treaty could be changed. Although he learned that the peace was already binding, Clearidas returned to Amphipolis with slightly but significantly modified orders: he was to "restore Amphipolis, if possible, but if not, to withdraw whatever Peloponnesians were in it."[5]

These orders were a clear breach of both the spirit and the letter of the peace. The treaty required the Spartans to restore the city to Athens, not to abandon it to the enemies of Athens. The restoration of Amphipolis was Athens' foremost material aim in making peace, and the Spartans not only failed to deliver it but tacitly condoned their governor's conspiracy to keep it out of Athenian hands. Sparta's first action was not likely to inspire trust among the Athenians.[6]

The continued resistance of Sparta's nearer allies further threatened the chances for continued peace. Clearidas' visit to Sparta must have come at least two weeks after the signing of the Peace of Nicias, but the allied delegates were still there.[7] The Spartans must have spent the intervening time trying to persuade them to accept the treaty, but with no success. Each ally had good reasons for rejecting the peace. Megara had suffered repeated ravages of her farmland and an attack on the city that almost put it into Athenian hands. Worse yet, its main port on the Saronic Gulf, Nisaea, had fallen under Athenian control and the peace did not restore it. This loss threatened both the economy and security of Megara (see Map 2). Elis rejected the peace because of a private quarrel with Sparta.[8]

The Boeotians' refusal to accept the peace is harder to explain. Thucydides' narrative reveals that they refused to restore to the Athenians either the border fortress of Panactum, which they

---

[5] 5.21.3.

[6] Eduard Meyer (Forsch. II, 353) argued that Clearidas was not able to turn Amphipolis over to Athens, but the account of Thucydides makes it clear that he could, but did not want to, alleging his inability as a pretext: οὐδὲ ὁ Κλεαρίδας παρέδωκε τὴν πόλιν, χαριζόμενος τοῖς Χαλκιδεῦσι, λέγων ὡς οὐ δυνατὸς εἴη βίᾳ ἐκείνων παραδιδόναι. See Busolt, GG III:2, 1200, n. 1, and HCT III, 690.

[7] 5.22.1; Busolt, GG III:2, 1200, n. 2.

[8] 5.31; Kagan, Archidamian War, 335.

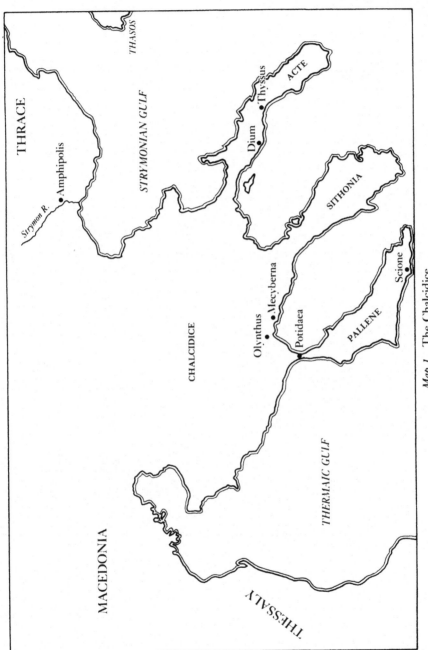

Map 1. The Chalcidice

Map 2. Attica and Boeotia

had seized in 422, or the Athenian prisoners taken in the Archidamian War. But these were not reasons for the Boeotian unwillingness to accept the peace, merely evidences of it. Though Thucydides explains the motives of the other recalcitrant allies of Sparta he does not do so for the Boeotians, so we can only speculate. The Boeotians, led by the Thebans, seem to have acted out of fear. Theban power, prestige, and ambition had grown greatly during the war. In 431, or soon thereafter, the citizens of Erythrae, Scaphae, Scolus, Aulis, Schoenus, Potniae, and many other small unwalled towns had migrated to Thebes and settled down, doubling the size of the city[9] (see Map 2). In 427 the Spartans gained control of Plataea and turned it over to their Theban allies. Within a short time the Thebans destroyed the city and occupied its territory.[10] Probably then, or soon after, the number of Thebes' votes in the Boeotian federal council was increased from two to four; "two for their own city and two on behalf of Plataea, Scolus, Erythrae, Scaphae," and a number of other small towns.[11]

The power and influence of the Thebans had been further increased by the leading part they played in the victory over the Athenians at Delium.[12] They took advantage of this new power in the summer of 423 when they destroyed the walls of Thespiae on the grounds that the Thespians sympathized with Athens. "They [the Thebans] had always wanted to do this, but it was now easier to accomplish since the flower of the Thespians had been destroyed in the battle against the Athenians [at Delium]."[13] Since these gains had occurred while Athens was distracted by a major war against the Peloponnesians, the Peace of Nicias was a threat to the new Theban position. The end of

[9]*Hellenica Oxyrhynchia* XII, 3 = XVII, 3 in the Teubner edition of Bartoletti. See also I. A. F. Bruce, *An Historical Commentary on the Hellenica Oxyrhynchia* (Cambridge, 1967), 114.

[10]3.68.

[11]*Hellenica Oxyrhynchia* XI, 3 = XVI, 3. See also Bruce, *Historical Commentary*, 104-106, and J. A. O. Larsen, *Greek Federal States* (Oxford, 1968), pp. 37-38.

[12]4.91.1; Kagan, *Archidamian War*, 283-286.

[13]4.133.1. Larsen (*Greek Federal States*, 34 and 37) suggests that it may also have been at this time that the Thebans weakened their traditional enemy Orchomenus by removing Chaeronea from its control.

Sparta's treaty with Argos, and the discontent and disaffection of Corinth, Elis, and Mantinea guaranteed that the Spartans would be fully occupied in the Peloponnesus. They could not, even if they would, prevent the Athenians, newly freed from other concerns, from interfering in Boeotia. The democratic and separatist forces in the Boeotian cities would surely seek help from the Athenians, who might be glad to assist them in hopes of restoring the control over Boeotia which they had exercised between the battles of Oenophyta and Coronea. So frightened were the Thebans that, even while rejecting the Peace of Nicias, they negotiated an unusual, if not unique, truce with the Athenians whereby the original cessation of hostilities was for ten days; after that, termination by either side would require ten days' notice.[14] Such fears, along with great ambitions, made the Thebans hope for the renewal of a war that would lead to the defeat of Athens and the destruction of its power.[15]

Of all Sparta's allies Corinth was least satisfied with the peace. None of the grievances that had led the Corinthians to push the Spartans toward war in 431 had been removed. Potidaea was firmly in Athenian hands, its citizens, descendants of Corinthian colonists, driven from their homes and scattered. The island of Corcyra remained allied to Athens, and Megara was intimidated by the Athenian garrison at Nisaea. Corinth, moreover, had suffered territorial losses in the northwest. Sollium and Anactorium remained in hostile hands, and Corinthian influence throughout the entire region had been destroyed (see Map 3). Only the destruction of Athenian power would enable Corinth to achieve the restoration of her former position, so the Corinthians rejected the peace and sought to disrupt the diplomatic situation that emerged from it.

The continued refusal of their allies to accept the peace left the Spartans in a dangerous situation. They could not bring their allies into the treaty; they could not compel the Boeotians to

---

[14]5.26.2. Thucydides calls the truce an ἐχεχειρίαν δεχήμερον. I follow the very sensible interpretation of Andrewes in HCT IV, 11.

[15]We may get some idea of Theban war aims from the demand they made at the end of the Peloponnesian War that the city of Athens be destroyed (Xen. Hell. 2.2.19).

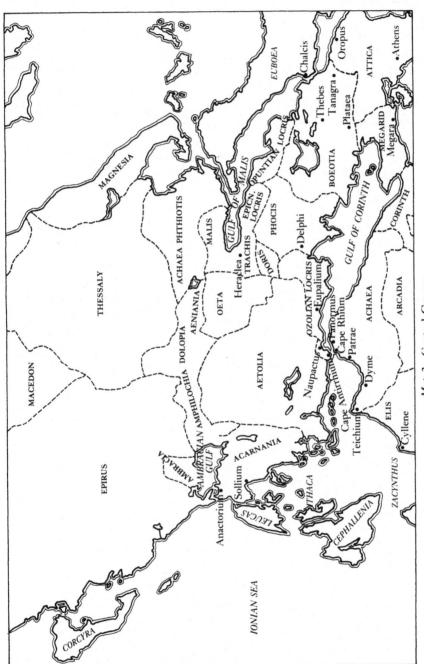

Map 3. Central Greece

restore Panactum; they would not restore Amphipolis. This dip-lomatic impasse threatened to produce an Athenian reaction against the policy of Nicias and a repudiation of his peace. Even if the Athenians were unwilling to go so far, they would cer-tainly refuse to restore Pylos and Cythera or, most important, to return the prisoners taken at Sphacteria. The alienation of Athens was especially dangerous for it would encourage the menacing ambitions of Argos, which had already indicated its unwillingness to renew its treaty with Sparta.[16] The prospect of an Argive-Athenian alliance, probably joined by such disaffected states as Elis and Mantinea, was a nightmare for the Spartans and it forced them to seek some way out of the situation that favored it.[17]

As a solution, the Spartans abandoned their attempt to per-suade their recalcitrant allies and instead offered a defensive al-liance to the Athenians. The alliance, like the peace, was in-tended to last fifty years. Each side promised to defend the other against attack and to regard the attackers as a common enemy. In addition, the Athenians pledged to assist the Spartans in case of a helot rebellion. A final clause permitted changes in the terms of the alliance by mutual consent.[18] As a token of good faith in their new allies the Athenians surrendered the Spartan prisoners whom they had held since 425.[19]

The language of Thucydides implies that the request for the alliance came from the Spartans and that it was a response to the immediate problem, rather than the fulfillment of a bargain made during the negotiations for the Peace of Nicias.[20] There is little reason to doubt either implication, for the peace negotiators could not have known that things would turn out so badly, and, as we have seen, the Spartans were in desperate need of the Athenian alliance.[21] The question is: why did the Athenians

[16]5.22.2.
[17]See Kagan, *Archidamian War*, 334-335.
[18]5.23.
[19]5.24.2.
[20]5.22.2: ὡς δ᾽ αὐτῶν οὐκ ἐσήκουον, ἐκείνους μὲν [the allies]ἀπέπεμψαν, αὐτοὶ δὲ [the Spartans]πρὸς τοὺς ᾽Αθηναίους ξυμμαχίαν ἐποιοῦντο.
[21]F. E. Adcock (*CAH* V., 253) and W. S. Ferguson (*CAH* V., 256) argue that the alliance had been prearranged during the negotiations for the peace.

agree to the alliance and hand over the prisoners who had been their security against invasion, even though the Spartans had failed to carry out their earlier agreements? Most Athenians, of course, still wanted peace, and without the alliance the Peace of Nicias was threatened with collapse. It has been suggested that the alliance at least guaranteed Athens against attack by the states that rejected the peace.[22] But if the Athenians retained the Spartan prisoners and the Spartans lived in fear of an Argive attack, there was no chance of Peloponnesian support for an attack by the Megarians, Boeotians, or Corinthians, and without that support they presented little danger. In fact, the ten days' truces that the Boeotians sought from the Athenians and the Corinthians' attempts to share them[23] are evidence that these dissident states feared attack by the Athenians more than vice versa. It has also been suggested that the Athenians may have hoped that the alliance would broaden the rift between the Spartans and their allies.[24] Although there is no doubt that the dissident allies cited the alliance as grounds for their discontent, this appears to have been only a pretext. Their dissent in fact predated the alliance and stemmed from more basic complaints. The rift would have widened in any case. It is even likely that the absence of an alliance would have encouraged Argos, Elis, and Mantinea to press forward more quickly and firmly.

Nicias and his Athenian supporters accepted the alliance with Sparta for reasons both deeper and less tangible. Nicias and the

---

This view is based on the belief that "Athens had won the war," but that "Sparta was not yet so reduced that she could be forced to face the risks of the Peace without the security of the alliance" (253). But Athens had not won the war, and it was Sparta that had forced Athens to accept the peace by threatening to establish a fort in Attica. (See 5.17.2 and Kagan, *Archidamian War,* 346–347.) Grote (VII, 4–5) suggests that Nicias and Laches may have proposed the idea to the Spartans. It is not unlikely that the Spartans discussed the matter with Nicias before making their proposal. It would be chiefly his job to persuade the Athenians, and his support was vital. Plutarch (*Nic.* 10.2) goes so far as to say that Nicias persuaded the Spartans and Athenians to add the alliance to the peace, but Thucydides' account seems preferable.

[22]Busolt, *GG* III:2, 1205.

[23]5.26.2 and 5.32.5.

[24]This point is made by Meyer, *Forsch.* II, 353, and accepted by Busolt, *GG* III:2, 1205.

politicians who surrounded him had strong personal and political reasons for wanting the alliance. Sparta's failure to hand over Amphipolis or to bring the major dissident states into the peace threatened to discredit both the peace policy and the men who advocated it, but we would be mistaken to think that such concerns were paramount. We have no reason to doubt that Nicias and his supporters welcomed the alliance for itself and looked upon it as a great achievement. Since her rise as an imperial power Athens had alternated between two different policies toward Sparta. First, under Cimon's leadership, the Athenians had maintained friendly relations with the Spartans, even offering help in time of need. Then, led by Ephialtes and Pericles, they had fought the First Peloponnesian War in the hope of achieving supremacy. When that war ended the Athenians were lucky to have escaped with their empire, army, navy, and fields intact. Between 445 and the outbreak of the great Peloponnesian War they had tried to keep the peace on the basis of mutually discrete spheres of influence. In the Archidamian War they reluctantly returned to fighting and emerged with a population reduced by a third, their homes, fields, trees, and vines destroyed, and their treasury depleted. As early as 425 Nicias had wanted to accept the Spartan offer of peace and an alliance, and intervening events must have led him to regret the lost chance more than ever. The idea of a Spartan alliance aroused visions of a return to the happy and glorious policy of Cimon.[25] The alliance offered by the Spartans in 421, in fact, might seem to have exceeded what Cimon had achieved. In Cimon's day the Spartans had been the unquestioned leaders of the Greeks while the Athenians were one among a number of allied states. The alliance of 421, on the other hand, was concluded by two powers, each claiming an equal part in the hegemony over the rest of Greece; furthermore, it was an alliance that the Spartans had been forced to seek in order to obtain Athenian protection.

The Cimonian policy had been good for Athens, allowing the Athenians to expand their Aegean empire and increase their prosperity free of warfare on the Greek mainland. But in 462 that policy had shattered on the rock of Spartan suspicion and

[25]The comparison with the Cimonian policy is made by Meyer, *Forsch.* II, 293 and 355; Beloch, *GG* II:21, 345; and Busolt, *GG* III:2, 1204.

jealousy.[26] There had always been a core of Spartans hostile to Athens and unwilling to recognize her empire or her equality with Sparta. In the early part of the century, and especially while the philo-Laconian Cimon was Athens' leading politician, these anti-Athenian Spartans were in the minority, but at crucial moments they could bring over the more placid and conservative Spartans and impose their policy.[27] They were able to do so in 446/45, when the rebellions of Megara and Euboea made Athens vulnerable.[28] In 440, when Samos rebelled, they were able to summon a meeting of the Peloponnesian League to consider joining with the Samians. Only the resistance of their allies led by Corinth prevented the Spartans from attacking Athens.[29] This same Spartan faction was, of course, able to persuade its countrymen to go to war against Athens in 431. Even more significantly, the Spartans rejected the Athenian offer of peace in 430.[30] Their own offer of peace and an alliance in 425 arose because of their defeat at Sphacteria and their desperation to recover the prisoners taken there.[31] Even if the majority of Spartans sincerely wanted peace and an alliance in 421 there was little reason to believe they would continue to do so after the immediate danger had passed. Ten years of hard fighting had not softened Spartan feelings toward Athens, and Spartan policy could be volatile. Each year new ephors were elected, and they could bring with them an entirely new outlook. The fact is that, even though the Athenians concluded the alliance and restored the prisoners, the new board of ephors that took office early in the autumn of 421 included at least two men hostile to the peace treaty.[32]

[26]Kagan, *Outbreak*, 72–73.

[27]For a useful discussion of the attitude of Spartans toward Athens see Ste. Croix, *Origins*, 169–210. Although I believe he overestimates the continuing influence of the faction hostile to Athens (he calls them "hawks"), he is right in saying that there was "at times a large and influential group of Spartans which deeply resented the transference from Sparta to Athens of the leadership of the anti-Persian alliance and the resulting growth of Athenian power, and wished to regain the hegemony by force" (169).

[28]1.114.

[29]1.40.5-6; 41.1-3. See also Ste. Croix, *Origins*, 200–203, and Meiggs, *Athenian Empire* (Oxford, 1972), 190, 461–462.

[30]2.59; Kagan, *Archidamian War*, 80–85.

[31]4.19.1, 4.18; Kagan, *Archidamian War*, 234.

[32]5.36.1; *HCT* IV, 38.

In 421 a Cimonian policy was no longer possible. Cimon and his Spartan counterparts had been able to build on the recent memory of glorious and successful collaboration between Athens and Sparta against the Persians. In 479 Athens was not yet a great imperial power and a threat to Spartan hegemony; the Spartans and Athenians had never fought a serious war against each other. After the Peace of Nicias all was otherwise. Recent memories were of long and bitter wars between the two cities and of continuing rivalry. There was little, if any, goodwill on which to build an enduring peace. Trust could not be assumed but must be earned. In that sense the alliance may even have damaged the chances for peace, for it allowed Sparta to continue to ignore its obligations under the peace treaty and thereby increased Athenian mistrust.[33]

Nicias and his associates did not view the situation so darkly. They had wanted to accept the Spartan offer in 425 and must have believed that events between 425 and 421 had proven them right. The failure of the Megarian and Boeotian campaigns and the defeats at Delium and Amphipolis showed the futility of further fighting. Why not, they might have reasoned, give peace a chance? Since Athens was in a stronger position and Sparta apparently was not willing to fulfill its commitment, did it not behoove the Athenians to act generously, to take the first step in the hope of creating a climate of mutual trust? Such feelings may be laudable and sometimes effective, but in 421 they were foolish. No mere gesture could make the Spartans restore Amphipolis, but until they did so, most Athenians would be disappointed, suspicious, and angry. The result must be to increase rather than reduce tension. It is hard to disagree with Grote's assessment that "there was never any public recommendation of Kleon . . . so ruinously impolitic as this alliance with Sparta and surrender of the captives."[34]

[33]Grote says that "the alliance, in fact, prevented the peace from being fulfilled" (VII, 7). My reliance on Grote here and throughout the volume will be evident. Although his understanding of Athenian politics is too rigid and formal, too reminiscent of the English politics of his own day, his understanding of the period is wonderfully shrewd and perceptive.

[34]Grote, VII, 8. For the most vigorous attack on Grote's interpretation see Meyer, *Forsch.* II, 352ff.

If the acceptance of the Spartan alliance was a mistake, it remains to ask what else Athens could have done. On the assumption that Spartan hostility and jealousy were bound to persist and that lasting peace was impossible without a major change in the balance of power, a rare, perhaps unique opportunity seemed to present itself. The Athenians could encourage a new coalition led by Argos and joined by the other democratic states of the Peloponnesus, Elis and Mantinea. They could join this new alliance themselves, send an army into the Peloponnesus, and force a battle in which the odds would no longer be powerfully against them. They could improve those odds by distracting the Spartans with helot raids launched from Pylos and raids on coastal towns from the sea. A victory in such a battle would probably put an end to the Peloponnesian League and to Spartan power, as the Theban victory at Leuctra did fifty years later. A defeat, though unpleasant, would not be a disaster. Such a policy soon appealed to some Athenians, but not in 421. War-weariness was still the dominant feeling and Nicias still the great figure in Athenian politics. Cleon might have chosen such an aggressive policy, as he had in 425, and he would have had the persuasive ability and stature to challenge Nicias. But Cleon was dead, and he had no successor of equal ability.[35]

If an aggressive policy was impossible in 421, could not the Athenians have made a better bargain? At least they could have insisted on the restoration of Amphipolis before making the alliance and returning the Spartan prisoners.[36] It is, however, unlikely that the Spartans would send an army to Thrace sufficient to capture Amphipolis, even with Athenian support. They had not done so during the Archidamian War and would surely

[35]Hyperbolus is treated in Old Comedy as the successor of Cleon. See Aristoph. *Peace* 679ff. and *Frogs* 570. He appears to have opposed the Peace of Nicias (*Peace* 918ff.) and in general to have supported an aggressive policy. See Gilbert, *Beiträge*, 209-215. The ancient writers treat him with a disdain they never show Cleon and suggest that he was never so effective. Thucydides, for instance, calls him a μοχθηρὸν ἄνθρωπον, and says he was ostracized διὰ πονηρίαν καὶ αἰσχύνην τῆς πόλεως ... (8.73.3). Alcibiades, whose family had close ties with the Spartans and had once been their *proxenoi* in Athens, had only recently been currying favor with the Spartans and had not yet turned against the peace (5.43.2; 6.89.2).

[36]Such is the suggestion of Grote, VII, 8.

not do so now, when the Peloponnesus was in turmoil. To offer an alliance in exchange for the Spartans' handing over Amphipolis would only emphasize Sparta's failure to carry out her commitments, anger the Athenians, and hasten a breach.

If neither an aggressive policy nor harder bargaining were attractive choices, there remained one other option: the Athenians could refuse the alliance without breaking the Peace of Nicias and allow events to take their course. This plan offered advantages. Without risking any Athenian lives or costing any money Athens could keep the pressure on Sparta. Possession of the Spartan prisoners and the new Argive threat would guarantee Athens against attack. The Argive League would come into being and challenge Spartan supremacy in the Peloponnesus. So long as Athens held aloof from Sparta, the Argives would not be deterred and would, in fact, be encouraged by the prospect of an alliance with Athens in the near future. Helots could escape to Pylos and, perhaps, foment a new rebellion. Further developments cannot be calculated; Sparta might or might not have regained the support of Corinth, Megara, and Boeotia in her struggle for Peloponnesian dominion. With or without these defectors she might or might not have been able to defeat her enemies. In any case, Athens could only have benefited from the turmoil, and an Athenian refusal to join with Sparta would have increased both that turmoil and the danger to Sparta. When we recognize that a course so moderate, so safe, and so promising was available to the Athenians, we can only marvel at their decision to make the alliance.[37]

[37]To Nicias and those who thought like him, however, even such a policy would not have been attractive. For them this was an opportunity not to be missed. If Athens refused the alliance and the Spartans defeated their enemies, there would be no renewal of the offer of the alliance that, they expected, would bring peace and an end to Spartan attacks on the Athenian Empire.

2. The Separate League

After the Spartan-Athenian alliance was concluded, the ambassadors from the Peloponnesian states that the Spartans had been unable to persuade to join in the Peace of Nicias left for home. The Corinthians were an exception. They went instead to Argos, where they held conversations with some of the Argive magistrates.[1] The Corinthians argued that the alliance between Athens and Sparta could have no good purpose, that it must be aimed at the "enslavement of the Peloponnesus," and that the Argives must take the lead in a new alliance to save the Peloponnesians from such a fate.[2] Corinth seemed to be instigating the formation of a separate league, a third force in the Greek world that could stand apart from the two older power blocs and resist their combined forces. Corinth's true motives and goals, however, are far from clear.

The motive that the Corinthians offered for the new coalition, i.e., to protect the Peloponnesians from enslavement by the two great powers, can only have been a pretext. It was evident to Thucydides, it is plain to us, and it could not have escaped the wily and well-informed Corinthians that the Spartan-Athenian alliance was no menace. The Spartans had made it for defensive reasons, to deter an Argive alliance with Athens. The Athenians had made it to save a peace that threatened to fall apart. There was a greater chance that the Athenians and Spartans would come to blows than that they might combine to attack other

---

[1] 5.27.2. I take τινας τῶν ἐν τέλει ὄντων to mean government officials rather than "certain important Argives" (G. T. Griffith, *Historia* I [1950], 237). For my reasons see *HCT* IV, 23.

[2] *HCT* IV, 23.

states in the Peloponnesus.[3] Nor could the Corinthians have intended to replace Spartan leadership of the Peloponnesus with an Argive hegemony. The Argives had no quarrel with Athens, and were not likely to launch a war against her. Corinth, on the other hand, could recover her losses and gain revenge only through such a war; this was why she had refused to join the peace. Moreover, Peloponnesian hegemony by neighboring Argos would be more dangerous to Corinthian autonomy than the preeminence of the Spartans.[4] One scholar has gone so far as to suggest that, for the moment at least, the Corinthians, enraged by Spartan neglect, abandoned the pursuit of their own interests and launched the new policy in search of vengeance.[5] But there is no reason to believe the Corinthians lost their wits on this occasion. They continued to pursue positive goals, the recovery of Sollium and Anactorium and the destruction of Athenian power, and had simply discovered new means to suit the changed conditions. The Corinthians needed to renew the war between Athens and Sparta, and the proposed Argive alliance was a means to that end.[6]

[3]Even Robin Seager (CQ LXX [1976], 249-269), who rejects the usual view of Corinth's motives, concedes that Corinth's story was more likely to be "pure propaganda" (254).

[4]Busolt, GG III:2, 1207.

[5]Seager, CQ LXX (1976), 254: "Corinth's behavior is intelligible only on the assumption that she temporarily set aside her positive aims and followed at this point a totally negative policy designed solely to diminish Sparta.... Corinth set out to take revenge by destroying the League and depriving Sparta of her hegemony within the Peloponnese. To the effects that these developments might have on relations between the Peloponnese and Athens she seems for the moment to have given no thought. Hatred of Athens no doubt sharpened her resentment of Athens, but it played no constructive part in framing her policy." This view implies that the Corinthians, who urged the Spartans on to war because of their grievances against Athens and who suffered further indignities at Athenian hands during the war, forgot all that in their anger at the Spartans. This seems less than plausible.

[6]Surprisingly little has been written about Corinthian motives in this period. Busolt, GG, III:2, 1207, shrewdly observed that the separate league aimed "womöglich die spartanische Politik auf andere Bahnen drängen." Westlake (AJP LXI [1940], 413-421) seems to have been the first to treat the question in depth. He concludes that the Corinthians meant to renew the war, "with the substitution of Argos for Sparta as the formal leader of the adversaries of Athens" (416). For the same view of Corinth's ultimate aim but a different understanding of her plan of achieving it, see D. Kagan, AJP LXXXI (1960), 291-310.

How an Argive alliance could help renew the war, however, is difficult to explain. No policy could guarantee success, and any policy contained an element of uncertainty and risk. The key to the situation lay in Sparta, in the quarrel between its factions and in the psychology of its people. The proponents of the Athenian alliance were the supporters of the Peace of Nicias. They had made the alliance out of fear of Argos, and as long as that fear was allayed Sparta would not be eager for war. If Corinth had taken no action there is good reason to believe that the Argive threat would have disappeared. The past had shown that fear was needed to move the Spartans to war, and no one knew this better than the Corinthians.[7]

One of Corinth's strongest weapons in influencing Spartan policy in the past had been the threat of secession from the Peloponnesian League and the implied threat of an alliance with Argos. The Corinthians had used that threat with great success in helping to goad Sparta to war against Athens in 431.[8] In 421 those Spartans inclined to peace must have thought it a mistake to have been taken in by Corinth's threat, and in brushing off Corinth's complaints about the Peace of Nicias, they called her bluff. If Corinth were to have any influence on Spartan policy, she must first show that the threat of an Argive alliance was real. If such an alliance could be made to include solid oligarchic states like Megara, the Boeotian cities, and Tegea, it could frighten Sparta with the loss of Peloponnesian hegemony to Argos. Control of the Peloponnesian League was the most basic element in Sparta's policy and crucial for her survival; fear of its loss might make the Spartans willing to take up the cause of their disaffected allies and resume the war against Athens. The plan might not succeed, but no other plan had any chance of achieving Corinth's ends.

Such, we may conjecture, was the thinking of those Corinthians who, apparently on their own initiative and without offi-

---

[7]See 1.23.6: τὴν μὲν γὰρ ἀληθεστάτην πρόφασιν, ἀφανεστάτην δὲ λόγῳ, τοὺς Ἀθηναίους ἡγοῦμαι μεγάλους γιγνομένους καὶ φόβον παρέχοντας τοῖς Λακεδαιμονίοις ἀναγκάσαι ἐς τὸ πολεμεῖν. The emphasis is mine. For an account of how the Corinthians had worked upon Spartan fears see 1.68–72 and Kagan, Outbreak, 287–292, 309–310.

[8]1.71.4; Meyer, Forsch. II, 314–315; Kagan, Outbreak, 292, 309–310.

cial sanction, opened discussions with the Argives. If we have understood their purpose rightly, a useful alliance required the membership of at least some of the oligarchic states mentioned above. A league consisting of Argos, Elis, and Mantinea, even joined by Corinth, would not constitute a threat sufficient to outweigh the advantages of Sparta's alliance with Athens. But the Corinthian negotiators had still another reason for persuading oligarchic states to join the new separate league, a reason arising from domestic politics at Corinth.

Although Thucydides' account of the period of the Peace of Nicias gives us a rare insight into the factional struggles within a number of Greek states, he gives us no direct information about internal politics at Corinth. Yet common sense and analogies with other Greek states suggest that there must have been differences of opinion, especially about a major change in policy like the Argive alliance, and that these must sometimes have taken the form of factional divisions. Such divisions certainly appear after the Peloponnesian War,[9] and, though conditions were now different, the later situation may shed some light on Corinthian politics after the Peace of Nicias.

At the outbreak of the Corinthian War in 395, Corinth was governed by a moderate oligarchy, as it had been since the overthrow of the Cypselid tyranny in the sixth century.[10] In 392 the oligarchs, who had brought Corinth into the coalition against Sparta, were challenged by a philo-Laconian group that wanted to end the war and rejoin the Spartan alliance. A plot by their enemies led to a massacre of the pro-Spartan faction. The survivors fled to exile in Sparta, where they spent the rest of the war fighting on the Spartan side against their native city.[11] Xenophon describes this group as *beltistoi*, "the best men," and

---

[9]See Xen. *Hell.* 4.4.1-13; Diod. 14.86 and 91; *Hellenica Oxyrhynchia* II, 3 = VII, 3. See also Kagan, *Historia* XI (1962), 447-457, and C. D. Hamilton, *Historia* XXI (1972), 21-37.

[10]For the character of the oligarchic regime the evidence is in Nicolaus of Damascus in *FGrH* 2A, 60, p. 358. For the interpretation of that passage see Busolt, *GG* I, 658, and Gustav Gilbert, *Handbuch der Griechischen Staatsalterthümer* (Leipzig, 1865), II, 87. For its mildness and moderation see Pindar O.13, and Hdt. 2.67.

[11]Xen. *Hell.* 4.4.

says that they were driven to seek peace in part because "they saw their land being devastated." It seems reasonable to refer to them as landed aristocrats. Their opponents, the ruling oligarchs, were hostile to Sparta and willing to continue the war in spite of the cost to Corinthian agriculture. It is tempting to connect these two groups with somewhat different economic interests: the aristocrats with agriculture and the oligarchs chiefly with commerce.[12] However that may be, there were indeed two factions in respect to foreign policy and relations with Sparta in 392. Although Corinth's problems were less serious in 421, there is no reason to doubt that a similar, if less intense, disagreement arose when the Corinthian ambassadors attempted to form an alliance led by Sparta's traditional enemy. Whatever their goal might have been, their means to achieve it involved a revolution in Corinthian policy, defection from the security of the Peloponnesian League, and alliance with democratic states. Such a program was certain to meet with opposition from conservative, less imaginative Corinthians. The expectation of such resistance helps explain many peculiarities of the Corinthians' behavior, especially their concern to enroll oligarchic states in the new league.

The Corinthians' overtures to the Argives were unusual. There is no evidence that the Corinthian negotiators were empowered to speak for their city; they came to a selection of powerful Argives, not to the assembly or a government council, and they offered a suggestion, not an alliance. No doubt simple caution could help explain both their failure to promise to join the new alliance immediately and their eagerness to keep the negotiations secret,[13] but political problems within Corinth must have played a part as well. The Corinthian activists could not hope to persuade their more cautious fellow citizens to join in an Argive alliance until it was bolstered by some comfortably oligarchic states. The specific procedures that the Corinthians recommended to the Argives were therefore aimed at making it easier for such states to join. They suggested that the Argives vote to

[12]As I did, perhaps too confidently, in *AJP* LXXXI (1960), 291–310, and more fully in *Parola del Passato* LXXX (1961), 333–339.

[13]5.28.2.

allow any autonomous Greek state "to make an alliance with the Argives for mutual defense of their territories, and to appoint a few men with full powers, and not to hold discussions before the people, so that anyone who does not persuade the assembly will not be revealed [as having sought an alliance]."[14] These provisions for secrecy, which enabled states to avoid Spartan anger should negotiations fail, would of course encourage applications to the Argive alliance. They would also allow a faction in some of the cities to test the waters before seeking to bring domestic opponents around to their policy.

The Argives accepted the Corinthian suggestion swiftly and with little alteration. The official bodies voted the necessary decree and appointed twelve men with full powers to negotiate with any state that wished to make an alliance. The only exceptions were Athens and Sparta, which could make alliances only with the consent of their popular assemblies.[15] The Argives greeted the Corinthian proposal as both opportune and welcome. Argive hostility to Sparta went back at least to the middle of the sixth century.[16] The most serious tangible source of dispute was Cynuria, a borderland that lay between the Argolid and Laconia. The Spartans had taken it from Argos in the sixth century, and the Argives had never given up hope of winning it back (see Map 4). Since the Spartans would not accept their demand for the return of Cynuria, and the Thirty Years' Peace between Sparta and Argos was on the point of expiration, the Argives knew that war was inevitable. The years of peace which they enjoyed while the combatants wore each other down in the Archidamian War had enriched the Argives and stimulated their ambition; in 421

[14] 5.27.2.

[15] 5.28.1.

[16] In the fourth century Argive-Spartan enmity was a commonplace and thought to go back much further in history. Xenophon (*Hell.* 3.5.11) has a Theban spokesman ask the Athenians, "Have not the Argives been hostile to the Spartans always?"; Ephorus (in Diodorus 7.13.2) dates warfare between Sparta and Argos to the eighth century B.C.; Aristotle (*Pol.* 1270a) speaks of a war between Sparta and Argos earlier than the Second Messenian War, i.e., prior to the mid-seventh century. Thomas Kelly (*AHR* LXXV [1970], 971–1003, and *CP* LXIX [1974], 81–88) argues that Argive-Spartan hostility was neither so long-standing nor so intense as the ancient sources say, but even he concedes a war between those states in 546 and again in 494.

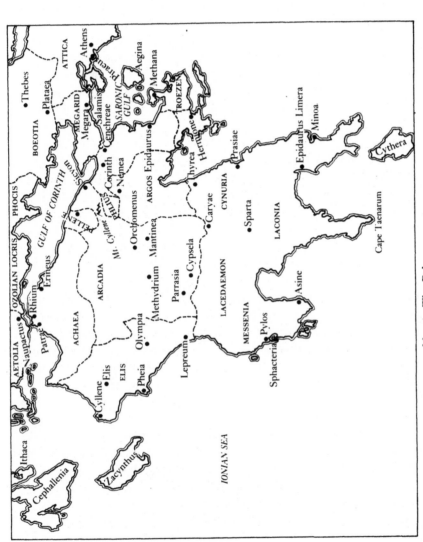

Map 4. The Peloponnesus

they sought nothing less than the hegemony of the Peloponnesus.[17] The barrier to achieving such a position remained Sparta's hoplite army, which despite Sparta's current troubles and disrepute was unbeaten by any other hoplite force and seemingly invincible. To overcome this barrier, the Argives chose one thousand young men who were "strongest in body and in wealth."[18] Freed from all other services to the state and supported at public expense, these men were trained as an elite corps capable of facing the Spartan phalanx. With such means and ambitions the Argives gladly took the road pointed out by the Corinthians.

Mantinea was the first state to make an alliance with Argos. The Mantineans feared an attack by Sparta, for they had expanded their territory at the expense of their neighbors, fought the Tegeans, and built a fort on the Laconian border during the Archidamian War.[19] The alliance with Athens seemed to give Sparta a free hand to punish them, but now Argos loomed as a powerful source of protection, so the Mantineans eagerly made the alliance, the more readily because Mantinea, like Argos, had a democratic constitution. The news of Mantinea's defection caused a great stir among Sparta's allies in the Peloponnesus. Already suspicious of the Spartan-Athenian alliance, especially the clause allowing Sparta and Athens to alter the peace treaty without consulting them, the allies were now impressed by Mantinea's change of sides. They concluded that the Mantineans "knew something more"[20] than they. Increasingly fearful of Spartan and Athenian intentions, they were eager to join the new Argive alliance.

The Spartans soon became aware of what was happening and of the Corinthians' role as instigators. They sent ambassadors to Corinth to complain and to put an end at least to Corinth's role in the intrigue. They accused the Corinthians of starting the whole matter and reminded them that an alliance with Argos would violate the oaths that bound Corinth to Sparta. In fact, since they

[17]5.28.2-3; Diod. 12.75.
[18]Diod. 12.75.7.
[19]5.33.1; Kagan, *Archidamian War*, 334.
[20]5.29.2: νομίσαντες πλέον τέ τι εἰδότας.

had agreed to accept the decision of the majority in the Peloponnesian League, the Corinthians were already violating those
oaths by refusing to accept the Peace of Nicias.[21] Not unprepared for the Spartan embassy, the Corinthians summoned representatives from the other dissident cities to hear both Sparta's
complaints and their own reply. Clearly not all the Corinthians
favored the risky policy supported by the more daring faction,
for even after the rejection of Sparta's complaints and demands
the Corinthian activists were unable to bring their city into the
Argive alliance without delay.[22]

Rising to answer the Spartan attack, the Corinthian activists
directed their remarks to both the conservative Corinthians and
the representatives of the other cities. They had a difficult task.
The oligarchic allies and the conservative Corinthians had both
been loyal followers of Spartan leadership, and they now had to
be persuaded to pursue a policy openly condemned by Sparta.
At this point Thucydides gives us a glimpse of Corinth's true
motive in these complicated maneuvers; she had neither regained
Sollium and Anactorium nor seen the rectification of any of the
other damages done her.[23] But Corinth's spokesmen knew that
complaints about the city's selfish interests were unlikely to sway
the allies, and therefore they kept those concerns to themselves.
Instead, "they offered as a pretext their unwillingness to betray

[21] 5.30.1. That this agreement of the members of the Peloponnesian League
dates from well before the outbreak of the war is demonstrated by 5.30.4: τῶν
παλαιῶν ὅρκων. The point is well made by Andrewes in HCT IV, 25–26. Ste.
Croix (Origins, 101–102) was right to criticize my neglect of this passage in my
description of the Peloponnesian League (Outbreak, 9–30). His arguments,
however, do not alter my belief that the League had few constitutional provisions and that its behavior was determined by practical realities rather than
legal forms. The behavior of Corinth in 421 is good evidence of that. In general,
I would not object to Ste. Croix's formulation: "there were a few basic 'constitutional' rules governing the behaviour of members of the Peloponnesian
League, and that we can clearly identify some of them, even if on occasion they
were ignored or overridden either by Sparta herself or by allies whose position
was strong enough to make it unwise for Sparta to attempt to coerce them"
(122–123). I would merely emphasize that the rules were few and the occasions
when they were ignored or overridden many.

[22] 5.30.5.

[23] 5.30.2: οὔτε Σόλλιον σφίσιν ἀπέλαβον παρ' Ἀθηναίων οὔτε Ἀνακτό-
ριον εἴ τέ τι ἄλλο ἐνόμιζον ἐλασσοῦσθαι.

their allies in Thrace."[24] Their argument may be paraphrased as follows: "We have given our oaths to the Potidaeans and our other Chalcidian friends in the Thracian region. They are still in bondage to the Athenians, and if we agree to the Peace of Nicias, thereby accepting that situation, we will be in violation of our oaths to the gods and heroes. In addition, the oath we took to accept the majority decision includes the clause 'unless there be a hindrance on the part of gods and heroes.' To betray the Chalcidians would surely be such a hindrance. Not we but you are breaking your oaths by abandoning your allies and collaborating with the enslavers of Greece."[25]

This attractive argument portrayed the new alliance as a continuation of the struggle against Athenian tyranny, a means of keeping faith with trusting allies betrayed by Spartan selfishness, not, as it really was, a tool in the policy of aggressive Corinthians.[26] Such an argument was meant to impress and persuade the delegates from the dissident Peloponnesian states, but it was also aimed at those Corinthians still reluctant to adopt the new policy. Perhaps it was also intended to provide ammunition for those Spartans who were opposed to the peace, men who would soon make their presence felt.

After the Spartan ambassadors had left for home, some Argive ambassadors who were present urged the Corinthians to enter into the alliance without further delay. Corinth's power, wealth, and strategic location, coupled with its influence on other states, made it a potentially important partner. The Corinthians' fiery rejection of Sparta's recriminations seemed to make it plain that they were ready to move, but again Corinth delayed. The best the Corinthians could do was ask the Argives to return for another meeting of the assembly.[27] This further delay cannot be attributed entirely to cautious foreign policy.[28] The Corinthians had invited the dissident states to hear their denunciation of

---

[24] 5.30.2: πρόσχημα δὲ ποιούμενοι τοὺς ἐπὶ Θράκης μὴ προδώσειν.

[25] 5.30.3-4. I have elaborated slightly on the spare account of Thucydides by filling in some things he clearly implies or mentions in adjacent passages.

[26] Compare this clever rhetorical performance with the similar one at Sparta in 432 (Kagan, Outbreak, 286-293, 307-309).

[27] 5.30.5.

[28] As Seager (CQ LXX [1976], 254-255) tries to do.

Sparta and their defense and support of the new league. The perfect moment to announce Corinthian membership in the Argive alliance was before the conference at Corinth disbanded. Such an action would encourage others to follow suit; further delay could only make the Corinthians appear ridiculous and raise doubts about their seriousness and honesty. The Corinthians did not move because they could not. The likeliest reason is that the conservatives at Corinth still held back, waiting for more states to join, especially some with comparable constitutions.

The next state to enter the new coalition was Elis, not an oligarchy, but a popular government of a "moderate and stable type—a democracy consciously preserving aristocratic elements, and still more aristocratic in practice than in theory from the fact that it was based not on a close civic but on an open country life."[29] Elis seems to have belonged to that class of states described by Aristotle, in which "the farmer class and the class holding moderate property are sovereign in the state which is governed according to the laws."[30] Although not technically an oligarchy, it seems to have been one of those states in which "the formal constitution is more democratic, but in its social system and customs it is constituted more like an oligarchy."[31] The Eleans were being manipulated by the aggressive faction in Corinth, for they came to make an alliance with the Corinthians before moving on to Argos to conclude an alliance there, "as they had been instructed."[32] If their appearance in Corinth was meant to reduce resistance to Corinthian participation in the new coalition, it served its purpose. "Immediately after [the Eleans]" the Corinthians joined the Argive alliance, taking with them the loyal and fiercely anti-Athenian Chalcidians.[33]

At this point Corinthian plans began to go awry. When ap-

[29]A. H. Greenidge, *A Handbook of Greek Constitutional History* (London, 1896), 213. Aristotle (*Pol.* 1292b 25–35) describes a rural democracy of this type.

[30]Arist. *Pol.* 1292b.

[31]Arist. *Pol.* 1292b.

[32]5.31.1: καθάπερ προείρητο. On the reasons for Elean hostility to Sparta see also Kagan, *Archidamian War*, 335.

[33]5.31.6. For the continued close association between Corinth and the Chalcidians see Westlake, *AJP* LXI (1940), 417.

proached, the Megarians and Boeotians, apparently working together, continued to hold aloof and wait upon events, put off by
the democratic constitution of Argos.[34] Now the Corinthians
turned to Tegea, a solid oligarchy strategically located, whose
defection, they thought, would bring over the whole Peloponnesian League. At least a faction seems to have been willing,[35] but
the Tegeans declined, striking a serious blow at the plan. "The
Corinthians, who had worked eagerly up to then, slackened in
their zeal and became afraid that no one else would join them."[36]

The Corinthians made one last effort to save their scheme.
They asked the Boeotians to join them in the Argive alliance and
"to take other actions in common." This was part of a wily
maneuver, for they had no reason to think the Boeotians had
changed their minds. The Corinthians further asked that the
Boeotians come with them to Athens and obtain for them the
same ten days' truce that the Boeotians had with the Athenians.
Finally, they asked the Boeotians to give assurances that if the
Athenians refused this request, Boeotia would renounce its own
armistice and make no further truce without the Corinthians.

The Corinthians must have acted out of desperation, for their
ploy was obvious and the Athenian answer was bound to be
negative. If the Boeotians agreed to Corinth's request, they
would find themselves unprotected against Athens, tied to
Corinth, and drawn into the Argive coalition. The Boeotians
were not deceived, but received the Corinthian request in a
manner that was friendly but cautious. They continued to delay
a decision in regard to the Argive alliance, but they agreed to go
to Athens and request a truce for Corinth. The Athenians, of
course, refused, answering that if they were indeed the allies of
the Spartans, the Corinthians already had a truce. The Boeotians
continued their own truce with Athens, angering the Corinthians, who in turn claimed that the Boeotians had broken a

---

[34]5.31.6.

[35]In 418 some Tegeans were prepared to hand their city over to the Argive
coalition, forcing Sparta's friends in the city to call on the Spartans to come
quickly or "Tegea would go over to Argos and her allies and was all but in
rebellion already" (5.62; 64.1).

[36]5.32.4. The Tegeans may have been influenced in their refusal by their
recent war against Mantinea (4.134).

promise. The Corinthians had not obtained a truce with Athens, but there was in fact no need for one. The friends of peace controlled Athenian policy, and there was no chance of a resumption of hostilities.[37] Corinth's attempt to renew the war by means of an Argive coalition had failed.

While these complicated diplomatic negotiations went forward, the Athenians finally completed their siege of Scione, killing and enslaving its survivors[38] in accordance with the decree proposed by Cleon in 423. This act of terror still required apology in the fourth century,[39] but it did not restore order in the Chalcidice and the Thracian district of the empire. Amphipolis remained in hostile hands and, later in the summer, the Dians captured the Chalcidic town of Thyssus on the promontory of Athos, though it was allied to Athens.[40] Still, with the friends of peace in control, Athens took no action. It is remarkable that Nicias and his colleagues could not or would not persuade the Athenians to rescind Cleon's decree of harsh punishment for Scione.[41] Perhaps to appease a guilty conscience, perhaps to remind themselves and others that the Spartans had been the first to give an example of such measures, they did not keep Scione for themselves but settled the survivors of Plataea there.[42] Next they tried to allay divine displeasure by returning to their native island the Delians whom they had removed in 422.[43] Having thus tried to appease both men and gods, the Athenians did not, however, try to regain their lost colony on the River Strymon. The recovery of Amphipolis would have required a siege no less difficult, protracted, and expensive,

[37]5.32.5-7.
[38]5.32.1 speaks of enslaving the women and children, though 4.123.4 says Brasidas evacuated them to Olynthus.
[39]Isoc. 4.100, 109; 12.63.
[40]5.35.1. See Map 1.
[41]Diodorus (12.76.3) tells us that the Athenians, "wanting to strike fear in those they suspected of planning rebellion, made an example for all in the punishment they inflicted on the Scioneans." Cleon's policy of calculated terror to deter rebellion in the empire seems to have persuaded the Athenians, for they retained it even after his death, and their motives for passing the original decree were presumably those that moved them to execute it.
[42]5.31.1.
[43]5.1.1.

perhaps, than the one at Potidaea. That siege had lasted two and one-half years and cost more than 2,000 talents.[44] Small wonder that no Athenian seems to have urged an attack on the rebellious colony, but there must have been great frustration and growing anger at the Spartans' failure to deliver Amphipolis to Athens.

The Spartans, meanwhile, were busy trying to restore their position in the Peloponnesus. They sent King Pleistoanax with the full Spartan army into Parrasia, a district in Arcadia to the west of Mantinea which the Mantineans had subjugated during the war (see Map 4). They had also built in the region a fort that threatened northern Laconia.[45] The Spartan army ravaged the Parrasian territory, thus invoking the defensive alliance between Mantinea and Argos. While the Argives guarded the city of Mantinea, the Mantinean army tried in vain to protect the threatened territory. The Mantineans could defend neither the Parrasian towns nor their fort at Cypsela; the Spartans restored Parrasian independence, destroyed the fort, and retired.[46] Turning next to Elis, they sent a garrison to settle Lepreum, the region between Elis and Messenia and the source of their quarrel with the Eleans. This policy was carried out despite the fact that Sparta had only recently declared the Lepreans autonomous.[47] These actions lent security to Sparta's frontiers and the helot country, and must have increased her reputation even as they diminished that of the Argive coalition.

But the Spartans were faced with internal problems as well. Clearidas brought back the army Brasidas had taken to Amphipolis, an army which included 700 helots. Because of the service they had rendered Sparta they were set free and allowed to live wherever they liked. Seven hundred helots moving freely about Laconia soon unsettled the Spartans and set them search-

[44]See Kagan, *Archidamian War*, 97, n. 83.
[45]5.33.1. For a discussion of the geography see *HCT* IV, 31–34. See Map 1.
[46]5.33.2-3.
[47]See Map 4. For the quarrel of Elis, Lepreum, and Sparta see 5.31.1–5. Andrewes (*HCT* IV, 36) suggests that the Lepreans might have rejected autonomy and moved into Elis, leaving their land to be occupied by the Spartan garrison. In light of the hostility between Elis and Lepreum, that seems unlikely. More probably, the Spartans simply took part of the Leprean land for their own purposes.

ing for an alternative solution. At the same time there was a different class of men in Laconia whose presence made the Spartans nervous, the *neodamodeis*. These men are mentioned for the first time in Spartan history at this point,[48] and it is possible that their status was a recent invention.[49] They were liberated helots who seem to have lived freely. We do not know how or why they were freed, but it seems likely that they too received their emancipation for military service well done. They probably were no less alarming to the Spartans than Brasidas' veterans. Still another problem for the Spartans was the continuing shrinkage of the citizenry from which they drew their army. For whatever reason, the number of "equals" who were eligible for the training that produced Spartan hoplites dropped sharply throughout the fifth and fourth centuries. From 5,000 at Plataea in 479 the size of the full Spartan army dropped to about 2,500 (or 3,360) at Mantinea in 418 and 1,050 at Leuctra in 371.[50] The need to place a garrison at Lepreum allowed the Spartans to alleviate both problems at once. They sent both Brasidas' veterans and the *neodamadeis* to settle the land on the Elean frontier.

One further problem remained. The men who had surrendered at Sphacteria and spent years as prisoners in Athens were now back in Sparta. At first they simply returned to the often high and influential positions they previously had held in Spartan society; some of them even held public office. The Spartans came to fear that the restored prisoners would cause trouble, and perhaps they were right. These men, after all, had shocked the Greek world by choosing surrender instead of death and had sullied Sparta's reputation in the process. Thucydides says that their fellow citizens thought the returned prisoners would fear a formal lowering of their status, and so become a dangerous element. Even if formal action were not taken against them, they would surely feel uncomfortable. Xenophon gives a sense of the humiliations they must expect to suffer:

[48]5.34.1.

[49]Such is the suggestion of Andrewes, *HCT* IV, 35.

[50]The figures are given by W. G. Forrest, *A History of Sparta, 950–192 B.C.* (London, 1968), 134. For a discussion of the reasons for the decline see 135–137.

In other states when a man proves to be a coward he is only called a coward. . . . But in Sparta a man would be ashamed to dine with a coward or to wrestle with him. Often when sides are chosen for a ball game he is left out; in the chorus he is shunted off to the most dishonorable place; in the streets he must make way for anyone; he must give up his seat even to a younger man; he must support the unmarried girls in his family at home and explain to them that the cause of their spinsterhood is his cowardice.[51]

Perhaps the Spartans feared that such dishonor would goad the returned prisoners to revolt even if they were allowed to keep the rights of citizenship. As a result they were disfranchised, deprived of the rights to hold office and to engage in any business transactions.[52]

Such internal threats to the Spartan order help explain why most Spartans continued to support a cautious and peaceful foreign policy. The recently improved security on the Elean and Mantinean frontiers, the diminished threat from the Argive coalition, and the pacific behavior of the Athenians, all encouraged the peace faction in Sparta. At the same time, however, resentment at Sparta's failure to carry out the Peace of Nicias continued to grow in Athens. Corinth, Boeotia, and Megara still refused to accept the peace despite repeated Spartan assurances that she would join Athens in coercing them. The Spartans would set a date for taking action, but not under oath, and refused to sign a binding agreement, fearing that it would turn the dissident states against both Athens and Sparta. As each deadline approached, however, the Spartans delayed further. The coercion of these states must have been a major Athenian goal in making the alliance, and, with each Spartan delay, Athenian suspicions grew.[53] The Athenians regretted giving up the prisoners and held on to Pylos and the other places they had agreed to return in the peace.

The Athenians also came increasingly to resent Sparta's ac-

---

[51]Xen. *Resp. Lac.* 9.4-5.

[52]5.34.2. Thucydides tells us their rights were later restored.

[53]5.35.2-3. My interpretation follows the persuasive suggestion of Andrewes, *HCT* IV, 37.

tions at Amphipolis. Clearidas' behavior there had been open to question, and Sparta's decision to evacuate his army instead of handing over the city was a violation of the peace treaty.[54] In the atmosphere of growing suspicion, many Athenians must have come to appreciate that fact and been angered by it. Some scholars have dismissed Athenian expectations as unrealistic: "[The Spartans] had already promised Athens that if necessary they would use force, but they could not seriously be asked now to compel their old allies by war to please Athens and thereby bring their reputation in Greece to an end. Still less was it possible for them to force the Chalcidians to accept the peace and even to turn over so populous a state as Amphipolis to Athens. Even if they had the will such an act would have trampled their honor underfoot. If the Athenians really expected the Spartans to carry that out they were indulging in childish illusions in the old way."[55] The view quoted here derives more from its author's hatred of Athenian democracy[56] than from an objective analysis of the situation. The simple fact was that in the Peace of Nicias Sparta had promised to restore Amphipolis to Athens and had sworn on behalf of her allies as well. The Athenians had been reluctant to accept the peace, and some of them, at least, must have voted for it because they were assured on these points. Both the Spartans and the Athenian supporters of the peace probably used an argument much like the modern assessment quoted above. If this is so, then the Spartans, and probably their Athenian friends, never expected to carry out these difficult provisions; they had persuaded the Athenian people by fraud. The moral implications of that fact are, perhaps, less important than its practical results. When Spartan duplicity was revealed it

[54]See above, pp. 19–20.

[55]Meyer, *Forsch.* II, 353–354. He is followed by Busolt (*GG* III:2, 1212), who also calls Athenian expectations that the Spartans would keep their commitments *Illusionen.*

[56]Meyer's dislike of democracy in general and Athenian democracy in particular is apparent throughout his scholarly work, as well as in his writings on modern and contemporary events. One typical example may be found on pages 355–356 of the essay quoted in the previous note, concluding: "a radical democracy is by its nature incapable of conducting a purposeful and steady foreign policy."

caused a great revulsion in Athenian public opinion. The Athenians "suspected the Spartans of evil intentions," and refused to restore Pylos. They "even regretted that they had restored the prisoners from the island and kept holding on to the other places, waiting until the Spartans should carry out their promises."[57]

The Spartans argued that they had done whatever they could, but could not restore Amphipolis. They promised to try to bring Corinth and Boeotia into the peace, to convince the Boeotians to return the border fort of Panactum to the Athenians,[58] and to persuade them to return the Athenian prisoners still in Boeotian hands. In return Sparta asked Athens to restore Pylos or, failing that, at least to remove the Messenians and escaped helots currently living there. Sparta was offering nothing but new promises in place of the old, unfulfilled ones, but the peace forces at Athens were still strong enough to extract further concessions from their fellow citizens. The Athenians agreed to withdraw the Messenians and helots from Pylos and settled them on the island of Cephallenia.[59]

This Athenian gesture was intended, no doubt, to strengthen the peace faction at Sparta, for Thucydides tells us that by now some Spartans too were suspicious of the peace.[60] At the beginning of autumn, 421, new ephors took office.[61] At least two of them, Xenares and Cleobulus, reflected the growing sentiment against the peace, for Thucydides says flatly that "they were most eager to break off the treaty."[62] They had not been in office

[57] 5.35.4.

[58] Panactum was betrayed to the Boeotians in 422 (5.3.5).

[59] 5.35.5-8.

[60] 5.35.2: ὑπώπτευον δὲ ἀλλήλους εὐθὺς μετὰ τὰς σπονδάς. Thucydides (5.25.2) says that it was only the Spartans who provoked suspicion. Andrewes (HCT IV, 37) says that the two passages are clearly contradictory and "were not thought at the same time." I agree and believe that Thucydides was indicating a change in Spartan opinion; he "would have removed the contradiction if it had come to his attention."

[61] 5.36.1. For the date when the ephors took office see HCT IV, 38, and Ste. Croix, Origins, 320-321.

[62] Thucydides says that τινες of the new ephors were against the peace treaty, and that Xenares and Cleobulus were οὗτοι οἵπερ τῶν ἐφόρων ἐβούλοντο μάλιστα διαλῦσαι τὰς σπονδάς. I think that they were the only two to hold such extreme views, for if there were a majority of ephors in favor of their policy the elaborate and secret maneuvers that they undertook would probably

long before they set in motion a plan intended to renew the war against Athens. A conference had been called at Sparta to which the loyal allies, the Boeotians, Corinthians, and even the Athenians, came, presumably to try once more to achieve a general acceptance of the peace. It was probably the failure of this conference that encouraged Xenares and Cleobulus to try their complicated scheme. The two ephors seem to have reasoned that the Spartans had made peace largely because of the threat from Argos and their desire to recover the prisoners and Pylos and that these same reasons had led them to bolster the peace with an Athenian alliance. Now, since the prisoners had been returned, it remained only to recover Pylos and remove the Argive threat. Then, Xenares and Cleobulus concluded, Sparta would be ready to resume the war against Athens.[63] Acting privately and secretly, the two ephors spoke to the Corinthian and Boeotian ambassadors, who were about to leave Sparta. They proposed that the Corinthians and Boeotians should act in concert, that the Boeotians should make an alliance with Argos and then try to

---

not have been necessary. I say that the ephors "reflected" the new suspicion rather than "represented" it, for two reasons. (1) We do not know when the ephors were chosen; it may have been so early as April or so late as September. The earlier their selection, the less likely they were chosen because of their bellicose policy. (For a discussion of this question see Ste. Croix, *Origins*, 321.) (2) We are not fully informed of the procedure whereby ephors were chosen, but it might not have been possible to select them on the basis of their views and policies. Plato speaks of the process of selection as resembling a lottery (*Laws* 692a, 5–6). Aristotle (*Pol.* 1294b29–34) says that the people elect the *Gerousia* but share in the Ephorate, ἔτι τῷ δύο τὰς μεγίστας ἀρχὰς τὴν μὲν αἱρεῖσθαι τὸν δῆμον, τῆς δὲ μετέχειν (τοὺς μὲν γὰρ γέροντας αἱροῦνται τῆς δ᾽ ἐφορείας μετέχουσιν), which implies that they do not elect the ephors. He also says that the ephors were selected from the entire population ἐξ ἁπάντων and that the method of selection is "too childish," παιδαριώδης γάρ ἐστι λίαν (*Pol.* 1270b25–27). On at least three occasions, moreover, he refers to the ephors as "people chosen by chance" (*Pol.* 1270b29, 1272a30, 1272b35–36). In the last passage he contrasts the ephors, who are chosen at random, with the Carthaginian Magistrates, the Hundred and Four, who are chosen for their excellence. I am grateful to Paul A. Rahe for calling these passages and their significance to my attention. For a fuller discussion, see his article in *Historia* XXIX (1980), 385–401. For these reasons we may not assume that the ephors were chosen on the basis of any program they proposed. This is not to say that they were not influenced by public opinion, but that such opinion took effect after the election rather than before.

[63]This is my amplification of Thucydides' account of their thinking in 5.36.

move the Argives into an alliance with Sparta. The Argive alliance, they pointed out, would make it easier to fight a war outside the Peloponnesus.[64] They also asked the Boeotians to give Panactum to the Spartans so that they in turn could exchange it for Pylos, "and so more easily be in a position to go to war against Athens."

The proposals of the two ephors present many problems to the historian. The Corinthians and Boeotians were asked to join the Argive alliance and try to bring it over to the Spartan side, but why should they believe the Argives would go along? The Argive quarrel was with Sparta, not Athens. Some Argives, to be sure, were enemies of the democracy and willing to accept an alliance with Sparta in exchange for oligarchy at Argos.[65] In 420, however, they had little or no prospect of coming to power. The Boeotians were asked to give back Panactum, which Sparta would then use in its attempt to regain Pylos, but why should the Boeotians trade a piece of their security to please Sparta? The ephors' answer was that such a sacrifice would facilitate the renewal of a war that was in the Boeotian interest. But why should the Boeotians believe that a faction so weak that it must conduct its business unofficially and secretly, that had not been able to prevent the conclusion of an alliance with Athens, could now bring about a reversal in Spartan policy? Finally, why should anyone believe that removing the main sources of Sparta's fear, the threat of Argos and the Athenian control of Pylos, would promote the renewal of an adventurous Spartan policy instead of a relapse into her more traditional conservatism?

Regardless of such problems, the ephors proceeded with their plan. On their way home from Sparta the Corinthian and Boeotian ambassadors were stopped by two Argive magistrates of the highest rank, who asked the Boeotians to join the Argive alliance.[66] Having been rejected once, the Argives this time put the offer more diplomatically: "employing a common policy,

---

[64] 5.36.

[65] For a discussion of the Argive oligarchs see Kagan, *CP* LVII (1962), 209-218.

[66] 5.37.1.2. These may have been *artynai* mentioned in 5.47.9 or generals mentioned in 5.59.5. For useful discussions see *HCT* IV, 58-59, 121-123.

they could make war against or a treaty with the Spartans or with any one else they might choose." We have no reason to believe that the Argives making this proposal represented either interests or a policy different from those of the magistrates who had organized the alliance in the previous year. They appear still to have been aiming at a new Peloponnesian alignment by which they and their allies could more effectively challenge Spartan leadership. The ambiguous language about the Spartans and other unnamed enemies or allies may have been meant merely to sugarcoat a rather bitter pill; such language committed Argos to nothing.[67]

The Boeotians received the invitation with pleasure, "for by luck the Argives had asked them to do the same thing their Spartan friends had instructed them." When they received the news, the Boeotarchs, the magistrates of the Boeotian League, were equally delighted and for the same reasons. The Boeotians' delight, however, was unjustified, for the Spartans and Argives only appeared to urge the same course of action. Both favored an Argive alliance with Boeotia, but for entirely opposite purposes.[68] The Boeotian leaders may have been pleased because they saw the Argives walking into what they hoped would be a trap, but at no time had their aims coincided. When the Argives sent ambassadors with formal proposals for an alliance, the Boeotarchs agreed to them and promised to send ambassadors to Argos to conclude the alliance;[69] the Boeotian constitution required that they first consult the federal council.

The ancient writers give us no direct account of Corinthian thinking about these developments; Thucydides merely reports Corinth's actions. The Corinthians had been party to all the negotiations and raised no objection to them, yet there is reason to think that they did not approve the methods suggested to try

---

[67]Thomas Kelly (*Historia* XXI [1972], 162) suggests that the Argive magistrates were pro-Spartan and acting in concert with the Spartan ephors. Seager (*CQ* LXX [1976], 258) thinks that the Argives were tempting the Boeotians to turn against Sparta. Neither suggestion seems likely, though we can not be certain that Xenares, Cleobulus, and the Argives were not in communication with each other.

[68]*HCT* IV, 41.

[69]5.37.5.

to renew the war. The Spartan and Boeotian magistrates might
be convinced that Argos could be brought over to Sparta and
that Sparta would then turn against Athens, but the Corinthians
had reason to doubt it. They had always counted on fear, not
security, to move the Spartans to fight.[70] A powerful Argive
alliance independent of Sparta might goad the Spartans to action, but Argos safely allied to Sparta and her friends would
not.[71] The Corinthians' problem in 420 was to prevent precisely
the alliance between Boeotia and Argos that they had sought the
year before. Yet they could not reveal their opposition without
alienating the war faction in Sparta—the very faction on which
they must ultimately rely. Thus, their immediate goal must have
been to work for delay in the hope that something would arise
from the inherently unstable situation to upset the difficult secret
negotiations.

Thucydides tells us that after the Argive ambassadors had
gone home to await an official embassy from Boeotia, "the
Boeotarchs, the Corinthians, Megarians, and the ambassadors
from Thrace decided first to swear oaths to each other to assist
any one of them who needed defense, should the occasion arise,
and to make neither war nor peace without a common agreement; and that only then should the Boeotians and Megarians
(for they pursued the same policies) make a treaty with the Argives."[72] There can be no doubt that the Corinthians were behind this proposal. The Chalcidians in Thrace, of course, were
only satellites of Corinth, as were the Megarians of Boeotia. The
Boeotians themselves had no need of such an agreement, for they
were ready to join with Argos and, since Corinth was already an
Argive ally, the common agreement did Boeotia no further good.
Finally, this scheme for joint action is only an enlarged version of
the earlier one proposed by the Corinthians, without success.[73]

The Corinthians understood the Boeotian constitution and

---

[70]See above, pp. 35-36.
[71]This point of view is accepted by Kelly (*Historia* XXI [1972], 162-163).
Cf., however, Westlake (*AJP* LXI [1940], 418), and Seager (*CQ* LXX [1976],
258).
[72]5.38.1.
[73]See above, pp. 43-44.

political mood well enough to realize that their proposal would cause trouble. At best it would destroy the delicate negotiations; at the very least it might delay them. The Corinthians knew that the Boeotians in general did not trust them, for they had seen through the earlier Corinthian ploy and rejected it. They looked upon the Corinthians as rebels from the Spartan alliance and feared that an agreement with Corinth would offend Sparta.[74] They had heard that Corinth had publicly defied the Spartans and then rejected Spartan complaints. Knowing all this, the Corinthians may well have hoped to capitalize on the distrust toward them felt by the ordinary Boeotian, who was not privy to the secret plans of the Spartan ephors.

The Boeotarchs, in any case, badly miscalculated the situation. They put before the Boeotian federal council, which was the sovereign power, resolutions for concluding the common agreement with Megara, Corinth, and the Chalcidians in Thrace.[75] They did not, of course, reveal the complicated and secret plans behind the proposal, for Xenares and Cleobulus would have been in serious trouble if word of their private negotiations had reached Sparta. The Boeotarchs seemed to be counting on their own authority to secure the passage of the proposal. No doubt, the federal council normally accepted the unanimous recommendations of the Boeotarchs, but these were not normal times and the council rejected the proposal, "fearing that they might be acting against the Spartans by swearing oaths with rebels from their alliance."[76] This rejection, unforseen by the Boeotarchs but perhaps not by the Corinthians, put an end to the discussion. The Corinthians and the Chalcidians went home, and the Boeotarchs did not dare bring up an Argive alliance. No envoys went to Argos to negotiate a treaty, "and there was neglect and a waste of time in the whole business."[77]

---

[74] 5.38.3.

[75] 5.38.2. The constitution of the Boeotian federation is described in *Hellenica Oxyrhynchia* XI, 2 = Bart. 16.2. Technically, there were four separate councils, but joint sessions of the four were needed for making decisions. See *HCT* IV, 42.

[76] 5.38.3.

[77] 5.38.4.

The war faction at Sparta had failed in its first attempt to create conditions that would allow a renewal of the war, but rather than give up, it conceived another plan, this time focusing on Boeotia instead of Argos. As before, Xenares and Cleobulus conducted these negotiations unofficially and secretly, and even as the negotiations moved toward their ineffective conclusion, public and official conversations between Athens and Sparta continued. The friends of peace in Sparta, no less than the advocates of war, were eager to recover Pylos. They continued to believe that if they could get the Boeotians to restore Panactum and the Athenian prisoners that they still held, the Athenians would restore Pylos to Sparta. Since they continued to hold that view after many talks with the Athenians, they must have been encouraged in it by the Athenian negotiators, presumably Nicias and his associates. With both factions in favor, the Spartans sent an official embassy to Boeotia asking that Panactum be restored to Athens along with the Athenian prisoners.

The Boeotians' response indicates that the faction eager to renew the war had devised a new plan. The Boeotians said they would not return Panactum unless the Spartans made a separate treaty with them like the one Sparta had with the Athenians. The Spartans knew that this would be a breach of the treaty with Athens, since that treaty implied that neither state could make either peace or war without mutual consent.[78] But a breach with Athens was precisely what the war faction wanted, so of course it supported the proposal for a Boeotian alliance. Not constituting a majority, the war faction needed some support from the friends of peace. Much as all Spartans may have wanted to regain Pylos, why should anyone think the Athenians would deliver it, especially when confronted with the treachery of a Spartan treaty with Boeotia? The only plausible explanation is that the Spartans put their faith in the apparently limitless patience of the

---

[78] 5.39.3. Some scholars have suggested that, since the treaty as Thucydides reports it contains no such clause, (1) Thucydides is wrong or (2) his text is faulty or (3) a clause was later added to the treaty, but Thucydides does not report it. None of these theories is necessary, for the impropriety of Sparta's separate alliance with Boeotia is implicit in her repeated promises to get Boeotia to accept the Peace of Nicias. Andrewes (HCT IV, 45), however, may be right in suggesting an oral commitment by Sparta in the general form reported by Thucydides.

peace faction at Athens and its capacity to maintain control of Athenian policy. In early March of 420 the Spartans made the treaty with Boeotia.

This new pact guaranteed the Boeotians against an Athenian attack by promising the tacit or even active support of Sparta. The Boeotians welcomed the treaty as a step in breaking up the alliance between Sparta and Athens, but there is yet another reason why the Boeotians were willing to reverse their policy: they meant to deceive their Spartan allies. No sooner had they made the alliance than they began to demolish the fort at Panactum.[79] This act not only deprived Athens of a valuable border fort, but also had distinct political advantages: it was certain to put further strain on the Athenian alliance with Sparta and the Peace of Nicias itself.

Thucydides tells us that the demolition of Panactum was carried out "by the Boeotians themselves," without the knowledge of the Spartans.[80] The idea may have come from the Boeotians, but past performance suggested that they were incapable of such subtle and effective maneuvers. Xenares and Cleobulus may have been party to the plot;[81] more likely, the Corinthians were behind it. The Spartan ephors, after all, wanted to secure Pylos before resuming the war, and the demolition of Panactum ruled that out. The Corinthians, on the other hand, believed that grievance and fear, not comfort and security, were likely to goad Sparta to fight.

Meanwhile, the Argives waited for Boeotian ambassadors to negotiate the promised alliance, but none came. Instead they received frightening news: Panactum was being demolished and Sparta had made a treaty with Boeotia. They assumed that they had been betrayed, that Sparta was behind the whole affair, knew of the destruction of Panactum, and had persuaded the Athenians to accept it by bringing Boeotia into the alliance with Athens. The Argives were in a panic; they could no longer make a treaty with Boeotia or with Athens and they feared that their

[79] 5.39.3. See Map 2.
[80] He makes it clear (5.42.1) that the official Spartan delegation sent to take command of the fort and the Athenian prisoners was taken by surprise when it found the fort destroyed.
[81] Such is the suggestion of Kelly (*Historia* XXI [1972], 164–168).

own coalition would break up and go over to Sparta. Their nightmare was that they would soon have to face a coalition of the Peloponnesians led by Sparta, the Boeotians, and the Athenians. In terror of such an outcome, the Argives sent two envoys to Sparta "as quickly as possible" to try "to make a treaty however they could so that they might have peace."[82]

The information that the Argives had received was largely true, their interpretation of it false. The question is, where did their information come from, since they learned of the destruction of Panactum before either the Spartans or Athenians?[83] The Boeotians could not have been the source, for there had been no contact between them and the Argives by the time the news reached Argos. The likeliest source is the team of Xenares and Cleobulus. The two ephors had close and confidential relations with the leading Boeotian magistrates and with the active Corinthian negotiators. They were not part of the conspiracy to destroy Panactum, but it was easy for them to learn what was happening. They, on the other hand, had the best motive for rushing to Argos with the news and using it for their own purposes. If the Argives were simply left to learn about the Boeotian-Spartan treaty and Panactum when everyone else did, they would learn at the same time of the Athenians' angry reaction. There would be no need for panic and a Spartan alliance, for an Athenian alliance, which was preferable, would still be available. If the Spartan ephors brought the news beforehand, however, and added to it the false item that the Athenians were aware of the events and complicit in them, all would be different. Then the Argives would have good reason for panic and for acting as, in fact, they did. We must suppose that it was the ephors' intervention that led the Argives to seek a Spartan alliance so urgently.[84]

---

[82] 5.40.3.

[83] 5.42.1. Andrewes (*HCT* IV, 45) thinks that Thucydides' evidence for Argive knowledge of the destruction of Panactum "looks like a slip." I agree with Kelly (*Historia* XXI [1972], 159, 165ff.) that we should accept his evidence as correct.

[84] Kelly's article (*Historica* XXI [1972]) is fundamental for an understanding of these difficult maneuvers. Although I differ from his interpretation on several points, my debt to his work is considerable.

The Argive negotiations for an alliance with Sparta reflected eagerness on both sides. Argos wanted arbitration over Cynuria by a third party; Sparta wanted a simple renewal of the old treaty which left the disputed territory in her hands. The Argives offered to accept the fifty years' treaty for the present, provided that at any time in the future either side could request a battle of limited scope to decide control of Cynuria.[85] The Spartans thought this was absurd, but after thinking it over, they agreed to the terms and signed the treaty, "for they were eager to have Argive friendship, regardless."[86] The Argive negotiators then went home to seek ratification by the popular assembly. They were to return to Sparta with that approval during the Hyacinthian festival, perhaps as late as the end of June.[87] The delay was long enough to allow developments in Athens to alter the course of events.

[85] 5.41.1-2. This was a revival of the idea of a battle between champions which the Argives had fought against the Spartans in the sixth century. Herodotus (1.82) reports the story in which 300 soldiers on each side fought for Cynuria.

[86] 5.42.3.

[87] That is the date suggested by Andrewes (HCT IV, 485). Busolt (GG III:2, 1217, and II, 722, n. 2) suggests May.

3. The Alliance of
Athens and Argos

While waiting for the Argive negotiators, the Spartans sent envoys to take charge of Panactum and the Athenian prisoners in Boeotian hands so that they could restore both to the Athenians. They found that the Boeotians had destroyed the fort, but they received the prisoners and proceeded to Athens to make the best case they could for the restoration of Pylos. They handed over the prisoners and argued that Panactum was properly restored, even though demolished, for it could no longer harbor hostile forces.[1] This bit of sophistry did not impress the Athenians. They insisted that Panactum should have been restored intact, and they were especially annoyed to learn of Sparta's alliance with Boeotia. This blatant example of Spartan perfidy not only violated the promise to make no new alliance without consultation, but it also exposed the deceit of Sparta's promises to coerce its dissident allies. The Athenians "answered the envoys angrily and sent them away."[2]

These events were a blow to Athenian supporters of the peace and encouraged its enemies to a more active policy. Since the death of Cleon, Athenians who favored an aggressive policy had been without leadership as effective as his. We know of one man who followed Cleon's tradition and who achieved a position of leadership with the Athenian people: Hyperbolus, son of An-

[1] 5.42.1.
[2] 5.42.2.

tiphanes, of the deme Perithoidae.[3] In the *Peace*, performed at the Great Dionysia in March, 421, Aristophanes' protagonist answers the question, "Who now rules over the Bema on the Pnyx?" by saying, "Hyperbolus now holds the place."[4] He was one of only eight fifth-century politicians, among them Cleon and Cleophon, called by contemporary writers *prostates tou demou*.[5] His significance is suggested both by the frequency with which he was attacked by the comic poets and by the number of different poets who attacked him.[6] He was a trierarch, an active member of the assembly who moved and amended decrees, and he may have been both a member of the *boule* and a general.[7] An ancient tradition treats him as a ridiculous and unworthy scoundrel, by implication beneath even the other demagogues. Thucydides calls him "a rascally man who was ostracized not because of fear of his power and importance but because of his baseness and because he was a disgrace to the city."[8] The very fact of his ostracism, however, and the fact that in 411 the oligarchic rebels found it necessary to murder him while he was in exile at Samos,[9] emphasize his eminence.

Hyperbolus was clearly a member of the aggressive faction. Aristophanes no doubt exaggerated when he attributed to him imperial aims that reached as far as Carthage,[10] but the joke must have had some basis in fact in order to get a laugh. Hyperbolus is also singled out as an enemy by both the peace-loving hero and the chorus in Aristophanes' *Peace*.[11] We may assume that he had

[3]For Hyperbolus see H. Swoboda, *PW* IX (1916), 254-258, and F. Camon, "Figura e ambiente di Iperbolo," *RSC* IV (1961), 182-197. See also above, Chap. 1, n. 35.

[4]Aristoph. *Peace* 680-681.

[5]O. Reverdin, *Museum Helveticum* II (1945), 201-212.

[6]The comic butt of Eupolis' *Maricas* is Hyperbolus. Other poets who allude to him, besides Aristophanes, are Cratinus, Leucon, Hermippus, Himerius, and Plato Comicus. For useful discussions of the evidence of the poets for Hyperbolus' career see Gilbert, *Beiträge*, 209-216, and W. R. Connor, *The New Politicians of Fifth-Century Athens* (Princeton, 1971), 79-84.

[7]Connor, *The New Politicians*, 81-82.

[8]8.73.3. The same theme is sounded repeatedly by Plutarch (*Arist.* 7, *Nic.* 11, *Alc.* 13).

[9]8.73.3.

[10]Aristoph. *Knights* 1302-1305.

[11]Aristoph. *Peace* 921, 1319.

been a leading voice in resisting the peace in 421 and the alliance with Sparta that followed it. His failure to carry the day is not surprising, for though he was a trained and skilled speaker, he had neither the military reputation of Cleon nor the personal stature and influence of the rich and pious Nicias. The recent Spartan treachery no doubt revived his cause, however, and he might have emerged as leader of the war faction had his position not been usurped by a potent and unexpected competitor.

Thucydides tells us that Alcibiades son of Cleinias was one of the faction that was pressing to break off the peace. He was "a man still young in age, as these things are thought of in other cities."[12] Between thirty and thirty-three years old in the spring of 420, he was elected general even though thirty seems to have been the minimum age for the office.[13] There were several reasons for Alcibiades' early prominence. He was rich, and as the careers of Cimon and Nicias had shown, wealth was a valuable asset in the Athenian democracy.[14]

Alcibiades was rich enough to enter 7 chariots at the Olympic festival of 416, more than any other private citizen had entered before.[15] He was, moreover, extraordinarily handsome, so much so that "he was hunted by many women of noble family" and sought after by men as well.[16] He was also a talented and trained speaker who sought instruction from the best rhetoricians of his time and whose ability was praised by no less a judge than the great Demosthenes.[17] His reputation for intellectual ability was attested many years after his death by Aristotle's successor Theophrastus, who said that Alcibiades was "the most capable of all men in discovering and understanding what was necessary."[18] Even his flaws seem to have helped him as much as they hurt

[12]5.43.2.

[13]For Alcibiades' age see Hatzfeld, *Alcibiade*, 27–28, 62–65. For the legal age for generals see Hignett, *HAC*, 224; Alcibiades' generalship is attested by Plutarch (*Alc.* 15.1) and accepted by Beloch (*AP*, 307) and Fornara (*Generals*, 62).

[14]For Cimon see Kagan, *Outbreak*, 66–67.

[15]6.16.2. For the date see *HCT* IV, 246–247.

[16]On Alcibiades' good looks see, e.g., Plut. *Alc.* 1.3, Xen. *Mem.* 1.2.24, and Plato *Prt.* 309 a. The quotation is from Xenophon.

[17]Dem. *Meid.*, quoted by Plut. *Alc.* 10.2.

[18]Plut. *Alc.* 10.2-3.

him. He had a speech defect, but people found it charming. He was willful, spoiled, unpredictable, and outrageous, but his boyish antics won him at least as much admiration as envy and disapproval. Most of all, these actions brought him attention and notoriety, which facilitated his early entry into public life.

Plutarch observes that Alcibiades' association with Socrates contributed significantly to his reputation, and we cannot doubt that his place in the Socratic tradition is one of the main reasons we are so well informed about him.[19] But there is little reason to believe that Socrates affected the young man's public career in any way. Alcibiades may have believed, as Plato has him say, that Socrates' effect on him was greater than that of Pericles, but Alcibiades was surely referring to an emotional and private response.[20] The universal evidence of the Socratics, moreover, is that the influence of their master on Alcibiades was not lasting.

His family exerted the greatest influence on Alcibiades' career and, as Thucydides points out, it was the fame of his ancestors which enabled Alcibiades to reach a position of eminence in Athens so rapidly.[21] Through his father he belonged to the noble clan of Salaminioi. His great-great-grandfather, also called Alcibiades, was an ally of Cleisthenes. His great-grandfather Cleinias fought as a trierarch at Artemisium on his own ship manned at his own expense. His grandfather Alcibiades (II) was an important enough political figure to be ostracized, perhaps in 460. His father Cleinias (II) was an associate of Pericles and probably the mover of the decree (that modern scholars call by his name) regulating the collection of tribute in the empire. He died fighting at the Battle of Coronea in 447/46. The name Alcibiades is Spartan and was acquired at least as far back as the sixth century as a result of the establishment of a guest-friendship with a Spartan family in which the names Alcibiades and Endius alternated each generation. This relationship made the family of Alcibiades Sparta's *proxenoi* in Athens, but Alcibiades (II) renounced this special connection with Sparta,

---

[19]Plut. *Alc.* 1.2. For a useful discussion of the relationship between Alcibiades and Socrates see Hatzfeld, *Alcibiade*, 32–58.

[20]Pl. *Symp.* 215E.

[21]5.43.2.

probably because of the outbreak of the First Peloponnesian War. This action did not, however, affect the relationship with the Endius-Alcibiades family in Sparta.

Alcibiades' mother Deinomache was an Alcmaeonid, descendant of a family whose importance is well known and whose fame dates from the seventh century. When Cleinias died his two sons Alcibiades and Cleinias (IV) were given into the guardianship of relatives on the maternal side, Pericles and his brother Ariphron. This is evidence for the close relationship between Alcibiades' father and Pericles, for the guardianships would normally have gone to the father's closest male relation.[22] From about the age of five, then, Alcibiades and his wild and uncontrollable younger brother were raised in the house of Athens' leading statesman.[23] We need not believe that Pericles spent much time with either boy, nor is there any evidence that he thought of the young Alcibiades as his successor.[24] But the boyhood of Alcibiades coincided with the height of Pericles' career, the period when he stood alone and almost unchallenged as the most influential man in Athens. The talented boy, his ambition already whetted and his expectations elevated by the tradition of his father's house, conceived greater ambitions by observing the power and glory of his guardian. Even great public success was not enough for the son of Cleinias and the ward of Pericles, and flatterers were not lacking to encourage his bold visions. As Plutarch put it: "It was . . . his love of distinction and love of fame to which his corrupters appealed, and thereby plunged him all too soon into ways of presumptuous scheming, persuading him that he had only to enter public life, and he would straightway cast into total eclipse the ordinary generals and public leaders, and not only that, he would even surpass Pericles in power and reputation among the Hellenes."[25] His family connections filled Alcibiades with the desire to play a great role in Athenian

---

[22]This discussion of Alcibiades' family depends largely on *HCT* IV, 48–50, and Davies, *APF*, 9–18.

[23]Plato (*Alc.* 1.118 and *Prt.* 320a) is our source for the character of young Cleinias. Davies' description of him as a "psychotic delinquent" (*APF*, 18) is stronger and more clinically precise than the evidence warrants.

[24]See Hatzfeld, *Alcibiade*, 28–32.

[25]Plut. *Alc.* 7.3-4. Translated by B. Perrin in the Loeb edition.

public affairs; in the still deferential democracy of the fifth century they also gave him a great advantage over his competitors.

By 420 Alcibiades could boast of a fine military record, having
served with distinction at Potidaea and Delium as a cavalryman.
His election to the generalship, therefore, although unusual for
one so young, was by no means frivolous. His ambition to play a
great role in public affairs showed itself some time after the
Spartan surrender at Sphacteria. He paid careful attention to the
Spartan prisoners, playing on his family's old Spartan connections and hoping to renew the Spartan proxeny. When the Archidamian War drew to its close, he hoped to be the Athenian
with whom the Spartans negotiated and who would receive
credit for the resulting peace, but the Spartans preferred to deal
with the experienced and reliable Nicias. Feeling slighted and
insulted, Alcibiades reversed his position. He now attacked the
Spartan alliance on the grounds that the Spartans were insincere,
allying with Athens only to obtain a free hand against Argos;
once Argos was dealt with Sparta would again attack the isolated
Athenians. Thucydides tells us that this was not mere rhetoric,
that Alcibiades sincerely preferred an alliance with Argos to one
with Sparta; certainly his assessment of Sparta's motives did no
injustice to Xenares, Cleobulus, and their supporters.[26]

Until the spring of 420 Alcibiades' opposition to the friends of
peace was in vain, but the demolition of Panactum and Sparta's
alliance with Boeotia changed everything. Nicias' policy was
now vulnerable, and Plutarch gives us a summary of Alcibiades'
attack: "He raised a tumult in the assembly against Nicias, and
slandered him with accusations all too plausible. Nicias himself,
he said, when he was general, had refused to capture the enemy's
men who were cut off on the island of Sphacteria, and when
others had captured them, he had released and given them back
to the Lacedaemonians, whose favour he sought; and then he did
not persuade those same Lacedaemonians, tried friend of theirs
as he was, not to make a separate alliance with the Boeotians or
even with the Corinthians, and yet when any Hellenes wished to
be friends and allies of Athens, he tried to prevent it, unless it were

[26]5.43; Plut. *Alc.* 14.1-2.

the good pleasure of the Lacedaemonians."[27] While these public attacks prepared Athenian opinion for a new policy, Alcibiades acted privately to bring Argos into the Athenian fold. He sent a message to the leaders of the popular party in Argos, urging them to come with Elean and Mantinean ambassadors and conclude an alliance with the Athenians: "the opportunity was ripe, and he himself would cooperate to the fullest."[28]

Alcibiades' message arrived in time to prevent the Argive alliance with Sparta. Only the mistaken belief that Athens and Sparta were working together had driven the Argives to seek such an unwelcome alliance, and now that the truth had been revealed they abandoned all thought of the Spartan tie and rejoiced at the prospect of an alliance with Athens, "thinking that it was a city that had been friendly to them in the past, that it was a democracy like theirs, that it had a great power on the sea, and that it would fight on their side if war should break out."[29] Envoys from Argos, Elis, and Mantinea at once set out to negotiate an alliance with Athens.

The Spartans learned of the new turn of events soon enough to attempt preventive action.[30] They sent a delegation of three men whom the Athenians regarded highly: Leon, Philocharidas, and Endius, the last a member of the family connected with that of Alcibiades. Their mission was to prevent the Athenians from making an Argive alliance and to ask that Pylos be exchanged for Panactum. They were also to explain that the recent Spartan alliance with Boeotia did not in any way threaten Athens.[31] Both factions in Sparta must have supported this mission, for neither wanted Argos and Athens allied.

---

[27]Alc. 14.4–5. We do not know what source Plutarch had for these remarks, but they are plainly the kind of arguments an able opponent of Nicias would find suitable.

[28]5.43.3. The detail that Alcibiades' message was sent to the leaders of the popular faction comes from Plutarch (Alc. 14.3), and there is no reason to doubt it.

[29]5.44.1.

[30]Since Alcibiades' message was private, unofficial, perhaps even secret (Plut. Alc. 14.3), it is not obvious how the Spartans learned of it so quickly. The likeliest guess is that the oligarchic, pro-Spartan faction in Argos was the source. For the existence of such a faction see 5.76.2. For its previous connection with Sparta and its allies see Kagan, CP LVII (1962), 210.

[31]5.44.3.

Thucydides' account of what follows is so remarkable that some have found it hard to believe.[32] He tells us that the Spartan envoys came to the council and announced that they had full powers to settle all differences. This alarmed Alcibiades, who feared that if they spoke to the assembly in the same way they would persuade it and thus prevent the Argive alliance. To avoid this possibility, he convinced the Spartan envoys not to admit to the assembly that they had come with full powers. In return he promised to use all his influence on their behalf; he would restore Pylos and settle all other differences. In the assembly the Spartans were taken thoroughly by surprise and rendered helpless. In response to Alcibiades' question about their powers, they avowed that they were limited. He turned on them with a loud and angry attack. Acting as though he had been betrayed, he assailed their honesty and the purpose of their mission. The assembly was soon inflamed and ready to bring the Argives in to make an alliance. Nicias was stunned and embarrassed, for he had been unprepared for this turn of events. Alcibiades, no doubt, had sworn the envoys to maintain secrecy, and especially to avoid contact with Nicias. Only the occurrence of an earthquake prevented completion of the Argive alliance on the spot.[33] The Spartan envoys had neither time nor opportunity to complain of Alcibiades' trick, and Athenian anger gave them no reason to think that its exposure would do any good. They probably left for Sparta quickly, for we find no evidence that they were present at the assembly the next day.

This puzzling story raises a number of questions.[34] Why did the Spartan envoys accept the advice of Alcibiades and trust him instead of working with Nicias? They knew, after all, that Alcibiades had been hostile to them. How did Alcibiades persuade

---

[32]The other ancient accounts (Plut. *Alc.* 14.6-9; *Nic.* 10.4-6) do not differ from Thucydides substantially, merely adding more or less plausible details. Modern scholars expressing astonishment at the story are legion. Hatzfeld (*Alcibiade*, 91-93) believes that the account is incorrect and is followed, with some hesitation, by Andrewes (*HCT* IV, 51-53). P. A. Brunt (*REG* LXV [1952], 66-69) suggests that Thucydides' source was Alcibiades himself and that the story aims at magnifying the role of Alcibiades.

[33]5.45.4; Plut. *Alc.* 14.8-9.

[34]The problem is laid out neatly and economically by Andrewes in *HCT* IV, 51-53, and I have followed his organization in part.

them that changing their story before the assembly would advance their cause? Why did the Spartans not reveal that Alcibiades had tricked them? Finally, we know that Endius and Alcibiades worked together closely in 413/12, but wonder how this can be if Alcibiades had tricked Endius in 420.[35] To understand the situation we must grasp the difficulty of the task facing the Spartan envoys. Despite their "full powers" they had almost nothing to offer the Athenians and much to ask. Their "full powers," in fact, merely gave the envoys the right to make a binding commitment for Sparta if the Athenians agreed to the proposals the envoys were authorized to make.[36] The Spartans still would not restore Amphipolis, they could no longer restore Panactum intact, and they were unwilling to break off their treaty with Boeotia. All they could offer were lame excuses and promises of goodwill in the future. Nicias, though still in favor of the peace and the Spartan alliance and still an important political force, could not achieve the Spartan purpose. The Athenians were angered by Sparta's recent actions and their anger encompassed Nicias as well.

Alcibiades, on the other hand, offered a new hope. He may already have been elected general for the coming year,[37] but even if not, his popularity was such as to make his election likely. It was precisely his prominence, moreover, as a leading voice in opposition to Sparta, that made his offer of assistance attractive. If Alcibiades' voice had been added to that of Nicias in favor of cooperation with Sparta, no political force in Athens could have resisted their combined influence. Nor should the Spartans' faith in Alcibiades' sincerity surprise us. They knew him to be an ambitious young man with special ties to Sparta who in the past had tried to serve as the link between Sparta and Athens, hoping to derive political benefit from that service. They knew that he had turned against Sparta when spurned in favor of his rival Nicias. Why should they doubt his capacity to change again in new circumstances? Now, by saving the threatened peace and, in the process, replacing Nicias as the Athenian politician trusted

[35] 8.6.3 and 12.
[36] See Hatzfeld, *Alcibiade*, 91–92, and Andrewes, *HCT* IV, 52.
[37] Such is the suggestion of Andrewes (*HCT* IV, 52, 69) and I think it likely.

and publicly honored by the Spartans, he might hope to emerge
as the leading figure on the political scene. In any case, the
Spartans had little to lose in trusting Alcibiades, for without
him, or with him in opposition, they had almost no reason to
hope for success.[38]

Plutarch records the explanation Alcibiades gave the Spartans
for denying their full powers before the assembly: he told them
that the council was customarily courteous and moderate
whereas the assembly was much more demanding. If informed
of the envoys' full powers the assembly would make impossible
demands, but if it believed that any agreement must be returned
to Sparta for ratification, it might be more reasonable.[39] We have
no reason to doubt the accuracy of Plutarch or his source on this
point. Alcibiades may have been correct in his description of the
behavior patterns of the council and the assembly, but even if he
were not, the Spartans were in no position to dispute him. Having decided to accept his support, they now had no choice but to
follow his instructions; they were in his hands.[40]

We may now turn to the matter of Endius and his later collaboration with the same Alcibiades who had treated him and his
colleagues so badly. One explanation is that in eight years men
may forget past wrongs, especially if there are present benefits.

[38]Some scholars, under the influence of Plut. Nic. 10.4, have read 5.45.1: τὸν
'Αλκιβιάδην ἐφόβουν μὴ καί, ἢν ἐς τὸν δῆμον ταῦτα λέγωσιν, ἐπαγάγωνται
τὸ πλῆθος ... to mean that the Spartans had already persuaded the council and
Alcibiades feared they would do the same in the assembly. I agree with Andrewes (HCT IV, 52) that there is no reason to do so. Plutarch's remarks here
look much like an expansion of Thucydides based on an incorrect reading of his
text. Brunt (REG LXV [1952], 67) asks if "Alcibiades' manoeuvres in fact
achieved anything at all; was it not the diplomatic and military position that
threw Athens and Argos together rather than the adroitness of one man?" An
answer to this is that both the situation and the man were needed, for Alcibiades' action in sending the message to Argos suggesting an Athenian alliance was vital in timing and consequence. It is true, however, that the trick
that deceived the Spartans was probably not necessary to defeat their mission.
It was needed, however, to propel Alcibiades into the limelight as the man to
see through the "perfidy" of the Spartans and denounce it publicly in the
assembly.

[39]Plut. Alc. 14.6-7.

[40]Andrewes (HCT IV, 51-52) rejects the reliability of Plutarch's account,
but his arguments are not compelling. Some of his objections are met by the
reconstruction offered here.

The circumstances of 413/12 may have been propitious for am-
nesty.[41] It is also possible that Endius and Alcibiades were
coconspirators in 420. The difficulty is that the sources provide
no motive for Endius' complicity.[42] However that may be, Alcibiades' later relationship with Endius should not stand in the
way of the explanation we have offered for Alcibiades' trick. It
was a device invented on the spur of the moment aimed not only
at achieving a new foreign policy but also at bringing prominence
and credit to its champion.

The next day the assembly meeting that had been interrupted
by the earthquake resumed. Nicias, still unaware of what had
prompted the strange behavior of the Spartans, did what he
could to recover his position. He asked that a decision on the
Argive alliance be postponed. He argued that friendship with
Sparta was preferable to friendship with Argos and asked that an
embassy be sent to Sparta to clarify Spartan intentions. Alcibiades' intervention, after all, had prevented the Spartans from
saying what they had come to say. Nicias advanced one further
argument that clearly reveals his outlook and temperament:
peace was good for the Athenians because they were in good
condition, their good fortune and security at a high point, their
honor unsullied. Sparta, on the other hand, in bad repute,
threatened, and insecure, would benefit from the opportunity to
fight a quick battle to set things right. These were the words of a
conservative pessimist who expected to lose. Others might argue
the opposite, pointing out that now, when Sparta was weakened
and threatened by a powerful coalition, might be just the time to
finish with Sparta and thus eliminate the threat it had posed to
Athens for so many years. But Nicias' influence was strong
enough to persuade the assembly to postpone the Argive alliance
and instead to send an embassy to Sparta with himself as one of
its members. The embassy was instructed to ask the Spartans to
restore Panactum intact, to give back Amphipolis, and to aban-

---

[41]Such is the suggestion of Andrewes, *HCT* IV, 51.

[42]R. C. Kebric (*Mnemosyne* XXIX [1976], 72–78) has attempted to supply
one: an attempt to overthrow the Spartan monarchy, as Lysander tried to do
later. There is no evidence for such an attempt and no reason to believe in it.

don the alliance with Boeotia unless the Boeotians agreed to the Peace of Nicias. The ambassadors were also told to point out that if Athens had any evil intentions it would already have made an alliance with Argos. After completing their speech, according to these instructions, the Athenian ambassadors announced that if the Spartans did not give up the Boeotian alliance Athens would make an alliance with Argos. We should not believe that this is the speech that Nicias would have delivered had he been free to choose his own message. No doubt, he hoped that the friends of peace at Sparta would come forward and at least abandon the Boeotian alliance as a way of avoiding a renewal of the war. But Alcibiades and his associates must have helped draft the embassy's instructions. The tough, demanding tone of the Athenian message destroyed any hope of conciliation. Xenares, Cleobulus, and their faction, "the Boeotian party" as Plutarch calls them,[43] carried the day and the Spartans refused. For Nicias' sake, and perhaps to appease the peace faction at Sparta, they agreed to renew the oaths of the Peace of Nicias, but it was an empty gesture. Sparta would hold to the Boeotian alliance, and Athens was expected to join with Argos.

The embassy returned and reported the failure of its mission. Alcibiades took advantage of the Athenians' rage to bring in the ambassadors from Argos, Elis, and Mantinea, and Athens concluded a treaty with the three democratic states from the Peloponnesus. The treaty, which was for one hundred years, provided for a mutual non-aggression pact and a defensive alliance on land and sea between the three Peloponnesian democracies and their dependencies, on the one hand, and the Athenians and their subject states on the other. Argos, Elis, and Mantinea were bound to come to Athens' aid if she were attacked, and the Athenians were likewise bound to send aid to the Peloponnesian democracies when they were invaded.[44]

The agreement was a triumph for Alcibiades and it set Athens on a new course, but neither ancient authors nor modern

---

[43]*Nic.* 10:7: τῶν βοιωτιαζόντων.
[44]For the full details see 5.47.1-12 with commentary in *HCT* IV, 54-63.

scholars agree on its virtues. Thucydides makes no explicit judgment, not even an equivocal one such as he makes on the Sicilian expedition,[45] although he may have meant us to include it among the many blunders that he attributes to the successors of Pericles. It is noteworthy, however, that in 415, even after the Spartans had defeated the new alliance at Mantinea, a far from embarrassed Alcibiades boasted of his role in creating it. "I put together the most powerful states of the Peloponnesus without great danger or expense to you and made the Spartans risk everything on a single day at Mantinea; because of that, even though they won the battle, to this day they no longer have secure confidence."[46] Though we must make allowance for the self-serving purpose of his speech and for rhetorical exaggeration, Alcibiades could not have made his boast if most of his fellow citizens thought the Argive alliance foolish or disastrous.

In 420, of course, some Athenians still clung to the hope of friendship with Sparta and rejected the idea of an Argive alliance. The ancient writers give us little indication of their arguments,[47] but Eduard Meyer has tried to fill that gap. In his view the Argive alliance was of no value to Athens because Argos was not a useful ally, as the earlier association in 461 had shown and as defeat at Mantinea would show again. On the contrary, the alliance only burdened Athens with Argos' troubles and distracted Athenian attention, energy, and resources from more important tasks. Athens needed peace chiefly to restore her wealth and population. The only proper sphere of Athenian activity was the northern Aegean, where Athens must restore her lost subjects in the neighborhood of Amphipolis. If Athens had rejected the Argive alliance and stayed close to Sparta, all would have been well. The turmoil in the Peloponnesus would have driven Sparta completely into Athens' arms. Athens must do whatever was necessary to keep the pro-Athenian party in power in Sparta. The split in the Peloponnesus would widen of its own accord. Even if the Spartans finally defeated their

[45] 2.65.11.
[46] 6.16.6.
[47] Nicias' speech against the Sicilian expedition of 415 may contain some parts of his general argument against an active policy (6.10).

enemies they would need a decade to do so. Meanwhile Athens would have recovered enough strength so as not to fear any threat from the Peloponnesus. Such a policy, of course, required a leader like Pericles, "not a pretender to the throne like Alcibiades who wished to fish in troubled waters to make himself king of Athens and of all Greece."[48]

Such is Meyer's argument. Its flaws are apparent. The earlier Athenian alliance with Argos had not followed a number of Spartan defeats and disgraces; it had not been accompanied by a general defection of Sparta's allies and the creation of a new coalition challenging Spartan hegemony. The new Argos was better prepared militarily and diplomatically to challenge the Spartans. The Argive alliance of 420, moreover, was an excellent guarantee against any Spartan invasion of Attica. So long as Argive, Mantinean, and Elean armies stood together ready to attack, no Spartan army would leave the Peloponnesus. Should the Athenians choose to use it, the new alliance offered a weapon with which to destroy Spartan power once and for all. The risk, as Alcibiades pointed out, was small as was the expense. Meyer's analysis, moreover, completely ignores the political realities in Sparta. The war party was not interested in friendship with Athens, and conditions guaranteed that this faction would gain control at some time. So long as the Spartans did not fulfill their commitments, Athens could not be asked to fulfill hers. While there were Athenians or Messenians at Pylos, the Spartans could not be at peace. Peaceful coexistence between the two great powers, no matter how desirable, was impossible. If the Athenians had rejected the Argive overtures, the results for them would have been unwelcome. Either the Argives would renew the Spartan alliance, as they had almost done already, or Argos would face a war in which the three Peloponnesian democracies would oppose the other Peloponnesians and Boeotia as well. Meyer may have thought that such a war could last a decade, but the Argives' own actions and the battle of Mantinea suggest otherwise. In either case Athens would soon face a united Peloponnesus allied with Boeotia, a repetition of the forces she

---

[48]I have summarized Meyer's argument in *Forsch.* II, 354-356.

had confronted in the Archidamian War, but now Athens' population was decimated and her treasury drained. Whether the Argive alliance was meant as a defensive measure or as a turn to the offensive, and Athenians may have supported it for either reason, it was an intelligent and necessary step that fully deserves Plutarch's praise: "It divided and agitated almost all Peloponnesus; it arrayed against the Lacedaemonians at Mantinea so many warlike shields upon a single day; it set at farthest remove from Athens the struggle and all its risks, in which, when the Lacedaemonians conquered, their victory brought them no great advantage, whereas, had they been defeated, the very existence of Sparta would have been at stake."[49]

In spite of the grave deterioration in relations between Athens and Sparta and the separate alliances each had made that violated at least the spirit of their own alliance, neither state renounced that alliance. Presumably neither wished to give the other a pretext for aggressive action or to assume the responsibility for breaking the peace. In the meantime, the Corinthians, instigators of so much of the trouble, continued to play a tricky game. They refused to join in this new Argive alliance with Athens as they had refused to join in the offensive and defensive alliance that Argos had earlier concluded with Elis and Mantinea.[50] "The Corinthians pulled back from their allies and inclined once again to the Spartans."[51] If we have understood the Corinthians' motives rightly this action should not surprise us. They had achieved what they had wanted: Sparta and Athens were at odds, the war party was in charge at Sparta, the war seemed about to resume. We need ask only why they continued to hold to the defensive alliance they had made with Argos, Elis, and Mantinea. Caution may provide part of the answer; the instability of Spartan politics might require further maneuvers. Beyond that, the Corinthians' ambiguous position in respect to the Peloponnesian democracies might allow them to intervene at some crucial moment in the future.

[49]Plut. Alc. 15.1, translated by B. Perrin.
[50]This full alliance is not mentioned earlier by Thucydides. See HCT IV, 63–64.
[51]5.48.

The Athenian alliance with the Peloponnesian democracies did immediate damage to Spartan prestige, encouraging actions that insulted and injured the Spartans. The first of these occurred at the ninetieth Olympic festival, held in the summer of 420. Although the very first clause of the Peace of Nicias had provided for free access to the common sanctuaries,[52] Olympia was in Elis, the Eleans presided at the games, and because of their quarrel with Sparta they barred the Spartans from making sacrifices or competing. They justified the ban on the grounds that Sparta had violated the sacred truce by attacking an Elean fort and sending troops into Lepreum after the truce had been announced. The Spartans claimed that they had taken these actions before the truce had been proclaimed. The rights and wrongs of the complaint are not totally clear nor do they seem important. The Eleans clearly intended to use the Olympic games to achieve their political ends. The Olympic court, composed of Eleans, found against Sparta and imposed a fine. When the Spartans objected, the Eleans offered to waive half the fine and pay the other half themselves if the Spartans would restore Lepreum to them. When the Spartans refused, the Eleans sought at least to humiliate them, asking them to swear an oath at the altar of Olympian Zeus before all the assembled Greeks that they would pay the fine later. When the Spartans still refused, they were banned from temples, sacrifices, and competition in the games. The Eleans would have dared none of these highly provocative actions without outside support. As it was, they were afraid the Spartans would force their way in by arms. They guarded the sanctuary with their own armed troops aided by a thousand men each from Argos and Mantinea. In addition, Athens sent a troop of cavalry which took up a position at Harpine, not far from Olympia.[53]

Tension at the Olympic games, already high, was increased by the provocative behavior of a single Spartan, Lichas, son of Arcesilaus. Lichas was one of the rare Spartans who stood out among the "Equals." His father had been an Olympic victor twice. Lichas himself was rich enough not only to race a chariot

[52] 5.18.1.
[53] 5.49.1-50.3; HCT IV, 64-66.

at the games but even to serve as host for the foreigners who came to view the festival of the Gymnopaediae at Sparta.[54] He was *proxenus* of the Argives and, as we shall see, had close relations with the Boeotians. It is tempting to identify him with the policy of Xenares and Cleobulus, for nobody was better suited to conduct the private negotiations that took place among Spartans, Argives, and Boeotians.[55] His action at the Olympic games of 420, at any rate, reveals a bold and defiant spirit. The Elean action barring the Spartans had been a blow to Sparta's prestige, and Lichas was determined to show that Sparta would not accept it supinely. He gave his own chariot over to the Thebans and raced it in their name. When it came in first Lichas entered the race course and placed a crown on the victorious charioteer, making it clear to all that the chariot was his. This act of defiance infuriated the Eleans, and they sent the games' attendants to scourge him with whips and drive him out. This further humiliation heightened the fear that the Spartan army might make an appearance, but Sparta took no action, leaving other Greeks to believe that it had been intimidated by Athens and its Peloponnesian allies.[56] The allied show of force may have been aimed at Corinth as well as Sparta, for just after the Olympic festival the Argives again approached the Corinthians and asked them to join in the new full alliance that included Athens. They probably hoped that the demonstration of Spartan weakness would sway the Corinthians to look in their direction again. The Spartans were present in Corinth, presumably to argue against the proposal, and extended conversations took place. Sparta's apparent weakness may have made the Corinthians reluctant to break off the talks, but a convenient earthquake interrupted the conference before it could take any action.[57]

But Sparta's humiliations continued. In the winter of 420/19 her colony at Heraclea in Trachis was attacked by the peoples of the neighborhood (see Map 3). Since the colony's establishment in 426,[58] the local populations had been hostile to it, and during

[54]Paus. 6.2.2; Xen. *Mem.* 1.2.61.
[55]For his proxeny see 5.76.3.
[56]5.50.4; Xen. *Hell.* 3.2.21; Paus. 6.2.2.
[57]5.50.5.
[58]See Kagan, *Archidamian War*, 195–197.

this winter they defeated the Heracleotes, killing their governor, Xenares son of Cnidis, presumably the warlike Spartan ephor of the previous year. Driven back within their walls, the Heracleotes sent for help to the Thebans, who sent 1,000 picked hoplites to save the city.[59] Early in March of 419[60] the Thebans took advantage of the weakened condition of the Heracleotes to take control of the Spartan colony. They dismissed the new Spartan governor Hegesippidas, alleging misgovernment. Thucydides tells us that they acted from fear that the Athenians would capture the colony, since the Spartans, distracted by their troubles in the Peloponnesus, could not defend it.[61] No doubt this fear was real, but we may guess that the Thebans, increasingly bold and independent since their victory at Delium, were pleased at the chance to reduce Spartan influence in central Greece and to increase their own. "The Spartans, nonetheless, were angry at them."[62] It seems fair to assume that the Aenianians, Dolopians, Malians, and Thessalians had been encouraged to attack Heraclea by news of the Athenian league with the Peloponnesian allies. They probably did not reckon with Theban intervention and without it they likely would have succeeded. Even so, the campaign created tension between the Spartans and the Boeotians. Although Sparta had suffered little material harm, the Athenian alliance with Argos, Elis, and Mantinea was achieving results even before Athens took any important action on its behalf.

[59] 5.51. The information about the Theban assistance comes from Diodorus (12.77.4) and is not mentioned by Thucydides. I agree with Andrewes (*HCT* IV, 68) that this precise detail comes from a non-Thucydidean source, probably Ephorus. There is no reason to doubt its accuracy, especially in light of the events of the next spring.

[60] Thucydides says: τοῦ δ᾽ ἐπιγιγνομένου θέρους εὐθὺς ἀρχομένου (5.52.1). For the date of the beginning of summer see *HCT* III, 699–706, especially 705–706.

[61] 5.52.1.

[62] 5.52.1.

4. The Challenge of the
Separate League

Athenian goals in making an alliance with the Peloponnesian democracies were far from clear. Different Athenians, in fact, may have supported the compact for different reasons. Some may have seen it as chiefly defensive, as a check to prevent any Spartan activity outside the Peloponnesus. Others may have hoped that by committing only small numbers of Athenian men and ships they might support a movement that would destroy the Peloponnesian League at little or no risk to Athens. Bolder Athenians may have hoped to bring on a single battle in favorable circumstances that would destroy Sparta's power. Thucydides does not tell us the motives of the Athenians or even of the architect of the alliance, Alcibiades. To resolve these matters we must examine the actions of the Athenians in detail.

Early in the summer of 419, Alcibiades, who had been reelected as general,[1] led a small force of Athenian hoplites and bowmen into the Peloponnesus. The expedition was planned in concert with the Argives and the other Peloponnesian allies and was strengthened by some of their troops. Thucydides tells us that Alcibiades "passed through the Peloponnesus with his army," presumably landing near Argos and marching to Mantinea and Elis, "settling matters concerning the alliance."[2] From there he went to Patrae on the coast, outside the Corinthian Gulf, where he

[1] 5.55.4; Fornara, *Generals*, 62. Andrewes (*HCT* IV, 69) places the date in the spring but suggests that the month was Hekatombaion, which is usually thought to begin about July 1.
[2] 5.52.2. The route is suggested by Gomme, *HCT* IV, 69.

persuaded its people to make an alliance with Athens and to build walls to the sea which would keep communications open with Athens and permit resistance to Spartan attack (see Maps 5a and 5b).[3] The Athenians also intended to build a fort at Rhium in Achaea, opposite Naupactus at the narrowest point of the Gulf of Corinth but the Corinthians, Sicyonians, and others in the neighborhood prevented the construction.[4] Gomme called this expedition "a grandiose scheme for an Athenian general at the head of a mainly Athenian army," to march through the Peloponnesus thumbing his nose "at Sparta when her reputation was at its lowest. Its daring, such as it was, its theatricality, and its small practical value, were alike characteristic of Alcibiades."[5] Other scholars, though taking a less harsh view of the expedition, have treated it as inconsequential and unrelated to other events, but Alcibiades had more in mind than a parade through the Peloponnesus: his march was part of a strategic plan.[6]

To be sure, the very fact that a hostile army could march unhindered through the Peloponnesus was valuable propaganda that advertised the weakness of Sparta and the strength of the new league. Nor should we underestimate the importance to Athens of "settling matters concerning the alliance." Political factions in Argos made it less than a perfectly reliable ally. Elis and Mantinea were newly associated with Athens and might doubt the seriousness of the Athenian commitment. It was, moreover, important to establish personal contact with the leaders in each state if the alliance were to function smoothly. The main purpose of the expedition, however, was something still more important.

The alliance with Patrae and the attempt to build a fort at Rhium were intended to gain fuller control of the mouth of the Corinthian Gulf. Alcibiades' task at Patrae was not as easy as

[3]5.55.2. That Alcibiades must have made an alliance was seen by J. K. Anderson, *BSA* XLIX (1954), 84.

[4]5.52.2.

[5]*HCT* IV, 70.

[6]For typical treatments of the expedition see Grote, VII, 63-64, and Ferguson, *CAH* V, 268. Hatzfeld (*Alcibiade* 97-98) places a higher value on it; the best understanding of the expedition's significance is provided by Busolt, *GG* III:2, 1232-1233, and *Forsch.*, 149-151. My own account owes much to his understanding of events.

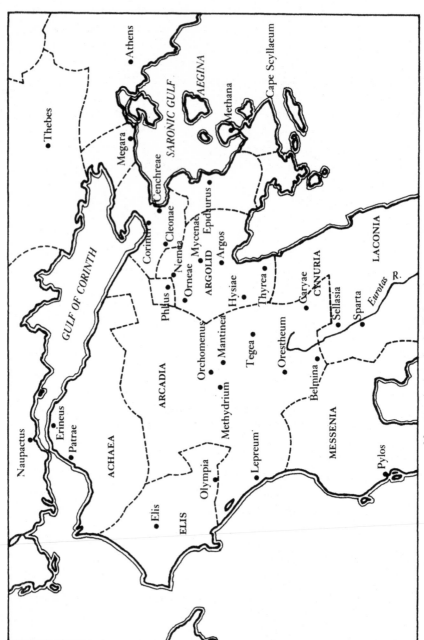

Map 5a. Actions in the Peloponnesus, 419/18

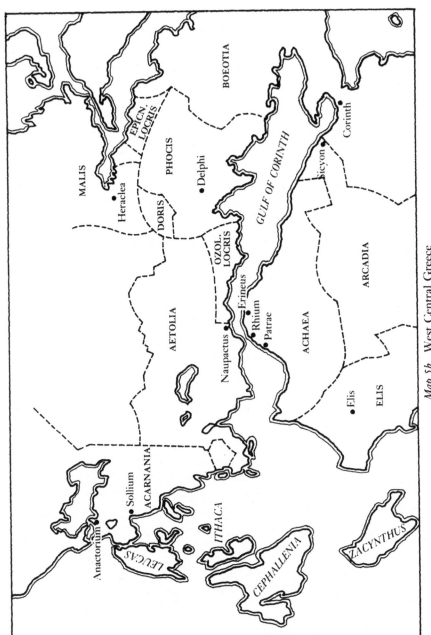

Map 5b. West Central Greece

Thucydides' laconic narrative might indicate. Pericles had taken over Achaea and brought it into alliance with Athens by means of a naval expedition during the First Peloponnesian War, but the Thirty Years' Peace of 446/45 made the Athenians relinquish it.[7] Most of the Achaean cities were neutral during the Archidamian War, though Cleon demanded the return of Achaea in 425 as one of his conditions for accepting the Spartan peace offer.[8] When Alcibiades came to Patrae in 419, the city seems still to have been neutral and to have had a democratic government. On the other hand, there appears to have been an oligarchic faction, and opinion in the city was divided.[9] Whereas Pericles had arrived with a large fleet, Alcibiades had only a small force of soldiers and no navy. The people of Patrae were free to reject his offer without danger. Their acceptance was undoubtedly influenced by the lowered reputation of Sparta and the ascendancy of Athens and its continental allies—an ascendancy demonstrated by Alcibiades' recent march through the Peloponnesus. If we may believe an anecdote reported by Plutarch, Alcibiades' debating skill also helped his cause. When someone objected to the alliance on the grounds that the Athenians would swallow Patrae up, Alcibiades responded: "Perhaps, but little by little, and feet first. But the Spartans will swallow you head first and all at once."[10]

The second part of Alcibiades' strategy was the conquest of Epidaurus, which the Argives began to undertake in the same summer. In 430 Pericles had led a large force against Epidaurus. Thucydides says nothing about the purpose of that campaign, though we may believe it was meant to increase the pressure on the Peloponnesians and encourage them to make peace.[11] He is more informative about the campaign of 419. The Argives offered as the *casus belli* the usual complaint of a religious violation by the Epidaurians. Their real motives, however, were to provide a shorter route by which the Athenians could come to their

[7]1.111.3; 1.115. I see no reason to reject the opinion of the scholiast that Pericles was responsible for the alliance, *pace* Anderson, *BSA* XLIX (1954), 81–82.

[8]4.210.

[9]Anderson, *BSA* XLIX (1954), 84.

[10]Plut. *Alc.* 15.3.

[11]2.56; Kagan, *Archidamian War*, 72–76.

aid[12] and, most important, "to keep Corinth quiet."[13] We may suppose that this expedition was one of the subjects Alcibiades discussed at Argos on his march through the Peloponnesus.

The campaigns in Achaea and Epidaurus were two aspects of a plan meant to threaten and isolate Corinth. The alliance with Patrae made it easier to interfere with Corinth's trade and communications with her western colonies. If Epidaurus fell, the psychological impact on Corinth would be great. Even though Epidaurus was not well situated for launching an attack on Corinth, its fall would threaten the Corinthians with attack from two sides and demonstrate that Argos and Athens were willing and able to attack and defeat the Peloponnesian states allied to Sparta. The next time, with Epidaurus safely in hand, the Argives might march against Corinth by the Nemea road while the Athenians landed on the Corinthian coast, as Nicias had done in 425.[14] The allies may have hoped that such a threat would force the Corinthians out of their alliance with Sparta. If they would not join the new league, at least they would remain neutral. Corinthian neutrality would have important strategic consequences, preventing extra-Peloponnesian allies like Boeotia and Megara from supporting the Spartans against the new league. It would also put Megara in a vulnerable position, menaced by Athens but unable to obtain Peloponnesian support. In time Megara, and perhaps other Peloponnesian states, might conclude that it was wise to seek neutrality rather than to continue supporting a weakening Sparta against the ever more powerful new league.

If we have judged Alcibiades' plans for the alliance rightly, we can conclude that its investment of Athenian men and money was low and that it ran a low risk. Rejecting battle as a primary device, the alliance used the armed forces as a means of applying diplomatic pressure, aiming neither to bring the enemy to battle, nor to exhaust his resources, but only to convince him to alter his course of action. It is striking that the two actions Alcibiades took in 419 had been undertaken by Pericles at earlier times;

[12]See Map 6. The Athenians could send aid by way of Aegina, to Epidaurus, then overland to Argos, thus avoiding the trip around the promontory of Scyllaeum.

[13]5.53.1.

[14]4.42-44.

indeed, the similarity between the general strategic approaches of each man is marked. We may guess that Alcibiades had studied the career of his guardian closely and rejected not only the ineffective quietism of Nicias but also reckless adventures on land or sea. His plan might or might not work, but it was rational and prudent.

The Argive invasion of Epidaurian territory had scarcely begun when King Agis led the Spartan army out in full force. He marched toward the Arcadian border in a direction which would allow him to move toward Elis in the northwest, Mantinea to the north, or even northeast to Argos. The Spartan army's objective may have been to attack any one of the allied cities or to create a threat that would keep Elean and Mantinean forces at home where they could not aid the Argives. Thucydides does not relate the purpose of the Spartan expedition, for on this occasion he surely did not know it. In fact, "no one knew where they were marching, not even the cities from which they were sent."[15]

Agis' real goal was never to be revealed, for when he made the usual sacrifices at the border the omens proved unfavorable. The Spartans turned to go home and sent word to their allies to prepare to march again after the coming month, the Carneian, which was a Dorian holiday. Modern scholars do not agree on the sincerity of Spartan religious scruples on this and other such occasions. Some argue that this Spartan withdrawal and the one that followed soon after[16] were the result of genuine religious feeling.[17] We need not doubt that the Spartans were sincerely religious and that unfavorable omens, especially earthquakes or other natural phenomena, sometimes affected their policy, but our suspicion is aroused by the coincidence in the summer of 418 of two consecutive occasions on which omens were said to prevent the Spartan army under Agis from attacking the Argives or their allies. That suspicion is not allayed when we notice that

[15] 5.54.1. For an excellent discussion of the extraordinary secrecy in both military and diplomatic spheres during this period see Busolt, *Forsch.*, 152–153. He makes the point that we must assume that Thucydides' many silences about these matters result from his lack of information.

[16] 5.55.3.

[17] H. Popp, *Die Einwirkung von Vorzeichen, Opfern und Festen auf die Kriegführung der Griechen* (Würzburg, 1957) 42–46, cited approvingly by Andrewes, *HCT* IV, 74.

later in that same summer the Spartans, fearing that the Peloponnesian League might collapse, decided to take action and were not prevented by any unfavorable omens. Nor did such omens delay them when they hurriedly sent an army to prevent Tegea from going over to the Argives.[18] We must agree with Busolt that the unfavorable frontier sacrifices were merely a "pretext by which the sudden withdrawal was explained to the army."[19]

If divine intervention does not explain Agis' actions, we must seek their human motives by assessing political, diplomatic, and military considerations. We have already seen that the faction to which Cleobulus and Xenares belonged sought an alliance with Argos as a step toward renewing the war against Athens. Recent events could only confirm their view that Sparta could not easily defeat an Athens supported by Argos and its allies. Sparta had almost succeeded in winning over the Argives in 420,[20] but a campaign against Argos now offered no guarantee of success and, even if successful, was likely to cost many Spartan lives. It was also likely to strengthen the new league, which had not yet acted together against the enemy. A Spartan attack on any allied city was bound to bring the others into the field and likely to bind them together more closely. There was, on the other hand, an oligarchic faction in Argos which was friendly to Sparta.[21] It seems likely that its members had taken the lead in trying to arrange a Spartan alliance in the previous year. They were, at any rate, prepared to carry out a coup d'état against the democracy and to join the Spartan alliance after the battle of Mantinea in 418.[22] The withdrawal of the Spartan army may have been caused by a decision on the part of Agis and others to delay a confrontation with Argos in the hope that these oligarchs might bring about a change that would make such a conflict unnecessary. Since he had been ordered out to fight, Agis could not merely withdraw, even in the face of unfavorable omens. The Epidaurians and their friends among the allies, as well as the

[18]5.64.
[19]Busolt, Forsch., 154.
[20]See above, Chap. 3.
[21]5.76. See also Kagan, CP LVII (1962), 209–218.
[22]5.81.

many Spartans who wanted to engage the enemy, could not be restrained forever. The order to reassemble after the Carneian month emphasized the pious motives for delay, gained time for the Argive oligarchs, and reassured those clamoring for action.

The Argives, aware of the Spartans' withdrawal and certainly informed of the plan to resume hostilities after the holy month, were eager to attack Epidaurus before then. Although they too were Dorians, they were not deterred by religious scruples. Someone in Argos, however, must have raised the religious question, for the Argives found it necessary to resort to a subterfuge. They launched their invasion of Epidaurus on the twenty-seventh day of the month before Carneius and proceeded to call every day they remained in Epidaurian territory the twenty-seventh of that month, thus avoiding violation of the Carneian holiday. The Epidaurians called on their allies, that is, the members of the Peloponnesian League, for help. Their response demonstrated the great impact both of Alcibiades' policy and of Spartan hesitation. Some of the allies did not appear at all, pleading the holy month as an excuse, while others advanced to the Epidaurian frontier but would come no further.[23]

A combined allied assault during Carneius (about August) of 419 might have brought the fall of Epidaurus, but before any Argive ally could take part the Athenians had called a conference at Mantinea to discuss peace.[24] It is generally thought that this intervention was the result of a change in the Athenian political situation which allowed Nicias to gain power for the moment and issue the call for a peace conference.[25] If we have judged Alcibiades' plan correctly, however, such a conference is perfectly in accord with it and need not be ascribed to Nicias. The Argive invasion of Epidaurus and the failure of Sparta and its allies to provide aid gave Alcibiades an opportunity to persuade the Corinthians to abandon Sparta before they, like the Epidaurians, were themselves abandoned. An unsuccessful battle or a

[23] 5.54.

[24] 5.55.1.

[25] See, e.g., Busolt, *Forsch.*, 155; Grote, VII, 68; Ferguson, *CAH* V, 268; Gomme, *HCT* IV, 76. Andrewes, however (*HCT* IV, 76), thinks that the meeting could just as easily have been called by Alcibiades to serve as a sounding board for Athenian propaganda and complaints prior to declaring that the Spartans had broken the Peace. Hatzfeld (*Alcibiade*, 10) also credits Alcibiades with calling the meeting.

campaign that lasted until after Carneius might bring the Spartans into the conflict and stiffen Corinthian resistance. The conference, we can conclude, was meant to crown Alcibiades' Argive policy, not to undermine it.[26]

Everything hinged on the Corinthian reaction, and the Corinthians, as always, were tricky. The Corinthian spokesman Euphamidas accused the allies of hypocrisy, pointing out that while they claimed to speak of peace, the Argives were in arms against the Epidaurians. He demanded that both armies be disbanded before the congress could go forward.[27] Euphamidas may have expected the Argives to refuse (the Corinthians had refused a similar request from the Corcyraeans in 433),[28] thereby giving him a pretext to break up the congress. It is clear, in any case, that the Corinthians were unwilling to accept peace on the allied terms, for even after the Argives had withdrawn from the field and the conferees had reassembled no agreement was reached.[29] The Corinthians must have understood that their withdrawal from the Spartan alliance would probably lead to the collapse of that alliance and the triumph of Athens. Their rejection of peace terms put an end to the conference and to Alcibiades' hopes for a diplomatic victory.

With the collapse of peace negotiations the Argives resumed their ravaging of Epidaurus. Once again the Spartans marched to their border, toward Caryae on the road to eastern Arcadia and Argos (see Map 5a).[30] This time there was no doubt where the army was going. When Alcibiades learned of the Spartan expedition, presumably from his Argive connections, he persuaded the Athenians to send him with 1,000 hoplites to protect his Argive allies.[31] The Argives themselves, having ravaged a third of the Epidaurian lands, withdrew to protect their own city. No fight-

[26]Nothing in the ancient evidence points to the resurgence of Nicias at this point and no ancient writer speaks of it.

[27]5.55.1.

[28]1.28; Kagan, Outbreak, 226.

[29]5.55.2. The Argive willingness to withdraw seems further evidence that the conference was the work of Alcibiades and not Nicias. Certainly it is hard to imagine the Argives leaving the field and wasting precious time in the Carneian month at the behest of Nicias.

[30]Gomme, HCT IV, 76.

[31]5.55.4. I accept the reading suggested by Fr. Portus and defended by Andrewes (HCT IV, 76-77); καὶ Ἀθηναίων αὐτοῖς χίλιοι ἐβοήθησαν ὁπλῖται

ing resulted, however, for when the Spartans reached the frontier the sacrifices once again produced unfavorable omens, and the army returned home. The mere threat of a Spartan attack had relieved the pressure on Epidaurus, and that, we may suppose, allowed Agis and his associates to risk once again postponing the confrontation with the Argives which they still hoped to avoid entirely. When Alcibiades heard of the Spartan withdrawal he took his own troops back to Athens. The Peloponnesian campaign of 419 came to an end with Corinth still allied to Sparta. More than diplomacy would be needed to destroy the Peloponnesian League.[32]

During the winter of 419/18 relations between the two leagues were further strained. The Spartans demonstrated their concern to help the defenders of Epidaurus by undertaking what was for them a daring enterprise. They dispatched 300 men to reinforce the garrison in the city, sending them by sea under the command of Agesippidas.[33] Agesippidas presumably sailed from Cenchreae, Corinth's harbor on the Saronic Gulf, and his route took him near Athenian bases at Aegina and Methana (see Map 6).[34] This gave the Argives, presumably disappointed with the level of Athenian involvement up to that time, grounds for complaint. Their treaty with Athens had provided that enemies of either Athens or Argos were not to be allowed to cross their respective territories. The Argives therefore complained that in not preventing the Spartans from sailing through the waters off Aegina, the Athenians had allowed them to cross Argive territory. The Argives now asked Athens to make amends by restoring the helots and Messenians from Naupactus to Pylos, a point from which they could harass the Spartans. Whether or not Alcibiades urged the Argives to make this demand, he certainly took the

καὶ Ἀλκιβιάδης στρατηγός, πυθόμενος τοὺς Λακεδαιμονίους ἐξεστρατεῦσθαι, which assumes that δὲ has been interpolated into the manuscripts after πυθόμενος.

[32] 5.55.3-4. Thucydides leaves unclear the chronology of the Spartan march and withdrawal, the Argive withdrawal, and the Athenian march to Argos. The above account represents an interpretation that is not in conflict with his narrative, but others are possible.

[33] 5.56.1. There is no reason to doubt that this Agesippidas was the same man who was expelled by the Boeotians from Heraclea the previous winter. His appointment here indicates that the Spartans did not hold him responsible for its loss and judged the Boeotians' charges against him to be mere pretexts.

[34] Andrewes, HCT IV, 77.

Map 6. Northeast Peloponnesus

lead in persuading the Athenians to comply. On his motion the Athenians inscribed on the bottom of the stele on which their treaty with Sparta was recorded that the Spartans had not carried out their oaths. Citing this betrayal as their excuse, the Athenians returned the helots who had been removed from Pylos, and they proceeded to ravage the countryside. The Athenians did not, however, formally denounce the treaty, which we may take as evidence of how delicate the political balance within Athens was. A majority of Athenian voters may have supported the Argive alliance, but there was no steady majority to support the renewal of a full-scale land war against the Spartans. The influence of Alcibiades was sufficient to commit the Athenians to activities in which others, be they Argives, Eleans, Mantineans, Messenians, or helots, would do the fighting. But if a real war involving Athenian soldiers loomed, Alcibiades' support waned. This division in Athens, which prevented the pursuit of a consistent policy for either peace or war, would be a source of great trouble to Athens for years to come.

The political division in Sparta also persisted. Though none of the Athenian actions, not even the restoration of the helots to Pylos, was technically in violation of the treaties, they were all clearly provocative. Athenian assistance to the Argive attack on a Spartan ally, at any rate, could not be ignored. Still, the Spartans did not declare the treaties broken and made no formal response to the Athenian declaration. Influential Spartans must have continued to desire peace, while others wanted a renewal of the war but may have differed as to the best tactics. Some clearly favored a direct and immediate confrontation with Argos and its allies, including the Athenians if necessary. Others, if we have reasoned correctly, hoped to detach Argos by diplomacy and treason before resuming the war on Athens. Neither Athens nor Sparta took further part in the Epidaurian campaigns during the winter. The Argives continued their depredations without bringing on a pitched battle. With the Epidaurian army scattered in an attempt to defend the countryside, the Argives tried to take the city by storm. The defenders, bolstered by the Spartan garrison, held them off, and the winter ended without a military decision.[35]

Early in March of 418 the Athenians elected generals to take office in July. The new board included Nicias, Nicostratus, Laches, Autocles, Euthydemus, Callistratus, and Demosthenes.[36] It did not include Alcibiades.[37] Demosthenes had

[35] 5.56.

[36] For the list of generals and the evidence for it see Fornara, *Generals*, 62–63, but see also next note.

[37] Thucydides (5.61.2) and Diodorus (12.79) make it clear that Alcibiades was not general at the time of Mantinea. Some scholars have tried to restore his name in a fragmentary inscription recording payments from the treasury of Athena for different purposes in the year 418/17 (Tod, I, 75, p. 289); the

been a most aggressive general in the Archidamian War and may have been in favor of the Argive policy; we simply do not know. We know little about Callistratus. Euthydemus signed both the Peace of Nicias and the alliance with Sparta[38] but perhaps should not be associated with Nicias merely on that account. Nicostratus, Laches, and Autocles, however, are regularly associated with Nicias.[39] When we couple the election of Nicias and his associates with Alcibiades' failure to be reelected, we must believe that many Athenians had changed their minds since the previous summer. The removal of Alcibiades and the predominance of his rival Nicias and his faction represented a vote for caution and against adventure, especially against the easy commitment of Athenian troops to Peloponnesian battlefields. The change, however, was not decisive. The Athenians did not abandon the Argive alliance, so they were still committed to help their Peloponnesian allies, but they wanted their troops to be under more conservative leadership.

In the middle of the summer of 418, King Agis led the Spartan army in full force against Argos; accompanied by the Tegeans and the other Arcadians still loyal to Sparta, they numbered almost 8,000 hoplites.[40] Sparta's other allies, both inside and outside the Peloponnesus, were ordered to gather at Phlius. They numbered about 12,000 hoplites as well as 5,000 light-armed troops and 1,000 cavalry and mounted infantry from Boeotia.[41] This extraordinarily large army had not been gathered to make a show of force and then return without a fight; it was Sparta's answer to the menace posed by Alcibiades' policy.

---

restoration is accepted by S. Accame, *Rev. Fil.* LXIII (1935), 346, n. 3, and Fornara, *Generals*, 63. I agree with Meiggs and Lewis (*GHI*, 235) that the restoration is too uncertain to accept. In any case the restorers argue that Alcibiades became general late in the year in an election to fill a vacancy, so he was not elected in March of 418.

[38] 5.19.2 and 5.24.1.

[39] For the association of these men with Nicias and with one another see Kagan, *Archidamian War*, 169, 179-181, 218, 260, 261, 305, 307, 313.

[40] Busolt (*GG* III:2, 1238, n. 1) estimates 4,200 Spartans, about 1,500 Tegeans, and about 2,000 Arcadians. Henderson (*Great War*, 304) makes essentially the same estimate.

[41] Thucydides gives us the number of Boeotian forces, including 5,000 hoplites. He also tells us that Corinth sent 2,000 hoplites. The rest came from Phlius, Megara, Epidaurus, Sicyon, and Pellene. See Henderson, *Great War*, 304.

Thucydides tells us that the Spartans launched the campaign, "because their allies the Epidaurians were in distress, and of their other Peloponnesian allies, some were in rebellion and others ill disposed. They thought that if they did not take action swiftly the trouble would go further."[42] This explanation in turn raises the question of why, if the emergency were so grave, the Spartans waited until mid-summer instead of launching their campaign early in the season. One suggestion is that the Spartans, aware of the results of the elections to the new *strategia* in Athens, were waiting for the friends of peace to take office in the hope that they might execute their obligations to the Argives without zeal and without using their full resources.[43] That would be a good reason for delay, but internal considerations in Sparta may have played a role as well. Agis and his supporters may have continued to hope that political developments in Argos would make a major battle unnecessary, and so delayed to let events take their course. When nothing happened in Argos and the Athenians stood by their alliance with the Argives, the pressure from Sparta's allies to act must have become irresistible. We may suspect that some of that pressure came from the Corinthians, who anticipated a great battle that would simultaneously eliminate the threat of the dissolution of the Peloponnesian League and bring the Spartans into battle against Athens.

For the Argives, too, there seemed to be no escape from a major confrontation. They learned that the Spartan army was marching towards a rendezvous with their northern allies at Phlius, and they gathered their own forces and those of their allies. The Argives are estimated to have had about 7,000 hoplites. The Eleans sent 3,000, and the Mantineans with their Arcadian allies brought about 2,000 more, for a total of about 12,000 troops.[44] The Athenians were also asked for help, and a force of

---

[42] 5.57.2.

[43] Such is the suggestion of Busolt, *Forsch.*, 162–163. Similar answers are given by Beloch (*AP*, 53) and Meyer (*Forsch.* II, 365). Gomme denounces all interpretations based on any political calculations in an uncharacteristically heated comment. His own suggestions are not persuasive. Andrewes' sensible observations soften Gomme's exasperated remarks (*HCT* IV, 78–79).

[44] 5.58.2. For estimates see Busolt, *GG* III:2, 1238, n. 1, and Henderson, *Great War*, 304. The rest of the chapter follows my article in *CP* LVII (1962), 209–218.

1,000 hoplites and 300 cavalry was ultimately sent, but it arrived too late to be of any use. The Spartans had done well to delay their campaign until the change of generals.[45] The Argive generals realized that if they allowed the two enemy armies to join, they would be badly outnumbered: 20,000 hoplites from the Spartan alliance against 12,000 of their own and 1,000 cavalry and 5,000 light-armed men against none. Their strategic task was plain: they must cut Agis off before his army could reach the northern army at Phlius. The Argives marched westward into Arcadia, relying no doubt on scouts and friendly Arcadians to keep them apprised of the Spartan route.

The most direct route from Sparta to Phlius went through Tegea and Mantinea, but Agis could not take it since he needed to avoid battle before joining the northern army. Instead, he took a more westerly route which went through Belmina, Methydrium, and Orchomenus.[46] At Methydrium he was met by the Argives and their allies who took up a position on a hill blocking the Spartans' path. The allied position also blocked the way to Argos and Mantinea, for if Agis moved eastward his army would be isolated in hostile territory and forced to fight unaided against a numerically superior enemy. The Argives had achieved a great tactical success, and Agis could do nothing but occupy another hill facing the enemy. When night fell Agis' situation seemed desperate. He must either fight against bad odds or retreat and disgrace himself.[47]

When morning came, however, the Spartan army had disappeared. Agis had marched by night, eluding the Argives, and was on his way to the rendezvous at Phlius. Henderson, an able military historian, renders this judgment: "the carelessness of the Argive watch defies language fitly to describe it."[48] This would be far from the only time that carelessness explains military lapses, and simple incompetence may be explanation enough. Yet this was the first of a series of military blunders committed

---

[45] For the arrival of the Athenian contingent see 5.61.1.

[46] See Map 5a. See also HCT IV, 81, and Henderson, *Great War*, 305.

[47] 5.58.2; Henderson, *Great War*, 305–306. Although I am not in complete agreement with a number of his interpretations I am indebted to Henderson's account for its treatment of tactical details.

[48] Henderson, *Great War*, 306.

by the Argive generals, and these, combined with political actions taken both before and after the affair at Methydrium invite the suspicion that other considerations were at work.

There can be no doubt that there were two political factions in Argos, democrats and oligarchs.[49] We can be sure that most democrats favored Athens and most oligarchs Sparta, and that Argive neutrality in the Archidamian War may have reflected some kind of balance between them. More likely, prudence led both sides to stand aside and profit from the war without taking risks. In spite of the official neutrality, however, there is evidence that some Argives worked for the Spartan cause. In 430 Peloponnesian envoys had traveled to Persia to convince the Great King to make an alliance with Sparta and furnish money. With them went Pollis of Argos, in a private capacity.[50] Friendship between Argos and Persia dated back to 480, and Pollis must have been thought a useful advocate. Again in 425 the friendship of some Argives for the Spartan cause became plain. On that occasion the Athenian attack on Corinth had relied on secrecy for success; it failed because the Corinthians were warned "from Argos."[51]

Both incidents show that there were in Argos men who hoped and worked for Spartan victory. They must have been oligarchs, for the democrats had nothing to gain and much to fear from a Spartan triumph. The Spartans were proven enemies of democracy and replaced it with oligarchy wherever they could. The average Argive may have been less interested in factional and even constitutional questions than in the power and glory of his city. Such a man certainly must have preferred an Athenian victory, for Sparta was the traditional enemy and still held Cynuria. An Athenian victory would provide an opportunity for revenge and the recovery of lost territory and prestige. Most Argives were neutral in deed, but they must have hoped that Athens would win the war. The oligarchs could not hope to come to power without Spartan help, so they collaborated with the Spartans.

By 421 the great majority of Argives wanted to take advantage

[49] 5.76.2.
[50] 2.67.1.
[51] 4.42.3..

of Sparta's troubles to recover their lost territory and regain the leadership of the Peloponnesus. They refused to renew their treaty with Sparta and were ready to join with Athens. The oligarchs were most unhappy with such a policy and tried to reverse it. They were the ones, no doubt, who suggested a treaty with Sparta in 420.[52] Though most Argives would have thought their goals and actions treasonous, the oligarchs themselves probably thought that they were acting patriotically. It was not unusual in Greek cities for party interest to be equated with the state's interest. Perhaps the oligarchs expected territorial concessions from Sparta in return for their cooperation, possibly in Cynuria. They may even have contemplated a sort of Peloponnesian dyarchy with Sparta and Argos as yokefellows.

Such thoughts, of course, had to be kept secret, for the democratic government of Argos wanted no friendship with Sparta in the years following the Peace of Nicias. When they formed their separate league to challenge Spartan hegemony, the Argives knew that they must do something to deal with Sparta's powerful hoplite army. For this reason they undertook the unprecedented and, for the democracy, dangerous step of forming an elite guard of 1,000 young aristocrats.[53] Their suspicion allayed by years of domestic peace, the democrats thus demonstrated their faith in the loyalty of the Argive upper classes. Future events would show that this faith was misplaced, for by creating this aristocratic army, the Thousand, the democrats had given their domestic enemies a weapon with which to regain power.

The early negotiations for the separate Argive League should not have troubled the oligarchs, for the talks were conducted with Corinth, Megara, Boeotia, and other oligarchies, and did not preclude an ultimate association with Sparta. When the complicated maneuvers were over, however, two opposing leagues had been created. On one side was the Peloponnesian League with the Corinthians, Megarians, and Boeotians back in the Spartan fold. On the other stood a new league composed of Argos, Elis, Mantinea, and Athens, all democracies. The Argive oligarchs could not have welcomed this situation. So long as Argos was part of such a coalition the oligarchs could not come to

[52]See above, Chap. 3.
[53]Diod. 12.75.7 and see above, Chap. 2.

power. Worse yet, the new league aimed at war against Sparta, to whom the oligarchs looked for support. In spite of their alarm and disappointment they seem to have concealed their feelings, for they continued to hold high positions in the state and to serve as generals of the army whose most potent force remained the elite Thousand. Nonetheless, they faced a dilemma: if they refused to cooperate in their city's policy they would lose their prestige and influence, perhaps endanger their own safety; if they continued to take part in state affairs, they would be working against their own interests. They chose to keep their influential positions and to steer a difficult and dangerous course between Scylla and Charybdis.

Such was the background of the Argive march to Methydrium. The Argive army was plainly commanded by oligarchic generals. Their role may be inferred from the fact that the aristocratic Thousand was the backbone of the army and becomes obvious in the later negotiations between Agis and Thrasyllus.[54] If the Argives and their allies fought the Spartans at Methydrium all possibility of rapprochement with Sparta would be ended, and any chance for a change of regime at Argos would be destroyed. If combat could be avoided, however, there remained the possibility of negotiation. Perhaps design, not oversight, explains why Agis was able to bypass Methydrium without a battle.

Agis arrived at Phlius and took command of what Thucydides calls "the finest Greek army assembled up to that time."[55] Some seventeen miles away lay Argos and its defending army, which had hurried home after the missed opportunity at Methydrium. Between the two armies lay rough mountain country penetrated by only one road suitable for cavalry, the Tretus Pass, which was entered south of Nemea and issued before Mycenae (see Map 7).[56] There was, however, a more direct path which led to the west of the Tretus past Mount Kelussa and into the Argive

[54] 5.59-60.
[55] 5.60.3.
[56] Curtius' map of Argolid in *Peloponnesos* II and map by Military Information Division of the British Army, 1897, sheet No. 4. For discussions of the terrain see E. Curtius, *Peloponnesos* (Gotha, 1851), II, 506, 510, 512 (Tretus), 468, 479 (Kelussa), and 478ff. (Orneae); Andrewes, *HCT* IV, 81-82; Ernst Meyer, *PW* XVI (1935), 2315.

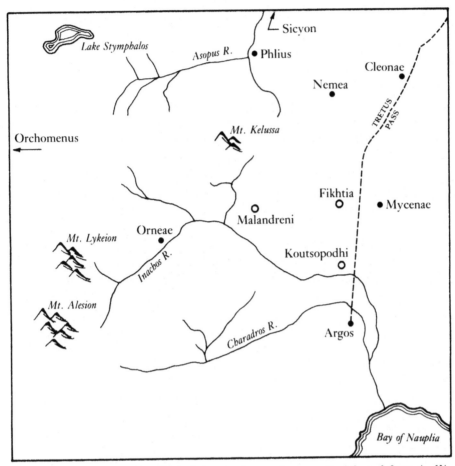

Map 7. Invasion of the Argolid and Approaches to Argos, 418. Adapted from A. W. Gomme, A. Andrewes, and K. J. Dover, *A Historical Commentary on Thucydides*, IV (Oxford, Oxford University Press, 1970), by permission of the publisher.

plain. Although this route was not suitable for cavalry, foot soldiers could use it to reach Argos from Phlius. The Argives could hardly have failed to know of it, yet their generals marched to Nemea where they deployed their forces to meet a frontal attack through the Tretus Pass, leaving themselves vulnerable to a flanking movement by way of Mount Kelussa. Henderson noted the strangeness of this maneuver: "A modern general defending Argos against attack from the north could hardly do otherwise than make Mycenae his headquarters, and content himself with throwing a strong advance guard forward to Nemea."[57] He explains this movement as another miscalculation by the Argives, who "may have relied on Agis doing the obvious thing, on the known presence of cavalry in the enemy army, which cavalry *must* use the Treton (*sic*) Pass, and on being so near to Mycenae that they could at once fall back in time to save themselves should they be threatened from the Kelussa Pass."[58]

A miscalculation it may have been, but if so it was the second serious blunder of the same type within a few days—both of them errors which avoided immediate battle. It may be that once again the Argive generals were playing for time in the hope that a reconciliation could still be effected.

Agis divided his forces into three columns. The Boeotians, Sicyonians, and Megarians and all the cavalry advanced through the Tretus Pass. The men from Corinth, Pellene, and Phlius proceeded by way of Mount Kelussa, probably reaching the plain near the modern village of Fikhtia. Agis himself led the Spartans, Arcadians, and Epidaurians by a third route, also steep and difficult. It may have taken him near the modern village of Malandreni; in any case, it led to a position still farther in the rear of the Argive army.[59] Once again Agis had made a successful march at night. In the morning word reached the Argive army at Nemea that Agis was in their rear ravaging the town of Saminthus and its neighborhood, probably near the modern Koutsopodhi.[60] Hurrying back to their city, the Argives were delayed by skirmishes with the Phliasians and Corinthians but broke through and placed themselves between Agis and the allied armies. Thucydides describes the precariousness of the Argive position: "The Argives were cut off in the middle: from the side of the plain the Spartans and those with them shut them off from the city; above them were the Corinthians, Phliasians, and Pellenians; on the side of Nemea were the Boeotians, Sicyonians, and Megarians. They had no cavalry, for the Athenians alone of their allies had not come."[61]

---

[57]Henderson, *Great War*, 307–308.

[58]Henderson, *Great War*, 308–309.

[59]I follow the suggestion of Ernst Meyer adapted by Andrewes in *HCT* IV, 81–82.

[60]5.58.5; *HCT* IV, 82.

[61]5.59.3.

Facing the Spartans who stood between them and their city, the Argives prepared for battle. Just as the two armies seemed about to meet, two Argives, Thrasyllus and Alciphron, went out to speak to Agis. To the surprise of all they returned with a four-months' truce, and no battle was fought. Stranger still was the reaction of the two armies. Each was angered by the lost opportunity for battle. The Argives believed from the beginning that "the battle was likely to be fought in favorable circumstances and that the Spartans had been cut off in their territory and close to the city of Argos."[62] When they returned to Argos they vented their rage on Thrasyllus, depriving him of his property and almost taking his life. The Spartans, on the other hand, "placed great blame on Agis because he had not conquered Argos when they thought the opportunity better than any they had before."[63]

Why did the Argives offer to negotiate? Why did Agis accept? How can the anger and disappointment of *both* armies be explained? Henderson attempts a purely military explanation:

Things had *not* gone "according to plan." Agis and his column had reached the plain. The centre column had marched and come into touch with the enemy. *But* the left column on which everything depended was not there. The Boeotians had failed him. No horse or foot pursued up the Treton Pass....

What now was his own position? He found himself isolated between an exultant enemy... and a hostile city.... No wonder the Argive troops, seeing nothing, knowing nothing of any peril of consequence in the hills behind them, stoned their craven generals.[64]

This interpretation contains several difficulties. The first and most serious is that there is no authority for the assumption that the Boeotians failed to appear. Thucydides says plainly that "the Argives were cut off in the middle... on the side of Nemea were the Boeotians." There is no reason to doubt the presence of the Boeotian column in its assigned position.[65] There is no possibil-

[62]5.59.4.
[63]5.63.1.
[64]Henderson, *Great War*, 314–316.
[65]Henderson's supposition that the Boeotians were absent (*Great War*, 315) is only conjecture. Andrewes (*HCT* IV) has also seen the flaw in Henderson's argument.

ity, moreover, that the Argives were unaware of the danger in the rear. They had faced the Boeotian contingent at Nemea[66] and had, in fact, based their entire policy on the expectation that the enemy's main force would come from that direction through the Tretus Pass.[67] Nothing could be plainer to them than the threat of a large force supported by cavalry approaching from the north. Finally, it is impossible to believe that the Spartans could have been angry with Agis if the Boeotians had truly failed him. The army and the magistrates who accompanied it would have been aware of the situation and could not have censured Agis for avoiding battle with an army that outnumbered the Spartans three to two and had him pinned against a hostile city.

Purely military arguments do not explain what happened, so we must examine political considerations. Thrasyllus and Alciphron were oligarchs who wanted to avoid a breach with Sparta.[68] They spoke to Agis on their own authority, without consulting the people. They were encouraged to think that their actions would be applauded by the people both because they would have extricated the Argive army from a patently dangerous situation and because the blame for the failure to engage and defeat the Spartans could be laid to the Athenians, who had failed to appear with hoplites and, more importantly, cavalry. The whole affair would undermine confidence in the reliability of Athens and cast doubt on the value of the Athenian alliance. It would once again raise the fear of a powerful Sparta, its alliance largely reunited, attacking an Argos bereft of major allies. The oligarchs could hope, once again, to bring about an alliance with Sparta. It must have been some such argument that Thrasyllus and Alciphron put before Agis: "Avoid battle now," they may have said, "and in a few months there will be no need of battle."[69]

Agis received the proposal privately, consulting only one of the magistrates who was with him, presumably an ephor. Since

---

[66]5.58.4. See also Busolt, *Forsch.*, 167.

[67]Busolt (ibid.) has already anticipated and disposed of the arguments of Henderson.

[68]Busolt (*Forsch.*, 168) and Ferguson (*CAH* V, 270) among others, have pointed out these men were oligarchs working to overthrow the democracy.

[69]For the best understanding of these events see, once again, Busolt, *GG* III:2, 1240–1242, and *Forsch.*, 75–181.

two ephors customarily accompanied the king on campaign,[70] it seems fair to conclude that Agis consulted the one who shared his view that war against Athens and Argos simultaneously must be avoided. Agis had much to fear. At any moment the Athenians might arrive with cavalry and a hoplite force of unknown strength. With the Spartan army engaged in the Argolid, the Athenians might seize the occasion to send a fleet to ravage Laconia; they might even raise a helot rebellion. To be sure, such tactics were not likely while Nicias and his friends held the upper hand, but the Athenian *demos* was unpredictable. If, on the other hand, Thrasyllus and Alciphron kept their promises, the Spartans could achieve their purpose of ending the threat from the new Argive league without fighting and, still better, destroy the deadly coalition between Athens and Argos. If he had such thoughts, Agis had to keep them secret, and the army, which knew nothing of his motives, could only censure him for letting a great opportunity slip by. It is noteworthy, however, that the Spartan government took no steps against Agis at this time; it must have seen the wisdom of his decision.[71]

There remains the problem of the Argive reaction. If the position of their army was precarious, why were the Argives outraged by the truce? On the surface their anger seems unjustified, yet when examined more closely it is not difficult to understand. Thrasyllus must have been the commander of the Argive forces, else he would not have had the authority to negotiate with Agis. As such he must have been responsible for the blunders that permitted Agis first to avoid battle at Methydrium and then to cut off the Argives between Nemea and Argos. In the light of his decision to avoid fighting in the Argive plain, these earlier errors must have seemed to be not the product of carelessness or honest error, but rather of cowardice. The entire sequence of events under the command of Thrasyllus now seemed shameful, and in their anger the Argives very likely underrated the danger that he had avoided.

That it was cowardice for which Thrasyllus was blamed and not treason seems certain, for the anger fixed on him alone, not

---

[70]Xen. *Hell.* 2.4.36 and *Resp. Lac.* 13.5.
[71]It was only later that Agis was punished (5.63.1-2).

on Alciphron or the oligarchic faction as a whole. The latter, in fact, seems to have exerted great influence immediately after the withdrawal of the rival armies. When the Athenians finally arrived, too few and too late, the Argive magistrates asked them to leave, refusing them the right to appear before the assembly. We may presume that these magistrates too were oligarchs.[72]

The behavior of the Athenians was embarrassing for their friends in Argos, and it is difficult for us to explain. They dispatched only 1,000 hoplites and 300 cavalry; the troops arrived late and were led by the generals Laches and Nicostratus and accompanied by Alcibiades in the role of ambassador.[73] Why did the Athenians send so few troops? Why were they so late? Why did they send two generals who were friends of Nicias and of peace and also Alcibiades, Nicias' rival and the architect of the war policy? The size of the Athenian force should not be surprising. It is true that they had sent 4,000 hoplites to Epidaurus in 430 and would send about the same number to Sicily in 415.[74] Since 430, however, the plague and the war had reduced considerably the number of available soldiers. The Sicilian expedition is not comparable because it was launched by an enthusiastic city full of self-confidence against despised enemies. We should also note that Athens sent only 300 cavalry to Epidaurus and none to Sicily. If we have judged Alcibiades' strategy correctly, even he would not have sent a force much larger. The idea was to obtain the greatest advantage possible with the smallest risk to Athens. Even 4,000 hoplites would not have evened the odds against the combined Peloponnesian forces, and the entire Athenian cavalry was not a match for the Boeotians. One thousand Athenian hoplites, the same number Alcibiades had brought the previous summer, was not an absurdly small number to send. If they had arrived in time they would have bolstered allied morale and, perhaps, made the Spartans more cautious.

[72]As Hatzfeld (*Alcibiade*, 103-104) puts it, "the oligarchic party at Argos, which doubtless was no stranger to these negotiations, claimed the right to forbid the Athenian ambassadors access to the popular assembly."

[73]Diodorus (12.79.1) says that Alcibiades came as a private citizen ($ἰδιώτης$), but Thucydides makes it clear that he held a formal appointment as ambassador, $πρεσβευτοῦ$ $παρόντος$ (5.61.2), and his version is to be preferred. Perhaps Diodorus meant to indicate only that Alcibiades was not a general.

[74]2.56.1 and 6.31.2.

But the Athenians did not arrive on time, and we can be sure that a conflict over policy caused the delay.[75] Thucydides tells us nothing of such a conflict, presumably because he did not have the facts. The Athenians faced a difficult problem in 418. Their commitment to the Argive alliance had brought only limited results. Corinth's resistance to pressure had defeated the goal of isolating Sparta in the Peloponnesus. During the winter of 419/18 it had become clear that the Argive alliance would require Athenian participation in a land war against Sparta to defend Argos. Athenian zeal for the alliance had cooled accordingly, resulting in the failure to elect Alcibiades and the victory of Nicias and his friends. Still, most Athenians were unwilling to abandon the new coalition which had seemed so promising and which continued to offer a significant deterrent to any invasion of Attica from the Peloponnesus. They could not, therefore, refuse the Argives' request for assistance; that would be a clear violation of the treaty. They could, however, send a force of moderate size and place it under the command of moderate, peace-loving generals who could be trusted to act cautiously and run as little risk as possible. To place the force under the command of Nicias would have been impolitic, for the Argives knew that he was the leader of those who opposed the Argive alliance and the author of the alliance with Sparta. The Athenians therefore sent Nicias' associates, but even they were suspect, as their reception by the Argives indicates. In an attempt to make their mission more acceptable to Argos, the Athenians also sent Alcibiades, not as a general, but as an ambassador. In the latter role he would not be in a position to risk the Athenian army, but he could smooth relations with the Argives.[76] It was up to the

[75]Andrewes' attempt at an explanation (*HCT* IV, 83) is weak: "their late arrival may be due only to the fact that sea transport, especially of horses, takes longer to arrange." The Athenians knew just how long it took to prepare for an expedition and for it to arrive in the Argolid; they had sent 4,000 men and 300 horses to Epidaurus in 430 by sea, and they had sent 1,000 men to Argos in 419.

[76]I have offered here a relatively simple explanation for what must have been a complicated series of decisions. The Athenians had to vote to send an expedition of a certain size, under particular generals. They had to vote to send Alcibiades as ambassador. They had to vote funds for the expedition. Each of these votes must have given rise to a debate. The more aggressive Athenians may have proposed sending a larger force and entrusting it to other generals, for

generals to decide when to embark the army.[77] There is no reason to suppose that they received the Argive request too late to arrive in time for the battle.[78] Their late arrival must have been intentional; they delayed in hope of arriving too late. Hatzfeld has articulated their probable expectations clearly: they would arrive at Argos after the battle, and "then they must come to terms with the winner; if, as was likely, Sparta were the victor, the two Athenian generals Laches and Nicostratus, always partisans of an alliance with Sparta, were well qualified to begin negotiations; and, in case of an Argive victory, Alcibiades had been added to the generals."[79]

If such was their thinking their plan almost failed, for the Argive magistrates came close to barring the Athenians from the Argive assembly. Only the intervention of the Eleans and Mantineans secured the Athenians a hearing. It was Alcibiades who spoke, and his audacious rhetorical skill did not desert him. Instead of apologizing for the Athenians' late arrival he took the offensive, complaining that the Argives had no right to make a truce without consulting the allies. Then he had the effrontery to say that, since the Athenians were there *opportunely*, the allies should resume the war. Elis and Mantinea and the other allies were easily persuaded and chose Orchomenus in Arcadia as the target for attack. The Mantineans were especially eager for the campaign, for the Spartans had placed some Arcadian hostages in Orchomenus. It was a good objective, moreover, because it was strategically located to interfere with forces moving into the

---

instance to Demosthenes. The decision to send Alcibiades at all may have been a sop that Nicias and his friends needed to throw to the opposition. Unfortunately, our sources tell us nothing about this.

[77]Diodorus (12.79.1) tells us explicitly that the army went by sea.

[78]Andrewes (*HCT* IV, 86–87) points out that, since the payment for the expedition does not appear in the accounts for 418/17 (*GHI* 77 = *IG* i². 302) it must have been ordered and paid for before the beginning of the official year, i.e., before about July 9. Since the Spartan march began "in the middle" of the summer the confrontation in the Argive plain could have occurred any time between early May and late July. See *HCT* IV, 271. More helpful is the fact that no ancient source even hints that the late arrival was caused by late receipt of the summons. Also telling is the angry Argive reception given the Athenian army and the failure of its generals to make any excuse.

[79]Hatzfeld, *Alcibiade*, 104.

central and southern Peloponnesus from the Isthmus of Corinth and beyond.[80] The Argives were also persuaded, Thucydides tells us, but did not march out with their allies. Only after some delay did they join the siege of Orchomenus.[81]

The Orchomenians did not hold out long because their walls were weak, they were badly outnumbered, and they did not expect help to come in time. They surrendered on condition that they should be received into the alliance of their besiegers. The loss of Orchomenus was a serious blow to Sparta, for it complicated communication between Sparta and her northern allies. Argos and Mantinea already hindered access from the north to both Laconia in the east and Elis in the west. The conquest of Orchomenus closed still another route (see Map 5a).

The capitulation of Orchomenus infuriated the Spartans, who only then undertook to punish Agis. They resolved to destroy his house and to fine him 10,000 drachmas. They were prevented from doing so only by his promise to wipe out the disgrace when he next took the field. Even so, the Spartans enacted an unprecedented law appointing ten *xymbouloi* to "advise" the young king. These advisers were to accompany Agis on his expeditions, and without their consent he could not lead an army out of the city.[82] This is further evidence that Agis' behavior in the Argive plain and the Spartan understanding of it were more political than military. If Agis had been to blame for the failure of his strategy or his nerve, the time for his punishment should have been immediately after his return to Sparta, not some time later. But his error was political rather than military. Agis' decision not to fight was based on the promise of the Argive oligarchs to bring their own city over to Sparta without bloodshed, an act that would mean the collapse of the new league. But the Argives had failed him, and the capture of Orchomenus proved the league's continuing vitality. The policy of Agis and his friends was discredited, and at this point his enemies demanded punishment.

Agis was embarrassed by the fall of Orchomenus and gave up

[80]Busolt, *GG* III:2, 1242–1243.
[81]5.61.3.
[82]5.63.4.

all hope of a rapprochement with Argos. He was eager to wipe out the memory of his errors and angry at the apparent treachery of the Argives. News of trouble at Tegea presented him with an opportunity. The successes of the new league and the hesitation of the Spartans had encouraged a faction that was ready to turn Tegea over to the Argives and their allies. The crisis was serious enough to prompt the Tegean faction friendly to Sparta to send word that unless the Spartans came quickly Tegea would go over to the Argive alliance.[83] For Sparta the loss of Tegea was unthinkable. An enemy in control of Tegea could trap the Spartans in Laconia, end their control of the Peloponnesian League, and even prevent them from maintaining the command of Messenia. As Tegea's entry into an alliance in the sixth century had marked the beginning of the Peloponnesian League and Sparta's power, so its defection would mean the end of both. Agis and the Spartans had no choice but to march north to save Tegea.

[83] 5.62.2; 64.1.

5. The Battle of Mantinea

Late in August of 418 Sparta learned of the threat to Tegea.[1] The Spartans responded with unprecedented swiftness,[2] sending word to their remaining Arcadian allies to assemble and meet them at Tegea. At the same time they sent messengers to their northern allies in Corinth, Boeotia, Phocis, and Locris to come to Mantinea as quickly as possible. The Arcadians could be counted on, but the northerners were a less reliable element. The most obvious difficulty was that since the fall of Orchomenus the obvious and easily passable routes from the north to Mantinea lay in hostile hands. The northern allies could hope to make their way south safely only if they first gathered all their forces, presumably at Corinth, and then overawed potential enemies with their numbers. The need for such unified action meant that considerable time must pass before the northern army would appear. With even the best will the northern allies could not expect to reach Mantinea in fewer than twelve to fourteen days after the dispatch of the Spartan request for help.[3] But there is reason to think that not all the northern allies were pleased by the

[1]There is general agreement about the time of the expedition and battle. Busolt (GG III:2, 1246, n. 1) gives a good and concise account of the arguments for the date.

[2]5.64.2. Thucydides tells us that the Spartans sent help to Tegea: πανδημεὶ ὀξεῖα καὶ οἷα οὔπω πρότερον. I agree with Gomme (HCT IV, 91), among others, that Thucydides means that only the speed of Sparta's response was unprecedented.

[3]I consider the chronological calculations of W. J. Woodhouse (King Agis of Sparta and his Campaign in Arcadia in 418 B.C. [Oxford, 1933], 154-155) reasonable here. If anything, I think the time he allows for the northerners to reach the battlefield somewhat too short.

invitation, and Thucydides' language hints that some of them found the summons inconvenient.[4] The Boeotians and Corinthians, moreover, had marched out to fight alongside the Spartans in the Argive plain just a few weeks before, only to turn back with nothing accomplished as a result of a truce the Spartan king had made without consulting them. A combination of reluctance and resentment might be expected to increase the delay in the arrival of Sparta's northern allies.

The foreseeable delay in the appearance of his allies added considerably to the problems facing Agis. Earlier that summer the forces under his command in the Argive plain, including the northern allies, had numbered about 20,000 against about 12,000 of the enemy. As he marched toward Tegea in August he could expect to find the enemy troops at Mantinea in almost the same numbers.[5] His own army at Argos had numbered about 8,000. To that force he now added some *neodamodeis*, including the men who had fought in Thrace under Brasidas. He must also have been strengthened by Tegean soldiers fighting in full force at their own city. These additions may have brought his numbers up to as many as 10,000 hoplites, but the enemy army would still be larger.

Apart from numbers, Agis faced another problem: the Spartans lacked confidence in his command. Since the death of his father Archidamus in the winter of 427/26, Agis had twice taken command of the Spartan army to invade and ravage Attica. In 426 he had marched only as far as the Isthmus of Corinth when an earthquake put an end to the expedition. The next year he invaded Attica, but the grain was too green to provide food for his soldiers, and unusually violent storms added to the dis-

---

[4]5.64.4: ἀλλὰ τοῖς μὲν ἐξ ὀλίγου τε ἐγίγνετο καὶ οὐ ῥᾴδιον, ἢν μὴ ἀθρόοις καὶ ἀλλήλους περιμείνασι διελθεῖν τὴν πολεμίαν (ξυνέκλῃε γὰρ διὰ μέσου).

[5]Since the Argives had been defending their own city on the former occasion they must have put their full force in the field, perhaps 7,000 men, including allies. In going to Mantinea they left their city behind, open to attack from Epidaurus. They must, therefore, have left a garrison of perhaps two or three thousand, reducing the army to four or five thousand. This would have been made up partially by the presence of the entire Mantinean army, only part of which would have gone to Argos for the same reason. Although there is margin for error in these estimates, Agis had reason to expect the enemy to number about 11,000 men.

comfort of his hungry men. After only fifteen days, the shortest incursion of the war, news of the Athenian fortification of Pylos forced Agis to lead his troops back to Sparta in haste.[6]

Neither campaign had given him any experience in battle and both were attended by unusually bad luck. The expedition to Argos in 418 did nothing to increase Spartan confidence in the young king. Twice he had been turned back at the frontier by evil omens. When at last he had the chance to fight an outnumbered and surrounded enemy, he rejected it. Any sympathy for his choice of diplomacy over war disappeared when the Argives and their allies captured Orchomenus, cutting the Spartans off from their northern allies. The bad news from Tegea must have increased the Spartans' displeasure, and only the fact that the other king, Pleistoanax, was discredited can explain their willingness to allow Agis to lead the army once again. Even so, as we have seen, they subjected him to the unprecedented and humiliating guidance of ten advisers. The Spartans had several reasons for suspecting Agis' leadership. Some may have disagreed with his policy; others may have doubted his courage; pious or superstitious Spartans may have thought him ill favored by the gods, or at least unlucky. To save himself from punishment after the fall of Orchomenus, he had promised that he would free himself from the charges against him "by a brave deed in battle; if not they could then do whatever they liked."[7] Mantinea was Agis' last chance; success would bring redemption, and failure would mean disgrace.

As Agis led his army out of Sparta he faced a tricky strategic problem. The crisis at Tegea required that he arrive to safeguard the city as soon as possible. Once there, however, the situation called for delay until the arrival of the northern army. During the interval, which would last at least a week, Agis would confront enemy forces that outnumbered his. Theoretically, he could spend the time within the walls of Tegea and refuse battle until his allies arrived, but this would allow the enemy to ravage

---

[6]For the date of Agis' succession see E. Meyer (*Forsch.* II, 506–507). For the two campaigns see 3.89.1 and 4.6.1-2.

[7]5.63.3: ἔργῳ γὰρ ἀγαθῷ ῥύσεσθαι τὰς αἰτίας στρατευσάμενος, ἢ τότε ποιεῖν αὐτοὺς ὅτι βούλονται.

the Tegean land, destroy farmhouses, approach the city, and hurl accusations of cowardice at the Spartans and their commander. Another general might be able to withstand all this and hold to his strategy; Agis certainly could not. He could not afford even the hint of a suggestion that he was unwilling or afraid to fight. Even before he left Sparta, therefore, he must have known that he would face a battle against superior numbers. That is why he took with him the entire Spartan army, reinforced by *neodamodeis*, and left his city undefended, even while the Messenians were perched at Pylos and were always a threat to launch a rebellion of the helots.

Agis did not march to Tegea by the shortest route, directly north by way of Sellasia and Caryae (see Map 5a). Instead he took a more westerly route along the Eurotas River, longer but easier both for men and the wagon train.[8] He stopped at Orestheum in the Maenalian district of Arcadia where he must have received the surprising and welcome news that the Eleans had not come to join their allies at Mantinea. After the conquest of Orchomenus the victorious allies had disagreed over their next objective. The Mantineans wanted to attack Tegea, their neighbor and ancient enemy, whereas the Eleans wanted to bring the allied army against Lepreum. The strategic importance of Tegea was clear to both the Athenians and the Argives, and both supported the Mantinean view. The Eleans, in their shortsighted selfishness, took offense and withdrew their 3,000 hoplites, refusing to join in the attack on Tegea.[9] Agis must have received the news at Orestheum, for that is the only way we can understand the action he took there.[10] He sent back one-sixth of his army, a portion drawn from the younger and older men, to guard Sparta. He could afford to relieve Spartan anxiety in this way because the Elean defection meant that his army, even without the 500 to 700 men sent back, would be larger than the

---

[8] 5.64.3. See *HCT* IV, 91–93, for discussion of the route.
[9] 5.62.
[10] Woodhouse (*Agis*, 108–109) saw the revolutionary impact of the news on Agis' strategy, but he believed that it came only after the Spartans reached Tegea. But Agis would not have sent part of his army back from Orestheum unless he already knew of the Elean defection.

enemy force, something over 9,000 Spartans and allies against about 8,000 for the Argive coalition.

The Elean defection completely altered the strategic outlook. Before the defection, strategic considerations had conflicted with Agis' personal requirements; now that conflict had disappeared. The pique of the Eleans could not last, however. Before long they were certain to realize the foolishness of their withdrawal and return to swell the ranks of the Argive coalition's army. They were, in fact, likely to rejoin their allies before Sparta's northern allies reached the area, if they ever did.[11] Thus conditions now argued for Agis' forcing his enemy into a pitched battle as soon as possible. Collecting his allies at Tegea, Agis marched into Mantinean territory and encamped at the sanctuary of Heracles (the Heracleum) more than a mile southeast of the city of Mantinea (see Map 8).[12]

The plain containing the ancient cities of Tegea and Mantinea rises to a height of about twenty-two hundred feet and is surrounded by mountains. At its longest, north and south, it is about eighteen miles, and at its widest east to west it is about eleven miles.[13] The plain slopes slightly from south to north, Mantinea being about one hundred feet lower than Tegea, ten miles away. A little more than three miles south of Mantinea the plain narrows to a gap almost two miles wide between two ridges, Mytikas on the west and Kapnistra on the east. There is little reason to doubt that the border between the two states was at this gap or just to the south of it.[14] Not far from Tegea the

[11]The Eleans arrived at Mantinea after the battle (5.75.5) along with 1,000 additional Athenian hoplites. We cannot be sure if Agis knew of the dispatch of these Athenian reinforcements. If he did, that would be further reason for him to seek battle swiftly. The Spartans' northern allies never got to Mantinea (5.75.2). We do not know where they were when they received the news that their services would not be needed.

[12]5.64.5.

[13]My understanding of the topography of the battle has been aided by the following accounts: W. Loring, *JHS* XV (1895), 25-89; G. Fougères, *Mantinée et l'arcadie orientale* (Paris, 1895), 39-52, 572-596; J. Kromayer, *Antike Schlachtfelder*, vol. I (Berlin, 1903), 47-76, vol. IV (Berlin, 1926), 207-220; A. Andrewes, *HCT* IV, 94ff; W. K. Pritchett, *Studies in Ancient Greek Topography*, Part II (Battlefields), (Berkeley and Los Angeles, 1969), 37-72.

[14]Andrewes, *HCT* IV, 95; Pritchett, *Studies* II, 43.

Map 8. Battle of Mantinea. Adapted from A. W. Gomme, A. Andrewes, and K. [
Dover, *A Historical Commentary on Thucydides,* IV (Oxford: Oxford University Press
1970), by permission of the publisher.

stream now called the Zanovistas rises and flows to the north into a *katavothra* (sinkhole) at the western edge of the Mantinean plain, north of Mytikas.[15] There is another stream, the Sarandapotamos, that flows north past Tegea, makes a sharp turn to the east through a pass, and empties into three *katavothrai* near the modern town of Versova, still in Tegean territory. Two roads ran south from Mantinea, one of them leading southwest to Pallantion while the other, located near the eastern end of the gap, ran south to Tegea. To the east of Mantinea stood a mountain that the ancients called Alesion. The Tegea road ran past it, and, where the mountain shaded into plain, there stood a temple of Poseidon Hippios. South of Mount Alesion was an oak forest called Pelagos which reached almost to Kapnistra and Mytikas. The Tegea road ran through this forest and the Pallantion road skirted it on the west.[16] The sanctuary of Heracles at which the Spartans made camp was located in the eastern part of the plain, south of Mount Alesion.[17]

Agis' first move was the classic gambit of ravaging the enemy's land to force him to defend it in a pitched battle. Unfortunately, the Spartans had arrived too late to exert the usual pressure. Mantinea's grain crops were harvested between the latter part of June and the end of July.[18] By the time Agis began his depradations, the crops, along with everything of value that could be moved, had been safely stored and the Spartans could do no

[15]Fougères, *Mantinée* 41–43, and Gomme, *HCT* IV, 98. Pritchett (*Studies* II, 42) appears to think that it empties into a *katavothra* at the "waist" of the plain, east of Mytikas, and never enters Mantinean territory. In this he seems to be unique.

[16]Pausanias (8.11.1,5) speaks of the forest in connection with Epaminondas' campaign in 362, but Thucydides, Xenophon, and Polybius make no mention of it in their descriptions of the Mantinean battles of 418, 362, and 207. There is no reason to doubt, however, Pausanias' clear and untendentious account of what he saw. Nor, in the absence of any evidence of afforestation instead of the usual deforestation in ancient Greece, should we doubt the existence of the woods in Thucydides' time. Andrewes (*HCT* IV, 96) argues for the presence of the Pelagos in 418, and his intelligent account of the battle assumes it.

[17]I follow the suggestion of Pritchett (*Studies* II, 46–49), who seems to be the first to have found archaeological remains that may have belonged to the sanctuary. For locations suggested by other scholars see Pritchett, p. 47.

[18]Fougères, *Mantinée*, 56.

unacceptable damage.[19] The members of the Argive coalition were drawn up in a strong defensive position on the lower slopes of Mount Alesion. They had chosen a place "steep and hard to get at,"[20] one from which they need move only if they wanted to. Furthermore, sound strategy dictated that they refuse battle except on their own terms. They were outnumbered by the Spartans, a situation that did not encourage an aggressive strategy. The burden of attack, moreover, belonged to Agis. It was he who needed a battle and a victory to relieve the pressure on Tegea and restore his own position in Sparta. If for any reason he withdrew once again without fighting, that would be a victory for the Argive coalition. Finally, we know that the Eleans had been asked to rejoin their allies and were on their way. We also know that reinforcements from Athens were coming; perhaps the generals of the confederacy knew it, too.[21] Once these reinforcements allowed them to outnumber the Spartans, the Argive generals could choose the proper moment to fight (they realized that the battle must occur before Sparta's northern allies could arrive). Until its reinforcements came, however, the forces of the Argive coalition had every reason to remain in their strong position and avoid battle, unless Agis was foolhardy enough to come to them.

But this is exactly what Agis tried to do. In spite of the insuperable difficulties facing a hoplite army in an uphill campaign, Agis led his men in a charge up the slopes of Alesion. This was the reckless act of a desperate man, for even with a small numerical advantage an uphill charge against a hoplite army in phalanx was doomed. The Spartans came "within a stone's throw or a javelin's cast"[22] when the advance stopped. Thucydides tells us that "one of the older men," seeing the impossibility of the situation, called out to Agis that what he had in mind was "to cure one evil with another." The wise elder may have been a member of the *gerousia*, perhaps one of the *xym-*

---

[19]The point is well made by Woodhouse, *Agis*, 110.
[20]5.65.1.
[21]5.75.5. The Eleans and Athenians arrived the day after the battle. On the day in question the Athenians must have been en route and the Eleans must at least have been preparing to go.
[22]5.65.2.

bouloi; we are not told. Clearly, he recognized that, with this impetuous and unwise action, Agis was attempting to erase the memory of his behavior at Argos. Agis took the elder's advice, either because he found it convincing or out of respect for the elder's authority, and led a rapid retreat before making contact with the enemy.[23] Some scholars have rejected Thucydides' description of the retreat as a last-minute change of plan, regarding it instead as a deliberate and successful feint intended to draw the enemy down into the plain,[24] but such a plan seems unlikely. Apart from the fact that Thucydides gives an entirely different impression, and no ancient source contradicts him, such a plan would have been reckless to the point of madness. To advance so close to the enemy and then turn and run was in effect to invite the enemy to fall upon the rear of the withdrawing army with devastating effect. Only the confederate generals' reluctance to be drawn into pursuit, a reluctance which could not have been foreseen with confidence, prevented such an outcome.

As Agis withdrew toward Tegea, he must have been more troubled and desperate than ever. His reckless charge had brought a reprimand and achieved nothing. So far as he knew the enemy army was still on the heights and would not come down until their reinforcements had arrived. It must have been immediately after his withdrawal that Agis sent to Sparta asking the garrison he had sent back from Orestheum[25] to join him again at Tegea. He now had to expect a battle against odds at a

---

[23] 5.65.2-3. Thucydides says that Agis may have been led to retreat by a last-minute recognition that his attack was mistaken rather than by the warning of the elder. This explanation seems far less likely. Thucydides, in any case, presents the warning as a fact; the least effect it could have had was to make Agis think again.

[24] Woodhouse (*Agis*, 111-113), rejecting the Thucydidean account as he does throughout, considers the charge and retreat as a carefully planned feint and part of a brilliant overall strategy. He has rightly won few converts. For a severe judgment of his interpretation see Gomme, *Essays*, 132-155. Woodhouse (*Agis*, 112) says: "The feint upon Alesion, pushed to within a hair's breadth of irretrievable committal, of achieving what, upon the evidence of Thucydides himself, it actually did achieve." The more prudent and reliable Andrewes (*HCT* IV, 97) says much the same thing: Agis "may have calculated that the assault so suddenly called off, followed by an apparent retreat, would have the effect which in fact it did."

[25] See above, p. 110.

time and place chosen by the enemy. To reduce those odds he must run the risk of leaving Sparta unguarded for some days. The Spartans at home took the matter seriously enough to send the army to him under the remaining king, Pleistoanax.[26]

Even if Pleistoanax should arrive as soon as the Eleans and Athenians, the Spartans would still be outnumbered, so Agis tried another plan to bring the enemy into the plain and force a battle before reinforcements appeared. For years the Tegeans and Mantineans had fought over control of the waterways that ran through the plain. All the streams and mountain torrents in the region emptied into caverns in the limestone beneath the soil, sinkholes or, as the Greeks call them, *katavothrai*. When the rain was excessive the sinkholes tended to become choked and Mantinea, because of the slope of the land, was in danger of being flooded. When this happened Mantinea "became a Holland."[27] The Mantineans would have found it difficult to inundate the Tegean plain, for stopping up whatever sinkholes would only have brought water into Mantinean territory. The only way to achieve a flood south of the Kapnistra gap was to close off the entire gap with some kind of temporary dam, the construction of which would be difficult.[28]

For the Tegeans the task was much easier. During the rainy

[26]5.75.1.

[27]Fougères, *Mantinée*, 41.

[28]Few have dealt with the question of how the Mantineans could flood the land of Tegea, and those who have do not provide a satisfactory explanation. Pritchett (*Studies* II, 43) assumes "that the Mantineians were in the habit of damming up the *katavothrai* at the frontier [which he believes to have been at a line of *katavothrai* just south of the Kapnistra gap], so as to make the water flood the Tegean plain, while the Tegeans would be equally anxious to keep the channels open until the waters reached the Mantinike." But even if all the *katavothrai* at the frontier were stopped, the water would, nonetheless, run downhill, that is, into Mantinean territory. Andrewes (*HCT* IV, 98) suggests that "Mantinea, of course, would damage Tegean territory by blocking the Zanovistas channel." That would result in the diversion of the water into another channel or channels, but, since water insists on running downhill, Mantinea, not Tegea, would receive any overflow. The only way that the Mantineans could flood Tegean land would be to build a dam all the way across the Kapnistra gap of a height and strength to force the water back uphill. This would appear to be a difficult undertaking, and it seems likely that in the quarrels over water described by Thucydides the Tegeans must usually have been the aggressors.

season they could stop up the sinkholes or divert the streams around them by digging simple ditches. Either way the overflow would be carried into Mantinean territory. Another device, which might be used together with or apart from these, was to flood the Mantinean plain by means of the Zanovistas. Of itself the Zanovistas poses little threat, for it holds little if any water outside the rainy season. The Sarandapotamos, however, is a more copious stream. In times of heavy rain it may flood the valley of Versova. The Tegeans, therefore, could have a double motive for diverting it into the bed of the Zanovistas, to spare their own crops in the region of Versova and to harm their neighbors and enemies, the Mantineans. This could be done by digging a canal of about a mile and a half between the rivers at their closest point. The likelihood is that at some time in the past they did so, kept the trench in being, and merely built a barrier across it when they wanted to allow the Sarandapotamos to return to its normal channel. Thus, in their repeated conflicts with Mantinea, the Tegeans could easily break down the barrier, divert the river, and flood Mantinean land.[29]

It seems likely, therefore, that Agis marched back toward Tegea to divert the Sarandapotamos into the Zanovistas. This does not, of course, rule out the possibility that he may also have sent men to fill up *katavothrai* on the frontier or to cut ditches that would lead the water around instead of into them, but such work alone would not have accomplished Agis' purpose. Thucydides tells us that "he wanted to make the men on the hill come down to help prevent the diversion of the water when they

[29]I follow the suggestion of Fougères (*Mantinée*, 43–44), as do Kromayer (*Antike Schlachtfelder* IV, 210) and Gomme (*Essays*, 138–139 and *HCT* IV, 98). Woodhouse (*Agis*, 49–50) rejects Thucydides' discussion of the diversion of the water and its significance as a "mere guess." Pritchett (*Studies* I, 122–134, and II, 42), with the aid and consultation of geologists, has formulated a theory of changes in the hydrology of the region since antiquity which, if correct, would make the diversion described above impossible. He reports the names of the experts he has consulted and reports the speculations they have made. He does not, however, cite any scientific publications by them or any one else in support of such views. Until other geologists and laymen can examine the arguments for the theory and the evidence on which they are based, it seems unsound to accept the theory. The assumption made here is that while many changes may have taken place in the plain of Mantinea and Tegea, the flow of the waterways has not changed radically.

learned about it and so to make them fight a battle on the plain."[30] Since the *katavothrai* were at some distance from Mount Alesion, where Agis had left the enemy army, and still farther from Mantinea, where the enemy might be expected to withdraw once the Spartan army had departed, and since the Pelagos Wood stood in between, the enemy probably would not learn of what was happening for some time. But for Agis, time was of the essence. The diversion of the Sarandapotamos into the bed of the Zanovistas would not be immediately apparent either, for in late August the bed of the Zanovistas was almost certainly dry. But within a day water would appear in the dry bed that wound its way well into Mantinean territory, and previous experience would tell the Mantineans that the Tegeans and their allies had diverted the water. For the moment that was no problem, but unless the Mantineans and their allies compelled their enemies to return the Sarandapotamos to its own channel before the advent of the rainy season, a matter of weeks, their land would then be flooded.

Agis' plan, we must emphasize, was based on hope, not certain expectation. Though the Mantineans must fight at some time in the next weeks, they could safely wait until the arrival of the Eleans and Athenians. Agis must have assumed that anger and fear would lead the enemy to march out immediately and seek a battle that they ought to delay. It was a gamble, but the best one available to a desperate man. He spent a day in the neighborhood of Tegea while the river was being diverted. The next day he led his army northward again toward the Heracleum in Mantinean territory. He probably expected to arrive there before the enemy saw the evidence of his previous day's work. He presumably wanted to take up the position he originally had chosen as the best place to fight, put his army in battle order, and await the advance that was sure to come when the enemy saw the menacing waters flow into Mantinean territory.[31]

But Agis never got to the Heracleum, for the enemy had not behaved according to expectations. The generals of the Argive confederacy had been astonished and puzzled by the strange

[30] 5.65.4.
[31] 5.66.1.

maneuvers of Agis' army, but they held to their original strategy and did not pursue, holding their commanding position on the heights while Agis' army withdrew into Tegean territory. At this point, however, political suspicion and distrust within the army of the Argive coalition played into Agis' hands. Thucydides' account reveals, as we should in any case expect, that the effective commanders of the army were Argives.[32] After the Spartan withdrawal, the troops began to complain of their generals' inaction: "On the previous occasion the Spartans, though nicely trapped near Argos, had been allowed to get away, and now, when they were running away no one pursued them; instead the Spartans were reaching safety without disturbance while we are being betrayed."[33] The last word is revealing. The complaining troops did not accuse their generals of cowardice but of treason (*prodidontai*). We may presume that the generals were still from the aristocratic Argive Thousand and that their earlier actions had made them suspect among the democratic citizens of Argos. The intensification of such suspicions and complaints now compelled the generals to abandon their sound strategy. They moved down from the hill and made camp in the plain in preparation for an advance against the Spartans.[34]

The next day the allied army lined up in the order in which they would fight if they came upon the Spartans. Meanwhile, Agis, leading his army toward the Heracleum, "saw that the enemy was close by and all in line already, in position away from the hill. On this occasion the Spartans experienced the greatest terror in their memory."[35] This account of the total surprise of the Spartans has caused much puzzlement and debate. Woodhouse, believing that Agis was a brilliant strategist whose every move was consequential and carefully planned, rejects Thucydides outright and argues that the Spartans were not surprised. Agis had been neither diverting rivers nor filling *katavothrai*; that was all the invention of Thucydides or his informants.

[32] 5.65.5.
[33] 5.65.5.
[34] 5.65.6.
[35] 5.66.2. For a discussion of the difficulties in this passage see *HCT* IV, 102–103. My translation follows the text and translation of Mme de Romilly in the Budé edition.

In Woodhouse's view, Agis' withdrawal to Tegea was merely a
feint meant to draw the enemy down from the heights, and it
worked. "*Reculer pour mieux sauter*—to draw back like a ram, in
order to butt the harder, as in after times Philip of Macedon put
it—that was the secret of his apparently strange proceedings."[36]
Woodhouse's readiness simply to throw out the best evidence we
have when it presents problems seems excessive, but he raises
some interesting questions. If the Spartans were indeed diverting
waters to flood the Mantinean plain, why didn't the allied army
intervene to prevent them? Why were the allies in battle order
when they came upon the Spartan army, since we are not told
they knew of Agis' movements? How can the Spartans have been
taken by surprise, since it was Agis' intention precisely to lure
the enemy down into the plain and force a battle? More particularly, how could Agis have been surprised since Mount Alesion
would have been visible from any part of the plain? No longer
seeing his enemy on the heights, Agis must have known that it
might be in the plain before him and ought to have been ready.
To this question must be added the one asked by both Gomme
and Andrewes: why didn't the Spartans post lookouts on the
heights of Kapnistra and Mytikas? If they did, why did they not
receive warning of the enemy movements?

These questions cannot be answered with certainty, but reasonable suggestions are available. The response to the first point
is easy enough: the diversion of the water took place quite near
Tegea, far enough away as to be unseen from Alesion.[37] The
Spartans' surprise is more difficult, but not impossible, to explain. First, the allied position on Alesion need not have been
visible from some places on the plain. Between the two armies
stood the Pelagos Wood. It may have been thick enough and tall
enough to conceal the allied movements from Agis. When Agis'
march began, moreover, the allies were already down from Alesion. They were probably moving forward from their camp on
the plain even as Agis was marching northward through the
wood by the Tegea-Mantinea road. There is every reason to

---

[36]Woodhouse, *Agis*, 55.
[37]This point is made by Gomme, *Essays*, 140.

believe that in such a circumstance he would have been fully
screened from any sight of the enemy. An objection to this is that
Agis ought to have seen that the enemy was no longer on Alesion
before he entered the forest. But even the absence of allied troops
on Alesion need not have told the Spartan king that the enemy
was in the plain preparing to offer battle. Another possibility
was that the allied army, seeing the Spartans in retreat, and
having no further reason to stand at arms on the mountain, had
withdrawn to more comfortable quarters within the city of Mantinea. Agis could have found such an explanation plausible, since
he knew nothing of the political suspicions that had forced the
Argive generals to leave the heights and because he knew that the
diverted waters would not yet have reached Mantinean territory.
To be sure, an experienced and cautious commander would have
anticipated another possibility, but Agis' previous record does
not require us to place him in that category.

There remains one further objection to the notion that Agis
could have been unaware of the enemy's movements. "If Agis
had on his first march got within a mile or so of Mantineia, he
presumably drove off Mantineian posts on those heights
[Mytikas and Kapnistra] and occupied them himself."[38] Agis had
hurried into the Mantinean plain to force a battle. Once through
the Kapnistra-Mytikas gap he had no need of lookouts; he could
see the enemy wherever he might be: on the plain, on Alesion, in
Mantinea. The only time he would have needed to post lookouts
was upon his retreat toward Tegea, but that maneuver had been
unplanned and taken in haste. There could have been neither
thought nor time for placing a watch on the heights, which,
moreover, were surely held, apparently strongly, by the Mantineans. A well-built watch tower has been discovered on the
easternmost shoulder of Mount Mytikas (see Map 8). It was built
in the fourth century B.C., and similar strongpoints probably
existed in the previous century.[39] Thus we can easily understand

[38]Gomme, *Essays*, 140, n. 1. Andrewes (*HCT* IV, 100–101) says, "I agree
with Gomme that Agis could not have failed to keep a watch on his enemies'
movements.... Surprise encounters (as opposed to contrived ambushes) are
rare, and the Spartan army is the least likely of all to neglect standard practice."
[39]Loring, *JHS* XV (1895), 82–83.

why the Spartans were not warned of the enemy's movement by observers posted on the heights.

As Agis marched his army northward from Tegea he may have noticed that the allied army was no longer at Alesion, but he could not have known where it was, whether at Mantinea or somewhere in the plain, but in either case he must go forward and take up a position north of the gap. If the enemy were in Mantinea, Agis would be forced to wait until the sight of water in the bed of the Zamovistas drew them out. If they were already on the plain, which he seems not to have expected, he could have his battle at once. Whatever his expectation, we can assume that he would be taken by surprise by the location of the enemy army.[40]

As his army emerged in column from the forest, intending to return to the Heracleum camp, he was shocked to discover his opponent close by, well away from the hills, and in full battle order.[41] The allied army had camped in the plain overnight, and their lookouts on the heights must have informed the Argive generals of Agis' march. As a result they were able to take up a position close to the place where the Spartans would emerge

[40]Thucydides' account does not make it sufficiently clear how and why Agis was taken by surprise. Therefore, unless like Woodhouse we are to reject Thucydides' testimony entirely, we must account for the surprise by interpreting and filling out that testimony. Gomme (*Essays*, 140–141, and *HCT* IV, 100) believes that the allied army made a night march through the Kapnistra-Mytikas gap, "and by next morning they deploy in the plain south of this line, ready for battle, barely five miles from Tegea itself; where Agis sees them, on his way back to his camp of the day before. If the wood did not play an important part, then they had marched by night. Is it any wonder that Agis was surprised?" (*Essays*, 141). But Thucydides says nothing of so difficult and unusual a maneuver, though he made a point of it on a previous occasion when Agis led his army on a march by night (5.58.2). Not to mention so crucial and peculiar an action would be a greater distortion than omitting to mention a topographic detail of a field he probably had never seen. For that reason, among others, I cannot accept Gomme's suggestion but prefer Andrewes' version, which emphasizes the presence of the Pelagos Wood and its role in obstructing the view of Agis (*HCT* IV, 101). I also agree with his general placement of the field of battle: "in the plain of Mantineia itself, well south of the city but north of the Mytikas-Kapnistra narrows, and north of the wood;... Thucydides probably worked from verbal descriptions of it, and had not inspected the site himself."

[41]5.66.2.

from the woods and be waiting in the battle order of their own choosing. Agis had walked into a trap.

The Spartan king's most immediate problem was to place his army, which was marching out of the forest in column, in line and in order of battle before the enemy could take advantage of its temporary disarray and attack. Here the unrivaled discipline and training of the Spartan army came into play. Agis needed only to give his orders to the polemarchs, the commanders of the six Spartan divisions (*morae*), and the chain of command did the rest. Unlike other Greek armies, the Spartan army "was composed of officers commanding other officers, for the responsibility of carrying out orders is shared by many."[42] The Argive generals apparently chose not to attack the enemy as it emerged from the forest or even to charge before the Spartans could form into line. Either tactic might have forced a Spartan retreat and led to another avoidance of battle, but, pressed by their soldiers' suspicions, the generals seem to have been determined to fight a pitched battle on that day. They were satisfied that the advantage was theirs; they had chosen the site of the battle and placed their troops in the array of their choice. The Spartans, hurrying into line, would not have time to put their troops in the most favorable order.

An examination of the disposition of both armies and the tactics pursued by each in the early fighting reveals the strategy of the Argive generals and the discomfiture of the Spartans. The allies placed their greatest strength on the right wing: the Mantineans fighting for their homeland, next to them the other Arcadians with a similar motivation, then the specially trained elite Argive Thousand. This right wing was meant to take the offensive and fight the decisive part of the battle. Next to them stood the ordinary Argive hoplites, and beside them the men of Orneae and Cleonae. On the left wing were the thousand Athenians supported by their own cavalry. The left wing was meant to stand on the defensive, to avoid encirclement and stave off a rout until the right wing could strike the decisive blow.[43] The Lacedaemonian alignment gives little if any clue that they pos-

[42] 5.66.4.
[43] 5.67.2.

sessed a calculated plan of battle. The left wing was held by the Sciritae, Arcadians who usually served as scouts or in connection with cavalry, and whose place on the left wing was traditional.[44] Then came the troops who had fought with Brasidas in Thrace and, along with them, some *neodamodeis*. The main Spartan army held the center and next to them were their Arcadian allies from Heraea and Maenalia. On the right was the army of Tegea supported by a few Spartans who held the very end of the line. The cavalry was split, protecting both wings.[45] The Spartan disposition was conventional and defensive, as we might expect from an army and a general taken by surprise. The initiative lay with the Argive generals.

The allied army numbered about 8,000 hoplites stretched across a front of about a kilometer, while the Peloponnesian forces, about 9,000 hoplites, formed a line about one hundred meters longer.[46] Because of their superior numbers, the Peloponnesian right wing, the Tegeans and the small band of Spartans with them, extended beyond the allied left, held by the Athenians. The slightly outnumbered allies, however, did not try to compensate by sending forces to the left. On the contrary, they extended their own right far beyond the enemy left, held by the Sciritae. The Spartans, moreover, advanced at their usual slow pace, keeping time to the measured rhythm of the flutes, but the allied army "advanced eagerly and impulsively," rushing into battle.[47] Plainly, the allied generals meant to have their best troops strike the decisive blow on the right and rout the enemy before their own left or center gave way.

On seeing his left wing in danger of encirclement, Agis ordered a change in the alignment of his troops. He signalled the Sciritae and the veterans of Brasidas' army on the left to break off contact with the rest of the army and to move further left to match the position of the Mantineans. This, of course, created a dangerous gap in the Peloponnesian line. He therefore ordered

[44] 5.67.1. Andrewes, *HCT* IV, 103–104.
[45] 6.67.1.
[46] I agree with the numerical estimates and the space allotted for the armies by Kromayer in *Antike Schlachtfelder* IV, 212–217. For a thorough discussion of the problem of numbers see Andrewes, *HCT* IV, 111–117.
[47] 5.70.

the polemarchs Hipponoïdas and Aristocles to take their companies, perhaps 1,000 Spartan troops altogether, from the right end of the main Spartan army to fill the newly created gap on the left.[48]

Such a maneuver seems to have been without parallel in the history of Greek warfare. To change the line of battle even as the armies approached one another, to open a gap in one's line deliberately, to open still another gap in order to fill the first—all of these actions were unheard of, if not impossible to carry out. Thucydides presents the maneuver as the result of a spur-of-the-moment decision by Agis: "Even as the two armies approached each other King Agis decided to do the following."[49] Thucydides reasons that Agis reached his decision when he noticed that the two armies were outflanking each other on the right, a situation that Thucydides claims was characteristic of all armies because of the natural tendency of hoplite phalanxes to move toward their unshielded side.[50] If Thucydides is correct, then Agis should have anticipated the movement and planned his tactics accordingly, without the need of a last-minute change. Thucydides, who had in the preceding paragraph emphasized the danger of an army's breaking order as it marches into battle,[51] makes it clear that Agis acted out of inexperience, underlining the point with his subsequent claim that the Spartans won the

---

[48]Thucydides (5.71.3) says the two Spartan companies were to come "from the right wing," and a number of scholars have taken the words literally to mean that he wanted two Spartan *lochoi* to come from the extreme right of his entire line. See, e.g., Kromayer, *Antike Schlachtfelder* IV, 218; Ferguson, *CAH* V, 273. The problem here is that Thucydides expressly tells us that only a few Spartans stood with the Tegeans on the right wing, and there is no reasonable way to interpret the "few" to be about 1,000 men. See the arguments of Woodhouse, *Agis*, 94ff. He suggests that Thucydides meant us to understand that the two *lochoi* were to come from the right wing of the Spartan contingent in the center of the phalanx (p. 99) and he is followed in this by Gomme (*HCT* IV, 119). This interpretation, too, is far from compelling, and further removed from the words of Thucydides, but no interpretation is fully satisfactory. I have, with considerable hesitation, followed the view of Woodhouse, though neither he nor Gomme sees that it makes Agis' orders even more surprising and dangerous.

[49]5.71.1.

[50]5.71.1.

[51]5.70.

battle by a great display of courage, "although they were strikingly inferior in every way in tactics."[52]

If, as Thucydides says, Agis' order was impromptu, we must reject some of the modern attempts to explain it. Agis' maneuver cannot have been part of a preconceived plan made in concert with the oligarchic leaders of Argos's elite Thousand, as one scholar suggests.[53] Nor can we believe that these last-second changes were really part of a carefully calculated strategy planned in advance by Agis, as argued by another.[54] Though Thucydides appears not to have known the terrain well nor to have been perfectly informed about this campaign, we have no reason to question his assessment. Taken by surprise, Agis was forced to fight before he was quite ready, on a field of his enemy's choosing. As the armies advanced he realized that his right wing was held not by Spartans, but only by Tegeans who must face Athenians supported by their own cavalry, just the force to delay an enveloping movement. He naturally feared that his left would be quickly outflanked and overrun by the enemy right, which was approaching on the double and eager to roll up or envelop his army while it was still engaged with the enemy center and left.

Agis' best plan would seem to have been to hold formation, have his right wing try to outflank and roll up the enemy left, throw his own powerful Spartan army against the unimpressive ordinary Argive contingent in the center, and hope that his left wing, bearing the brunt of the enemy onslaught, could maintain contact and hold off the enemy until he himself could bring relief. The real danger in such a strategy was that the Peloponne-

---

[52]5.72.2.

[53]D. Gillis (*RIL* XCVII [1963], 199-226) makes an interesting argument in favor of a political explanation of the strange tactics employed in the battle, but I think he goes too far. Political considerations appear to have come into play some time in the course of the fighting, but the case for collusion in advance is not substantial.

[54]Woodhouse (*Agis*, 80-82) argues that the gap on the left was meant to entice the Argive Thousand to charge into nothing: "the enemy's line would be fatally severed, torn asunder, as it were, by its own momentum. . . . The blow struck by the select corps would fall almost harmlessly in the air." The successful outcome "was the clearly foreseen and nicely calculated issue of tactics not in the least comprehended by Thucydides."

sian left would be outflanked and rolled up too soon. In the situation that surprise had forced on the Spartans, however, every alternative involved even greater risks. What Agis needed now was the judgment, confidence, and determination of an experienced commander, but, as his previous behavior shows, these were precisely the qualities he had yet to acquire. Instead he gave the unusual orders we have described.

We shall never know how Agis' maneuver might have worked. The left wing obeyed orders, moving out to prevent the flanking movement of the enemy and opening a gap between themselves and the Spartans in the center, but the Spartans from the right of that center did not move. The captains of the two companies, Aristocles and Hipponoïdas, simply refused to obey the order.[55] Such disobedience was as unprecedented as Agis' order, and we must ask what made the two captains behave in this unexampled way. Thucydides tells us that they were later condemned and exiled for cowardice,[56] and most scholars who have raised the question have accepted the verdict of the Spartan court, in the process inferring that Agis' order must have been feasible, even sensible.[57] But let us examine the actions of the two captains: they refused a direct order from their commander in the field, presumably an unprecedented act; they kept their companies in the original position in the phalanx, in the center where the battle was won; they did not flee or seek sanctuary afterwards but returned to Sparta for trial. These are not the actions of cowards. Nor should we be unduly impressed by the verdict of the Spartan jury. Almost every Spartan trial of which we know, certainly every one involving kings, was a political trial. Only the naïve will believe that the facts and the law alone determined the decisions in the trials of the following: Cleomenes I, the regent Pausanias after the Persian Wars, Pleistoanax in 445, King Pausanias after the Peloponnesian War, and Phoebidas and Sphodrias in the time of Agesilaus. When Aristocles and Hipponoïdas came to trial, Agis was on trial as well. If they were

[55] 5.72.1.
[56] 5.72.1.
[57] Kromayer (*Antike Schlachtfelder* IV, 220), for example, argues that the two captains would hardly have been punished as they were, "If Agis' order had been considered an obvious absurdity."

right he was wrong. But at the time of the trial he was a great hero, the victor of Mantinea, the man who had restored Peloponnesian hegemony to Sparta. For a Spartan court to find for the defendants, and thus to say that Agis' orders had been foolhardy or impossible, was out of the question. Whatever the facts, the Spartan victory at Mantinea had sealed the fate of the captains.

Still, to disobey a direct order in the field is no small matter anywhere in any circumstances, and especially in Sparta. The recusant captains must have known how dangerous their defiance was to them, yet they risked it. Their bold action can be at least partially explained by its timing. Before the battle these experienced soldiers had reason to believe that their army was led by an incompetent. Agis was so distrusted that, even before the campaign, he needed to be overseen by ten advisers. Since first encountering the enemy, he had led his men in a reckless and abortive uphill charge, led them back down after coming within a spear's throw of the enemy, and, finally, allowed the enemy to surprise him with a battle on a ground and in a formation of its choosing. A second reason for the captains' action may be that Aristocles was the brother of Pleistoanax, Agis' royal colleague.[58] He may have hoped for the effective protection of his brother and persuaded Hipponoïdas to go along. But ultimately the Spartan captains must have been moved to act by what seemed the sheer folly of Agis' orders and the terrible danger in which it would place the Spartan army. The Spartans won the battle even though the two captains had disobeyed Agis' orders, and it is possible that their refusal was a major factor in the victory. When the two armies joined in battle, there was no gap on the right side of the Spartan center, nor were the captains' two companies in question *hors de combat*, moving behind their

---

[58]5.16.2. Gomme and Andrewes question whether this Aristocles is Pleistoanax's brother, chiefly on the grounds that Thucydides does not mention the connection in this context (*HCT* IV, 120). In light of Thucydides' frequent silences and omissions this one carries little weight, and we have no reason to doubt that this Aristocles is the same one mentioned earlier in Book V. Aristocles was not a common Spartan name. See Paul Poralla, *Prosopographie der Lakedaimonier* (Breslau, 1913), 27–28.

own phalanx. They were instead strengthening the Spartan center and that was where the victory was won.

The Spartan victory also owed something to the enemy's mistakes. When Agis learned that he could not use troops from his right to close the gap he had created on the left, he reversed himself and ordered the left wing to close up the line again, but it was too late. The Mantineans routed the Spartan left wing and then, aided by the elite Argive corps, drove into the gap between the Spartan left wing and center. For the Argives and their allies this was the key moment in the battle and the great chance for victory. If they had ignored the disorganized Sciritae, *neodamodeis*, and Brasidaeans on the left wing, or sent a small force to occupy them, and turned left against the flank and rear of the Spartan center, they would almost surely have gained the victory, for the Spartan center was still engaged with the enemy directly before it. Instead the allies turned to the right and destroyed the Spartan left wing, thus losing their great opportunity and with it the battle.[59] While the allies needlessly pursued the Sciritae and freed helots, Agis and the Spartan center repulsed the unimpressive forces in front of them: the "five companies" of older Argives and the hoplites from Cleonae and Orneae. In fact, Thucydides tells us, "most did not even stand and fight but fled as the Spartans approached; some were even trampled in their hurry to get away before the enemy reached them."[60] Perhaps Thucydides' account reflects an aristocratic slander against the Argive masses,[61] but clearly they put up only feeble resistance.

By this time the Spartan right wing was beginning to encircle the outflanked Athenians on the allies' left. The cavalry prevented a rout, but still disaster loomed. The failure of the allies on the right to exploit their advantage had been decisive. Some scholars have pointed to this failure as further evidence of collusion between the Spartans and the Argive aristocrats, as part of a plan to insure that the oligarchic Argive Thousand would be

---

[59]5.72.3. For evidence of the right turn see Kromayer, *Antike Schlachtfelder* IV, 218 with n. 2.

[60]5.72.4.

[61]As Gomme (*HCT* IV, 123 and *Essays*, 153, n. 1) suggests.

allowed to destroy the expendable Sciritae and the dangerous freed helots but prevented from coming into conflict with the main Spartan army.[62] There is no evidence for such an interpretation; indeed, the explanation is probably purely military. The Mantineans and elite Argives charging through the opening in the Spartan ranks did the natural and easy thing. They turned to the right rather than to the left because to the right they faced the unshielded side of the enemy, a more tempting and safer target than the shielded Spartans to their left. We must also remember that the allies were probably surprised to see the gap open before them as they approached the enemy phalanx; it had, after all, not been there when they started their advance. Originally the allied generals must have ordered their right wing to concentrate all its force on the enemy left wing, to destroy it swiftly and totally, for only then could they hope to turn inward against the center. The allied soldiers must have had as their main goal the destruction of the enemy left wing—and that is what they did. The sudden opening of the Spartan left center called for a change in plan, but it was difficult if not impossible to change a battle plan once a hoplite phalanx was underway, as Agis discovered. Perhaps a great general commanding a homogeneous, well-drilled, and familiar army could have succeeded in such a maneuver, but we do not know who the allied general was, and his army had been assembled from different states. The allied army did what it was most likely to do, and the battle was lost.

Once the tide of battle had turned, Agis gave a number of orders that determined the character of the victory. Instead of allowing his right wing to finish off the Athenians who were retreating before it, he ordered his entire army to bring support to his defeated and hard-pressed left wing. This allowed the Athenians and a part of the ordinary Argive army to escape.[63] Agis' decision can be understood on purely military grounds; the Spartan king surely wanted to save his army from further losses and to destroy the flower of the enemy's army, the Mantineans and the elite Argives. This explanation does not, however, eliminate the possibility that he also had political motives. We

[62]Gillis, *RIL* XCVII (1963), 221-223.
[63]5.73.3.

must remember that, strange as it may seem, Athens and Sparta were still technically at peace. The Spartan destruction of the Athenian army at Mantinea would surely strengthen the hands of Sparta's enemies at Athens. News of the Spartan victory combined with evidence of Spartan restraint, on the other hand, might help persuade the Athenians to adopt a moderate policy and keep the peace while Sparta restored its power and prestige.

On the other end of the field the Mantineans and elite Argives soon lost their zeal as they saw the collapse of their forces and the approach of the entire enemy army. They turned to run for safety and the Mantinean casualties were heavy, but "most of the elite Argives were saved." It is hard to understand why of these two contingents fighting side by side one should have been almost annihilated and the other almost unharmed. Thucydides explains that their flight was not pursued hotly or for any great distance, "for the Spartans fight their battles for a long time and stand their ground until the enemy is routed, but when he is, pursuit is brief and only for a short distance."[64] This explanation rings hollow, for it does not tell us why the Mantineans were killed while the Argives escaped. It is almost as if Thucydides' source, probably a Spartan or an Argive oligarch, was aware that there was a different explanation and offered this weak substitute.

There is, in fact, another explanation in the account given by Diodorus:

After the Spartans had routed the other parts of the army, killing many, they turned on the Thousand elite Argives. Encircling them with superior numbers, they hoped to destroy them entirely. The elite troops, though much inferior in number, were outstanding in courage. The king of the Spartans, fighting in the front ranks, persisted against the dangers, and he would have killed them all—for he was eager to carry out his promises to his fellow citizens to make amends for his previous disgrace by accomplishing great deeds—but he was not allowed to carry out his intention. For the Spartan Pharax, who was one of the advisers, and had a great reputation in Sparta, commanded him to give an escape route to the elite troops and not, by taking

[64] 5.73.4.

chances against men who had given up hope of living, to find out about the courage of men deserted by fortune. So the king was compelled by the orders he had recently received to allow their escape in accordance with the judgment of Pharax.[65]

Gomme dismisses this account as "a foolish little story, so typical of the *civilian* Ephoros,"[66] but there is no reason for such skepticism. The story is not in itself improbable; it does not contradict any facts offered by Thucydides but adds some he omits and offers a different interpretation.[67] We should not be surprised that Agis wanted especially to destroy the Argive elite, for they were the source of his disgrace. Their destruction would be the clearest and most satisfying fulfillment of his promise to atone for his errors with noble deeds in war. Nor should we be surprised at the intervention of the *xymboulos* Pharax. The appointed adviser was plainly thinking ahead to the results of the battle and its effects on Sparta's position. To destroy the aristocratic elite when most of the ordinary, democratic Argives had escaped would be folly. It would probably mean the continued alliance of Argos with the other democracies, Athens, Elis, and Mantinea. If, on the other hand, the Argive elite were permitted to return in the aftermath of the great defeat of the anti-Spartan policy, it would be in good position to bring the city over to Sparta and destroy the dangerous enemy coalition. The headstrong, inexperienced Agis, determined to recover his honor, could not be expected to see this in the heat of battle, but that was why the Spartans had appointed advisers.[68]

---

[65] 12.79.6-7. Diodorus clearly believes that Agis had to obey the *xymbouloi*, but on an earlier occasion the Spartan commander Alcidas could reject the advice of the *xymboulos* Brasidas, because the latter did not have equal authority (3.79.3). Diodorus or his source may be right in thinking that the relationship between commander and advisers at Mantinea was different. Even if that view is wrong, however, Agis would have needed extraordinary boldness to reject their advice, given his special problems.

[66] Gomme, *Essays*, 151.

[67] Andrewes (*HCT* IV, 125), though not clearly accepting it, points out that the story is not inherently improbable and that Gomme exaggerates the difference between the two versions.

[68] The detail supplying Pharax's name is telling support for the reliability of the account. Though an active soldier (see Poralla, *Prosopographie*, 123) he was not a famous man of the sort around whom legends grow. There is no reason to

The battle of Mantinea did not destroy the defeated army,[69] but Thucydides was right to emphasize its importance: "This was an exceptionally large-scale battle, involving an exceptional number of important cities; and it was very long since a comparable battle had been fought."[70] The most important result of Mantinea for the Spartans was that they did not lose. Had the elite Argives exploited the gap in the Spartan line properly and defeated the Spartans and their allies, Spartan control of the Peloponnesus might have come to an end in 418 instead of 371. The blow to Spartan prestige, following the surrender at Sphacteria and Alcibiades' parade through the Peloponnesus, would have been fatal to Spartan hegemony. The loss of Tegea, which surely would follow an allied victory at Mantinea, would be a more tangible and deadly blow, destroying Sparta's strategic position. With Tegea in hostile hands, the Spartans would be cut off from all their allies and would even find it difficult to control Messenia. We must realize that an Allied victory at Mantinea would almost surely have put an end to the Peloponnesian War with a victory for Athens and her friends. Instead the Spartan victory restored Sparta's confidence and reputation: "The charges that the Greeks brought against them at that time, cowardice because of their disaster on the island Sphacteria, bad judgment and slowness on other occasions, were erased by this single action. Now it seemed they had suffered disgrace because of bad luck, but they were still the same in their resolve."[71]

The Spartan triumph was also a victory for the principle of oligarchy.[72] All the allied states were democracies. Victory at

---

put him into the story if he were not part of it and, therefore, very good reason to believe the story. The source may have been Ephorus, Diodorus' major source for this period. Ephorus wrote in the mid-fourth century and could have had access to reliable oral accounts. We know he used the *Hellenica Oxyrhynchia*, a good source for the late fifth and early fourth centuries. He may have had other good written sources unknown to us. There is no warrant for rejecting his accounts a priori.

[69] 5.74.2. Thucydides reports the allies' losses as follows: 700 from the Argives, Orneates, and Cleonaeans together; 200 Mantineans, 200 Athenians, including both their generals.

[70] 5.74.1. I have adopted the paraphrase of Andrewes (*HCT* IV, 126) of a passage I cannot translate satisfactorily.

[71] 5.75.3.

[72] The point is forcefully made by Busolt, *Forsch.*, 179–181.

Mantinea would have fortified democratic rule at Argos, Elis, and Mantinea, lending it a prestige that would probably have brought forth other democracies in the Peloponnesus. Defeat, instead, badly damaged democratic prestige and weakened the hold of the Peloponnesian democrats on their own states. The battle, as Busolt says, was "a turning point in the political development of Greece. . . . It introduced an oligarchic reaction which, after many fluctuations, finally gained dominion in all of Greece."[73]

The Spartans were not quick to follow up their victory. The time for the Carneian festival came soon after the battle, and the Spartans went home to celebrate it. The day before the battle the Epidaurians invaded Argos in the knowledge that it would be deserted or only lightly defended, and after the battle they were still attacking the Argive garrison. After the battle the 3,000 Eleans and the 1,000 Athenian reinforcements came to Mantinea. If they had arrived in time to fight and to strengthen the allied center, the battle would almost surely have had a different result. Now, however, they marched against Epidaurus to relieve the attack on Argos while the Spartans continued to enjoy their celebration of the festival. The allies began to build a wall around Epidaurus, but only the Athenians finished their part of the assignment, the others soon wearying of the work. They all contributed to the garrison that stayed and took shelter behind the fortifications the Athenians had built on a height containing a temple of Hera. The armies went home as the summer came to an end. The democratic alliance persisted, but morale was low and the alliance tenuous.[74]

About the beginning of November, after the allied armies had withdrawn, the Spartans took steps to reap the fruit of their selective restraint at Mantinea.[75] Although their target was Argos, the Spartans sent their army to Tegea, for they intended to secure their ends by diplomacy, not war. From Tegea they sent Lichas, the Argive *proxenus* at Sparta, to Argos with a peace offer. The army was kept at Tegea, presumably to make sure

[73]Busolt, *GG* III:2, 1251.
[74]5.75.4-6.
[75]For the date see Gomme, *HCT* IV, 130.

that the Argives listened carefully.[76] In relating these negotiations Thucydides reveals important information about internal
politics in Argos. He maintains that even before this time there
were men at Argos who were friends of Sparta, "and who wished
to destroy the [Argive] democracy." We may presume that the
elite Thousand were among them.[77] After their escape from
Mantinea they were the only significant military force in Argos.
Furthermore, their prestige had been enhanced by their brave
showing, that contrasted so sharply with the cowardice that the
mass of the army had demonstrated in the battle. The half-
hearted Athenian performance at Mantinea also embarrassed and
discouraged the Argive democrats. As Thucydides says, "after
the battle the friends of the Spartans found it much easier to
persuade the many to make an agreement with Sparta."[78]

Lichas came to the Argive assembly and stimulated a lively
debate with his proposals. Alcibiades, though still a private citizen, came to Argos in an attempt to salvage what he could of his
policy.[79] But now the oligarchs were confident enough to come
into the open and argue in favor of the Spartan proposal. Even
the eloquence and cleverness of Alcibiades were no match for the
new realities created by the outcome of Mantinea and the presence of an unopposed Spartan army at Tegea. The Argives accepted the treaty which required them to restore all hostages,
give up Orchomenus, evacuate Epidaurus, and join with the
Spartans in forcing the Athenians to do the same.[80] Since it was
no longer needed, the Spartan army returned home after the
Argives accepted the peace. This was only the beginning. Grow-

[76]Thucydides does not tell us who led the Spartan army. Perhaps it was
someone other than Agis.

[77]Diodorus (12.80.2) says flatly that these were behind the attack on the
democracy and that they aimed at establishing "an aristocracy made up of
themselves."

[78]5.76.2. Aristotle (*Pol.* 1304a 25) says "In Argos the notables (γνώριμοι),
having enhanced their reputations in the battle of Mantinea, destroyed the
democracy."

[79]Thucydides (5.76.3) says Alcibiades happened to be present (ἔτυχε γὰρ
καὶ ὁ Ἀλκιβιάδης παρών). There was, of course, nothing casual or fortuitous
about Alcibiades' presence. This passage sheds light on a similar one (1.72.1).
See Kagan, *Outbreak*, 294.

[80]5.77.

ing in confidence, the oligarchs persuaded the Argives to renounce the alliances with Elis, Mantinea, and Athens and
crowned their victory by concluding an alliance with Sparta.[81]

The Argive defection was fatal to the democratic league, especially when the Argives showed genuine zeal in cooperating with
Sparta. They refused to have any diplomatic contact with the
Athenians until they had evacuated their forts and withdrawn
from the Peloponnesus. They sent envoys to Macedon and
Thrace, where they were influential, urging their friends to join
with them and the Spartans. They demanded that the Athenians
withdraw from Epidaurus and, in the new circumstances,
Athens complied.[82] Mantinea was so weakened by the defection
of Argos and the collapse of the league that she too yielded and
made a treaty with Sparta, relinquishing control of a number of
Arcadian cities. Next the Argive Thousand joined an equal number of Spartans in an expedition to Sicyon, where a trustworthy
oligarchy was established in place of the former government.
Finally, the maneuvers of the oligarchs and their loyalty to the
Spartan cause were rewarded when the joint army returned, put
down the Argive democracy, and established an oligarchy.[83]

By March of 417, therefore, the Spartans, by war and subver-
sion, had shattered the democratic league, ending its threat to
Sparta's security and its control of the Peloponnesus. Success at
Mantinea averted disaster, but it did not guarantee safety for the
future. The Athenians were still powerful, and Alcibiades continued to favor an active and aggressive policy. Perhaps next time
the Spartans might not be so fortunate as to find their chief
opponent out of office on the crucial day. Nor were conditions in
the Peloponnesus entirely stable. Athens continued to hold
Pylos, which was a constant invitation to defection or rebellion
by the helots. Elis appears to have remained outside of Spartan

[81] 5.77-79.
[82] 5.80.3.
[83] 5.81.2. Diodorus adds details, saying that the oligarchs put the popular
leaders to death, terrorized the other citizens, and destroyed the laws (12.80.3).
There seems no good reason for rejecting the evidence of Diodorus here as
Busolt (GG III:2, 1255, n. 5) does.

control,[84] and events would soon show that the rule of the Argive oligarchs was far from secure. Finally, differences of opinion continued to divide the Spartans themselves. The final significance of the battle of Mantinea was yet to be determined.

[84]See Andrewes (*HCT* IV, 148).

6. After Mantinea: Politics and Policy at Sparta and Athens

In the summer of 417, probably in August, the Argive democrats broke out in rebellion against the ruling oligarchs.[1] Preparations for the revolt had been going on for some time, for the
rule of the Argive oligarchs seems to have been hard to bear. As
Grote pointed out, "an oligarchy erected by force upon the ruins
of a democracy was rarely of long duration."[2] Once the lower
classes of any Greek state became accustomed to the democratic
way of life, they could not peacefully accept the restoration of
oligarchic rule. The oligarchs, for their part, after long exclusion
from power, were likely to abuse the opportunity, and the Argive oligarchs had proven no exception. Diodorus tells us that
"first, taking hold of those accustomed to be popular leaders,
they [the oligarchs] put them to death; then, by terrorizing the
other Argives, they destroyed the laws and began to take public
affairs unto themselves."[3]

The popular leaders who replaced those who had been exe-

---

[1] 5.82.1. For the date see Busolt, *GG* III:2, 1263, and Andrewes, *HCT* IV,
150–151.

[2] Grote, VII, 98.

[3] Diod. 12.80.3. Pausanias tells the story of a specific outrage committed by a
certain Bryas, commander of the elite Thousand. In addition to his general
insolence to commoners he kidnapped a girl on her way to her wedding and
raped her. Pausanias makes this act the immediate cause of the rebellion
(2.20.2). Busolt (*GG* III:2, 1263, n. 2) and Andrewes (*HCT* IV, 150) are right to
reject the causal connection, but there is no good reason to reject the rest of the
story.

cuted waited as discontent grew and the people gained courage. They planned their rebellion to coincide with the Spartan ally's celebration of the festival of the Gymnopaediae and they struck with success. A battle broke out in the city, and the popular party was able to kill or exile many of the oligarchs. Argos was again in democratic hands. The surviving oligarchs appealed frantically and repeatedly to Sparta for help, but for some time the Spartans turned a deaf ear to their Argive friends and continued to celebrate the festival. When at last they broke off the celebration and dispatched an army, it got only as far as Tegea, where it learned that the Argive oligarchs had been defeated. In spite of the continued pleading of the Argive exiles, the Spartans returned home and resumed the Gymnopaediae.[4]

Sparta's response to the rebellion at Argos is surprising. After all their efforts to gain control of their troublesome neighbor and place it in friendly hands, why did the Spartans allow it to escape so easily? Perhaps they at first underestimated the danger; possibly they were still reluctant to commit themselves until they had a clearer idea of Athens' intentions.[5] But they did eventually break off their festival, thus acknowledging the danger. Then, having sent an army, they did not use it. Such vacillation must have stemmed from a division of opinion within Sparta. Until the democratic rebellion at Argos most Spartans must have been pleased to have an alliance with the Argives. For the friends of peace the alliance ended a threat of war in the Peloponnesus; for the advocates of war it removed a barrier to the renewal of war against Athens. Recent events in Argos, however, must have raised questions among those cautious Spartans opposed to war. Perhaps they now came to understand the intimacy of the relations between the Argive oligarchs and the aggressive faction in Sparta. Perhaps all Spartans were taken aback when the rebellion showed that only a small number of Argives were friendly to Sparta, while the great majority would always be in wait for an opportunity to rebel. That would mean constant trouble for Sparta; the discontented Argives would always look to Athens

[4] 5.82.1-3.
[5] Both suggestions are made by Busolt (GG III:2, 1264-1265) who alone seems to have seen the problem.

for help, and the Spartans must always be ready to intervene.
From the point of view of cautious Spartans an alliance with a
democratic but stable Argos would be preferable. Perhaps the
reluctance and opposition of such Spartans caused the delays and
hesitations in Sparta's response to the democratic rebellion in
Argos.

Such an interpretation helps to explain what happened next.
The Argive democrats sent ambassadors to Sparta, seeking to
establish not only their legitimacy, but also friendly relations and
probably an alliance.[6] The democrats were cowed by their isolated position and feared that the oligarchic exiles would persuade the Spartans to restore them by force. The Argive ambassadors presented their case to the Spartans and their assembled
allies, and the Argive oligarchs argued against them. The debate
was long, but at last the Spartans decided in favor of the
oligarchs and voted to march against Argos. Still, for some time,
"there were delays and postponements."[7] Thucydides' terse account of this assembly is reminiscent of the fuller accounts he
gives of the assemblies in 431 in which the Spartans voted to go
to war against Athens. The Spartans and their allies were divided on policy; they voted to take action but delayed.

After the Spartan rebuff, the democratic Argives once more
sought protection in an alliance with Athens. They made good
use of Sparta's hesitancy, taking Alcibiades' advice to begin
building long walls connecting Argos with the sea.[8] Evidently
the battle of Mantinea had not crushed the spirit of Peloponnesian resistance to Sparta, for some of the Peloponnesian cities,
presumably including Mantinea and Elis, "were accomplices in
the fortification."[9] Completion of the walls would have dramatically enhanced the security of Argos by keeping open a sea route
to Athens, and the Argives hurried to complete the work. They

---

[6] 5.82.4. Thucydides does not specifically mention the request for an alliance,
but his account seems to justify Busolt's assumption (GG III:2, 1264) that the
Argives made one.

[7] 5.82.4.

[8] 5.82.5. Although Thucydides does not mention Alcibiades, Plutarch (Alc.
15) says that the idea came from the Athenian. This time there is good reason to
believe him. See Busolt, GG III:2, 1265, n. 3.

[9] 5.82.6: ξυνῄδεσαν δὲ τὸν τειχισμόν. . . .

put their men, women, and slaves to work on the project, and the Athenians sent carpenters and masons. But Argos was about five miles from the sea,[10] and the job was not finished before the end of summer. By that time news of the Athenian alliance and the fortifications had goaded the Spartans to act. They sent an army of Spartans and Peloponnesian allies under King Agis against Argos, hoping to obtain support from oligarchs who were still within the city. They received no help from their oligarchic collaborators, but their army was able to destroy as much of the walls as had been constructed. Agis also captured Hysiae, an Argive town, killing all the free men who had been captured before he broke off the campaign and returned home. Thucydides relates this atrocity without comment.[11]

Among Sparta's allies only the Corinthians did not take part in the expedition, and their absence deserves an explanation. Not only did they fail to take part in Sparta's attack on Argos in 417, but they were the only allies absent from the attack of the following winter,[12] even though they continued to be hostile to Athens.[13] Busolt suggested that the Corinthians held back because they did not want to drive the Argives into the arms of Athens,[14] but the Argives were already in the Athenian embrace, and if this was not clear in 417 it certainly was a year later. As usual, Corinthian thinking is not disclosed by the ancient writers, so we must speculate. Perhaps the Corinthians, like the friends of peace in Sparta though for different reasons, changed their outlook because of the brief experience of oligarchic rule in Argos. The Corinthians owed their special position of influence in the Spartan alliance in considerable part to the menace that a powerful and independent Argos presented to the Spartans.[15] Under the oligarchs, however, Argos had been and always would be merely a Spartan satellite, for given their inadequate political base the oligarchs must rely on Spartan support. With

[10]Gomme, *HCT* IV, 152.
[11]5.83.2.
[12]5.83.1 (417), 6.7.1 (416).
[13]Thucydides (5.115.3) says that in 416 the Corinthians went to war with the Athenians "over some private differences."
[14]Busolt, *GG* III:2, 1264 and n. 2.
[15]E. Will, *Korinthiaka* (Paris, 1955), 628.

the Argive threat removed, Sparta's fear, and hence her need of Corinth, would diminish; as a result Corinth would be less able to manipulate the Peloponnesian League for its own purposes. Perhaps we see in Corinth's reluctance a hint of the suspicions about Sparta's interference in the internal affairs of its allies which would lead both Corinth and Thebes to break with Sparta after the Peloponnesian War.

The withdrawal of Agis' army left the Argives free to attack Phlius, where most of the oligarchic exiles had settled. Such attacks were repeated, and steps were taken to protect the democracy from treason. In 416 Alcibiades took a fleet to Argos and removed 300 men suspected of being sympathetic to the Spartans, scattering them among the islands. Even that did not end the insecurity, for later in the year the Argives arrested more suspects, and still others escaped into exile before they could be caught.[16] The Argives, however, continued to be subject to attack by the Spartans and to urge the Athenians to take a more open and active part, not only in defending them but in attacking Sparta.[17] Athens' alliance with Argos persisted, but after Mantinea it offered few opportunities and many dangers.

The battle of Mantinea had confused the political situation in Athens. Alcibiades and his policy were surely not helped by the defeat on the battlefield, the dissolution of the Argive alliance, and Argos' treaty with Sparta, yet no more than three years later Alciabiades looked back proudly on the policy that had brought on the battle.[18] He could certainly argue that the fault lay not with the policy but with its execution and with those Athenians who had failed to elect him general for 418/17. The execution had left much room for criticism: the initial Athenian contingent had been too small; the reinforcements (the very dispatch of which indicated that the Athenians recognized the inadequacy of their contingent) had arrived too late; the Athenians had not taken the opportunity to distract the enemy and divide his forces by launching seaborne raids on the Peloponnesus or by using the base at Pylos to stir up the helots; and finally, the generals at the battle were neither Alcibiades nor his friends but men who were

---

[16]Phlius: 5.83.3; 115.1, Argos: 5.84.1; 115.1.
[17]6.7.1-3 and 105.
[18]6.16.6.

at best lukewarm in their support of the entire undertaking. The defeat at Mantinea did as much to hurt Nicias and those Athenians known to be hostile to a forward policy as it did to hurt the aggressive faction whose policies had led to the battle.

The election of generals early in the spring of 417 revealed the uncertainty and division in Athenian politics. Both Nicias and Alcibiades were elected,[19] and each continued to pursue his own policy as best he could in the new circumstances. Alcibiades, as we have seen, continued to support and encourage his friends at Argos, but without the participation of Elis and Mantinea there was no hope of resuming an active Peloponnesian campaign, though the sanguine Alcibiades may not yet have completely abandoned the scheme of reviving the alliance and bringing on another decisive battle, only this time with himself in command. Nicias' policy was to recover the Chalcidian and Macedonian territories lost to the genius of Brasidas. This policy had the advantage of avoiding possible conflict with Sparta, but it was also prudent and practical. The region was crucial to Athens as a source of money and timber, but even more important was the need to recover lost territory, subjects, and prestige before the idea of rebellion spread any further. Since the peace in 421 there had, in fact, been further defections from Athens in the Chalcidice.[20]

The already strong case for an Athenian expedition to the Chalcidice and Amphipolis was strengthened further by the suspicious behavior of King Perdiccas of Macedon.[21] In 418 the Spartans, accompanied by Argive oligarchs, had persuaded Perdiccas to swear an alliance with them, even though he was still too prudent to break with Athens.[22] About May of 417 the Athenians forced the king's hand by planning a campaign against the Chalcidians and Amphipolis under the command of Nicias.[23]

[19]Fornara, *Generals*, 63. So were Teisias and Cleomedes (idem), but we know nothing of their political leanings.

[20]In 421 the Dians took Thyssus on the promontory of Athos (5.35.1); during the next winter the Olynthians took Mecyberna from its Athenian garrison (5.35.1); in 417 Dium revolted and went over to the Chalcidian rebels (5.82.1). See Map 1.

[21]For a useful account of Perdiccas' career see J. W. Cole, *Phoenix* XXVIII (1974), 55-72.

[22]5.80.2.

[23]5.83.4. For the date see Andrewes, *HCT* IV, 154.

In all such Athenian ventures to the north much depended upon the attitude adopted by Perdiccas. In this case he refused to play the part expected of him and, as a result, the Athenians were forced to abandon the campaign, although money to support it already had been taken from the public treasury and paid to Nicias.[24] The Macedonian king had frustrated Nicias' policy. The best the Athenians could do now was order their forces already in the neighborhood to impose a blockade on the Macedonian coast, but they must have known that such an action would have little effect on the renegade Perdiccas.[25] The Athenians could agree on no single, consistent policy, and the attempts of their two major leaders to pursue different policies alternately had produced only failure and deadlock.

The man who stepped in to break the impasse was Hyperbolus, and the device he used was the old one of ostracism. No one seems to have been ostracized from Athens in a quarter century, the last certain victim being Thucydides son of Melesias, in 443. Yet ostracism appeared perfectly suited to solve Athens' problems in 416, for it would give the Athenians a clear choice between the policies of Nicias and those of Alcibiades. The very nature of the institution, however, prevented either leader from introducing it. The cost of defeat was so high that only a statesman confident of a majority could favor an ostracism. Since the death of Pericles, however, no Athenian could have such confidence, and in 416 Nicias and Alcibiades had about equal support, thus neither was encouraged to gamble. Hyperbolus, on the other hand, appeared to have nothing to lose. The emergence of Alcibiades as leader of the aggressive faction seemed to have put him, as Plutarch says, "out of the reach of ostracism," for in the past only major political figures, the leaders of factions, had been ostracized.[26]

Plutarch tells us that Hyperbolus "hoped that when one of the

[24]Busolt (GG III:2, 1262 n. 1) and others have thought the expedition got so far as Thrace before being abandoned. Thucydides' language, however, will not bear that interpretation. See Andrewes, HCT IV, 154. For a useful commentary on the inscription recording the payment to Nicias see GHI #77, 229-236.

[25]5.83.4; Andrewes, HCT IV, 153-154.

[26]Plut. Nic. 11.4.

other men was exiled he would become the rival of the one who remained."[27] This may have been no more than a guess on Plutarch's part, but it was a good one. Hyperbolus had every reason to think that the removal of either Nicias or Alcibiades might enhance his own position. Despite his poor reputation among the ancient writers, he may have placed the well-being of Athens first, reasoning that the ostracism would result in a steadier and clearer policy. Whatever his motives, we have no reason to doubt that Hyperbolus was the man most responsible for persuading the Athenians to hold an ostracism in the sixth prytany, probably early in January of 416.[28] It is more difficult to understand how he was able to win a majority, since his major opponents were against the idea of an ostracism. Probably they were taken by surprise; after all, there had been no successful ostracism for a quarter century.

Our knowledge of the ostracism comes from Plutarch, but he offers three different versions. In one version only Nicias and Alcibiades are candidates for exile;[29] in another the competitors

[27]Plut. *Nic.* 11.4.

[28]Plut. *Alc.* 13.4. The date of the ostracism is usually thought to have been 417, chiefly on the basis of a fragment of Theopompus (*FGrH* 115 F96b) which reads in part: ἐξωστράκισαν τὸν Ὑπέρβολον ἓξ ἔτη, ὁ δὲ καταπλεύσας εἰς Σάμον καὶ τὴν οἴκησιν αὐτοῦ ποιησάμενος ἀπέθανε. . . . Since Thucydides tells us that Hyperbolus was killed in 411 (8.73.3), scholars have simply added ἓξ ἔτη to 411 and fixed the date of the ostracism in 417. A. G. Woodhead, however (*Hesperia*, XVIII [1949], 78–83), has interpreted an inscription to mean that Hyperbolus moved an amendment to a decree of the Athenian assembly in the tenth prytany of 417. Both his reading of the inscription and his interpretation of its significance have been supported by M. F. McGregor (*Phoenix* XIX [1965], 31 and 43–46). This would make it impossible for Hyperbolus to have been ostracized in 417, since the ostracism took place in the eighth prytany. A. E. Raubitschek (*TAPA* LXXIX [1948], 191–210), accepting the historicity of Andocides IV, has tried to make a case for placing the ostracism in 415, in close connection with the Sicilian campaign. The reasons for rejecting the speech attributed to Andocides have been known at least as far back as Grote (VII, 106, n. 1) and are neatly summarized by Charles Fuqua (*TAPA* XCVI [1965], 173–175). I am persuaded by Fuqua's arguments for the 416 date. Fuqua allows us to accept both the implications of the inscription and the evidence of Theopompus by pointing out that the Greeks often engaged in inclusive reckoning and suggesting that "the figure ἓξ ἔτη counts by means of inclusive reckoning of archon years starting with 417/16 and ending with 412/11" (168), giving us 416 as the date of ostracism.

[29]Plut. *Nic.* 11. and *Arist.* 7.3.

are Alcibiades and a certain Phaeax, not Nicias;[30] in the third all
three are involved.[31] Phaeax, according to Plutarch, was, like his
rival Alcibiades, of noble birth and still early in his career.
Thucydides tells us that in 422 he led a diplomatic mission to
Sicily and Italy. Since he commanded two ships he may already
have been a general.[32] He was said to be effective in private
conversation, but no match for Alcibiades as a public orator. His
father was named Erasistratus, as were his son and nephew.[33]
Since an Erasistratus, probably the son or nephew, appears on
the list of the Thirty Tyrants of 404,[34] it is generally thought
that Phaeax was sympathetic to oligarchy.[35] The ancient tradition about his role in the ostracism is confused. Modern scholars
have speculated about it, some arguing that Phaeax was a tool of
Alcibiades, others claiming that he was used by Nicias.[36] The
evidence is insufficient to support either interpretation, and if
Phaeax played a part it must remain a mystery. We would do
well at least to follow Plutarch's example in rejecting Theophrastus' views on the involvement of Phaeax.[37]

Once the decision to hold an ostracism had been taken, Nicias
and Alcibiades had no choice but to prepare for the danger that
faced them. As might be expected, Alcibiades took action, approaching Nicias and suggesting that they collaborate to turn the
ostracism against Hyperbolus. Although neither had the political
strength to be confident of safety in an ostracism without collusion, their combined forces guaranteed success against Hyperbolus; he was ostracized and died in exile.

The *ostrakophoria* of 416 revealed a fatal weakness in the institution: it could secure and confirm a leader or a policy supported by a clear majority, but it was useless where such clarity
was lacking. We may guess that this, not the unworthiness of

[30]Plut. *Nic.* 11.7. Plutarch's source for this version is Theophrastus.
[31]Plut. *Alc.* 13.
[32]5.4.
[33]For references to Phaeax in ancient writers see *HCT* III, 633–634.
[34]Xen. *Hell.* 2.3.2.
[35]Fuqua, *TAPA* XCVI (1965), 173.
[36]The former view is set forth by Hatzfeld (*Alcibiade*, 112–118), the latter by
J. Carcopino (*L'ostracisme athénien*, 2d ed. [Paris, 1935], 230–232).
[37]Plut. *Nic.* 11.7: "I am not unaware that Theophrastus says that Hyperbolus was ostracized when Phaeax, not Nicias, was the rival of Alcibiades. But
most writers tell the story as I do."

Hyperbolus as a victim, was the reason why ostracism was never used again at Athens.[38] Plutarch conjectures that had Nicias "run the risk of ostracism against Alcibiades he would either have won out and lived safely in the city after the expulsion of his rival, or, if he were defeated, he would have left before his final misfortunes and maintained his reputation for being an outstanding general."[39] From a less personal point of view, Athens would have benefited enormously if the major rivals had not made a private bargain; the ostracism of March 416 meant that Athens would remain without a consistent policy or leadership.

The elections for the generalship in Athens took place shortly after the ostracism of Hyperbolus. Both Nicias and Alcibiades were elected. We know the names of four others, Lamachus, Cleomedes, Tisias, and Philocrates,[40] but except for Lamachus, we have nothing that allows us to discern their views, policies or factional affiliations, and Lamachus himself appears to have been a soldier rather than a politician. The election seems to have reflected the continuing stalemate in Athenian politics.

To understand the behavior of the Athenians in these years we must imagine their great frustration after five years of alleged peace. Nicias' hope for a sincere rapprochement between the two great powers had been shattered by Sparta's unwillingness to carry out the terms of the peace. Alcibiades' bold scheme of defeating Sparta through a great Peloponnesian alliance lay in shambles. Nicias' more modest program of recovering Athenian losses in Thrace and the Chalcidice had never progressed beyond the planning stage. Peace had, however, allowed the Athenians to recover their financial strength; by 415 they may have had as many as 4,000 talents in the reserve fund.[41] A new corps of young men had matured, one without experience in war or sharp

---

[38]Plutarch (*Arist.* 7.3 and *Nic.* 11.6) says the institution was abandoned when it began to be used against base and ignoble men like Hyperbolus.

[39]Plut. *Nic.* 11.7.

[40]Fornara, *Generals*, 63–64.

[41]Andocides (3.8) says that as a result of the Peace of Nicias the Athenians had stored 7,000 talents on the Acropolis. The editors of *ATL* (III, 346–457) suggest that Andocides was speaking of the Athenian intention to repay all loans from the gods made during the Archidamian War. They believe that in 421 the Athenians made a payment of 1,000 talents, and thereafter they paid 500 annually. Their views are accepted by H. B. Mattingly, *BCH* XCII (1968), 461–462. See also Meiggs, *Athenian Empire*, 340–343.

memories of the Spartan invasions. Athens boasted an un-
matched naval power and had a considerable army available, yet
it seemed unable to use its strength and vitality either to gain a
true peace or to win the war. The Athenians needed an outlet for
their energy and frustration, and the attack on Melos in the
spring of 416 provided one.

Previous events and the mood of the Athenians may help explain the timing of the attack but not its target. Why Melos? The
Melians, alone of the Cycladic islanders, had refused to join the
Delian League. They enjoyed the benefits of the Athenian Empire without bearing any of its burdens. They were Dorians and,
during the Archidamian War, they seem to have given aid to the
Spartans, whose colonists they were. They fought off an Athenian attack in 426 and stubbornly maintained their independence,[42] although the Athenians included them on their assessment lists beginning in 425. A further conflict was inevitable,
for the Athenians could not long allow their will and authority to
be flouted by a small Cycladic island. The Melians relied on their
special relationship with Sparta for their security,[43] and, ironically, this may help to explain the timing of the Athenian attack.
Frustrated by Spartan arms in the Peloponnesus and by Spartan
diplomacy in the north, the Athenians may have been eager to
demonstrate that, at least on the sea, the Spartans were power-
less to do Athens harm.

Thucydides cites no immediate grievance as triggering the
attack; the long-standing grievances seem to have been reason
enough. The Athenians sent 30 ships, 1,200 hoplites, 300 archers, and 20 mounted archers of their own. Their allies, most of
whom were probably islanders, sent 8 ships and 1,500 hoplites.
The participation of such a high proportion of allies and islanders
suggests, as Andrewes says, "that the attack was not just an evidently monstrous outrage."[44] We are not told of any dissension
among the Athenians over the decision to attack Melos. Nicias
could hardly object to the resumption of a project he himself had

[42]Kagan, *Archidamian War*, 197–200; Meiggs, *Athenian Empire*, 327–328.
[43]5.104.
[44]5.84.1. For discussions of the number of islanders and its significance see
Andrewes, *HCT* IV, 157, and Meiggs, *Athenian Empire*, 437–438.

undertaken unsuccessfully in 426,[45] and we have no reason to doubt the approval of the aggressive Alcibiades. The expedition did not seem important enough to invite the participation of either man and could be left to lesser lights.

Tisias and Cleomedes led the allied forces. They made camp on the island and, before laying waste the fields of Melos, they sent ambassadors to the Melians to persuade them to surrender without a siege or a battle. The Melian magistrates refused to allow the ambassadors to address the people, presumably fearing that the masses would be willing to yield, and instead arranged for them to speak before the magistrates themselves and probably an oligarchic council.[46] Thucydides' account of the ensuing discussion has caused at least as much scholarly debate as any part of his *History*. Its form is unique in the work: a dramatic dialogue in which one speaker is identified as "the Athenians' ambassadors" and the other as "the Melian councilors."[47] Just as startling is the manner and content of the Athenians' argument. In language that is cruelly blunt, they point out that the disparity in power between Athens and Melos renders all discussion of justice or injustice irrelevant, for in the reality of human affairs discussions of this kind only arise when equality of power prevents one side from imposing its will on the other.[48] When asked to consider the possibility of divine retribution, the Athenians respond with a remarkable statement: "As to the divine favor we do not think we are at a disadvantage.... For of the gods we believe, and of men we know, that by a necessity of their nature they always rule wherever they have the power."[49]

The dialogue form, the abstractness of the discussion, and the frank immorality of the Athenian arguments have provoked

[45]Kagan, *Archidamian War*, 197–200.

[46]We do not know what constitution prevailed at Melos. Thucydides (5.84.3) speaks of τὸ πλῆθος whom the Athenians were not allowed to address, and ταῖς ἀρχαῖς καὶ τοῖς ὀλίγοις to whom they spoke. Even in a close oligarchy, such as Melos appears to have been, questions of war and peace were usually referred to a popular assembly of some kind. The Melian leaders plainly did not trust the populace to support their stubborn and dangerous policy.

[47]The form of the dialogue between Archidamus and the Plataeans provides the closest analogy (2.71-74).

[48]5.89.

[49]5.105.

questions about the authenticity of Thucydides' account. Scholars have doubted that he had access to reliable sources, but he could easily have learned what was said from the Athenian participants and even from those Melians who escaped the mass execution that consumed their fellow citizens.[50] The problems of the dialogue's style and structure are not difficult to resolve, but it is not easy to ascertain the motives for their selection. Although the Melian Dialogue is not a verbatim record of the proceedings, but a shortened, stylized, and dramatically heightened account, it can, nonetheless, be faithful to the general sense of what was actually said. What has aroused the doubts of the skeptics is the content of the dialogue itself, the hard, merciless arguments put forth by the Athenians. Surely neither the Athenians nor any one else could have spoken so, without any attempt at self-justification or palliation. The skeptics maintain that the dialogue cannot have taken place as reported and conclude that it must be a Thucydidean invention.[51]

Such skepticism is unjustified. We must remember that the discussion took place in private among small numbers of officials, not in a public forum. In such circumstances frankness is more common. Nor were frankness and toughness necessarily out of place in the practical mission undertaken by the Athenian ambassadors. Their purpose was to convince the Melians to surrender without fighting, and they may have hoped to achieve this more readily by menace than by any other device. Such an approach, at any rate, was perfectly in keeping with their recent harsh treatment of Scione, where the policy of mild treatment of fractious allies had been abandoned in favor of rule by terror.[52] History does not lack examples of similar plain speaking when the circumstances warranted. Grote's treatment of the dialogue should have stilled the skeptics' argument more than a century ago, but it has received curiously little attention. He reminded

[50]For the surviving Melians see Xen. *Hell.* 2.2.9. For an excellent discussion of the problems presented by the Melian Dialogue see Andrewes, *HCT* IV, 182–188.

[51]For a collection of some such opinions see M. Amit, *Athenaeum* XLVI (1968), 225–227.

[52]5.32.1.

his readers of the British attack on Copenhagen in 1807, an attack launched in peacetime and without provocation by a powerful Britain against tiny Denmark. When the Danish Prince Regent protested, the British spokesman "replied to this just indignation with an insolent familiarity, saying that war was war, that one must be resigned to these necessities, and yield to the stronger when one was the weaker."[53] Finally, the blunt, hard language of the Athenians is not unique to their dialogue with the Melians. Both Pericles and Cleon had been willing to term the Athenian Empire a tyranny in public speeches, and the Athenian spokesman at Sparta in 432 used language not unlike that found in the Melian Dialogue: "We have done nothing amazing or contrary to human nature if we accepted an empire that was given to us and then did not give it up, since we were conquered by the strongest motives—honor, fear and self-interest. And we are not the first to have acted this way, for it has always been ordained that the weaker are kept down by the stronger."[54]

For all these reasons we need not doubt the authenticity of the dialogue in its essentials, but the question remains: why did Thucydides choose to report it in this unique way? The steady increase in the number of studies that attempt to answer this question suggests the difficulty and complexity of the matter. In antiquity Dionysius of Halicarnassus condemned Thucydides for ascribing the language of pirates and robbers to the Athenians, and suggested that this had been done to discredit the state that had sent the historian into exile.[55] Some modern scholars suggest that Thucydides intended the Dialogue to show the moral decline of the Athenians in the course of the war.[56] Others, on the contrary, think that he has taken the opportunity to illustrate an unpleasant, but important, side of human behavior.[57] Another interesting interpretation is that Thucydides

---

[53]This is my translation of the account by L. A. Thiers, *Histoire du Consulat et de l'Empire* VII, p. 190, cited by Grote, VII, 110-111, n. 1.

[54]Pericles: 2.63.2; Cleon: 3.37.2; Athenians at Sparta: 1.76.2.

[55]Dion. Hal. *Thuc.* 37-42.

[56]J. Finley, *Thucydides* (Cambridge, Mass., 1942), 208-212.

[57]H. P. Stahl, *Thukydides* (Munich, 1967), 158-171; A. G. Woodhead, *Thucydides on the Nature of Power* (Cambridge, Mass., 1972), 3, 8-10.

uses the Dialogue as an opportunity to wrestle with the problem of empire and morality, an issue which he never fully resolves.[58]

Thucydides could have inserted such a general discussion at other places, when describing the decision to destroy Scione for instance, if he had been in the business of inventing speeches or topics. Presumably he reports the discussion at Melos because some such debate took place, and its importance caught his attention. It is also possible that some of the ironies in the situation appealed to him. Melian resistance to the Athenian demands was based on the Melian conviction that since their cause was just, the gods would protect them, on their confidence that the Spartans would come to their aid, and on their hope that in some unaccountable way fortune would bring success to their efforts despite Athens' superior power. We have already seen how the Athenians dealt with the argument that the gods protect the just. In a similarly pragmatic way they also dismissed the prospect of Spartan intervention. The Athenians acknowledged that the Spartans practiced virtue at home, but added that "most blatantly of all men we know, they believe that what is agreeable is noble and what is expedient just. But this disposition does not favor your unreasonable expectation that they will save you."[59] The Athenians asserted that the Spartans, more than anyone else, were moved to action only when convinced that they were superior in power, "so that it is not likely they will cross over to an island so long as we control the sea."[60] The Melian expectations would all be proved false while the Athenian predictions would be borne out by events. The Athenians expressed a similar contempt for the Melians' reliance on hope, but these remarks have an ironical ring both for us and for Thucydides. Less than a year after these events at Melos, the ill-fated Athenian expedition sailed for Sicily. Perhaps Thucydides wished to dramatize the condition of post-Periclean Athens, which could give such sound advice to others in one year and grossly ignore it in her own undertakings the next.

The Athenians, having failed to convince the Melians to yield,

[58]A. Andrewes, *PCPhS* n.s. VI (1960), 1–10.
[59]5.105.3.
[60]5.109.

set about the siege, building a wall and leaving part of the army to guard it. The small size of the encircling army allowed the Melians to break through with a night attack long enough to bring in some supplies and later even to seize part of the wall that the Athenians had built around the city. This led the Athenians to send reinforcements. The Melians, suffering from hunger, discouraged by the increased forces against them, and fearful of treachery from within, surrendered to the Athenians.[61] The Athenians voted to kill all the men and to sell the women and children into slavery.[62] Thucydides describes these events with no more comment than he gives to the atrocities at Scione and Hysiae. Later writers attribute the decree, or at least support of it, to Alcibiades, and we have no reason to doubt that he was in favor of it.[63] But at the same time we have no reason to believe that Nicias or any one else opposed it.[64] The Athenian treatment of Melos was only an extension of the policy that had destroyed Scione. Nothing in the ancient record reveals that either Athenian faction opposed the growing frightfulness of the war.

Within Athens, the competition for political leadership continued, especially between the two great figures, Nicias and Alcibiades. Their rivalry for popularity brings to mind more recent political campaigns in which issues are subordinate to personalities and each politician tries to project a favorable "image" by means of some spectacular activity. The image Nicias wanted to put forward was that of piety, and in 417 he gave a spectacular demonstration of his devotion to the gods. In that year the Athenians completed and dedicated a temple of Apollo at Delos which they had pledged eight years earlier.[65] Nicias used the ceremony as an opportunity to put on a great display. Previously

[61]5.115.4 and 116.3; Aristophanes jokes about the hunger of the Melians in the *Birds* (186), produced in the spring of 414.

[62]5.116.4. The sentence was carried out and Melos was later settled by Athenian colonists. Some of the Melians escaped, however, and were restored to the island by Lysander after the war (Xen. *Hell.* 2.2.9).

[63]Andocides (4.22) attributes the decree to Alcibiades, while Plutarch (*Alc.* 16.5) says Alcibiades supported it.

[64]Indeed, an ancient, if unreliable, tradition says that Nicias was the man who reduced Melos by hunger. See Andrewes, *HCT* IV, 190.

[65]For the date of the temple and Nicias' great display in connection with it see F. Courby, *BCH* XLV (1921), 174–241.

the custom had been for the choruses sent by the city to sing the praises of the god in a rather disorganized way. Nicias changed all that dramatically. He himself led the Athenian procession. The day before the scheduled landing of the choruses he took the Athenian contingent, along with sacrificial animals and necessary equipment, to the nearby island of Rheneia. He also brought with him a bridge of boats, built to fit exactly the distance between the two islands and decorated with the richest tapestries in glorious colors, and put it into position during the night. At sunrise he himself led the sacred procession across the bridge; the chorus, richly and beautifully costumed, sang as it went forward. After the sacrifices, choral contests, and banquets, Nicias dedicated to Apollo a bronze palm tree which soon became famous. In addition, he gave the god a piece of land that cost no less than 10,000 drachmas. The revenues from the cultivation of this land were to be used for sacrificial banquets at which the gods were to be asked to bring blessings down upon the donor. Plutarch, who describes this remarkable performance, does not question the piety of Nicias, but he does point out that "in all this there was much vulgar ostentation aimed at increasing his reputation and satisfying his ambition."[66] Most Athenians, however, would have been persuaded that the gods must favor a man so bountifully pious and would themselves be impressed by him.

In the next year Alcibiades put on a no less impressive display. At the Olympic games of 416 he entered seven teams in the chariot race, a number, as he later boasted, greater than any private citizen had ever put forward, and three of them came in first, second, and fourth.[67] Alcibiades made no secret of the political motive behind this great and expensive display at a religious festival; he sought not a reputation for piety but an opportunity to display Athenian power. As a result of this unprecedented show of wealth, "the Greeks believed our city to be more powerful than it was . . . though earlier they expected that we had been worn down by the war."[68] We can assume, however, that Al-

[66]Plut. *Nic.* 3.4-4.1.

[67]6.16.2. For the date see Busolt, *GG* III:2, 1268, n. 3 and Dover, *HCT* IV, 246-247. Dover also discusses the ancient tradition that Alcibiades' chariots came in first, second, and third.

[68]6.16.2.

cibiades meant to impress the Athenians no less than the other
Greeks. His exposition at Olympia was a response to Nicias'
extravaganza at Delos. To the image of mature piety he opposed
one of youthful dash. It was all part of a continuing political
campaign that had important implications for Athenian policy,
but for the moment neither competitor could achieve a significant and lasting advantage over the other. With the failure of
ostracism the Athenian constitution had no device to resolve the
dangerous division in the state. Thucydides, looking back at
Athens' troubles after the passing of Pericles, accused the great
leader's successors of acting out of private ambition and greed.
"Being more or less equal to one another in political power, and
yet each man striving to become first, they turned to pleasing the
masses and even handed over the management of public affairs to
them."[69] Neither Nicias nor Alcibiades was driven by greed for
money, nor was either eager to turn policy decisions over to the
masses. But both were ambitious to be first in the Athenian
state, and neither enjoyed the special political advantages that
occasionally produced a Cimon or a Pericles. The misfortune of
Athens was that although each man wanted to be the successor to
the Olympian Pericles, the best each could do was to interfere
with the plans of the other.

[69] 2.65.10.

Part Two

The Sicilian Expedition

Early in June of 415 a large and magnificent Athenian force sailed out of the Piraeus bound for Sicily.[1] Some two years later this and a second, reinforcing armament were wiped out; almost all the men were killed, and a great fleet was lost. Athens was never able fully to replace the losses, material and human, or to recover the prestige and confidence that she had enjoyed before the disaster. Thucydides names this defeat alone among "the many blunders" the Athenians committed after the death of Pericles which helped bring on Athens' final defeat, giving it special significance in this way. Most scholars agree that the destruction of the Sicilian expedition was the turning point in the war and a great mistake on the part of Athens. When dealing with these events, modern historians are more than usually prone to follow Thucydides' narrative and to accept his interpretation of events without much question.[2] This attitude is understandable, for the portion of the history describing the Sicilian expedition is the most polished of all Thucydides' work, the most carefully constructed for dramatic effect, the most hauntingly convincing.

But the historian has the inescapable obligation to put questions even to the most authoritative interpretation, and Thucydides' account of the Sicilian expedition clearly provokes such questions. We cannot even be sure what he thought of the

[1]For the date see Dover, *HCT* IV, 271–276.
[2]One distinguished scholar has gone so far as to say to Books VI and VII of Thucydides, "We can do little but paraphrase his famous narrative" (Ferguson, *CAH* V, 282n.).

expedition's prospects for success, for though he called it a blunder he qualified that description in the same sentence; it was "not so much an error of judgment with regard to the enemy against whom they sailed as a failure on the part of those who sent them out to support the first expedition."[3] This assessment is not only unclear in itself, but the second part of it seems to contradict Thucydides' own narrative of the campaign.[4] There is also doubt as to what he thought was the correct strategy for the Athenians' attack and how he assessed their leaders. For these and other reasons we must carefully examine Thucydides' account and his interpretations.

[3] 2.65.11.
[4] Among the many who have seen the apparent contradiction is Gomme, *HCT*, II, 195-196, and *JHS* LXXI (1951), 70-72.

7. The Decision to Attack Sicily

The great Athenian expedition against Sicily, like so many pivotal actions in the history of warfare, came about in response to an unforeseen opportunity. In the winter of 416/15 ambassadors representing the Sicilian city of Segesta (also Egesta) and a faction of Leontines asked the Athenians to help them in a war against the neighboring city of Selinus and its protector, Syracuse.[1] Segesta seems to have become an Athenian ally in the mid-fifth century;[2] Leontini may have joined with Athens at

[1]Diodorus (12.83.2) provides the detail of the joint embassy. Thucydides (6.6.2) has the Segestans speak on behalf of the Leontines. Diodorus's account is fuller and, in Sicilian matters, may well be reliable, for he had a close interest in Sicily and contemporary sources like Philistus and Antiochus of Syracuse.

[2]The date of the Athenian alliance with Segesta is much disputed, for it depends on the reading of a fragmentary inscription on a badly worn stone (IG²19 = GHI, 37). The date is established by the name of the annual archon, but only its last two letters (--ον) can be read with certainty. Five candidates, Habron (458/57), Ariston (454/53), Epameinon (429/28), Aristion (421/20), and Antiphon (418/17), seem possible. The greatest support has been won by Habron. Some support him because of what they have believed they saw on the stone (A. E. Raubitschek, *TAPA* LXXV [1944], 10–12, and B. D. Meritt, *BCH* LXXXVIII [1964], 413–415), others because of historical probability and the presence in the inscription of three-barred sigmas and tailed rhos, letter forms they judge to rule out a date after 445 B.C. (*GHI*, 37). Some epigraphers (e.g., W. K. Pritchett, *AJA* LIX [1955], 58ff.) have examined the stone and vigorously denied that any letters but the final ον can be read, but recently others have believed they can see a phi in the antepenultimate space, and have thus argued for Antiphon, dating the treaty in 418/17 (H. B. Mattingly *Historia* XII [1963], 267ff; J. D. Smart, *JHS* XCII [1972], 128ff; T. E. Wick, *JHS* XCV [1975], 186–190). Mattingly subsequently abandoned that position because of the uncertainty caused by the worn condition of the stone. The opposition has not been persuaded; see D. W. Bradeen and M. F. McGregor, *Studies in Fifth-Century Attic Epigraphy* (Norman, 1973), "The Alliance with Egesta," 71–81.

about the same time, but certainly made a treaty of alliance with her in 433/32.[3] The Athenians, of course, need not have involved themselves in the petty quarrels of these distant cities, but their interest in Sicily had not disappeared after the Congress of Gela had barred them from the island in 424.[4]

At the Congress of Gela the Syracusan Hermocrates had promulgated a kind of Sicilian "Monroe Doctrine" rejecting the interference of foreign states in Sicilian affairs. It was not long before the advantages of such a policy for Syracuse became apparent. Shortly after the Athenian withdrawal in 424, the democrats who ruled Leontini enrolled many new citizens and were contemplating the redistribution of the land to accommodate them. The departure of their Athenian allies left them vulnerable, and the move may have been made to strengthen the city against a possible attack from powerful Syracuse, located not far to the southeast (see Map 9). Instead, the democrats merely provoked the action they feared. The oligarchs of Leontini learned of the democrats' plans and called in the Syracusans to forestall them. The Syracusans drove the commons of Leontini from their city and scattered them. The oligarchs abandoned their own city and moved to Syracuse where they were given citizenship while the Syracusans established a fortress and placed a garrison at Leontini.[5]

This new arrangement did not last. The Leontine oligarchs, for whatever reason, became discontented with their lot at Syracuse. Soon some of them returned to their native city where they took possession of a section called Phoceae, as well as a fortress

---

Professor T. E. Wick has been good enough to write me to the effect that he has a photograph proving the presence of an antepenultimate phi which would confirm the reading of Antiphon and date the treaty to 418/17. Unfortunately he was unable to send me a print, but even if I had one I would not trust my ability to read and interpret it without the advice of those more experienced in epigraphy. I have, therefore, chosen to adopt an agnostic position as to the disputed letter and read only a final ον. If that is indeed all we may read, I find the arguments in GHI the most persuasive.

[3]GHI, 64. T. E. Wick (Historia XXV [1976], 288–304) believes these treaties were renewals of earlier ones made in 444/43.

[4]See Kagan, Archidamian War, 265–268.

[5]5.4.2–3; Thucydides does not mention the fortress and garrison, but Diodorus (12.54.7) does.

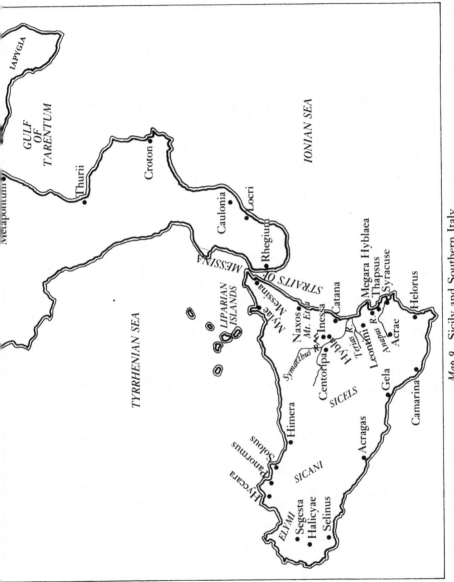

Map 9. Sicily and Southern Italy

called Bricinniae, which was located in Leontine territory. The prospects of restored Leontine independence and a return to their city and property seem to have led most of the Leontine democrats to forget their old differences with the oligarchs.[6] From their two strongholds the reunited Leontines waged war, dramatizing the menace presented by Syracuse and sustaining resistance to Syracusan influence.

By 422 news of these events had aroused interest in Athens. The Athenians voted to send Phaeax son of Erasistratus and two other ambassadors to Sicily and Italy. They went with only two ships, for their mission was exploratory and diplomatic. Their instructions were to try to persuade their own allies in Sicily and, if possible, the other Sicilian Greeks to join in a common attack against the growing power of Syracuse. In this way they might be able to save the people of Leontini.[7] On the way to Sicily Phaeax stopped first at Locri, near the southern shore of the toe of Italy, where he negotiated an agreement. The Locrians had no love for the Athenians and had refused to make any treaty with them after the Congress of Gela. At this time, however, Locri was at war with two of its nearby colonies and was glad to be on good terms with the Athenians.[8] After their success in Italy, the Athenian ambassadors landed in Sicily where they quickly won over Camarina and Acragas, but their reception at Gela was so cold as to discourage them from going farther. They marched inland through the territory of the Sicels to their ships at Catana, stopping on the way at Bricinniae to encourage the Leontines. Stopping again near Locri in Italy, Phaeax and his colleagues continued home to Athens.[9] They had not accomplished much, but their mission showed their continued interest in the west and their suspicion of Syracuse. This "showing of the flag" must have encouraged Syracuse's enemies to seek help from Athens in the future.

Such was the background to the appeal to Athens from

---

[6] 5.4.4. See Freeman *History of Sicily* III, 70-71, for the location of these places.
[7] 5.4.5.
[8] 5.5.2-3.
[9] 5.4.5-6.

Segesta and Leontini in 416/15. The appeal was the result of a dispute between Segesta and Selinus, two cities in western Sicily. In addition to the usual quarrel over land lying between the two cities there was a dispute over marriage rights between their citizens, for although Selinus was Greek and the Segestans were Elymian barbarians, they seem to have had rights of intermarriage.[10] When the Selinuntians won the first battle, Segesta sought help, first from nearby Acragas, then from Syracuse, and later from Carthage. They had no success, and Syracuse, in fact, joined with Selinus against the Segestans.[11] At last, pressed hard by Selinus and Syracuse on land and sea, the Segestans turned to Athens. Apparently they had little confidence in the persuasive power of their old alliance with the Athenians, for their arguments do not refer to it. Instead they took advantage of the troubles at Leontini and made common cause with those other allies of Athens who were fighting against Syracuse. The Segestan ambassadors reminded the Athenians of their alliance with Leontini, apparently renewed during Laches' expedition in 427, and emphasized the kinship between Athens and Leontini, both Ionian states.[12] Turning to more practical matters, the ambassadors put forward a solid reason for Athens to intervene in Sicily again: "If the Syracusans, who had depopulated Leontini, were not punished and, after destroying their allies who were still left, took power over all of Sicily there was the risk that at some time in the future, as Dorians to Dorians and as kinsmen and colonists of the Peloponnesians, they might send them help with a great force and help destroy the power of Athens." Finally, the Segestans offered to pay for the war with their own funds.[13]

It is important to notice that the Segestan invitation was couched in the most conservative terms, emphasizing traditional ties, obligations to allies, and defensive strategy. Thucydides represents the Athenian response as being of quite a different

[10]6.6.2.

[11]Diod. 12.82.6-7.

[12]For the renewal of the treaty see 6.6.2. Diodorus (12.83.3) presents the Leontine ambassadors themselves as making the argument from kinship. Thucydides has the Segestans make it on behalf of Leontini. Plutarch (Nic. 12.1) agrees with Diodorus.

[13]6.6.2.

order. The Athenians, he says, were happy to receive the request to aid their kinsmen and allies, but only as a pretext. Once again, as in his account of the outbreak of the Peloponnesian War, he maintains that "the truest explanation" of the Athenian response is that "they longed for the rule of the whole island."[14] This interpretation, made explicit at this point, had been foreshadowed, indeed anticipated, by Thucydides' earlier references to the great Sicilian enterprise. At the very beginning of Book Six he asserts that the purpose of the expedition was the conquest of the island.[15] Throughout his account he paints the picture of an undertaking aimed at the domination and exploitation of the entire island, an undertaking demanded by an Athenian mob hungry for power and greedy for gain but ignorant of the scope of the adventure and the difficulties and dangers it presented. "The many," he tells us, "were ignorant of the magnitude of the island and of the number of its inhabitants both Greek and barbarian and that they were taking on a war not much inferior to the one against the Peloponnesians."[16] After describing the first Athenian decision to send a force to Sicily, he attributes to Nicias the thought that "with a slight and specious pretext they meant to conquer all Sicily, a large undertaking."[17] Later he attributes to the "mob" the goal of securing money for the present and, for the future, additional imperial control which would provide an endless source of pay.[18]

Thucydides' interpretation, plain as it is, raises some questions, for it does not appear to accord fully with the Athenians' behavior as reported in his own narrative. Even if we grant that most Athenians had the motives Thucydides ascribes to them at the point of sailing in the summer of 415, it is far from clear that their motives had been the same from the first. We should remember that Thucydides makes a similar judgment about the motives that launched the first expedition to Sicily in 427: the Athenians were testing the waters to see if they could bring

---

[14]6.6.1: ἐφιέμενοι μὲν τῇ ἀληθεστάτῃ προφάσει τῆς πάσης ἄρξαι.
[15]6.1.1: ἐπὶ Σικελίαν πλεύσαντες καταστρέψασθαι.
[16]6.1.1.
[17]6.8.4.
[18]6.24.3. The words I have translated as "mob" are ὁ δὲ πολὺς ὅμιλος.

Sicilian affairs under their control.[19] Yet when the reinforced expedition failed to achieve any important goal and withdrew in 424, the Athenians did not pursue the matter further, however angry they were at their generals.[20] Apart from Thucydides' statement, we have no reason to believe that the Athenians who received the Segestan request for aid in 416/15 were planning to use it as an excuse to conquer Sicily.

Thucydides' charge that the Athenian people were entirely ignorant of both Sicily's geography and its population, and therefore that they underestimated the scope of the undertaking, is even more suspect. In 424, less than nine years before the great expedition sailed, some 60 Athenian triremes had returned from Sicily.[21] Some of their crews had been in Sicilian waters and on the island itself for three years, others for several months. At one time or another the Athenians visited Himera and Mylae on the north shore, the offshore Liparian Islands, almost every city on the eastern shore, Gela and Camarina on the southern shore, Messina on the strait dividing the island from Italy, and Rhegium and Locri in Italy itself (see Map 9). Phaeax had revisited some of these places in 422 and traveled to Acragas, on the southern coast of Sicily, as well. Like his predecessors, he had visited the non-Greek Sicels in the interior. Segesta itself, a long-standing ally, was located almost at the western tip of Sicily. Since each trireme carried about 200 men, the fleet that returned in 424 numbered about 12,000 men. Even if only half of them were Athenians (the others being allies) and not all of them survived until 415, there still must have been about 5,000 Athenian sailors and marines who knew the geography of Sicily intimately and had a rather good idea of its population. Each of them, of course, had friends and relatives, so the charge that most Athenians were ignorant of these matters seems improbable.

Nor does Thucydides' account of the Athenians' response to the request from Segesta and Leontini support the notion of

[19]3.86.4-5.
[20]See Kagan, *Archidamian War*, 265-270.
[21]The fleet sent in 427 under Laches (3.86.1) had 20 ships and the fleet sent in 424 under Sophocles and Eurymedon (3.115.4) had 40.

Athenian ignorance or rashness. They neither accepted nor rejected the invitation but voted to send a mission to Segesta, "to see if the money was there, as the Segestaeans said, in the public treasury and the temples, and, at the same time, to discover how the war against the Selinuntians was going."[22] The Segestans deceived the Athenian envoys by constructing, in effect, a Potemkin village. In their temple of Aphrodite they showed them impressive votive offerings which were more gaudy than valuable. They also entertained the Athenian sailors in private homes where they drank from gold and silver vessels that had been collected for the occasion from wealthy Segestans and even from neighboring cities. By passing these same evidences of wealth from house to house when needed, the Segestans succeeded in convincing the Athenians of their fabulous prosperity.[23] This successful imposture helped to convince the Athenian envoys, but surely more persuasive was the fact that the Segestans brought to Athens 60 talents in uncoined silver, a full month's pay for 60 ships.[24]

The Athenian envoys, with the Segestans and their money, returned home "at the beginning of spring," in March of 415.[25] The Athenians called an assembly to consider the appeal from Segesta again. Thucydides tells us that, hearing from both their own envoys and the Segestans that there was plenty of money to pay for the expedition and "other alluring things that were also not true," the assembly voted to send 60 ships to Sicily under Alcibiades, Nicias, and Lamachus. These generals were to have full powers to help Segesta against Selinus, to join in resettling Leontini (if that were possible), and "to settle affairs in Sicily in whatever way they judged best for Athens."[26]

Thucydides gives no more detail about the first of two meetings of the Athenian assembly that decided on the expedition to

---

[22] 6.6.3. Diodorus (12.83.3) adds the detail that the Athenian envoys were chosen from "the best men," τινὰς τῶν ἀρίστων ἀνδρῶν, but does not provide any names.

[23] 6.46.3-5.

[24] 6.8.1.

[25] 6.8.1; Busolt, *GG* III:2, 1276.

[26] 6.8.2. For the meaning of "full powers" (αὐτοκράτορας) see Dover, *HCT* IV, 228.

Sicily. Although he neither reports speeches nor summarizes arguments for or against the measures finally adopted, both probability and epigraphical evidence suggest that there must have been some debate. The brevity of Thucydides' account, however, has led some scholars to believe that all Athenians, even Nicias, were in agreement at this first assembly. One has gone so far as to suggest that Thucydides' account is totally distorted and not to be trusted, that it is constructed to conceal the fact that Nicias from the first sought a major expedition to conquer Sicily.[27] A more moderate view accepts Thucydides' account as essentially credible. It assumes that the measures taken in this first assembly were unopposed and that Nicias favored them because the intervention in Sicily was "a continuation of the traditional policy of Athens,"[28] whose involvement in Sicily went back to the 450s. In this view Nicias would have favored the expedition especially in 415 because the Spartan victory at Mantinea had upset the balance of power on which the Peace of Nicias rested. To restore it and Athenian prestige was vital. The same motive lay behind the attack on Melos in 416. Nicias would have been especially receptive to the Sicilian expedition because it promised to divert Athenian energies from moves against Sparta and so contribute "to maintaining that peace of which he himself had been the promoter and artificer."[29] Such an understanding of the situation, according to this view, has been obscured by Thucydides' decision to present the great Sicilian expedition as an unforeseen and unexpected action of Athenian imperialism, isolated from preceding events, instead of indicating their true continuity.[30]

It is clear that both these views arise from the inadequacy of Thucydides' account of the first assembly, but their improbable speculations are unnecessary. There is no good reason to doubt

[27]G. De Sanctis, *Riv. Fil.* n.s. VII (1929), 433-456 = *Problemi di storia antica* (Bari, 1932), 109-136. For responses to this theory see Hatzfeld, *Alcibiade* 149ff., and U. Laffi, *Rivista Storica Italiana* LXXXII (1970), 178ff.

[28]Laffi, *RSI* LXXXII (1970), 281.

[29]Ibid., 281.

[30]On the connection between the expedition and immediately preceding events see A. Momigliano, *Riv. Fil.* n.s. VII (1929), 371ff., an article that influenced both De Sanctis and Laffi.

Nicias' opposition to the action taken by the first assembly and considerable evidence that he spoke against it. Thucydides' apparent silence proves nothing, for he commonly omits such important facts as the position of leading figures in significant debates. He does not tell us what Pericles said or thought about the Corcyraean request for an alliance in 433, and we must rely on Plutarch who says that "[Pericles] persuaded the people to send aid" to Corcyra.[31] Thucydides does not even mention the meeting of the assembly and the debate that must have preceded the dispatch of a second fleet to reinforce the ten ships first sent to Corcyra. Again, it is Plutarch who supplies the arguments that his opponents used to force his hand.[32] Another example, the debate on the fate of Mytilene, presents an almost perfect parallel to Thucydides' account of the assemblies in 415. On that occasion, too, there was a first assembly in which important decisions were reached which were subsequently changed by a second assembly. There, too, Thucydides gives only a brief account, reporting no speeches but only the actions taken and the general mood that led the people to vote as they did. Only in writing about the second assembly does he mention that Cleon and Diodotus had been the chief opponents in the first assembly as they were in the second. He gives no account of what they said on the earlier occasion, though it is evident that Diodotus, at least, used different arguments each time.[33] Again, in his account of the Athenian expedition to Sicily in 427, he gives no account whatever of the assembly that must have voted it. There are no speeches, no arguments offered by proponents or opponents, no names of partisans of either position, only Thucydides' own statement of what were the pretended and real purposes of the expedition.[34]

As in these other instances, there is adequate evidence, in spite of Thucydides' reticence, to recover with a reasonable degree of confidence at least part of what took place at the first assembly of

[31] Plut. *Per.* 29.1.

[32] 1.50.5; Plut. *Per.* 29.2-3.

[33] 3.36.6, 3.41. For a discussion of these debates see Kagan, *Archidamian War*, 153-163.

[34] 3.86.

415. Thucydides himself provides the first clue when he tells us that Nicias was elected as general for the expedition "against his will, because he thought that the city had made a wrong decision."[35] This is an event, so far as we know, unique in Athenian history: a general accepting a command against his will. How was it known that on this occasion Nicias was unwilling not, of course, to continue in the office of general, but to undertake the expedition just voted?[36] Surely the likeliest source of information was what Nicias had said in the assembly when the assignment was made. It would not be the first time that he had offered to step aside and surrender a command to someone else. In 425 he had done the same, however ironically, in connection with the command at Pylos and Sphacteria.[37] We have good reason to believe that there was a debate in the first assembly as to who should be appointed general and that Nicias indicated his reluctance to serve because he disapproved the project.

Epigraphic evidence provides further support for this view. Eight fragments from at least two stelae found on the Acropolis in Athens contain inscriptions that epigraphers universally connect with the Sicilian expedition of 415.[38] One of the fragments speaks of a fleet of 60 ships and, even more to the point, considers the possibility of appointing only one general to command them. This fragment must belong to the first assembly, since that meeting concluded by appointing three generals to command the 60 triremes. Plainly, the choice of generals was a subject for debate.[39]

Later writers also provide us with evidence of what took place at the first assembly. Plutarch seems to have a distinct notion of the sequence of events. Even before the meeting of any assembly, he tells us, Alcibiades had captured the imagination of the

[35] 6.8.4.
[36] Dover, *HCT* IV, 230.
[37] 4.28.3. See Dover, *HCT* IV, 261–262.
[38] E.g., *GHI*, 78. See also Dover, *HCT* IV, 223–227.
[39] A troubling question arises which the epigraphers seem not to have asked. Why should the Athenians inscribe a decree that was necessarily invalidated by a subsequent motion at the same meeting which named the three generals to the command? A possible answer is that the inscription carried all the motions passed by the assembly that day, even those nullified by later enactments.

masses who, young and old, "sat in groups drawing the map of Sicily and of the sea around it and the harbors of the island." Next he tells us of the first assembly, in which Nicias spoke in opposition. He had few supporters and those he had were of little influence, but still he was chosen as one of the three generals. Finally, he speaks of the second assembly, where again Nicias rose to try to turn the Athenians from the decision they had taken.[40] There is no good reason to doubt the accuracy of Plutarch's account. Diodorus provides still another clue. His account is brief and compressed and speaks of only one assembly, but it reports arguments given by Nicias in opposition to the expedition. Most of these arguments are the same as those Thucydides reports in the speech Nicias made to the second assembly, but one argument does not appear in Thucydides at all. Diodorus reports Nicias as contending that the Athenians could not hope to conquer Sicily: "Even the Carthaginians who had a great empire had often fought wars for Sicily but had not had the power to subdue the island.... How could the Athenians, whose power was much less than that of the Carthaginians, do better?"[41] Diodorus or his source may, of course, have invented this argument, but we have no reason to believe so. More probably the report is an echo of the speech Nicias made at the first assembly. We have, therefore, good reason to believe that all aspects of the decisions taken at the first assembly were debated and that Nicias led the opposition to the entire expedition from the first.

It is instructive to try to reconstruct the course of the debate at this assembly, without making more than the most general claims for our scenario's accuracy. The first motion likely to have been put was one authorizing the sending of a fleet of 60 ships to assist Athens' Sicilian allies at Segesta and Leontini. The placing of this motion would allow a debate on the merits of the undertaking. Presumably Alcibiades spoke in favor and Nicias against, perhaps employing the comparison with Carthage's unavailing power, as later reported by Diodorus.

Another topic for debate was the choice of a commander or

[40]Plut. *Nic.* 12.
[41]12.83.6.

commanders. Some may have favored a single commander, presumably Alcibiades,[42] but neither the political situation in Athens nor the character of its leaders permitted such a choice. Alcibiades, as the foremost advocate of the undertaking, was the natural choice for a single command, but he did not have a solid majority in the assembly, and many Athenians who might otherwise support his policy would not trust him as the expedition's only general. The idea of adding Nicias would have appealed not only to his friends and supporters but also to those who thought it wise to balance Alcibiades' youthful, ambitious daring with the experience, caution, piety, and luck of Nicias. Nicias, in speaking against the expedition, must have indicated his reluctance to serve as general, perhaps he even spoke directly against the motion to put him in command. But in the end, it would have been unpatriotic or cowardly to refuse; when ordered to serve as general on the expedition he had no choice but to obey, regardless of his own opinions and wishes. The Athenians, of course, saw the impossibility of naming to one command two generals who were political and personal enemies and who disagreed on all aspects of the projected campaign. They therefore chose a third general, Lamachus son of Xenophanes. Lamachus was an experienced soldier, about fifty years old in 415, who had been appointed general as early as 425 or even before. Aristophanes presents him as a kind of young *Miles Gloriosus* in the *Acharnians* and teases him about his poverty.[43] He must have favored the expedition and could be counted on to support its general purpose while respecting the counsel of Nicias.

There must have been a lively debate over the instructions to be given to the commanders, for these would determine the purposes of the expedition. We have seen that Thucydides presents the Athenians as aiming from the outset at the conquest of all Sicily. He also tells us that Alcibiades intended to conquer not only Sicily but also Carthage, and later reports a speech made at Sparta in which Alcibiades spoke of using conquests in

[42]Such is the suggestion of H. Wentker, *Sizilien und Athen* (Heidelberg, 1956), 183, n. 510, and Dover, *HCT* IV, 225.

[43]For his age and the references to him in the comic poets see Busolt, *GG* III:1, 585, n. 2; III:2, 1058, n. 2, and 1277.

Italy and Spain as a basis to conquer the Peloponnesus and rule over all Greeks.[44] There surely were some Athenians at the first assembly in 415 who harbored grandiose goals (some seem to have had such goals as early as 427),[45] and perhaps Alcibiades had already raised his sights to encompass the goals ultimately attributed to him. Thucydides' opinion supports such an assumption, despite the fact that the historian was in exile from Athens at the time and could only have reached this conclusion considerably after the fact. What we can be sure of is that nobody advanced such ambitious goals at the assembly.[46] Thucydides, of course, makes no mention of any such reference. What is more telling is that Nicias was led to reopen the question of the whole expedition at the second assembly because he "thought that the city... with a slight and specious pretext meant to conquer all of Sicily."[47] He *thought* it, but he did not know it because nobody at the assembly had spoken of such a purpose.

At the first assembly of 415, in fact, the Athenians voted for very modest goals that fit the relatively modest force they voted to accomplish them, a force and goals comparable to those of the 427–424 campaign. To help Segesta against Selinus, to help restore Leontini, and "to settle affairs in Sicily" in the best interests of Athens did not require, and need not even imply, the conquest of the island. It may be argued that these stated goals were merely a pretext, as Thucydides says, a screen to conceal Athenian rapacity. The number of ships the Athenians voted for the expedition provides a satisfactory response. It was neither the small squadron of 20 sent out under Laches and Charoeades in 427 to prevent Syracuse from sending grain to the Peloponnese and as a "preliminary test to see if they could bring the affairs of Sicily under control,"[48] nor was it the vast armada that ultimately sailed in 415. Rather it was precisely the number dispatched in 424, when Sophocles, Eurymedon, and Pythodorus brought 40 triremes to reinforce the 20 already there. The total

[44]6.15.2; 90.2-4.
[45]See Kagan, *Archidamian War*, 184–186.
[46]Though, if Didorus is right, Nicias imputed such aims to others. See above, Chap. 7.
[47]6.8.4.
[48]3.86.4.

of 60 had been thought adequate to bring the war to a close, given the modest goals of that campaign.[49] There could have been no question of conquering Sicily with 60 ships in 424, and the Athenians had not intended to do so. Their decision at the first assembly in 415 to send a fleet of the same size indicates that again their intentions were limited.

This is not to say that the expedition voted by the first assembly had no aggressive intentions. Events in Sicily since the first Athenian intervention had shown the danger that Syracuse presented to the allies of Athens and to the freedom of the other cities on the island. Left to itself, Syracuse might develop a power that could one day lend important assistance to the Peloponnesians, especially to their mother city Corinth, a city so hostile to Athens. The Athenians who voted for the expedition may well have hoped for the conquest of Syracuse in order to forestall such possibilities. Sixty ships could be enough for such a purpose. A surprise attack directly on the city from the sea might succeed, as might an attempt to gain Sicilian allies who could bring Syracuse down by the show of considerable, if not overwhelming, force. In either event the risk to Athens would be low. In case of an assault on Syracuse by land, the Sicilian allies would do the fighting, for the Athenians were not sending an army. In case of an attack by sea, the Athenians could turn back if they found Syracuse well defended and resolute. Even if everything went wrong and the entire expedition were destroyed, that would be a misfortune but not a disaster. Many of the sailors would be allies, not Athenians, and the ships could be replaced. The one thing that could not result from the expedition voted by the first assembly in 415 was a major strategic defeat that could change the course of the war. We must take careful note of the fact that only after the second assembly did the Athenians incur such a risk, and we must ask how they came to do so.

Four days after the first, a second assembly met to consider "how the fleet could be equipped most quickly and to vote anything else the generals might need for the expedition."[50] Thucydides describes this meeting as fully as any in his *History*,

---

[49]3.115.4.

[50]6.8.3. Thucydides says the assembly met ἡμέρᾳ πέμπτῃ. I assume he is counting the days inclusively as the Greeks usually did.

directly recounting two speeches by Nicias and one by Alcibiades, and telling us about other things said in the assembly.
His account is rich with evidence of the kind of arguments used
by orators in the assembly, the character of whose speeches has
been well described in the following terms: "No statement or
prediction or factual implication in these speeches can be taken at
its face value; everything is coloured; everything is exaggeration,
insinuation or half-truth."[51] Nonetheless, these speeches tell us
much about the speakers, their purposes, and the situation in
which they spoke.

Nicias appears to have spoken first. This strategy imposed
itself, for he meant to turn the debate away from its stated purpose toward one that was unexpected and might well be improper. Although he conceded that the assembly had been called
to consider ways and means, he said, "I believe we should consider this question again: whether we should send the ships off at
all."[52] Clearly Nicias recognized the doubtful propriety of his
maneuver, for at the end of his speech he addressed the Prytanis,
that day's presiding officer, asking that he put the basic question
of sending out the expedition to a vote for a second time.[53] The
Athenians do not seem to have had any law forbidding *anapsephisis*, the act of proposing the repeal or annulment of a decree
just passed by the assembly. In fact, in 427 the assembly re-
pealed the decision to kill the men of Mytilene at a meeting called
specifically to reconsider it the day after the first vote, and no
one seems to have objected on legal grounds.[54] Still, proposing to
repeal a decree just passed by the assembly seems to have been
unusual enough to run the risk of a number of different legal
challenges, any of which might have proved dangerous to
Nicias.[55] His belief in the importance of the subject, however,

[51]Dover, *HCT* IV, 229.
[52]6.9.1.
[53]6.14.
[54]3.36.
[55]The mover of such a proposal might incur the *graphe paranomon*, an objection charging the proposal with being invalid in form or "contrary to the laws"
in substance. Although the Athenian constitution was unwritten and the
understanding of it vague, the term "contrary to the laws" appears to have been
roughly equivalent to the modern term "unconstitutional." The accused mover
of the proposal was tried before a popular court; if guilty he could be fined or

led him to run the risk. Nicias recognized that the Prytanis also might incur some danger by allowing a doubtful motion to be put, but persuaded him to do so, urging him "to become a physician for a state that has decided badly."[56]

Nicias began his speech with a conventional disclaimer that the policy he advanced would serve his own advantage. He himself, he pointed out, would gain honor by carrying out the command that had been voted him; he less than others feared for his own life. (He may have been referring to his relatively advanced age or to the kidney ailment that would plague him on the expedition.) Following the example of Pericles, Cleon, and presumably many others, he announced that he would not play the demagogue but would advise what he thought best, though he knew that the Athenians would not like his advice. Given the Athenian character, he said, there was no point in advising them to preserve what they already had and not to risk their present possessions for unknown future prospects. Instead his intention was to show that their haste to make the expedition was untimely and the prospects for its success not good.[57]

Next, he offered an assessment of Athens' diplomatic and military situation that must have surprised both his friends and enemies and should give pause to modern scholars who think that the Peace of Nicias was a victory for Athens. Athens, according to Nicias, could not afford to attack Sicily and so make new enemies, for she already had formidable enemies at home. Nor should the Athenians take any comfort in the peace treaty with Sparta, for even if the Athenians abandoned the expedition and stayed home, it was a peace in name only. For this he blamed the war parties in both Athens and Sparta.[58] The

---

even lose his civic rights. For a discussion of the *graphe paranomon* see C. Hignett, *HAC*, 210–213, and Busolt and Swoboda, *GS*, 1014–1015. For *anapsephisis* see K. J. Dover, *JHS* LXXV (1955), 17–20.

[56] 6.14. Some manuscripts and a scholiast offer the reading κακῶς βουλευσαμένης, but the better manuscripts omit κακῶς. Even without κακῶς the sense of the passage is that the Athenians have made a bad decision.

[57] 6.9.3.

[58] 6.10.2: οὕτω γὰρ ἐνθένδε τε ἄνδρες ἔπραξαν αὐτὰ καὶ ἐκ τῶν ἐναντίων. As Dover (*HCT* IV, 232) says, the reference must be to Xenares and Cleobulus in Sparta and Alcibiades and others in Athens.

Spartans had not made peace willingly but were forced to it by their misfortunes. Many aspects of the treaty, in fact, were still disputed. Some of Sparta's most important allies still had not accepted. If the Athenians should weaken their power in the homeland by sailing to Sicily, her enemies would attack, aided by the Sicilian reinforcements they had long coveted. The Athenians had no right to take the Spartans lightly, for they had gotten the better of their enemy contrary to their own expectations and because of the Spartans' bad luck.[59] The Spartans, however, were not convinced that they had been beaten and were only waiting for the right moment to erase their dishonor and recover their reputation.[60] The Athenians, on the other hand, were only just recovering from the loss of men in the plague and the expenditure of money in the war.[61] Before contemplating any Sicilian expedition, the Athenians should consolidate their present empire by recovering the rebellious cities in the Chalcidice and the Thraceward region. "We must not reach out for another empire until we have made the one we have secure."[62]

This evaluation of Athens' strategic situation lay at the heart of Nicias' policy, though he needed to raise questions about the security provided by his own peace treaty to support it. He must have made the same points at the first assembly, but they had not been able to win the debate. At this second meeting he also had to respond to the arguments advanced by the advocates of the expedition. We can sense the emphasis that the activists placed on some of their arguments by the amount and kind of attention Nicias gives to their rebuttal. Clearly, the wish to aid Athens' allies in Sicily played a prominent part in the debate, for Nicias goes far in refuting their claim on Athenian assistance. His first reference to the Sicilian allies and their cause sets the tone: "We should not undertake a war that is not our affair,

---

[59] 6.11.6: χρὴ δὲ μὴ πρὸς τὰς τύχας τῶν ἐναντίων ἐπαίρεσθαι. The underscoring is mine. It emphasizes that Nicias here accepts the Spartans' own explanation of their defeat at Pylos and its central role in bringing them to make peace. Not all Athenians would see things in this way.

[60] Idem.

[61] 6.12.1.

[62] 6.10.5.

persuaded by men of an alien race."[63] Nicias calls the Segestans "a barbaric people" who require help when they are in trouble but give none when the Athenians need it.[64] He dismisses the Leontines as fugitives and clever liars who supply only words while their allies take all the risks, who are ungrateful in victory and bring disaster to their friends in defeat.[65] Such impolitic and harsh language, even toward inconvenient allies, is unusual. It suggests that the supporters of the expedition must have put considerable weight on the appeal from the allies and thus compelled Nicias to answer forcefully.

The threat to Athens from a Sicily dominated by Syracuse appears to have been the main argument used by his opponents at the first assembly, for Nicias confronted it with a relatively long and complicated, even sophistical, rebuttal. He made it clear that the ambassadors from Segesta, especially, placed emphasis on the threat from Syracuse, if it were allowed to dominate the island. Nicias, paradoxically, asserted the exact opposite: "The Sicilians . . . would be even less dangerous than they are now if ruled by the Syracusans, for now they might attack us singly out of feeling for the Spartans, but if the Syracusans were in control it is not likely that an empire would attack another empire." He argued that if Syracuse joined with the Spartans to destroy the Athenian Empire, it could expect its own empire to be destroyed by the Spartans, as well.[66] All this, of course, was such nonsense as to require no refutation, and in fact, Alcibiades made no reference to it in his rebuttal. But Nicias' second argument may have been even weaker than the first. The Athenians, he said, could best frighten the Sicilian Greeks and thus deter them from joining in an attack on Athens by staying as far from Sicily as possible. If Athens attacked Sicily and lost, the Sicilians, in contempt of Athenian power, would quickly join the Spartans in an attack. The best thing for Athens to do would be not to go to Sicily at all; the next best would be to make a brief show of force and retire immediately: "for we all know that we

[63] 6.9.1.
[64] 6.11.7; 13.2.
[65] 6.12.1.
[66] 6.11.3.

marvel most at things that are the farthest away and least allow their reputation to be tested."[67] This argument, apart from its dubious psychological assumptions, ignores the possibility that the Athenians might win, thereby enhancing their reputation in a forceful way and acquiring a certain means of deterring an attack from Sicily. Again we have a foolish argument that opponents need not bother to answer. It is hard to believe that many Athenians would have been persuaded by such obvious sophistry. That Nicias was forced to address the question, although armed only with pitiful arguments, suggests that the fear of Syracusan domination of Sicily, followed by a joint attack with the Peloponnesians against the Athenians, played a central part in the debate at the first assembly.

In spite of Thucydides' own comment, it is surprising that Nicias had nothing direct to say about the idea of conquering all Sicily, although one or two of his remarks may be ambiguous enough to suggest a reference to such a notion.[68] The ambiguity may have been in the words of Nicias himself or supplied by Thucydides, but in neither case can we find anything

[67] 6.11.4.

[68] The only two passages that might refer to the conquest of Sicily are in 6.11.1 and 5. The former says that the Sicilians would be hard to rule because they are so many and so far away, εἰ καὶ κρατήσαιμεν. Crawley translates "even if conquered," and Rex Warner has it "even if we did conquer the Sicilians." In this context, however, κρατήσαιμεν means "conquer" only in the sense of "defeat in battle," as Jowett's translation, "even if we are victorious," and Mme de Romilly's "en triompherions-nous," and Smith's "even if we should get the better of them" show. The most obvious sense of what Nicias says in this context is, "Even if we defeat the Syracusans and their Sicilian allies they will be difficult to govern." There need be no implication of aiming at control over the entire island.

The latter passage warns the Athenians against overconfidence. "Having gotten the better of the Spartans, you despise them," καὶ Σικελίας ἐφίεσθε. According to Crawley's rather free translation, the Athenians' recent success has tempted them "to aspire to the conquest of Sicily." Smith says that the Athenians "aim even at the conquest of Sicily." Jowett has it "you . . . even hope to conquer Sicily." Mme de Romilly's translation is essentially the same as Smith's: "pour porter vos visées jusque sur la Sicile." ἐφίημι, however, cannot mean "conquer." It may mean "aim at" or "long for," but it may also mean simply "send against." Thus, to some Athenians Nicias' words may have meant: "The recent success of the Athenians has led them to hold the Spartans in contempt and even to send [an expedition] against Sicily." To others the last clause would have said "and even to aim at [the conquest of] Sicily."

straightforward against a plan of general conquest. If conquering Sicily had been put forward at the first assembly as a reason for sending the expedition, Nicias could not have failed to attack such a proposal. It was the most vulnerable possible target and would not have required the tortured reasoning that he was forced to rely on to combat other arguments. It seems reasonable to conclude, therefore, that no one at the first assembly openly offered the prospect of general conquest as a reason to go to Sicily, whatever private intentions may have been.

Perhaps Nicias was frustrated by his inability to attack what he would have liked to present as the true purpose of the expedition, and perhaps that is what led him to launch not only a personal attack but also one against an entire generation. "If someone," he said,

delighted by having been chosen to command, urges you to make the expedition—considering only his own advantage, all the more since he is still rather young to be exercising the command, considering how he may win admiration because of raising magnificent horses and, because that is very costly, how he might make some profit from his position—do not give this man, to the peril of the state, the chance to make a great display for his private interest. Consider instead that such men harm the interests of the state and squander their own property and that the matter is a great one and not of such a kind as to be decided and hastily managed by a young man. Seeing such young men sitting here now, who have been summoned by that same man, I am afraid, and I appeal on the contrary to the older men.[69]

No one could doubt that Nicias' target was Alcibiades. Apart from their political differences, there seems to have been considerable personal animosity between the two men. Nicias' attacks *ad hominem*, therefore, may have been simply an outburst of temper, but that would seem to have been out of character. The attack on Alcibiades and on his youthful supporters may have been a device to focus attention on the most radical advocates of the expedition and on the man who was both its chief proponent and probably the most distrusted man in Athens.

After Nicias others came forth to argue each side of the case.

[69]6.12.2-13.1.

Most of them favored the expedition, but the man who, according to Thucydides, was the most eager for the expedition was Alcibiades son of Cleinias. Although Alcibiades had played an important part in Athenian affairs since the Peace of Nicias, Thucydides chose this moment to introduce and characterize him and to evaluate the important role he played in the outcome of the war. He tells us that Alcibiades spoke in opposition to Nicias because of their political disagreement in general, because Nicias had attacked him personally, but chiefly because he wanted to be in command so that he might attack not only Sicily but Carthage as well, thereby winning both public glory and private wealth. In making such judgments, Thucydides, of course, endorses the charges that Nicias made in his speech. He also supports Nicias' accusation that Alcibiades wanted money to support the expense of raising horses and sustaining other costly activities with which he enhanced his reputation among the Athenians.[70]

But these expenditures and the conspicuous display they paid for had other, less favorable results, and Thucydides describes them in a remarkable passage that foreshadows the Athenian defeat not only in Sicily, but in the war as a whole. "And it was just this that later on did most to destroy the Athenian state. For the many were afraid of the extent of his lawless self-indulgence in his way of life and also of his purpose in each and every affair in which he became involved; they became hostile to him on the grounds that he was aiming at a tyranny. And so, although in public affairs he conducted his military functions in the best possible way, his activities in his private life offended everyone, so they turned the leadership of the state over to other men and before long brought the state to ruin."[71] Such a dramatic summary and anticipation of future events is matched only by Thucydides' famous encomium on and evaluation of the career of Pericles, a passage that has the function of providing a framework for the reader's understanding of the entire history.[72] This passage works in the same way, making clear to the reader

[70] 6.15.1-3.
[71] 6.15.3-4.
[72] 2.65.

how he is to understand future events. Alcibiades' extraordinary style of living will ultimately cause trouble, but it is not he who will be responsible for the Athenian defeat but rather the offended masses who fear him and will give the command to other and lesser generals.

Alcibiades' speech was, for the most part, a direct response to Nicias. He began with a rebuttal to the personal attack. The magnificent style of his private life brought not only glory to him and his family but also to his country. The unprecedented victories of his teams at Olympia had persuaded the other Greeks that Athens, far from being exhausted by the Archidamian War, was even more powerful than she really was. The magnificence of his displays at home, for instance the splendor of the choruses he provided at the dramatic festivals, excited jealousy among his countrymen, but, again, this same magnificence bolstered the impression of Athenian might in the eyes of foreigners. Boldly facing the charge, partly explicit and partly implicit, that he offended by setting himself above other men, he admitted it, arguing that the great achievements that went with such great claims were useful to the state. The benefit that he brought to the state, not the nature of his private life, was, he argued, the criterion by which to judge him. In that connection he pointed proudly to his part in bringing on the battle of Mantinea, for "without great danger or expense to the Athenians, the Spartans had been compelled to stake their hegemony on a single battle; because of that, although they had won the battle, they had not yet fully recovered their confidence."[73]

His response to the attack on his youth was both defiant and conciliatory. On the one hand, he cited his achievements as a general against the Peloponnesians as evidence that his youth did not signify incompetence, and he told the Athenians not to fear his lack of years. Still, since he knew that the argument against his youth carried weight, he reminded the Athenians that they had voted not for a single commander but for a board of three generals. "Make use of both of us," he said, "while I am still at peak and Nicias has the reputation of being lucky."[74] This was

[73]6.16.
[74]6.17.1.

not the last time that Nicias' presence among the team of commanders would be used to bring about the very expedition he so vigorously opposed.

An important difference between Nicias and Alcibiades lay in their respective estimates of the condition of Sicily. Alcibiades naturally deprecated the power of Sicily and the ability of its inhabitants to resist Athens. He pictured the island as teeming with instability, its populous cities filled with "a mixed mob" prone to frequent movement and constitutional overthrow. As a result, men did not take arms to defend their cities loyally and patriotically, as in the mother country, but were prepared instead to take the wealth that they had hoarded and move elsewhere. Alcibiades argued that such people were not likely to act in common and could easily be lured to the Athenian side. Earlier in the debate or at the first assembly, someone must have pointed out the great hoplite army that the Sicilians could field against the Athenians, for Alcibiades treated that subject defensively. The Sicilians, he claimed, did not have as many hoplites as was alleged. Besides, the Athenians could make use of the barbarian Sicels, who hated the Syracusans.[75]

Alcibiades' account of Sicilian affairs, though one-sided and exaggerated, was not entirely wrong. Early in the fifth century Sicilian tyrants had frequently transplanted populations, and the overthrow of the tyrannies caused similar upheavals.[76] The Congress of Gela, to be sure, had revealed that the Sicilians might unite and present a formidable opposition to Athenian plans, but the subsequent period demonstrated that such unity was unlikely to last. The fate of Leontini was good evidence of internal instability in the Sicilian towns, and the war between Selinus and Segesta revealed the continuing divisions between states.

It was easy to rebut Nicias' warning against undertaking a distant naval expedition while the Spartans threatened the homeland. Nicias had portrayed the Spartans and their allies as eager to resume the war, needing only an opportunity to pounce, but

[75]6.17.2-6.
[76]For references see Dover, *HCT* IV, 249–250; see also Freeman, *History of Sicily* III, 100.

Alcibiades pictured them as having less hope than ever before. The Spartans' failure to take any aggressive action to recover Argos or to renounce the Peace of Nicias, in spite of Athenian provocation, showed that Alcibiades was closer to the truth. But even if the Spartans had been strong and bold, Alcibiades argued, all they could have done was invade Attica by land, something which they could do at any time. They could not, however, hurt the Athenians in the way that counted, at sea. Even with an Athenian fleet bound for Sicily, the reserve fleet at home was still a match for the enemy.[77] Again, Alcibiades was right, especially when we remember that when he spoke the Athenians were contemplating sending to Sicily only the 60 ships they had already voted.

Having dismissed the arguments that the expedition could not succeed and would leave Athens open to attack, Alcibiades turned to one of his strongest arguments, and one that was most embarrassing to Nicias—Athens' obligations to her allies. First, there was the moral argument: "What plausible excuse could we give ourselves for shrinking back, or what defense could we offer to our allies in Sicily for not coming to their aid? We must assist them, for we have given our oath."[78] But interest as well as honor dictated that the Athenians keep their commitments and send help to their allies. Athens had not made the Sicilian alliances in order to be able to summon help from that quarter to the homeland, but instead to keep its enemies in Sicily off balance so that they could not attack the Athenians. Allies like Segesta and Leontini were, in fact, a first line of defense for Athens.

In addition to the arguments of honor and interest, Alcibiades maintained that the very nature of the Athenian Empire required an active policy on behalf of allies. "That is how we have acquired our empire and that is how others who have had empire acquired theirs—by always coming eagerly to the aid of those who called upon us, whether Greek or barbarian."[79] To change now to a policy of quiet and restraint, to draw distinctions

[77] 6.17.7-8.
[78] 6.18.1.
[79] 6.18.2.

among allies on the basis of race, to set arbitrary limits on the extent of the empire—all these would be disastrous. Such a policy not only would prevent further growth, but would even threaten the empire's present security. Other states might pursue a policy of peace and inactivity, but the Athenians could not adopt such a policy without giving up their way of life and their empire, and the Athenians could not abandon their empire without running the risk of becoming the subjects of others.[80] Alcibiades' argument is quite similar to that advanced by Pericles in his last recorded speech: "It is not possible for you to withdraw from this empire, if any in the present situation out of fear or from love of tranquillity has decided to become honest." Pericles had put the main point more bluntly than Alcibiades dared: "By now the empire you hold is a tyranny; it may now seem wrong to have taken it, but it is surely dangerous to let it go," for "you are hated by those you have ruled."[81]

At that point, for the only time in the speech, and probably for the first time in the entire debate, Alcibiades revealed the grander purposes he had in mind for the Sicilian expedition. If the expedition succeeded, "as seems likely," the Athenians might gain control of all Greece, since their power would be reinforced by the addition of Sicily.[82] This ambitious statement was not so un-Periclean as it might seem. When Pericles was challenged by the men who in his time advocated a peaceful and passive policy, the *apragmones,* he told the Athenians: "You are the absolute masters of the entire sea, not only as much of it as you now rule but however much more you wish. And there is no one, while you have the fleet you do, who will prevent you from sailing on it, not the Great King nor any nation such as now exists."[83] Pericles, however, spoke his bold words at a time when he found the Athenians "unreasonably discouraged," and he intended not to undertake a new expedition but merely to encourage them to persevere in the war in which they were already engaged.[84] Alcibiades, like Pericles, called his opponent's policy *aprag-*

[80]6.18.2-3.
[81]2.63.1-2.
[82]6.18.4.
[83]2.62.2.
[84]For a discussion of the speech and its context see Kagan, *Archidamian War,* 85–89.

mosyne,[85] but the circumstances in which he spoke were different. On the one hand, Athens was at least formally at peace and could better afford a distant campaign. On the other hand, the Athenians, according to Thucydides, were already excessively confident and ambitious. Thucydides, no doubt, had this comparison and contrast in mind, wishing his readers to notice the difference between Pericles, the great statesman who worked against the grain to moderate the passions of his people, and Alcibiades, the demagogue who exploited these passions for his own purposes.

But Alcibiades was prudent enough to know the danger of dwelling too long on the dangerous and controversial question of the conquest of all Sicily. We should remember, moreover, that his reference to such a conquest was made in the context of sending a force of 60 ships and no hoplites, a low-risk operation that depended more on surprise, psychology, and diplomacy than on the fortunes of battle. He was careful to bracket his suggestion of more ambitious war aims with others that were strictly defensive. The boldness of the attack on Sicily during the present uncertain peace would further reduce the confidence of the Spartans, and presumably, though Alcibiades does not spell it out, this would deter them from resuming the war and attacking Athens. Even if the Athenians did not conquer Sicily, moreover, the expedition could at least do damage to Syracuse, and this would benefit both the Athenians and their Sicilian allies.[86]

Alcibiades next turned to exploit the mistake Nicias had made in criticizing the young men of Athens and asking the older men to oppose them. Nicias' remarks had provided an opening for an able orator. Deploring Nicias' divisive counsel, he could easily establish himself as the guardian of conservative values by extolling the good old days when young and old consulted together. We thus find the clever Alcibiades pronouncing such comforting bromides as: "youth and age could accomplish nothing without each other," and "strength is best achieved when the simple, the very keen, and the moderate are mixed together."[87]

Having thus gained the moral advantage, Alcibiades con-

[85] 6.18.6.
[86] 6.18.4-5.
[87] 6.18.6.

cluded with the subtle and unusual argument that Athens must pursue an active rather than a passive policy because that was her nature. It was not merely that an extended period of peace would dull the skills by which Athens had gained and maintained her empire, while continued activity would sharpen them. Beyond that, Alcibiades asserted, "It seems to me that a city which is not passive (*apragmon*) would quickly be destroyed by a change toward passiveness and that those men are safest who make political decisions that are least in conflict with existing habits and institutions."[88] That assertion justified, indeed required, continued expansion of the kind Alcibiades had in mind. It conflicted directly with the policy of Pericles, which had aimed at the maintenance without further expansion of an empire acquired through the habits and institutions alluded to by Alcibiades. Even after Pericles' death the ward continued the debate with his guardian.[89] Again, Thucydides probably meant his reader to consider the contrast.

In the assembly of 415 Alcibiades' speech was effective, especially when supported by renewed pleas from the Segestans and Leontines to keep Athenian oaths and send help to Sicily. Given such pressure, "[the Athenians] were even more eager than before to make the expedition,"[90] but Nicias did not yet give up his attempt to prevent it. He came forward to speak again, but this time he abandoned straightforward opposition, resorting instead to guile. Thucydides tells us that Nicias "knew he could not deter them with the same arguments but thought he might change their minds by the size of the expedition, if he proposed a large one."[91] Such a tactic is a risky parliamentary maneuver at any time, requiring good organization of support and skillful rhetoric. Nicias, for whom subtle and tricky argument was hardly a strong suit, appears to have made no preliminary arrangements with supporters. Instead he seems to have conceived his plan on the spur of the moment.

Nicias began with a direct, personal, and sardonic rebuttal of

[88] 6.18.7.
[89] For an earlier debate see Xen. *Mem.* 1.40-46.
[90] 6.19.1.
[91] 6.19.2. Thucydides repeats the same attribution of motive to Nicias in 6.24.1. We have no reason to doubt that he understood Nicias' intention.

Alcibiades' picture of Sicily. Alcibiades had concluded his description of the wretched state of the Greek cities of Sicily with the words, "so I learn from what I hear." Nicias began his account of the condition of those cities with almost the exact words, "as I learn from what I hear," and we can almost hear the sarcastic tone and see the speaker looking at Alcibiades as he speaks.[92] What Nicias has heard is that the Greek cities of Sicily are neither in turmoil internally, nor in conflict with one another, nor are they demoralized. They are, however, large, numerous and, except for Naxos and Catana, ill disposed to Athens. They are well equipped with hoplites, archers, javelin throwers, triremes, and rowers. They also have plenty of money, some public and some private; Syracuse even collects tributes from barbarians. The Greeks of Sicily also have two important things that the Athenians going to Sicily will lack: many horses and grain that need not be imported.[93]

If these cities joined together they would make up a great power against which the pitiful force that the Athenians had already voted would be inadequate. With that fleet the Athenians might make a landing, but the enemy, with its cavalry, could confine them to the beachhead and force them to send home for supplies or to return in shame. The Athenians must realize that they are undertaking something unprecedented for them, fighting at such a distance that in winter even a messenger might take four months to arrive from home.[94] To succeed they must send many hoplites (Athenians, allies, subjects, and mercenaries), as well as light-armed troops to harass the enemy cavalry. There must also be more warships to guarantee control of the sea and supply. In addition, the Athenians must take grain with them in merchant ships, for no force of such a size could expect to live off the land, especially since the Sicilians could not be trusted. They had better take plenty of money, too, for talk of money from Segesta would turn out to be just talk.[95]

[92]Alcibiades' words are ἐξ ὧν ἐγώ ἀκοῇ αἰσθάνομαι (6.17.6). Nicias says ὡς ἐγὼ ἀκοῇ αἰσθάνομαι (6.20.2). For a good discussion of the special character of the speeches in this debate see Dover, *HCT* IV, 229.

[93]6.20.

[94]6.21.

[95]6.22.

Nicias, no doubt, hoped this list of requirements would daunt his audience, and he went on to paint an even darker picture. Even if we mount an expedition, he said, which is greater than the combined forces of the Sicilian Greeks, "except, of course, for their hoplites, the force that does the real fighting, we will not find it easy to defeat them or even to guarantee the safety of our own forces."[96] The Athenians must realize that they are like colonists going out to found a new city in dangerous foreign lands where they must establish control immediately or face hostility from all the natives. Such an expedition required careful planning and, even more important, the good luck that mere mortals cannot count upon. Nicias therefore preferred to rely for safety on the best and most careful preparation. "I think that the preparations I have suggested provide the greatest security for the state and safety for those of us who go out on the expedition. But if any one thinks otherwise, I offer to give up my command to him."[97]

We can understand most of Nicias' speech in light of his basic aim, to prevent the sailing of the Sicilian expedition. By demanding a much larger armament than the Athenians had voted and pointing out that even this will guarantee neither the success nor even the safe return of the expedition, he hoped to deter them from going. But why, after trying to frighten the Athenians, did he suggest that the adoption of his proposals would make it safe, and why did he offer to resign his command? Both ploys suggest that he expected someone to deny his fundamental assumption, that the mission to Sicily would be terribly difficult to accomplish, and to deny the conclusion he drew from it, that a vast and expensive force would be required if the mission were attempted. He might well have expected Alcibiades or someone else to say that Nicias was exaggerating the problem and the danger and that proper use of the force already voted would insure success. If that view seemed popular, Nicias could then honorably ask to be relieved on the grounds that his advice had been rejected and that he was unwilling to lead Athenians to

[96] 6.23.1. This is a difficult passage, especially the clause about hoplites. My translation is based on Dover's text and his interpretations of its meaning (*HCT* IV, 259–261).

[97] 6.23.

their deaths on an impossible mission. To carry our conjecture
farther, Nicias may have hoped that his resignation would sober
the assembly, forcing it to realize that it was losing the experienced and lucky general it had appointed to tame the wild and
ambitious youth. Failing that, there might still be long debate
and, perhaps, delay, during which the excited populace might
cool off and reflect.

We cannot, of course, be sure of Nicias' expectations, but
Thucydides makes it clear that they were not realized. A certain
Demostratus rose to challenge him in an unexpected and embarrassing way.[98] Though he came from a noble family, Plutarch
calls him "foremost among the demagogues in urging the Athenians to war."[99] He told Nicias "not to make or cause delays but
to say at once and before them all what forces the Athenians
should vote him."[100] Nicias was not prepared for such a question. He answered that he would rather discuss the matter with
his colleagues at leisure, and even this he said unwillingly.[101] But
the bluntness of Demostratus permitted no delay, so Nicias put
forward his estimates: at least 100 triremes from Athens, of
which some should be troop transports, and others from the
allies; a combined force of Athenian and allied hoplites of no fewer
than 5,000; and a proportional number of light-armed troops.

Thucydides makes it clear that Nicias' speech had an effect
opposite to what he had intended. After he finished, the Athenians "were not turned away from their eagerness for the expedition by the burdensomeness of the preparation but became more
eager for it, and things turned out the opposite of what Nicias
expected. For they thought he had given them good advice and
that now the expedition would be very safe. And a passion came
upon all of them equally to sail off. The older men thought that
either they would conquer or at least that such a great force could
not come to harm. Those who were in their prime longed for
distant sights and spectacles, being confident that they would be
safe. The mass of the people and the soldiers hoped to get money

---

[98]Thucydides (6.25.1) does not mention Demostratus but speaks only of "a
certain Athenian." Plutarch (*Nic.* 12.4, and *Alc.* 18.2) provides the name.
[99]Plut. *Nic.* 124. On Demostratus see Busolt, *GG* III:2, 1282, n.2.
[100]6.25.1.
[101]ὁ δὲ ἄκων μὲν εἶπεν (6.25.2).

at the moment and to make an addition to their empire from which they would have a never-ending source of income."[102] Thucydides represents the enthusiasm of the majority as great enough to intimidate the opposition into not voting against the expedition lest they be thought disaffected from the state. The Athenians then voted—Thucydides' implication is that they were unanimous—to give their generals full powers in determining the size of the expedition and "to act in whatever way seemed best to them for Athens."[103]

Nicias' clever maneuver had failed disastrously. His performance reminds the reader of his similar action during the assembly in 425 which dealt with the Spartans trapped on Sphacteria. On that occasion Nicias had offered to relinquish his command to the inexperienced and apparently incompetent Cleon. He expected Cleon to refuse and so be discredited, but Nicias misread the character of the assembly, which egged Cleon on until he could not reject the offer. The results could have been disastrous for Athens, for Thucydides tells us that the "sensible men" thought it likely that Cleon would lead his troops to defeat. That scene ended comically, with Cleon's brash promises causing the assembly to burst into laughter, but in the end Cleon made good his boast and brought the Spartan prisoners home to Athens.[104]

Karl Marx said that history repeats itself, the first time as tragedy and the second time as farce. Nicias' career seems to illustrate the opposite principle. The first time he had tried an ironic maneuver in the Athenian assembly the results were comical but fortunate; the second time they were tragic. His behavior in the second assembly was decisive in converting into a vast enterprise an expedition that, publicly, had involved limited objectives and run limited risks. Now capable of attempting the conquest of Sicily, the Athenian expedition was of such a size that its defeat could mean almost total disaster. If Nicias had said nothing at the second assembly or had confined himself to the stated topics of ways and means, the Athenians would have sent only 60 ships

[102]6.24.3.
[103]6.26.2.
[104]For a discussion of this incident see Kagan, *Archidamian War*, 239-247.

to Sicily. His reopening of the question invited the effective and encouraging speech of Alcibiades. In his own second speech he suggested an investment of men, money, and ships which no other Athenian politician would have dared to propose—and in two assemblies none had. Thucydides' portrait of the Athenian masses, greedily eager from the outset to conquer Sicily and ready to make a vast expedition for that purpose, is not justified by any of the evidence that he gives.[105] We have no reason to doubt the accuracy of this picture, however, after the second assembly. What moved the Athenians from a cautious and limited venture to a bold and unlimited commitment was the assurance they had received from the pious, fortunate, and cautious Nicias. Such assurance from such a source swept all before it, kindling new ambitions and heightening those which had already been voiced. Without Nicias' intervention there would have been an Athenian expedition against Sicily in 415, but there could not have been a disaster.

[105] A striking sample of the contradiction between his interpretation and his narrative is this: at the very beginning of Book VI he tells us that the Athenians "wanted to sail against Sicily again with a force bigger than the one led by Laches and Eurymedon." The force brought back by Eurymedon and his colleagues in 424 consisted of 60 triremes, exactly the number the Athenians voted to send to Sicily in the first assembly of 415. Dover (HCT IV, 197), noting that the number of ships on both occasions is identical, suggests that the bigger force mentioned by Thucydides "must therefore refer to the greater scale of land forces now envisaged." But there is no reason to believe that the assembly that voted to send 60 ships to Sicily in 415 voted to send greater land forces than accompanied the earlier expedition.

8. Sacrilege and Departure

Preparations for the Athenian expedition to Sicily went forward with enthusiasm. Allied contingents were summoned, and at Athens there was money in the treasury and a fresh crop of soldiers who had grown to manhood in time of peace.[1] But not everyone looked forward to the expedition with hopeful anticipation, and in the two months or so between the decision to sail and the departure for Sicily several kinds of opposition appeared.[2] Plutarch tells us that "the priests" were opposed to the expedition without saying what priests he means or how many they were. In any case, Alcibiades readily supplied contrary religious authority, bringing forward "seers" who cited ancient prophecies that the Athenians would win great glory in Sicily. The religious competition continued when envoys returned from the shrine of Zeus-Ammon in the Libyan desert with an oracle saying that the Athenians would capture all the Syracusans. They also carried omens with the opposite import, but these they suppressed for fear of bringing bad news to a people who did not want to hear it.[3]

Some evil omens could not be suppressed. An unknown man,

---

[1] 6.26.2.

[2] There is not perfect agreement on the chronology of the important events of the year 415. Good discussions may be found in Douglas MacDowell's edition of Andocides's speech (*Andokides on the Mysteries* [Oxford, 1962], 181–189) and in *HCT* IV, 264–276. They come to conclusions that are not far apart but that differ on some important points. I accept MacDowell's date for the assembly that voted to go to Sicily as mid-April. He believes that the fleet sailed "in the later part of June." Dover prefers "early June." For our purposes the difference is not significant.

[3] Plut., *Nic.* 13.102.

presumably mad, leaped onto the Altar of the Twelve Gods and castrated himself with a stone. News came from Delphi that the gold palladium set on a bronze palm tree, which the Athenians had dedicated in honor of their brave deeds in the Persian War, was being pecked to pieces by ravens. Most Athenians dismissed the story as one invented by the Delphians at the persuasion of Syracuse, but others must have found it disquieting. These latter must have been further impressed when the priestess of Clazomenae was brought to Athens by order of an oracle and her name turned out to be *Hesychia*, one of the synonyms for Peace. "This," Plutarch tells us, seemed to them "what the divinity advised the city in the present circumstances, to keep the peace."[4] Some Athenians were also made uneasy because the preparation for the expedition took place at the same time as the ritual of Adonis. These rites commemorated the death of Aphrodite's beloved and included the public display of images of the god laid out for burial to the accompaniment of the wailing of women. People affected by such things were quick to connect them with the impending expedition and to fear that it too would end badly.[5]

None of these things deterred the Athenians from the Sicilian project, but shortly before the fleet was due to sail the Athenians were confronted with an event that completely overshadowed all the other omens. On the morning of 7 June 415 they awoke to

[4]Plut. *Nic.* 13.3-4.

[5]Plut. *Nic.* 13.7. Plutarch also tells us of two very different individuals who foresaw disaster for the expedition, Meton the astrologer and Socrates the philosopher (*Nic.* 13.5-6). Aristophanes (*Lys.* 387-397) has one of his characters speak of hearing women wail for Adonis during an assembly in which Demostratos spoke in favor of an expedition to Sicily. According to the chronology accepted here, that would place the festival of Adonis in mid-April, not in the time shortly before the sailing in June, when Plutarch puts it (*Alc.* 18.3). The date for the Adonia cannot be fixed with confidence (Dover, *HCT* IV, 371) but some scholars would put it well past the June date for the fleet's departure. See O. Aurenche, *Les groupes d'Alcibiade, de Léogoras et de Teucros* (Paris, 1974), 156-157. The reference to Zacynthian hoplites in the *Lysistrata* (594) has led H. D. Mattingly (*BCH* XCII [1968], 453-454) to associate the Adonia not with the expedition of 415 but with the reinforcing expedition under Demosthenes that sailed in 413, for Thucydides specifically mentions the enrollment of Zacynthians on the latter occasion (7.31.2-57.7). The likelihood is that Aristophanes, not writing history but comedy, is mixing up a variety of things that took place at different times for his own purposes.

find that the stone statues of Hermes which stood on square pillars all over Athens, both in front of private houses and in the sanctuaries of the gods, had been mutilated.[6] It is hard to imagine and difficult to exaggerate the effect that this had on the Athenian people, though Grote's brilliant evocation helps us to understand it.

If we could imagine the excitement of a Spanish or Italian town, on finding that all the images of the Virgin had been defaced during the same night, we should have a parallel, though a very inadequate parallel, for what was now felt at Athens, where religious associations and persons were far more intimately allied with all civil acts and with all the proceedings of every-day life; where, too, the god and his efficiency were more forcibly localized, as well as identified with the presence and keeping of the statue. To the Athenians, when they went forth on the following morning, each man seeing the divine guardian at his doorway dishonored and defaced, and each man gradually coming to know that the devastation was general, it would seem that the town had become as it were godless; that the streets, the market-place, the porticos, were robbed of their divine protectors; and what was worse still, that these protectors, having been grossly insulted, carried away with them alienated sentiments, wrathful and vindictive instead of tutelary and sympathizing.[7]

In a society where no real separation existed between religion and the state, the sacrilege had political significance. A considerable number of perpetrators had been required to carry out the systematic mutilation of most of the Hermae in the city,[8] and a conspiracy of such scope was likely to have political aims. The targets, moreover, had immediate and specific political significance. Hermes was the god of travelers, and the mutilation of his statues was plainly a warning against the imminent expedi-

---

[6]Thucydides (6.1) mentions only mutilation of faces, but Aristophanes (Lys. 1094) makes it clear that the more obvious means of mutilation, knocking off the erect phallus, was also employed. I accept the arguments of MacDowell (Andokides, 188) for the date. Dover (HCT IV, 274-276) sets it about May 25.

[7]Grote, VII, 168-169.

[8]Thucydides (6.27.1) says οἱ πλεῖστοι were mutilated. Diodorus (13.2) implies they were all so treated. Andocides (De Myst. 62) says the one near his own family home was spared.

tion to Sicily. Suggestions that the whole thing was a prank committed by drunken young men or even by the Corinthians on behalf of their Syracusan colonists were dismissed.[9] Thucydides tells us the Athenians "took the matter seriously. For it seemed to be an omen for the voyage and to have been done on behalf of a conspiracy to make a revolution and destroy the democracy."[10]

In such a mood the Athenians took steps to discover the perpetrators. The assembly met frequently in the next few days and voted to offer great rewards for their discovery; in addition, immunity was offered to anyone, citizen, metic, or slave, who might come forward with information about this or any other sacrilege that had been committed.[11] At the same time, most likely, the assembly voted to give the council full powers to conduct an investigation, and the council in turn set up a commission of inquiry that included Diognetus, Peisander, and Charicles, the latter two men at that time leading democratic politicians.[12] The invitation to informants was dangerously broad and tempting, given the heated atmosphere, and it soon brought results. A meeting of the assembly was called to conduct final discussions with the generals prior to the fleet's departure for Sicily; Lamachus' flagship was already afloat in the harbor. A certain Pythonicus, otherwise unknown to us, rose and accused Alcibiades and his friends of putting on a performance of the Eleusinian mysteries in a private house. He offered to prove his allegation if immunity were granted a slave who had witnessed the proceedings. The offer was accepted, and the slave Andromachus came forward to testify that he and others had seen the mysteries performed in the house of Pulytion. He claimed that Niciades, Meletus, and Alcibiades had played the principal parts, and he named seven other participants as well.[13]

[9]Plut. *Alc.* 18.3-4.
[10]6.27.3.
[11]6.27.2.
[12]And. *De Myst.* 14, 15 and 40; Plut. *Alc.* 18.4.
[13]And. *De Myst.* 11-13. Thucydides (6.28.1) says that information, not about the Hermae but about other mutilations and about performances of the mysteries in houses, was given "by certain metics and slaves" (ἀπὸ μετοίκων τέ τινων καὶ ἀκολούθων). This first information came from a slave; the second one came from Teucrus, a metic, probably after the expedition sailed. Hatzfeld

These charges had nothing to do with the desecration of the Hermae, but the involvement of Alcibiades and the excitement of the people gave them a disproportionate importance. The participation of Alcibiades in a mockery of a religious ritual was all too plausible. Thucydides speaks of the popular suspicion of "his lawless self-indulgence in his way of life"[14] and Plutarch's *Life of Alcibiades* is full of anecdotes that justify that suspicion. There was even a story that he had staged a mock murder, directed the members of his *hetairia*, his political club, to pass by the presumed corpse, and even asked them to help him conceal the crime, before one of them at last discovered the hoax.[15] The charges, therefore, were quickly taken up by Alcibiades' political enemies, among them Androcles, a leading democratic politician. Thucydides speaks of these men as "those most jealous of Alcibiades as an impediment to their own positions of leadership of the *demos*, who thought that if they got rid of him they would be first."[16] They connected the alleged profanation of the mysteries with the mutilation of the Hermae and charged that Alcibiades was involved in both, that he aimed at "the destruction of the democracy."[17]

Alcibiades rose to deny the charges and to defend himself. He offered to stand trial immediately on all charges, asking that if he were acquitted he should be permitted to retain his command. His main concern was that the trial take place at once, before the departure of the fleet. He was concerned, of course, not to have a serious charge hanging over his head while he was off in Sicily and afraid that his enemies would trump up newer and more serious charges against him in his absence. Both he and his enemies knew that at the moment he was very popular with the sailors and soldiers of the expedition, not least because he was

---

(*Alcibiade* 163, n. 5) suggests Thucydides has "arbitrarily put together" the evidence of Andromachus, of Teucrus, and of others denouncing the mutilation of other statues, "carried away by his habits of generalization and synthesis." Dover (*HCT* IV, 274) is less generous to the historian, arguing that in this passage he has "sacrificed accuracy to indignant rhetoric."

[14]6.15.4.

[15]Polyaenus *Strategemata* 1.40, cited by Hatzfeld, *Alcibiade*, 164.

[16]6.28.2. Thucydides does not mention any names; Androcles' is supplied by Plutarch (*Alc.* 19.1).

[17]6.28.2: ἐπὶ δήμου καταλύσει.

thought responsible for the participation of Argive and Mantinean contingents in the expedition. While he demanded an immediate trial that would either clear his name or bring about his
death, his enemies were determined to delay the trial until after
he was gone for the very reasons he feared. They arranged for
speakers who were not known to be hostile to Alcibiades, but
who in fact hated him as much as the others, to argue against
delaying the expedition to holding a trial at once. "Let him sail
off now with good luck," they said. "When the war is over let
him come back here and defend himself. The laws will be the
same then as now."[18] The assembly was persuaded that he
should sail at once and "come back and be tried within a specified
number of days."[19] Alcibiades had no choice but to accept their
decision. He was being forced to sail off to Sicily with the charge
still pending and his enemies in control of the assembly. He
could only hope that the passage of time would cool passions in
Athens and that success in Sicily would make him invulnera-
ble.[20]

The Athenian contingent of the great expedition to Sicily embarked soon after, probably in the latter part of June.[21] The allied
triremes, the supply ships, and smaller craft had already been
given orders to gather at Corcyra and wait for the Athenians to
arrive. The Athenian force, though not greater in numbers than
the expedition Pericles had led against Epidaurus in 430, "was
the most expensive and glorious armament coming from a single
city with a purely Greek force that put to sea up to that time."[22]
Not only public funds but also private expenditures by the
trierarchs provided for ships that were both efficient and beauti-
ful, and even the hoplites vied with one another in the beauty
and quality of their equipment. The whole city and the foreign
allies who were in it went down to the Piraeus to see the great
spectacle. "It looked more like a display of power and wealth
before the rest of the Greeks than an expedition against
enemies."[23]

[18]Plut. Alc. 19.4.
[19]6.29.3.
[20]6.29; Plut. Alc. 19.
[21]MacDowell, Andokides 189.
[22]6.31.1. For the numbers involved see below, p. 210.

On the morning of the departure the high spirits of the Athenians were somewhat chastened by the reality of saying farewell to sons, relatives, and friends who were about to sail off on an expedition made unprecedentedly dangerous by the long distance involved. Perhaps they were also uneasy because of the recent sacrilege and the various evil omens. They were cheered, however, by the extraordinary power and brilliance of the force that they were dispatching.[24] At last, when all was ready, the blare of a trumpet brought silence to the vast crowd. The prayers customary before putting out to sea were offered in unison by the entire army and navy with the crowd joining from the shore. "When they had sung the paean and finished the libations they set out, at first in column, then, as they sailed off, they raced each other as far as Aegina."[25] From there they headed for Corcyra to meet their allies before going on to Sicily.

The departure of the expedition did not stop the council's investigating committee from pursuing its work with undiminished zeal, and soon their searches produced results that once again threw the city into turmoil.[26] A metic named Teucrus, after prudently withdrawing to Megara, told the council that he had himself taken part in a performance of the mysteries and was prepared to name his associates in the deed, that he also had information about the mutilation of the Hermae, and that he was prepared to return to Athens to testify if he were first granted immunity. The council agreed and Teucrus kept his promise, naming eleven men, besides himself, as profaners of the mysteries and eighteen, himself not one of them, as mutilators of the Hermae.[27] Neither list included the name of Alcibiades, but the list of profaners of the mysteries carried the name of Diognetus, a member of the council's investigating committee and a brother of Nicias.[28]

Andocides tells us that after the testimony of the slave An-

[23]6.31.4.
[24]6.30.2; 31.6.
[25]6.32.2.
[26]6.53.2.
[27]And. De Myst. 14, 15, 34, 35.
[28]And. De Myst. 14, 15; for his relationship to Nicias see MacDowell, Andokides, 74–75, and Davies, APF, 404–40.

dromachus, Polystratus, one of the accused, was arrested and executed, while all the others named fled the country and that all those denounced by Teucrus also ran off.[29] Some time later a certain Diocleides testified before the council about the mutilation of the Hermae. He told a strange story. Awakened before dawn by a full moon, he had set out from the city on some private business. As he passed the theatre of Dionysus he saw a large group of men in the orchestra. Taking cover, he saw that they were about three hundred in number, and in the moonlight he was able to identify some of them. The next day he heard about the sacrilege and concluded that the men he had seen were the perpetrators. Back in Athens, he discovered that the council was offering 100 minae as a reward for information. Hoping to do better, he approached some of the people he had identified, seeking a bribe greater than the public reward. His negotiations involved Andocides, his father Leogoras, and Euphemus, the brother of Callias who was brother-in-law to Andocides. As Andocides told the tale, Diocleides was promised two talents for his silence, but when the money was not paid during the next month as agreed, Diocleides gave his information to the council. Among the forty-two men he named, Mantitheus and Apsephion were members of the council and thus present at the denunciation.[30]

This testimony was more alarming than the earlier ones. It inculpated two councilors, and Andocides, Leogoras, Euphemus and Callias were all wealthy aristocrats. Among the others named were Charmides son of Aristoteles, the father probably later a member of the Thirty Tyrants; Taureas, probably a choregus, and therefore a rich man; his son Nisaeus; Eucrates, a brother of Nicias; and Critias, later the leading member of the Thirty Tyrants.[31] Their alleged involvement provided substance

[29]And. De Myst. 14–15. Although Andocides' evidence must always be examined with care, there seems little reason to doubt the general accuracy here. It is true that Alcibiades, one of those named by Andromachus, did not flee Athens, as Grote (VII, 196, n. 1) and Dover (HCT IV, 280, n. 1) point out. But this should not cast doubt on his account, for he probably failed to exclude him from those fleeing because he assumed everyone knew he had sailed off with the expedition.

[30]And. De Myst. 37–42.

[31]And. De Myst. 47. For the identification see MacDowell, Andokides, 97, and Davies, APF 29–32, 326, 328.

to the fears of an oligarchic plot. The growing panic allowed Peisander to move the suspension of a law forbidding the torture of Athenian citizens while the council shouted approval. He meant to wrack each of the forty-two accused so as to get the names of all the conspirators before dark. With difficulty Mantitheus and Apsephion persuaded their colleagues to allow them to stand trial instead of being tortured, and to accept sureties for their appearance. Their immediate flight to enemy territory, either Megara or Boeotia, increased the general fear, particularly when a Boeotian army soon appeared on the Athenian frontier.[32] This may have been at the same time that a small Spartan army came as far as the Isthmus of Corinth in connection with some arrangements with the Boeotians.[33] These external threats increased the sense of internal danger from traitorous Athenians working with the enemy. All Athens trembled with fear of a conspiracy to overthrow the democracy and install either an oligarchy or a tyranny.[34]

The remaining forty accused were placed under close arrest. In both the city and the Piraeus the frightened Athenians spent the night awake and armed, while the council took refuge on the Acropolis. The informer Diocleides was hailed as savior of the city, crowned with a wreath, and taken in honor to the Prytaneum where he dined at public expense. In their excitement and gratitude the Athenians noted neither his attempt to suborn a bribe nor his delay in seeking public safety.[35]

The triumph of Diocleides, however, was short-lived. After a time in prison Andocides was persuaded by his cousin Charmides and other relatives to tell what he knew of the mutilation of the Hermae and so refute what they knew to be Diocleides' false testimony. Receiving a grant of immunity from the council, Andocides revealed that the *hetairia* of which he was a member had done the deed. His list of the guilty agreed with the names supplied earlier by Teucrus, all of whom were by now either dead or off in exile; the four he added to the earlier list likewise

[32]And. *De Myst.* 43-45.
[33]6.61.2.
[34]6.28, 53, 60, 61.
[35]And. *De Myst.* 45.

fled at once.[36] Andocides' testimony exculpated his family and himself; in the case of his family this was probably just, but in the case of Andocides himself, we are less sure.[37] The council and the investigating committee summoned Diocleides, and he quickly confessed that he had lied, saying that he had been persuaded to do so by Alcibiades of Phegus, a cousin of the great Alcibiades, and a certain Amiantus of Aegina.[38] The two men fled into exile. Those accused earlier, including Andocides, his family and friends, were released from prison, and those who had fled were invited to return. Diocleides' request for pardon was denied, and he was put to death.[39]

At this point the Athenians were satisfied that the mutilators of the Hermae had been found and breathed a sigh of relief believing, as Andocides says, that they had been "freed from many evils and dangers."[40] The lists of Teucrus and Andocides coincided, naming only twenty-two culprits, all of whom were now either dead or in exile with a price on their heads.[41] It was reassuring that there were only twenty-two, apparently a single *hetairia*, instead of a large conspiracy including at least three hundred men, as Diocleides had claimed. The new list, moreover, contained few men of note and seemed less threatening in that way, as well.[42] But if the matter of the Hermicopidae had been cleared up to suit the Athenian people, the profanation of

[36]And. *De Myst.* 48–61. Plutarch (*Alc.* 212) says Andocides was persuaded by a certain Timaeus.

[37]And. *De Myst.* 61–66. For recent discussions of the guilt of Andocides in the mutilation of the Hermae see MacDowell, *Andokides*, 173–176 (not guilty), and J. L. Marr, *CQ* n.s. XXI (1971), 326–338 (guilty).

[38]And. *De Myst.* 65; for the identification of Alcibiades of Phegus see Mac-Dowell, *Andokides*, 104, and Davies, *APF* 17. This may be the place for Plutarch's story (*Alc.* 20.5) that Diocleides was proved a liar when his tale of recognizing the perpetrators by moonlight was rejected, since there was no moon on the night in question. Dover (*HCT* IV, 274–276) rejects Plutarch's story, but MacDowell (*Andokides*, 187–188) offers a plausible defense of it.

[39]And. *De Myst.* 66. Andocides (*De Myst.* 20) tells us that the law provided that a witness giving testimony under a grant of immunity was subject to the death penalty if he lied.

[40]And. *De Myst.* 66.

[41]6.60.4. My discussion here owes much to the fine account of Hatzfeld (*Alcibiade*, 173–177), though we do not agree on all points.

[42]The twenty-two names can be conveniently seen in the valuable list of all those accused of either sacrilege which was compiled by Dover, *HCT* IV, 277–280.

the mysteries remained to be dealt with, and the investigations continued.

Soon, another denunciation was forthcoming, and this time not from a metic or slave but from an aristocratic Athenian lady, Agariste, the wife of Alcmaeonides.[43] Both her name and that of her husband indicate her connection with the great Alcmaeonid family. She reported a profanation of the mysteries performed by Alcibiades, his uncle Axiochus, and his friend Adeimantus in the house of Charmides, presumably the son of Aristoteles, Andocides' cousin.[44] Next, a slave named Lydus produced new information. He testified before the council that his master Pherecles of Themacus had celebrated the mysteries in his own house; Pherecles also had been named as a Hermocopid by Teucrus. Lydus produced a list of participants that included Leogoras, the father of Andocides, but Leogoras was able to clear himself of the charge. The others accused took flight.[45]

By now scores of men had been charged with one or both of the misdeeds.[46] Those not cleared by Andocides' testimony had either fled into exile or been executed. At the height of the panic the atmosphere was full of the kind of terror that accompanies political witch hunts. In their fear the Athenians readily connected the sacrileges with plots to overthrow the democracy. Though there was no solid evidence of such an undertaking, all Athens trembled with fear of a conspiracy to install either an oligarchy or a tyranny.[47] Frightened Athenians accepted accusations from disreputable witnesses, were careless in examining them, and, on the basis of such dubious evidence and without trial, arrested and imprisoned reputable citizens. This mood had not yet disappeared when the testimony of Agariste and Lydus revealed that the mysteries had been mocked repeatedly and that

[43]And. De Myst. 16. She had previously been married to Damon, possibly the friend and adviser of Pericles. For Agariste see Davies, APF, 382–384.

[44]And. De Myst. 16. For the identifications see MacDowell, Andokides, 76.

[45]And. De Myst. 17–18.

[46]Dover (HCT, IV, 277–280) lists sixty-eight by name and indicates an unknown number from the list of Lydus, since that list does not appear in the ancient evidence. Twenty-eight others were named by Diocleides and released after the testimony of Andocides. The total of those accused by name may have approached one hundred.

[47]6.53.2; 6.60.

Alcibiades had taken part in that sacrilege. His enemies seized on this new evidence and once again asserted that the profanation was part of "a conspiracy against the democracy."[48] The recent movements of the Spartans and Boeotians lent some weight to these allegations. About the same time suspicions were spread about Athens that Alcibiades' friends in Argos were planning a coup to overthrow that city's democracy. These unfounded and unlikely rumors gained so much credence that the Athenians returned their pro-Spartan Argive hostages to Argos, where they were put to death.[49] Thucydides tells us that "suspicion gathered about Alcibiades from all sides," and thus the decision was made to recall him and make him stand trial.[50]

Plutarch quotes the charge made before the council that led to Alcibiades' recall: "Thessalus, son of Cimon, of the deme Laciadae, impeaches Alcibiades, son of Cleinias, of the deme Scambonidae for committing crimes against the goddesses Demeter and Cora by imitating the mysteries and displaying them to his companions [hetairoi] in his own house, by wearing the same kind of robe worn by the hierophant when he displays the sacred objects and calling himself hierophant, Pulytion torchbearer, Theodorus of Phegaea herald, and proclaiming the other companions [hetairoi] initiates and initiates into the higher mysteries, contrary to the laws established by the Eumolpidae, Kerykes, and priests of Eleusis."[51] The detailed nature of the indictment suggests that it was based on good evidence, and its gravity is indicated by the name of the impeacher, Thessalus, son of the great Cimon. The enemies of Alcibiades now plainly included not merely demagogues but important aristocrats as well. Probably toward the end of July the state trireme *Salaminia* was sent to Sicily to bring Alcibiades back to Athens to answer the indictment; others on the expedition who had been implicated by the several informers were to be returned as well.[52]

Such is the account we can construct of the unusual events

[48]6.61.1: τῆς ξυνωμοσίας ἐπὶ τῷ δήμῳ.
[49]6.61.2-3.
[50]6.61.4.
[51]Plut. *Alc.* 22.3. On the nature of the legal process see Hatzfeld, *Alcibiade*, 176.
[52]6.61.4. I deduce the date from the estimates of Dover, *HCT* IV, 272–276.

that occurred in Athens in the spring and summer of 415. We cannot be sure of either the relative or absolute chronology, nor can we give certain answers to the questions: who was guilty of each sacrilege? what were the motives for each? Thucydides was far from convinced that the investigations and trials had solved the crime of the mutilation of the Hermae; after all the testimony, confession, trials, exiles, and execution, "it was still unclear whether those punished had been treated unjustly." And further, "neither then nor later could anyone say with certainty who had committed the deed."[53] But Thucydides was away from Athens in exile during these events, and he probably did not have access to the speech of Andocides, as modern scholars do. The property of those convicted of mutilating the Hermae and profaning the mysteries was confiscated and a record of its subsequent sale inscribed on a number of stelae set up in the Athenian *agora*. Considerable fragments of the lists containing the names of the convicted are now available and can be checked against the names supplied by Andocides.[54] Thucydides probably never saw the inscriptions; he certainly made no use of them in his *History*. For these reasons, among others, it seems reasonable to try to answer the important questions as best we can.

The profanations of the mysteries seem to present no great problem. They were parodied many times in private houses by many different people, frequently at meetings of *hetairiai*. These *hetairiai*, or clubs, had a long history in Athens, going back at least to the sixth century.[55]

Athenian clubs usually comprised men of the same age group, though there were exceptions. Although it seems to have been possible to have belonged to more than one club, we cannot tell how widespread the practice of multiple membership was. The membership of a club rarely exceeded twenty-five, and most

---

[53] 2.60.2 and 4.

[54] Some of the fragments are published in *GHI* #79, 240-247. The original publications are by W. K. Pritchett in *Hesperia* XXII (1953), 240-249, XXV (1956), 276-281, XXX (1961), 23-25; A. Pippin, *Hesperia* XXV (1956), 318-325 and D. A. Amyx, *Hesperia* XXVII (1958), 163-310. See also D. M. Lewis, *ASI*, 177-191.

[55] For general discussions of these clubs see G. M. Calhoun, *Athenian Clubs in Politics and Litigation* (Austin, 1913), and F. Sartori, *Le eterie nella vita politica ateniese del VI e V sec. a.C.* (Rome, 1957).

were probably smaller, for the clubs were social organizations, among other things, which held banquets and drinking parties in private homes which rarely could hold so many men. The clubs were secret societies with initiation rites and oaths of allegiance. This practice of taking oaths explains why the word *synomosia*, or "union of oath-takers," is often used as a synonym for *hetairia*. The former word often has negative political connotations and should sometimes be translated "conspiracy." This points up the political character of many, if not all, of the Athenian clubs.

Thucydides tells us that the clubs worked to influence elections and the law courts.[56] Though different clubs held different opinions, most seem to have leaned toward oligarchy, especially toward the last part of the war. Clubs played a vital part in the oligarchic revolution of 411 and the establishment of the Thirty Tyrants in 404. None of this should occasion surprise, for the clubs all had aristocratic origins and recruited their members from the upper classes.

The events of 415 allow modern scholars to identify three clubs with a reasonable degree of confidence: one included Alcibiades, his cousin Alcibiades of Phegus, Callias, Charmides, and Alcmaeonides, among others; a second included Andocides, his father Leogoras, and Critias; and a third with Teucrus and Nicias' brother Diognetus.[57] Though the three clubs had different leaders, their members had much in common. Most of them were rich aristocrats who derived their wealth chiefly from the land. Sometimes a club was knit together by bonds of kinship among certain of its members. Perhaps membership in the same tribe or residence in the same deme may help to explain membership in a particular club, although the evidence does not allow confidence.[58]

All three clubs took part in mimicry and profanation of the mysteries in 415.[59] Such behavior is not surprising in the "enlightened," critical atmosphere created by the sophists who taught in Athens in the late fifth century, especially from the

[56] 8.54.4.
[57] The division, suggested by O. Aurenche (*Les groupes*) is serviceable, but the assignments of particular individuals to each group is far from certain. For useful criticisms see E. Will, *Revue de Philologie* LI (1977), 92–96.
[58] Aurenche, *Les groupes, passim.*
[59] Aurenche, *Les groupes,* 164–165.

rich aristocratic youths who were their chief customers. Participation in the sacrilege may, in some cases, have been part of an
initiation ritual into a club, a pledge by which each member
opened himself to denunciation by any of the others and thereby
assured them of his loyalty.[60] In any case, these profanations
could not have had any political meaning, for they were all done
in private, indeed in secret, and could not have been meant to
influence outsiders in any way. They were intended as "a kind of
charade, with the added spice of illegality," or were like "the
celebration of a black mass in seventeenth-century France."[61]

The mutilation of the Hermae was quite a different matter.
The scope of the activity alone makes it plain that it could not
have been a drunken prank undertaken on the spur of the moment by a few men. Many men were needed to deface so many
statues, and the entire operation must have been planned in
advance.[62] The timing of the sacrilege and its target, both clearly
connected with the Sicilian expedition, make it certain that the
purpose was political. But who committed the outrage, and
why? There is good reason to accept the testimony of Andocides, since it confirms that of Teucrus and is confirmed, in
some cases, by the names of the convicted which appear on the
stelae in the *agora*. We may follow Andocides' account with
general confidence when he tells us that the plot was inspired
and organized by Euphiletus and Meletus and carried out chiefly
by the members of his own *hetairia*.[63]

It remains to seek the motive for the desecration. Some
modern scholars have revived the opinion of the Athenian minority that thought it the work of drunken youths engaged in van-
dalism for the fun of it, and therefore concluded that it was
without any political significance.[64] For reasons already mentioned this seems highly unlikely, and we would do well, like the

---

[60]And. *De Myst.* 67, and Dover, *HCT* IV, 286.

[61]The former analogy is made by MacDowell, *Andokides*, 192, and the latter
by Aurenche, *Les groupes*, 171.

[62]And. *De Myst.* 67.

[63]And. *De Myst.* 60–68; Hatzfeld, *Alcibiade* 186; Aurenche, *Les groupes*, 165–
171.

[64]Plut. *Alc.* 18.4; Gilbert (*Beiträge*, 252) called it "the deed of insolent
youths"; Eduard Meyer (*GdA* IV, 506) called it "a boy's trick, no political
maneuver."; he is followed by Henderson (*Great War*, 357).

Athenian people, to take the matter more seriously. There is no reason, however, to agree with them that the sacrilege was part of an oligarchical plot to overthrow the democracy. There is no evidence for this view in the ancient sources; they report not a single informer, truthful or mendacious, who mentioned such a plot, though the overheated atmosphere was receptive to such testimony.[65] We must understand the fear of such a plot as a natural, if unjustified, reaction to an unprecedentedly bold outrage, a reaction seized upon and intensified by opportunistic politicians for their own purposes.

The Athenians thought that the mutilation of the Hermae was "an evil omen for the expedition,"[66] and at least some of them, those, for instance, who blamed the Corinthians, thought that its purpose was to prevent the expedition. That view has won considerable support among modern scholars,[67] but objections have been raised: (1) the sacrilege had little chance of preventing the expedition, and, in fact, did not come close to doing so; and (2) such a motive is improbable, for the groups that opposed the expedition because they favored peace must have realized that an attack on Sicily would not be a breach of the peace with Sparta, and that refraining from the expedition was no guarantee of that peace in a world as strained as Greece in 415. Besides, the men performing the mutilation would be running terrible risks for the common good without prospect of personal gain, and "such selflessness is most uncharacteristic of fifth-century Athenian politics."[68]

The response to the first objection is that the mutilators could

---

[65]MacDowell (*Andokides*, 193) offers a reasonable argument why the idea of a plot to overthrow the democracy is unlikely: "an anti-democratic revolution would have been far more likely to succeed when the fleet was absent from Athens, as it was in 411, and . . . an action designed to prevent the Sicilian expedition would be the worst possible beginning for it."

[66]6.27.3.

[67]E.g., Grote, VII, 171–172; Hatzfeld, *Alcibiade*, 187–188; MacDowell, *Andokides*, 192–193; Aurenche, *Les groupes*, 173.

[68]These objections are raised by J. L. Marr in the appendix to his article, *CQ* n.s. XXI (1971), 331–338. He also raises the question of timing, accepting Dover's date for the mutilation, which is about two weeks earlier than the one accepted here. Even if he were right about the date, there is no good reason why the mutilators would need to wait for the eve of the departure to try to stop the expedition.

not have known that their plot would fail, and conspirators often are more optimistic than the facts warrant. If we rid ourselves of the advantage of hindsight, in fact, we may believe that they had some reason to hope for success. The pious Nicias was one of the generals of the expedition. For all his inability to stop the Athenians from voting to attack Sicily, he remained a popular and respected man, especially in matters of religious piety. The Greeks, and even the Athenians, frequently aborted public business because of such omens as thunderstorms and earthquakes. It must therefore have seemed likely that Nicias, honestly alarmed by so unique and terrifying an omen as the mutilated Hermae, would, with the aid of priests and seers, convince the Athenians that they must postpone or abandon the dangerous expedition that he himself opposed on other grounds.[69] The conspirators, moreover, did not know that they would be exposed or their sacrilege confused with the several profanations of the mysteries. In the hysteria of charges and countercharges, two of Nicias' brothers, Diognetus and Eucrates were named. Diognetus appears to have been guilty and Eucrates innocent, but it hardly matters. Once their names were aired publicly in connection with any sacrilege, it would have been impossible for Nicias to act without raising suspicions of collusion between the brothers for political purposes. It is doubtful that Nicias could have persuaded the Athenians to abandon the expedition in any case, but there had at least been a chance. After the revelations that chance was gone.

The second objection is even less persuasive. Friends of peace would readily believe that the attack on Sicily increased the chances of general war, but regardless of that, the Sicilian expedition itself was war with most of its disadvantages. It might not immediately bring a Spartan army to ravage the lands of Attica, as in the Archidamian War, but it required Athenians to risk their lives in foreign places. If the expedition succeeded it would bring new wealth to support the democracy and bring glory to their enemy Alcibiades. The *hetairia* of Andocides, Leogoras, Euphiletus, Charmides, and Critias was composed of wealthy

[69]The point is made by Grote, VII, 171-172.

aristocrats with oligarchic leanings.[70] They would have shared the disinclination of men of their class and political views to see the expedition, with all its attendant risks, sail, especially since they could expect to pay for it through additional impositions of the *eisphora*, if the war did not bring immediate success.[71] Reasoned argument, Nicias' attempt at clever politics, and all other legal means had failed. We need not be astonished that the opponents of the campaign turned, at last, to more bizarre means.

Alcibiades was not involved in the mutilation of the Hermae; he seems to have been guilty of profaning the mysteries. Again the truth was less important than appearance. His enemies painted a picture with broad strokes: oligarchic plots were at work, and Alcibiades was involved in them. Alcibiades and the soldiers and sailors over whom his rhetorical skill exerted such great influence were away in Sicily. Opponents of the expedition, democratic politicians who were his rivals, and aristocratic political clubs, all joined against the common enemy and recalled Alcibiades to what seemed certain doom at the trial that awaited him in Athens.

[70]On this group see Aurenche, *Les groupes*, 89–101, and Hatzfeld, *Alcibiade* 186–188; for information on some of the men denounced see Dover, *HCT* IV, 286–288. This Critias may not be the same as the notorious leader of the Thirty Tyrants, for that Critias later proposed the recall of Alcibiades (Plut. *Alc.* 33.1).

[71]E. Will, "Review of Aurenche, *Les groupes*," in *Revue de Philologie* LI (1977), 94.

9. Athenian Strategy and the Summer Campaign of 415

During these upheavals in Athens the great armada was bound for Sicily. The Athenian contingent joined the allies at Corcyra, and the commanders mustered their forces for a final review. The navy consisted of 134 ships, 100 from Attica and the others from Chios and other allied states. Sixty of the Athenian ships were fighting triremes, the remaining 40 being troop carriers.[1] The main land force was the corps of 5,100 hoplites. There were 1,500 Athenians from the regular list, and 700 thetes serving as marines. The Argives sent 500 hoplites and there were 250 mercenaries, some of them from Mantinea. All the rest, some 2,150, came from Athens' subject allies. The force of light-armed troops included 400 archers from Athens and 80 from Crete, 700 slingers from Rhodes, and 120 light-armed exiles from Megara. There was also one horse transport with 30 cavalrymen. In addition there were 30 cargo ships carrying food, supplies, and bakers, together with stone masons, carpenters, and tools for building walls.[2] This was the largest body of hoplites the Athenians had used during the war, except for the group sent to ravage the land of Megara.[3]

---

[1] For the relationship between triremes and troopships see Dover, *HCT* IV, 308–309.

[2] 6.43-44.1; Diodorus (13.2.5) gives somewhat higher figures, but there is no reason to prefer his account here.

[3] The invasion of Megara used 13,000 hoplites, but they ran little risk of fighting (2.31.1). The attack on Epidaurus in 430 used 4,000 hoplites, all of them Athenians (2.56).

At Corcyra the fleet was divided into three divisions, one of which was assigned to each general to facilitate better control and to avoid a situation in which the entire fleet landed at once, overtaxing the local water and food supply. Three ships were sent ahead to Italy and Sicily to discover what type of reception the Athenians might expect in each place.[4] After that the whole force sailed across the Ionian Gulf to the Iapygian peninsula, the heel of the Italian boot, and then along Italy's southern shore.[5] They met a cold reception; some towns would neither allow them inside nor set up a market for them outside, permitting them only an anchorage and drinking water. The major cities of Taras and Locri would not allow even those courtesies.[6] At last the expedition came to Rhegium, where they were not admitted into the town but were allowed to beach their ships, make camp outside the walls, and purchase supplies at a market set out by the Rhegians.

The Athenians expected much from the Rhegians, who were not only allies of long-standing but also Chalcidians by descent, like the Leontines to whose aid Athens was sailing.[7] Rhegium had a good anchorage and was strategically based to allow forays along both the eastern and northern coasts of Sicily and to put pressure on Messina across the narrow strait. During Athens' first Sicilian campaign (427-424) Rhegium had cooperated fully, serving as the Athenians' main base of operations; but this time the Athenian generals were bitterly disappointed for the Rhegians declared their neutrality, saying that "they would do whatever the other Italiote Greeks would decide upon."[8] Since there was no machinery for common deliberation among the Greek cities of Italy, and since most of those cities had already made their hostility plain, the Rhegians' answer amounted to a polite refusal of the Athenian requests. The Rhegians may have been "astonished and intimidated by the magnitude of the newly-arrived force," as Grote suggested,[9] for there appears to be no

[4] 6.42.
[5] See Map 9.
[6] 6.44.2. Diodorus (13.3.4) says they were warmly received at Thurii and provided access to a market at Croton.
[7] 6.44.3. For the alliance see GHI, 63, 171-175.
[8] 6.44.3.
[9] Grote, VII, 181.

other reason for their change in attitude since 424. The Athenian force originally voted, the same number of ships as had finished the earlier Sicilian campaign, would probably not have affected the Rhegians in the same way. The chagrin of the Athenian generals was increased when they learned of the aforementioned Segestan trick; the additional money that they had expected from Segesta did not exist, all that could be found was 30 talents. Thucydides says that Nicias was not surprised, but the other commanders were shocked. "The generals immediately became dispirited because the first thing they tried had gone against them and because the Rhegians refused to join them."[10]

The three Athenian commanders then held a council of war to determine what strategy they should follow in light of the disappointments that they had encountered. Nicias recommended that the whole force sail to Selinus; if the Segestans agreed to furnish money for the whole Athenian force "they would consider the matter further."[11] If not, they should demand money to pay for the 60 ships the Segestans had originally requested and then stay on the scene until a peace was arranged between Segesta and Selinus "either by force or agreement." After that, they should sail along the Sicilian coast making a display of Athenian power and so showing their commitment to their Sicilian friends and allies. Then they should sail home "unless they happened to find some quick and unexpected way to help the Leontines or bring over any of the other cities. But they should not endanger the state by spending its own resources."[12] There was, of course, no chance that Segesta could or would pay for the maintenance of the vast Athenian armada, so what Nicias was proposing was to settle matters at Segesta in some way and then go home, for there was unlikely to be a quick and costless way to help Leontini. His plan would achieve one of the expedition's objectives, at most, without even risking a battle on land or sea. He must have been emboldened to suggest this do-little scheme by the bad news the Athenians had received. As Nicias had predicted, Segesta did not supply the promised money, and the

[10]6.46.2.
[11]6.47: πρὸς ταῦτα βουλεύεσθαι.
[12]6.47.

Athenian force was not received by important cities in Italy.[13] If, on their return to Athens, the generals were blamed for achieving nothing, Nicias could answer that the fundamental assumptions on which the expedition rested had proven to be wrong.

Alcibiades, of course, had a different opinion. He pointed out that for so great a force to go home without accomplishing anything would be a disgrace. He may also have said that it would destroy Athenian prestige in Sicily and damage it in the rest of Greece. It would leave Athens' Sicilian allies at the mercy of their enemies and increase the chance of Syracusan domination of the island. The very thing that the Athenians had sought to avoid by the two Sicilian expeditions would be brought about if they now followed Nicias' suggestion. It might have been right not to have sailed against Sicily at all, but it could not be right to sail away without accomplishing anything of note. Alcibiades instead suggested a diplomatic campaign in which Athenian envoys would try to enlist the friendship of Sicilian cities and win the native Sicels away from Syracuse. Such friends could provide valuable grain and soldiers. He placed special emphasis on winning over Messina because of its strategic location. After they had succeeded in bringing these allies over to their side, the Athenians could attack Syracuse and Selinus, "unless Selinus came to terms with Segesta and Syracuse permitted them to restore the Leontines to their homeland."[14]

The plan was characteristic of Alcibiades. Essentially diplomatic in nature, it relied more on skills of persuasion than on military ability and even left open the possibility that Selinus and Syracuse would yield without a fight.[15] If there were fighting, moreover, much of it would be done by others on behalf of the Athenians. This must have been the same plan that Alcibiades had in mind when he supported the Sicilian expedition at the first assembly in Athens. Since that original plan had provided for only 60 ships and no hoplites, there could have been

[13]6.22.
[14]6.48.
[15]Laffi (*RSI*, LXXXII [1970], 294, n. 71) doubts that Alcibiades took this possibility seriously but Liebeschütz (*Historia* XVII [1968], 292–293) argues that "had everything gone according to plan the ultimatum to Syracuse to restore Leontini might eventually have been accepted."

no thought that Athenians would bear the brunt of the fighting. The expedition must have been intended to allow precisely the kind of maneuvering that Alcibiades now proposed. The great increase in Athenian forces brought about by Nicias' intervention had not affected Alcibiades, who still wanted to follow the original plan, but the present size of that force did make a difference and probably worked against the prospects of Alcibiades' plan. A force of 60 Athenian triremes without infantry might well have gained the support of Sicilian cities, hostile to and frightened of Syracuse and seeking to use the Athenian force in their own interests. They could not fear that Athens would try to conquer the island with such a force. The larger armament that arrived in 415, however, seemed to most Sicilians a greater threat than Syracuse. Even if Alcibiades had not been recalled his scheme was unlikely to have worked. The augmented Athenian force was large enough to spoil the original diplomatic strategy but not large enough to provide security for an Athenian force on Sicily, particularly because of the lack of cavalry. The Athenians could sail from city to city, but if the natives did not yield to blandishments or threats, there was little the Athenians could do about it. A siege of any length involved the risk of exposing the army to superior numbers and especially to harassment by cavalry, and there is no reason to think that Alcibiades contemplated such a siege.[16] Neither is there any reason to think that he understood the significance of the increase in Athenian forces and the threat that it posed to his strategy.

Lamachus proposed a different course of action. He wanted to sail directly to Syracuse and force the issue at once, thereby taking full advantage of the unpreparedness of the Syracusans and of the terror they would feel at facing an enemy that forced a battle suddenly, before they were psychologically ready to fight. Lamachus appears to have envisioned three possible courses of action, each depending on the nature of the Syracusan reaction to the appearance of the Athenian expedition. The most optimistic possibility was that the Syracusans would be so unprepared and frightened that they would surrender without a fight. If that

[16]See Liebeschütz, *Historia* XVII (1968), 289-294.

did not occur, the Athenians would force a hoplite battle by drawing up close to the city. Presumably, the Syracusans would not refuse battle; they would come out and be defeated by the Athenian army. If, however, the Syracusans refused to fight and stayed behind their walls, a swift Athenian landing near the city would find many Syracusans and much of their property on their farms outside the city walls. By trapping these Syracusans on their farms, the Athenians would be able to maintain a steady flow of supplies while they invested and besieged the city. The swiftness and boldness of the Athenian action would impress the other Sicilian cities and bring them into the Athenian alliance. Lamachus also recommended that if a blockade was needed, they make a base at the deserted site of Megara Hyblaea, not far along the coast to the north of Syracuse.[17]

Most scholars have criticized Alcibiades' strategy and rated Lamachus' as the best,[18] a choice that is not surprising, for Thucydides seems to have held the same opinion. There can be little doubt that he agreed with Demosthenes' later assessment that the delay in besieging Syracuse was what saved the city,[19] but it is important to remember that even Demosthenes had the benefit of hindsight. Lamachus' strategy could not have been the original one. The force initially voted had consisted of only 60 triremes and no hoplites, and such a force could not have been

[17]6.49. I accept Böhme's emendation ἐφόρμησιν τά for the reading ἐφορμηθέντας in the MSS in 6.49.4.

[18]For a list of modern opinions see Laffi, RSI LXXXII (1970), 295, n. 72. Laffi himself and Liebeschütz (Historia XVII [1968], 289-294) support the plan of Alcibiades.

[19]7.42.3. See G. Donini, Hermes XCII (1964), 116-119. Liebeschütz (Historia XVII [1968], 299-302) believes that Thucydides, though he appears to agree with Demosthenes, did not, because the historian's narrative of the events does not seem to support such an interpretation, yet Thucydides' strategic analyses of the Sicilian expedition are impressive. "It is highly unlikely," says Liebeschütz, "that Thucydides intended the parenthetic and inexactly framed generalization 7,42,3 to contradict so carefully composed an argument. The passage must be intended to have less wide scope than it would have if considered in isolation or in the context of another author" (301-302). Dover's analysis of the passage (HCT IV, 419-421), however, supports Donini's. There is no good reason to disagree with his conclusion: "We must therefore regard the parenthesis as expressing Thucydides' own judgement, not merely his report of Demosthenes' judgement, though the two may largely have coincided."

expected to terrify the Syracusans into surrender, to conduct an infantry battle before the city, or to undertake a siege. There is no evidence, in fact, that Lamachus or anyone else conceived this bold set of plans in Athens, even after the increase in forces had been voted. Lamachus probably invented it only when the coldness of Rhegium and the failure of Segestan support made the original plan more expensive and less likely to succeed.[20]

His new plan was also open to criticism, however. A well-planned assault on Syracuse required a secure naval base not far from the city. Megara Hyblaea, destroyed by Gelon of Syracuse in 483/82 and never reoccupied, had a good harbor and, as Lamachus pointed out, was not far from Syracuse either by sea or land.[21] But a good base must be able to supply its army with sustenance either by trade or by control of an agricultural hinterland, and the deserted site of Megara could not do this.[22] Another problem with Lamachus' plan was that the Athenians' disadvantage in cavalry would hamper them both in a hoplite battle and during a siege; in any case there was a good argument for delay until cavalry reinforcements could come from Athens.[23] These considerations may help explain why Lamachus did not prevail in the debate, but they do not vitiate his judgment, which is supported by Demosthenes and Thucydides. No strategy could guarantee victory in Sicily, but the best plan was to strike at Syracuse while it was unprepared materially and psychologically. Thucydides believed that the Syracusans would have fought in response to an Athenian attack and been defeated. They would then have been unable to pre-

[20]Liebeschütz, *Historia* XVII (1968), 294.

[21]On the virtues of Megara as a base see P. Green, *Armada from Athens* (New York, 1970), 141.

[22]Laffi, *RSI* LXXXII (1970), 296. Liebeschütz (*Historia* XVII [1968], 292, and n. 18) suggests that the inability of an ancient force to make an opposed landing presented another obstacle to Lamachus' plan. He overlooks the fact that the Athenian fleet dominated the sea completely and so could land the army unopposed on one of the several places about Syracuse where a landing was possible. There are several such places in the Great Harbor of Syracuse, and the Syracusans were not numerous enough to prevent landings at all of them. Even if they could, the Athenians could have reached Syracuse by land from Megara.

[23]Laffi, *RSI* LXXXII (1970), 295.

vent the Athenians from building a wall to cut the city off by land, as their fleet already did by sea. In those circumstances Syracuse would not even have sent abroad for aid, but yielded to the siege.[24] Although there are questions to be asked of this assessment Lamachus' strategy might well have worked.

Lamachus, however, did not persuade his colleagues. Perhaps his plan was too bold and his eloquence inadequate; perhaps he lacked weight and authority, as Plutarch says, because of his poverty.[25] More likely he never had a chance to persuade his colleagues; Nicias wanted to do nothing and could only have been appalled by the prospect of an attack on Syracuse. Alcibiades had his own plan and would hear of no other. This meant that Lamachus, unwilling to accept Nicias' feeble plan, had no choice but to lend his support to the scheme of Alcibiades.[26]

A crucial requirement for the success of Alcibiades', and now Athens' strategy, was the possession of a large, secure, and well-located base from which to launch diplomatic missions and naval expeditions. With Rhegium unavailable Messina was the most desirable substitute, and Alcibiades sailed there in his own ship to negotiate an alliance. Just like the Rhegians, however, the Messinians offered to provide a market, but would not allow him into the city, much less make an alliance with Athens.[27] This was a serious and embarrassing rebuff for Alcibiades. The Athenians could not even stay in Sicily without a proper base, but for the moment their entire force was camped outside Rhegium in temporary quarters provided reluctantly and temporarily by the nervous Rhegians. Alcibiades sailed back to Rhegium. Taking 60 ships and one other general, presumably Lamachus, he sailed along the east coast of Sicily to the next possibly ally, Naxos. The Naxians were Chalcidians, the founders of Leontini and long-standing enemies of Syracuse, so they received the Athenians into their city.[28] He might have expected a similar reception

[24]7.42.3.
[25]Plut. Alc. 21.6.
[26]6.50.1.
[27]6.50.1.
[28]6.50.2. For the Chalcidian origins of Naxos and its foundation of both Leontini and Naxos see 6.3.

at Catana, for it too was Chalcidian and a Naxian colony, but a pro-Syracusan faction was in power and shut the gates to the Athenians. They were compelled to make camp at the Terias River north of Leontini and spend the night.[29]

The next day the fleet sailed along the coast toward Syracuse. Ahead of the rest went 10 ships which sailed into the Great Harbor of the city to see whether a fleet were anchored there. Finding none, they carried out the rest of their orders, proclaiming from the ships that they had come to restore the Leontines to their own country on the basis of their kinship and alliance with them and inviting any Leontines who were in the city to come over to their Athenian friends and benefactors. The Athenian announcement amounted to an ultimatum. When no answer came from Syracuse the ultimatum could be considered as rejected. The two states were openly at war. The Athenians carefully examined the harbor, the city, and the countryside where they would have to fight before sailing out unhindered.[30]

The Athenians found no Syracusan fleet in the harbor, because none had been fitted out. In fact, all the Athenians, perhaps excepting Lamachus, would have been astonished at how unprepared the Syracusans were. The sailing of the Athenian armada had brought many reports of its intentions to Syracuse, but for a long time they were not taken seriously. The Athenian fleet had already reached Corcyra before the Syracusans called an assembly to discuss the rumors that were coming in from all sides.[31] In 415 Syracuse was a moderate democracy of the sort that Aristotle could call a *politeia*. It seems to have elected its generals and magistrates, and most of these, as in Athens, appear to have come from the upper classes. At one time Syracuse had an institution called petalism, like the Athenian ostracism, whereby men thought excessively powerful or dangerous to the constitution were expelled from the state. Abuse by demagogues, however, had led to its abandonment. Still, the Syracusan assembly in 415 appears to have had much the same powers as the one in Athens, although the Syracusan *demos* was probably

[29] 6.50.3. See Map 9.
[30] 6.50.4-5.
[31] 6.32.3; Busolt, *GG* III:2, 1299.

still as deferential to the upper classes as the Athenians had been to theirs before the reforms of Ephialtes and Pericles. It was only after their great victory over Athens that the Syracusans introduced the lot and a more thorough democracy. In Syracuse the Athenians were attacking a rich, powerful, and expanding democracy much like their own, but somewhat behind Athens in constitutional development, wealth, and power.[32]

The Syracusan assembly engaged in a lengthy debate in which many speakers affirmed or denied that the Athenians were coming against Sicily, and Thucydides conveys the sense of the exchange by reporting two of the speeches. The first of these was given by Hermocrates son of Hermon, the man who had dominated the Congress of Gela in 424, which had united the Sicilians in order to exclude Athens from the island.[33] He seems to have been an aristocrat, but in the moderate polity of Syracuse there is no more reason to doubt his acceptance of democracy than to doubt Pericles' in Athens.[34] He claimed to have reliable information that a large Athenian force was sailing to Sicily on the pretext of helping the allies of Athens but that its real intention was the conquest of Syracuse and all of Sicily. Though the expedition was powerful, he was confident that if the Syracusans acted promptly, they could defeat the invaders and win glory for themselves as Athens had done in defeating the Persians.

Most of his speech urged specific actions that should be taken immediately for the defense of the city. Envoys should be sent to the cities of Sicily and Italy to seek allies, and even to Carthage, which might draw from its great wealth to help because of its own long-standing fear of Athens. They should also send to Corinth and Sparta asking them to send help to Syracuse and to stir up war against Athens in metropolitan Greece. Finally, Hermocrates urged the Syracusans to take the offensive, to send a fleet to Taras and the Iapygian peninsula in Italy. From there

---

[32]For the constitution of Syracuse see Dover, *HCT* IV, 430-431. H. Wentker (*Sizilien und Athen* [Heidelberg, 1956], 51-53) argues that Syracuse was not a democracy until the reforms of Diocles in 412. He is ably refuted by P. A. Brunt in his review of the book (*CR* VII [1957], 243-245.)

[33]4.58-65.

[34]For a discussion of his career see H. D. Westlake, "Hermocrates the Syracusan," in *Essays*, 174-202. For his politics see 184-185.

they could either intercept the Athenian armada in the open sea or attack the Athenians in Italy when they were still weary from the crossing. A show of force at such a forward position might even deter the Athenians from making the crossing, for Hermocrates had heard that "the most experienced of the Athenian generals" was reluctant to make the expedition and might seize on the evidence of resistance to abandon the project. He recognized that his proposal was bold and urged his listeners at least to take the other steps he recommended at once, if they were unwilling to run the greater risk. "The enemy is certainly coming against us, and I am sure that they are already under sail and almost here."[35]

Most of what Hermocrates said was unquestionably sound. His information about the Athenian expedition, its movements, and the attitude of Nicias was correct. His opinion about Athenian goals was at least plausible; in any case Syracuse was certain to be a target. His advice about diplomatic actions was beyond reproach, but his final suggestion is of a different character. Most modern scholars have condemned it as impractical and dangerously mistaken.[36] During the earlier Athenian action in Sicily, all the Sicilians combined had never put many more than 30 ships to sea at once. As we have seen, when the Athenians arrived in 415, the Syracusans had no fleet at all. Even in 414, after receiving help from the Peloponnesians, the Syracusans were able to launch only 80 ships, which were quickly defeated by 60 Athenian triremes.[37] That defeat was not surprising, for the Athenians were incomparably superior to the enemy in naval tactics, and Syracuse had not fought a naval engagement for many years. In 415, of course, the Athenian armada far outnumbered anything the Sicilians could have sent against it. We must agree with Dover that "if Hermokrates' proposal had been adopted ... the probable outcome was the annihilation of the Sikeliot fleets and the rapid imposition of Athenian rule on Sicily and South Italy."[38]

[35]6.33-34.
[36]See especially Busolt, GG III:2, 1300–1301, and Dover, HCT IV, 299.
[37]4.25.1; 6.49.52; 7.21-24.
[38]Dover, HCT IV, 299.

But there is something else wrong with the bold plan of Hermocrates. Its hope of deterring the Athenians with a show of force before they could even cross over from Corcyra was simply impossible. The armada was already gathered at Corcyra as Hermocrates spoke. It would take at least two months to build, gather, and train a Sicilian fleet, by which time the Athenians would certainly be at Rhegium.[39] All the strategic advantages he claimed for his plan were mythical, not merely because he gravely underestimated Athenian numerical and tactical superiority at sea, but because his plan was chronologically impossible. What is more, Hermocrates must have known it, as the closing words of his speech make clear: "they are already under sail and almost here." How, then, can we account for his recommendation? The most plausible suggestion is that the bold plan was merely a rhetorical device. Knowing that the Syracusans were reluctant to take any action and certain that they would in any case do less than what was suggested, he advanced his daring plan in the hope that they would at least initiate the diplomatic campaign he thought vital.[40]

The Syracusan reaction showed that some device other than a simple and straightforward expression of opinion was needed, for other speakers continued to dismiss as false and even ridiculous all reports that the Athenians were coming. Among these speakers was a certain Athenagoras.

Thucydides represents Athenagoras as a demagogue, describing him in terms strikingly similar to the ones he uses for Cleon. He was "leader of the *demos*" and "most persuasive to the masses."[41] His language was violent, his logic was dubious, and his facts, as the reader knows, were completely wrong. He considered his opponents not mistaken but treasonous and cowardly. He offered arguments from probability to show that if the Athenians came they would easily be beaten, and concluded that since the Athenians were reasonable people, they could not be

[39]Busolt, *GG* III:2, 1301, n. 1.

[40]Such is the suggestion of Westlake (*Essays*, 182–183), who reminds us of the similar, though differently motivated, rhetorical maneuver tried by Nicias at the second assembly in Athens.

[41]6.35.2: δήμου τε προστάτης ἦν καὶ ἐν τῷ παρόντι πιθανώτατος τοῖς πολλοῖς. For the description of Cleon see 3.36.6 and 4.21.3.

coming. Why, then, did reports allege that the Athenians were on their way to Sicily with a great force? Such rumors were termed the inventions of wicked Syracusans, who aimed to overthrow the democracy and establish oligarchy or tyranny. Athenagoras was referring especially to young aristocrats whom he pictured as impatient to wield political power. Presumably they were inventing the stories of an Athenian attack to frighten the people and thus make them put aside ordinary democratic procedures, perhaps even appoint these ambitious youths to military commands with which they could gain control of the city.[42] In response to these ambitious youths, Athenagoras offered a concise and vigorous defense of the theory of democracy, and urged the people to take measures to forestall the plot.[43]

Though Thucydides pairs this speech with that of Hermocrates, it could not have been a direct response to the latter. The experienced statesman Hermocrates was not one of the young, ambitious oligarchs whom Athenagoras was accusing, and there was nothing in his speech to provoke a defense of democracy. Probably one of the many other speakers had alleged that democracy was indolent and incompetent, and perhaps had even suggested special measures that provoked the suspicion and anger of Athenagoras.[44] The demagogue's approach—both his reference to ambitious young men and his warning of plots that aimed at oligarchy and tyranny—is starkly reminiscent of recent events at Athens, and Thucydides may intend that we understand this as behavior typical of democracies in time of crisis.

After Athenagoras' speech, one of the generals addressed the assembly. He is not named, but he must have been a man of great authority, for he made it clear that he would be the last speaker and was obeyed.[45] Without naming Athenagoras he de-

---

[42]Athenagoras does not explain how he thinks the conspirators mean to use the false crisis they are allegedly creating to gain power. The version offered here seems the likeliest interpretation of his meaning.

[43]6.36-40.

[44]Grote, VII, 184.

[45]6.41.1. ἄλλον μὲν οὐδένα ἔτι εἴασε παρελθεῖν does not imply that he had any constitutional power to prevent others from speaking but, like Pericles' action in preventing the Athenian assembly from meeting in 430 (see 2.22 and Kagan, *Archidamian War*, 55-56), it shows that he had the political influence and personal authority to have his way.

plored personal attacks in the assembly. Turning to the substance of the debate he pointed out that taking measures for
defense would do no harm whether the reports about the Athenians were true or false. He advocated putting Syracuse in a state
of preparedness for war and sending out the diplomatic missions
already suggested. Indeed, he said that the generals had already
undertaken some of these steps. He promised that they would
report back to the assembly whatever further they learned.
About an expedition to Italy, he said nothing. When he was
finished, the assembly dispersed.[46]

Still, the Syracusans were not quick to provide for their defense. Only when undeniable reports reached them that the
Athenians were at Rhegium did they abandon their skepticism
and take steps in earnest. They sent round to the Sicels, fearing
lest they go over to the enemy. To their subjects they sent
guards; to other Sicel communities they sent ambassadors;[47] and
to the forts on their own borders they sent garrisons. In Syracuse
itself they held inspections of arms and horses, "and they took all
other measures on the assumption that war was coming swiftly,
indeed was almost upon them."[48] These measures, of course, did
not include the preparation of a fleet, for when the Athenians
sailed into Syracuse harbor under Alcibiades and Lamachus they
were unopposed.

From Syracuse they sailed back to Catana. Once again the
natives would not open their city to the Athenians, but this time
they allowed them to send their generals to make their case
directly to the Catanian assembly. While the population listened
to Alcibiades, a force of Athenian soldiers broke into the town
through a faulty and unguarded gate. When members of the
pro-Syracusan faction saw the Athenians walking in the *agora*,
they slipped away in fear. The Catanian assembly now voted to
make an alliance with Athens and invited the Athenians to bring
their entire force from Rhegium to Catana. With this the Athenians acquired a base suitable for an attack on Syracuse or for

---

[46]6.41.

[47]For an appreciation of Syracuse's relations with the Sicels see Freeman,
History of Sicily III, 139 and n. 2.

[48]6.45.

conducting the kind of diplomatic warfare envisioned by Alcibiades.[49]

At Catana the Athenians received two reports, one good and one bad, but both, as it turned out, false. They were told that Camarina was ready to join them if they went there and that Syracuse was manning a fleet. It seems likely that both stories came from a pro-Athenian faction in Camarina which wanted to bring the Athenians to the city and perhaps seize power for itself. The Athenians were taken in and moved their entire army, going first to Syracuse. Finding no sign of a fleet there, they moved on to Camarina, where they were not admitted. To avoid making the day's sail a total waste, they landed in Syracusan territory and made some raids. During the Athenian retreat some straggling light-armed troops were cut up by Syracusan cavalry, an omen for the future.[50]

Back in Catana the Athenians found the state trireme *Salaminia* waiting to bring Alcibiades and the others indicted for mutilating the Hermae or profaning the mysteries back to Athens to stand trial. The men of the *Salaminia* had orders to tread softly, for those who had sent them were afraid that the arrest of Alcibiades might cause trouble. They feared a mutiny in the great armada, especially among the Argives and Mantineans, who had a special relationship with Alcibiades. Perhaps if he had resisted there might have been some support for him. Plutarch, in fact, says that he could have caused a mutiny had he wanted to.[51] Possibly, as he says, the men were dispirited at Alcibiades' departure and troubled by the realization that the campaign would be drawn out under the leadership of Nicias, since Lamachus would have little influence. But on the other hand, most of the summer had passed in pursuit of Alcibiades' strategy under his own leadership and there was little to show for it. Naxos and Catana had been won to the alliance, but the

[49]6.51. Polyaenus (1.40.4) depicts the Athenian break-in as part of the plan of Alcibiades. Freeman (*History of Sicily* III, 152) understood the value of Catana to the Athenians well: "The Athenians had now a station much nearer to Syracuse than Rhegion or even than Naxos, a station from which the long hill of Syracuse may be clearly seen."

[50]6.52.

[51]Plut. *Alc.* 21.6.

more important cities of Rhegium and Messina had not, and lesser cities in both Italy and Sicily had shut their gates to the Athenians. Nothing had been done for Segesta or Leontini, nor had any important action been taken against the main enemy, Syracuse. Alcibiades' popularity with the troops may already have waned when the *Salaminia* came for him; certainly we have no evidence of any complaint from the army when he was taken away.

Alcibiades himself went quietly, agreeing to follow the *Salaminia* back to Athens in his own ship along with the other accused.[52] He knew of the excited condition of the Athenians at the time of his departure from Athens, and he probably learned of all that had happened in the interim from the men on the *Salaminia*.[53] He seems to have decided at once not to return for trial and certain condemnation but to escape. He followed the *Salaminia* as far as Thurii, where he abandoned his ship and disappeared. The *Salaminia*'s crew hunted for him in vain, then gave up and sailed home, and soon thereafter Alcibiades sailed over to the Peloponnesus. When he failed to appear in Athens, the indictment brought by Thessalus went forward, and Alcibiades was convicted by default.[54] He and the others recalled were condemned to death, their property was confiscated, their names were enscribed on a stele of disgrace erected on the Acropolis, and a reward of a talent was promised to anyone killing any of them.[55] A further decree ordered that Alcibiades' name, and presumably the names of the others, be cursed by the Eleusinian priests.[56] With Alcibiades thus convicted, condemned, disinherited, and accursed, his enemies must have

---

[52]6.61.5.

[53]Diodorus (13.5.2) tells us that Alcibiades ἀκούσας τῶν πρέσβεων τὰ δόξαντα τῷ δήμῳ ... ἐξέπλευσεν. It does not stretch τὰ δόξαντα too far to think it includes more than merely the wording of the decree recalling the accused.

[54]6.61.5-7.

[55]For the conviction by default and condemnation see 6.61.7; Plut. *Alc.* 22.4; Diod. 135.4. Philochorus (*FGrH* 328, frg. 134) tells us about the stele, the confiscations, and the reward. For further references to the stele see Hatzfeld, *Alcibiade*, 204, n. 1.

[56]Plutarch (*Alc.* 22.4) applies the command to all the priests and priestesses in one place, but his later reference to the Eleusinian priests only (*Alc.* 33.3) is probably more accurate.

thought that they were rid of him, but when word of the death penalty that had been passed against him reached Alcibiades, he announced, "I will show them I am alive."[57]

With Alcibiades out of the way Nicias became the de facto commander of the expedition.[58] He appears to have tried to return to his own strategy, although the best psychological moment for it had passed after the receipt of the bad news at Rhegium. Since that time the Athenians had spent time, money, and some lives on the Sicilian campaign. The troops would probably have complained if asked to return without achieving anything important, and almost certainly the Athenian assembly would have taken a dim view of the general in charge. Still, Nicias sailed with the entire armada toward Segesta and Selinus, "wanting to know if the Segestans would pay the money and also to investigate the state of affairs at Selinus and to learn what differences they had with the Segestans."[59]

This led him to sail from Catana north through the Straits of Messina and to coast along the northern shore of Sicily toward its western tip, "as far as possible from the Syracusan enemy," as Plutarch says.[60] The armada tried to put in at Himera, the only Greek city in the region, but was turned away. Sailing past the Carthaginian cities of Solous and Panormus, the Athenians attacked Hyccara, a town of native *Sicani* who were hostile to Segesta. The Segestan cavalry helped in the attack, and their city was given the town to keep. The Athenians enslaved the inhabitants, put them on ships, and sent them back to Catana. The main army, since their ships were occupied, marched inland through the Sicel territory ruled by Athens' friend Archonides on their way back to Catana. Nicias himself had gone directly to Segesta from Hyccara even before the siege was over. Thucydides tells us he went to collect the promised money and to transact unspecified "other business." It is hard to imagine what business he could have had in Segesta other than diplomacy. Presumably he wanted to find out the details of the quar-

[57]Plut. *Alc.* 22.2.
[58]Plut. *Nic.* 15.1-3.
[59]6.62.1.
[60]Plut. *Nic.* 15.3.

rel with Selinus and the prospects for settling it peacefully. The answers must have been completely discouraging, for at this point Nicias abandoned his own strategy. He never went to Selinus, but simply collected 30 talents from Segesta, presumably all there was, and rejoined his army at Catana. The Athenians sold their captives for the considerable sum of 120 talents, which more than made up for Segesta's default. By now the Athenians had approached almost every Greek city in Sicily. So far as we know they did not appeal to Gela or Acragas, probably because they knew it would be futile to try. The strategy of Alcibiades had also failed. All that was left was to turn to Athens' Sicel allies and ask for troops. The summer ended with a futile assault on the small town of Hybla Geleatis not far from Catana.[61]

The summer campaign of 415 must have been a great disappointment to the Athenians. Their allies had failed them in a number of ways, and they had been rejected by most of the Greek cities in the west. Although Alcibiades' strategy had been far from successful, his removal made the situation even worse. The expedition was left in the hands of a man who did not believe in its purposes and who no longer had a strategy of his own to achieve them. Plutarch probably did not exaggerate much when he described the situation: "Nicias, though theoretically one of two colleagues, held sole power. He did not stop sitting about, sailing around, and thinking things over until the vigorous hope of his men had grown feeble and the astonishment and fear that the first sight of his forces had imposed on the enemy had faded away."[62] In such a mood the Athenian forces had now to confront the main enemy at Syracuse.

---

[61]6.62; for the friendship of Archonides see 7.1.4.
[62]Plut. *Nic.* 14.4.

10. The First Attack on Syracuse

The only strategy left to the Athenians was that of Lamachus, but though its author was present, the real leader of the army was Nicias. Thucydides makes clear how much the delay in putting Lamachus' plan into operation had already cost the Athenians. The longer they delayed the attack on Syracuse, the more Syracusan courage revived. News that the Athenians had sailed away from Syracuse to the western end of the island and then failed to conquer it roused the Syracusans to contempt, and the excited mob demanded that their generals lead them in an attack against the Athenians at Catana. Syracusan cavalrymen rode up to the Athenians and insulted them by asking "have you come to settle here with us on someone else's land instead of resettling the Leontines on their own?"[1]

By now, however belatedly, Nicias knew that he must act. The problem was to transfer his forces to a good position near Syracuse. Landing from the sea against an armed opponent was impossible, and since the Syracusans had been forewarned, they would not be taken by surprise, as they might have been by an earlier attack. They might be expected to guard the several places in the Great Harbor where an unopposed landing could succeed. If, on the other hand, the Athenians marched overland against Syracuse, they would be discovered long before they neared the city. For an army of hoplites such premature detection would normally not be a great problem; in formation they had little to fear from anything but an equivalent hoplite force

[1] 6.63.

and if the Syracusans preferred to fight nearer to Catana than Syracuse, well and good. But the Athenians had many light-armed soldiers and a vast mob of bakers, masons, carpenters, and other camp followers who would be endangered by the unopposed Syracusan cavalry.

The Athenians, therefore, resorted to a stratagem. A man from Catana whom the Syracusans trusted was really, to use the jargon of modern espionage, a "double agent" working for the Athenians. They sent him to the Syracusan generals having coached him to tell the following story. He claimed to represent the remainder of the pro-Syracusan faction at Catana, a faction whose names the generals knew and which was in fact still loyal to Syracuse. He reported that these Catanians sympathetic to Syracuse had observed that the Athenians habitually spent the night within the city, leaving their armor and weapons outside.[2] He revealed that the Catanians would lock the unarmed Athenians within the gates of the city and set fire to their ships, "if the Syracusans would come with their entire army at dawn on a fixed day." After that it would be a simple thing for them to capture the whole Athenian army, for they would get help from many Catanians.[3]

We might expect that the Syracusan generals would have examined this gift closely before accepting it, but they were full of confidence and eager for an opportunity to act, particularly one as tempting as that offered by the Catanian spy. They did not even send to Catana to confirm his story, but immediately fixed a day for their march and began to ready their forces. The Syracusan generals were emboldened to leave their city and march their entire army to Catana because their allies from Selinus and elsewhere had arrived to assist them. The allies could defend Syracuse while her troops attacked the Athenian force. On the appointed day, the army of Syracuse marched northward toward Catana, almost forty miles away. They spent the first night near the Symaethus River, in Leontine territory but not far south of Catana (see Map 9). The Athenians, of course, were well informed about the Syracusans' movements long before the army

[2] 6.64.3. This seems the correct sense of ἀπὸ τῶν ὅπλων.
[3] 6.64.2-3.

reached its first encampment. At the right moment they loaded their forces, and those of the Sicels who had come to join them, on the ships. They sailed by night and made their way unseen into the Great Harbor of Syracuse.[4]

At dawn the Athenians were able to land at their leisure. They chose a beach, designated by Syracusan exiles who had come over to the Athenian side, south of the Anapus River and opposite the temple of Olympian Zeus whose remains "even today... dominate the skyline as one enters the Great Harbour from the sea or looks across from Ortygia."[5] (See Maps 10 and 11.) By now the Syracusans had learned that they had been

[4] 6.65.1-2.

[5] 6.65.3; Syracusan exiles 6.64.1. The quotation is from Dover (*HCT* IV, 480) from whom I have learned much about the topography of Syracuse and its environs. Thucydides may or may not have seen the Syracusan battlefields, but there appears to be no way to reconstruct the battles he describes which perfectly reconciles the topographic details that Thucydides gives with the topography now visible. In locating the relevant sites for the battle between the Athenians and Syracusans in the fall of 415, I follow the generally excellent account of Peter Green (*Armada from Athens*, 155–163). He differs from Dover chiefly by locating the Athenian landing and the battle south of the River Anapus instead of having the landing and the fighting occur on both sides of the river. Dover's major objection to having everything to the south of the Anapus is contained in a series of rhetorical questions: "If the Athenians landed south of the river... how did the Syracusans cross the river to fight them (the bridge was destroyed), why did the Syracusans fight with the barrier of the river between themselves and the city, and why is the river never mentioned in the course of the battle as an impediment either to the Syracusan retreat or the Athenian advance?" (483). To these questions Green supplies a simple answer (though he wrote before seeing Dover's work): the Anapus "is easily fordable, even in depths of winter. I found no difficulty doing so towards the end of December" (157 and n. 3). It would present even less of a barrier in October, about the time of the battle, before the autumn rains. Dover's second objection to locating the battlefield south of the river is that an Athenian army facing northwest or north, as it must have if it stood south of the river, could not have had a λίμνη (6.66.1) i.e., a lake or body of still water, on its right, for he believes that in antiquity such a lake stood just north of the mouth of the river. Dover cites a seventeenth-century observer who saw standing water "at the mouth of the Anapos in wet weather" but does not say on which bank it was or whether it was on both. Dover is inclined to reduce that observation to refer only to "the pools which are there now," again without saying on what side of the river those pools stand. Today there are salt pans south of the Anapus, and the water near the shore is shallow and reedy. It hardly matters, for λίμνη need not imply anything so grand as a lake but can mean merely a marsh, a swamp, or other wet land. The present condition of the land near the mouth of the river

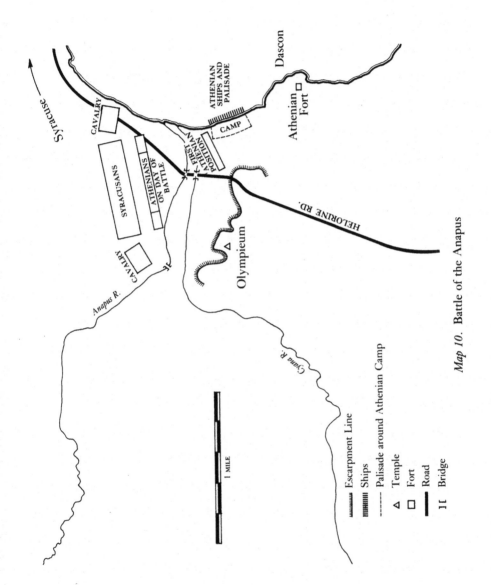

Map 10. Battle of the Anapus

Map 11. Siege of Syracuse

tricked, but the Athenians had plenty of time to make their preparations before the enemy returned to the city. They drew their ships onto the beach just south of the river and built a palisade to protect them.[6] On the coast at Dascon they constructed a fortification of stones and timbers to prevent a Syracusan landing and attack on their position from the south. To hamper access from the north, they destroyed the nearest bridge over the Anapus. The Athenians placed their army so as to be least vulnerable to the Syracusan cavalry. Their right wing was positioned near walls, houses, trees, and the swampy land near the mouth of the Anapus, while their left wing was protected by the sharply rising land leading up to the temple of Zeus.

While the Athenians made these preparations, the Syracusan allies in the city made no move to disturb them. The allies must

---

does not prevent us from believing that it was wet enough in October 415 to justify the title λίμνη and to deter attacks from hoplites or cavalry. None of the maps available to me is thoroughly satisfactory. I have combined features of Dover's Map 5 (opposite p. 481), Green's (184), and several of those in H.-P. Drögemüller's, *Syrakus Gymnasium* Beiheft VI (Heidelberg, 1969), especially #11 on p. 55, to construct my own (Map 10). Dover's map does not locate either the Athenian camp or fleet. I am not persuaded by his placement of the Athenian palisade (σταύρωμα) or fence (ἔρυμα), but for these points see below. Drögemüller makes no attempt to deal with this battle on his maps.

[6]6.66.2. Dover (*HCT* IV, 480–481) accepts the reading of the MSS: παρά τε τὰς ναῦς σταύρωμα ἔπηξαν καὶ ἐπὶ τῷ Δάσκωνι, ἔρυμά τε, ᾗ εὐεφοδώτατον ἦν τοῖς πολεμίοις ... ὤρθωσαν, translating it "They planted a palisade along by their ships and ἐπί Dascon, and erected a strong point where it was easiest for the enemy to attack them." He takes ἐπί to mean not "on" or "at" but "to protect" or "to neutralize," which leads him to place the palisade "between the spur of Caderini and the rising ground to the west in order to impede an enemy attack from the south." (See his Map 5, opposite p. 481.) This interpretation requires a strained sense of ἐπί and is inconsistent with παρά τε τὰς ναῦς σταύρωμα ἔπηξαν, for in no way could the palisade placement suggested by Dover be described as "along by their ships." (The problem is not apparent on Dover's map, for he does not locate the Athenian ships.) Krüger's amendment, ἔρυμά τι, adopted by Jones in the Oxford text, would make more sense, placing the palisade by the ships and the ἔρυμα, or stronghold, at Dascon, either on the promontory or on the beach to the south. But it is unnecessary to emend the text to get the required sense, as Mme. de Romilly has pointed out. She accepts the reading of the MSS but places no comma after Δάσκωνι, and translates the passage: "ils plantèrent une estacade le long de leurs vaisseaux; sur le Dascon, au point où le terrain était le plus ouvert à l'ennemi." As she rightly says, "the place of τε ... καί is, in Thucydides, free enough that we need not correct it." (*Thucydide Livres VI et VII*, 49 and n. 2).

have been completely surprised by the landing, and when they recovered they could see they were no match for the Athenian force. When the Syracusans finally arrived, their cavalry preceding their infantry, they gathered their forces and "drew near the Athenian camp," challenging the Athenians to fight. It is likely, however, that they did not cross the Anapus but instead waited for the Athenians to make the first move. The situation recalls the anecdote, possibly true, in which Plutarch reports Hermocrates encouraging the Syracusans by saying, "Nicias is ridiculous in using his generalship to avoid battle, as if he had not sailed to Sicily to fight a battle."[7] When the Athenians did not advance, the Syracusans withdrew and made camp for the night.[8]

The Athenians launched their attack the next morning. Nicias had arrayed the main army in a phalanx at the usual depth of eight, with the Argives and Mantineans on the right, the Athenians in the center, and the other allies on the left, where the danger from the cavalry was greatest.[9] This was only half the Athenian force, the rest being arranged three deep in a hollow square, within which stood the supply-carrying civilians. This square was placed in the rear, near the Athenian camp, as a reserve to support the front line wherever it might falter. Before moving forward Nicias addressed his troops, being careful to speak to each allied contingent as well as to the Athenians. Characteristically, he did not try to encourage false hopes but emphasized the negative, hoping that fear of the cost of losing would encourage them to fight well. He reminded them that although the Athenians and their allies were superior to the enemy in experience, skill, and generalship, the enemy was fighting in and for its homeland. If the Syracusans lost the battle they could simply retreat to safety behind the walls of their city. The Athenian army, on the other hand, must win, for if it lost, its soldiers would find escape difficult, particularly since the enemy could pursue with its large cavalry. Nicias concluded his

[7] Plut. *Nic.* 16.4.

[8] 6.66. I agree with Green in assuming that the bridge the Athenians destroyed was closer to the sea than another, further upstream, that probably led to the temple of Zeus (*Armada*, 158 and n. 4).

[9] Though we do not agree on every point, my debt to Green's account of the battle (*Armada*, 159-163) will be obvious.

THE FIRST ATTACK ON SYRACUSE

address with this not very encouraging exhortation: "Attack the enemy eagerly and with the thought that our present necessity and lack are more fearsome than our opponents."[10]

The Syracusans had not expected the Athenians to advance north across the river, especially since they had refused battle on the previous day. The Syracusan camp was so close to the city that some soldiers had even gone home for the night and had to turn back when the fight broke out, falling in wherever they could. "They did not expect the Athenians to attack first and were forced to defend themselves in haste." On this occasion and afterwards the Syracusans would show themselves to be brave and eager warriors, but in this first battle especially, their indiscipline, inexperience, and multiple leadership cost them dearly.[11] The Syracusans and their allies must have had about as many hoplites as the entire Athenian army, for they arranged their phalanx sixteen deep to face the forward army arrayed eight deep. Thus, the Athenians on the front line confronted a force with twice the weight of its own. In addition Syracuse's cavalry, including that of their allies, numbered about 1,500; the Athenians apparently had none.

The fighting began with inconclusive skirmishing between the light-armed troops. Then the sacrifices were made and the trumpets sounded for the main event, the clash of the phalanxes. After crossing the river the Athenian line must have taken up a position at an angle to it, so that its left wing was protected by the river bed.[12] Presumably the right was protected by marshy land, still nearer the river mouth. That appears to be the only explanation of the Syracusan cavalry's failure to outflank the Athenians and attack them from behind, for the conflict between the hoplites went on for a long time.[13] The Athenian slingers, archers, and stone-throwers, after their earlier exercise, must have taken up positions on the wings where, assisted by the marshy ground and the river, they could fight off the enemy

[10]6.68.4.
[11]6.69.
[12]See Map 10.
[13]6.70.1: ἐπὶ πολὺ ἀντεῖχον ἀλλήλοις. The other accounts I have seen do not seem to ask why the Syracusan cavalry played no part in the battle itself.

cavalry. In spite of the depth of the Syracusan phalanx and the individual bravery of its soldiers, the superior discipline and experience of the Athenians and their allies carried the day. During the fighting a severe rainstorm broke, accompanied by thunder and lightning. This terrified the Syracusans who, never having fought before, naturally found fighting in a thunderstorm uncomfortable and frightening; they probably also thought the storm an evil omen.[14] The experienced Athenians, on the other hand, had seen this sort of thing before and took it in stride. The storm probably helped break the Syracusan spirit; in any case, the Argives drove the enemy left wing back and the Athenians repulsed the center. Soon the enemy line broke, and the Syracusans and their allies fled.

This was a critical moment for the Athenian cause. If they had been able to pursue the helpless enemy effectively, they might have been able to inflict casualties heavy enough to discourage the Syracusans from continuing the war, or at least sufficient to render defense against an Athenian siege difficult, if not impossible. But an armed hoplite phalanx was too encumbered to sustain the rapid pursuit of individual soldiers who had dropped their burdensome shields and thus enjoyed a great advantage in speed. Effective pursuit generally required cavalry, and the Athenians had none. On the contrary, the Syracusan cavalry, not having played an important part in the battle, was intact and helped check the pursuit even more quickly than would otherwise have been possible.[15] The Syracusans were able to regroup on the Helorine Road and send a garrison to the Olympieum to protect the treasures in the temple of Zeus before retiring to the city. The Athenians could do nothing but set up a trophy of victory on the battlefield. The next day they gave back the bodies of the 260 dead to the Syracusans; the Athenians and their allies had lost 50 of their own. After collecting the spoils of victory, the Athenians sailed back to their base at Catana.[16]

Thucydides gives us the reasons for the Athenian withdrawal, and they are clearly those set forth by Nicias: "It was winter, and

[14]See Dover, *HCT* IV, 345.
[15]6.70.3.
[16]6.70-71.1.

it did not yet seem possible to carry on the war from where they were. First they must send to Athens for cavalry and recruit some from their allies in Sicily so that they would not be completely dominated by the enemy cavalry. At the same time they must gather money from Sicily and get some from Athens, as well. Also, they should bring over to their side some of the cities that they expected would be more likely to obey them after the battle; finally, they should prepare grain and whatever else they might need for an attack on Syracuse the next spring."[17]

From antiquity to modern times Nicias has been blamed for failing to exploit his victory immediately. Only a few months after the battle, Aristophanes' comedy *The Birds* was performed in Athens, and one of the characters pronounced the following lines:

> by Zeus, there is no more time
> For drowsiness and Nicias-delays.

Although Nicias must long have had the reputation for caution and hesitation, it seems probable that the line had special point after the news reached Athens of Nicias' withdrawal from Syracuse.[18] Demosthenes, who came to reinforce Nicias in 413, was sharply critical of his delay, as was Thucydides himself: "Demosthenes believed that he must not fall back into the same difficulties that Nicias had experienced. For Nicias was an object of terror when he first arrived, but when he failed to attack Syracuse immediately and spent the winter in Catana he came to be despised, and Gylippus anticipated him by coming with an army from the Peloponnesus. The Syracusans would not even have sent for this army if he had attacked immediately, for they would have thought their own forces sufficient and would not have learned they were inadequate until they were already walled in. Even, therefore, if they had then sent for help, it would

[17]6.71.2.
[18]The lines are 639-640: καὶ μὴν μὰ τὸν Δί οὐχὶ νυστάζειν ἔτι
ὥρα ὁτὶν ἡμῖν οὐδὲ μελλονικιᾶν
μελλονικιᾶν is a pun which also means "delaying victory." *The Birds* was performed at the Great Dionysia of the City in Elaphobolion (probably March) 414.

no longer have had the same effect."[19] Plutarch also commented on Nicias' delay after his victory at Syracuse: "Everyone blamed Nicias for this, since by calculating too carefully and delaying and being overly cautious he destroyed the opportunity for action. After he was in action no one could find fault with the man, for once in motion he was energetic and effective, but in getting up nerve to act, he was hesitant and timid."[20]

The shrewdest modern analysts of the battle and its consequences are Grote and Busolt. The former argues that "the victory was barren; we may even say, positively mischievous, since it imparted a momentary stimulus which served as an excuse to Nicias for the three months of total inaction which followed, and since it neither weakened nor humiliated the Syracusans, but gave them a salutary lesson which they turned to account while Nicias was in his winter quarters."[21] Busolt's evaluation also deserves quotation:

After the defeat a depressed mood reigned in Syracuse. Scarcely any resistance would have been met at the beginning of the siege if the camp had been moved to a location closer to the city. With the help of entrenchments, ground would certainly have been gained before the arrival of the cavalry, work could have been done on the siege walls, and in this way the enemy could have been kept in turmoil. However that may be, in fact, in the operations of the next summer the Athenian cavalry took an effective part in the fighting only once. The tactical victory was not exploited, and the capably begun operation ended in a complete strategic failure. The Athenians had not traveled to Syracuse

[19]7.42.3. G. Donini (*Hermes* XCII [1964], 116-119) has shown that Thucydides endorses Demosthenes' opinion, and Dover (*HCT* IV, 419-421) and Westlake (*Individuals in Thucydides* [Cambridge, 1968], 182, n. 1) agree with him. E. C. Kopff (*GRBS* XVII [1976], 23-30) has argued that the quoted passage is by the Sicilian historian Philistus and was slipped into the text by someone who found it written in the margin by a learned reader. His argument has been controverted by M. W. Dickie (*GRBS* XVII [1976], 217-219). Kopff's rebuttal (*GRBS* XVII [1976], 220-221) is not persuasive. The main reason for doubting Thucydidean authorship of the passage in question is that it appears to contradict the Thucydidean narrative of events. If that were a sufficient criterion, we should have to delete significant portions of Thucydides' *History*.

[20]Plut. *Nic.* 16.8.

[21]Grote, VII, 223.

for the purpose of landing, striking, and withdrawing on the third day.[22]

Some modern scholars have defended Nicias' caution, pointing out that winter was coming and that the Athenians would have difficulty transporting supplies to the camp near Syracuse during the winter.[23] On the other hand, the mild Sicilian winter would probably have been a better time to conduct a siege than the hot summer that brought with it the threat of malaria from the nearby marshes.[24] As to the supply problem, that would always exist, whenever the Athenians began their siege. Still, the acquisition of food and other supplies did require money, and the protection of men and supplies would be aided by the arrival of Athenian cavalry. Indeed, this lack of the cavalry is the best explanation and defense of Nicias' judgment.

The significance of the Syracusan cavalry for defense against a siege has been greatly underestimated. The Athenian army could camp on the shores of the Great Harbor all winter, so long as it maintained its defensive position. Any detachments sent out to dig trenches or build encircling walls, however, would be vulnerable to attack by the Syracusan cavalry, and this threat would remain so long as the Athenians had no cavalry of their own. When the Athenians did begin their siege of Syracuse the following spring, the Syracusan cavalry rode out to prevent them from bringing stones and building the wall. By then, however, the Athenians had a cavalry of their own which drove off the Syracusan horsemen.[25] Without such help the Athenian masons

---

[22]Busolt, *GG* III:2, 1323, my translation.

[23]Eduard Meyer (*GdA* IV, 518) says "just as little was it possible to remain in that position near the Olympieum throughout the winter months without being reduced to serious distress." Adolf Holm (*Geschichte Siziliens im Alterthum* II, 27) makes the point that the autumn was not the time to begin a siege of Syracuse. On the incorrect assumption that the battle was fought south of the Anapus River and that the river was a significant barrier, Holm further justifies the Athenian withdrawal. If Holm's assumption were correct, Nicias could be blamed for having chosen such a bad place to fight.

[24]As Grote, VII, 222, and Busolt, *GG* III:2, 1323, point out.

[25]6.98.3.

would have been at the enemy's mercy, as would Nicias' men had they tried to encircle Syracuse during the winter of 415/14.

If the matter is viewed from a purely material and military point of view, Nicias, without cavalry and short of money, was probably right to withdraw from Syracuse over the winter. Demosthenes, however, based his criticism, which Thucydides supported, on psychological considerations. He believed that the Syracusans would overestimate their capacity, be defeated by the Athenians in battle, and find their city shut in by a wall before they had sent for help. At that point, Demosthenes presumed, they would surrender, and even if they did send for help so late, it would be to no avail once the city was walled in. But such estimates of human reaction are never certain. So talented a man as Pericles had planned his strategy to achieve the psychological exhaustion of the enemy and been badly disappointed.[26] Even if the psychological calculations of Demosthenes were correct, we must doubt whether the Athenians could ever have built a wall of circumvallation without the protection of cavalry, and so long as such a wall was not in place the Syracusans could always send for help, get it, and make good use of it.

It is possible to interpret the criticism of Demosthenes and Thucydides in a different way, to assume that they are criticizing the Athenian generals for choosing Alcibiades's strategy instead of Lamachus' and for not attacking Syracuse immediately in the summer of 415.[27] Such an interpretation is strained and unlikely, but even if it were correct the criticism would not be justified. To be sure, Lamachus' plan would have had a better chance of success than an attempt to begin a siege in the autumn of 415 because the psychological situation would have been even better. Even then, however, victory was not guaranteed if the Syracusans kept their nerve. Without cavalry the Athenians could no more have built the wall in the summer than in the autumn. Once the Athenians arrived in the west without cavalry and decided to attack Syracuse only one strategy was available: they must force the Syracusans into a battle, defeat them, and hope for a surrender. Failing that, they had no choice but to

[26]See Kagan, *Archidamian War*, 27–42 and 352–362.
[27]See the discussion of Dover, *HCT* IV, 419–421.

withdraw to winter quarters and wait for cavalry. Given the resources available to him, Nicias' generalship was outstanding. He evaluated the situation correctly, chose the correct plan, and executed it with skill verging on brilliance. His use of espionage to create a diversion and allow an unopposed landing was splendid. His understanding of the terrain and his disposition of his troops both before and during the battle were outstanding. His ability to surprise the enemy and bring on the battle on the most favorable terms was masterful. There is nothing to blame in Nicias as a tactician.

None of this, however, absolves him from making a strategic error that was probably the main cause of the expedition's failure. The key to the capture of Syracuse, as we have seen, was the presence of Athenian cavalry. If the Athenian army had been supported by cavalry when it had first arrived before Syracuse, whether in summer or fall, then, as Thucydides implies, the Syracusans would either have surrendered or been starved out; no outside help could have saved them. Nor have we any reason to doubt that Nicias would have begun such a siege immediately after his victory if cavalry had been available, for his vigor and skill in the conduct of the battle show that he had accepted the necessity of an attack on Syracuse. Indeed, Nicias himself had foreseen the need for cavalry, telling the Athenian assembly: "The thing in which the Syracusans most surpass us is in their possession of many horses and their use of grain that is home-grown and not imported."[28] Yet later in the same debate, when asked to name what forces the Athenians should vote for the expedition, Nicias had asked for ships, hoplites, bowmen, and slingers, but not for cavalry.[29]

On that occasion, of course, Nicias had been taken by surprise and may be excused for the omission, in spite of his own emphasis on the importance of cavalry. But there was a considerable time between that meeting and the departure of the expedition and, in fact, the assembly met a number of times in the interim.[30] There were many opportunities for Nicias to request

[28] 6.20.4.
[29] 6.25.
[30] 6.27.29; And. De Myst. 11.

cavalrymen and no chance that he would be refused, but he made no such request. As late as the council at Rhegium, when it should have been clear that a siege of Syracuse was likely, there was still time to send home for horsemen. In any case, there was no point in landing near Syracuse and forcing a battle without the cavalry needed to follow up victory. By that time, however, pressure from his troops was probably forcing Nicias to act. He could only hope that a victory would break the nerve of the Syracusans; if that failed, he would have to withdraw and try again the next spring. Nicias' great failure, therefore, was not in wasting time either in the summer of 415 or the winter of 415/14, but in failing to provide cavalry for the Athenians whenever they chose to fight and besiege Syracuse. It is possible to explain this failure as an error in judgment, and no more. But Nicias showed on a number of occasions that he was a practiced and careful general, unlikely to make such a mistake and least likely to forget an arm of warfare in which he knew the enemy was significantly superior. We may speculate that the oversight was more a failure of purpose than of judgment, that it resulted, at least in part, from his original disinclination for the expedition, from his hope that it would never be necessary to fight at all.

The Athenians did not intend to waste the winter of 415/14. They could not move against Syracuse until the arrival of cavalrymen, so they sent a trireme to Athens to request money and cavalry for the spring campaign. They could gather supplies and assistance from their allies in Sicily and by diplomacy and other means win over new allies. Immediately after reaching their base at Catana, the Athenians sailed to Messina, expecting that treason would deliver it to them. Messina was badly rent by faction, and there was a plot by the pro-Athenian group to turn the city over to Athens. There is reason to think that with the arrival of the Athenian force in the harbor of the city the plot would have succeeded, but now the Athenians began to pay the price for their condemnation of Alcibiades. Even as he dutifully stepped aboard his ship, ostensibly to return to Athens for trial, he was planning to flee and to get revenge on the Athenians, for on the way he stopped at Messina and revealed the plot to the pro-Syracusan faction. By the time the Athenians arrived civil war had broken out; the friends of Syracuse were in arms, had killed the conspirators, and were strong enough to bar the Athenians from the city. Though they stayed for thirteen days, the Athenians accomplished nothing and were compelled to retire by storms and a shortage of supplies. They withdrew to a new base at Naxos for the winter, building docks for their ships and a stockade to protect them and the camp.[31]

Meanwhile, the Syracusans were making use of the respite provided by the Athenian withdrawal. Hermocrates, whose political fortunes must have risen when his warning had proven to be true, addressed the Syracusan assembly. Although he has already appeared prominently in the *History*, Thucydides provides him with an introduction at this point, praising him in almost Periclean terms as "a man second to none in general intelligence" and as one who had shown himself "conspicuously competent in war because of his experience and courage."[32] Certainly, his speech to the Syracusans is characteristically Periclean. Finding them dispirited and lacking in confidence because of their recent defeat, he encouraged them and tried to lift their spirits. Their defeat, he told them, was not caused by any fundamental inferiority, but by inexperience, lack of discipline, and divided leadership. He urged them to provide arms to those below the hoplite census in order to increase the size of the hoplite army, to impose compulsory training on the army, and to select only a few generals in place of the fifteen who currently shared the command. These generals should be given full powers and be allowed to make decisions without consulting the assembly; indeed, the assembly should confirm their right to do so with an oath. This would provide not only a more effective leadership but also better protection for the secrecy of plans.[33]

The special powers that Hermocrates was asking for the generals would significantly curtail the Syracusan democracy, but Syracuse was in serious danger, and desperate measures seemed appropriate. The assembly voted everything that Hermocrates asked, choosing three generals: Heracleides son of Lysimachus,

[31] 6.74.
[32] 6.72.2.
[33] 6.72.3-5.

Sicanus son of Execestus, and Hermocrates himself. At the same time the assembly took the important step of sending ambassadors to Corinth and Sparta to ask for help. The Syracusans made two requests of the Spartans: send a force to help them defend Syracuse, and resume vigorous warfare in mainland Greece, thereby compelling the Athenians to abandon Sicily or, at least, reducing their capacity to reinforce the expedition already there.[34]

The Syracusans also took a number of material actions to improve their defenses. The most important of these was the extension of the city wall, which not only increased the enclosed area controlled by the Syracusans but also added considerably to the length of the wall of circumvallation that the Athenians must build if they laid siege to the city. The new wall jutted out to the west to include the suburban area called Temenites, then led east and north across the plateau of Epipolae, which overlooked the city, to a place called Trogilus.[35] They also placed garrisons at Megara Hyblaea and the Olympieum and built palisades at likely landing places along the coast. Knowing that the Athenians were at Naxos, they took the offensive and made a raid on the Athenian camp at Catana, burning the huts and ravaging the countryside.[36]

Next, the Syracusans had to use their diplomatic skills. They

[34] 6.73.
[35] 6.75.1. See Map 11. The topography of Syracuse and its environs and its relationship to the account of Thucydides has long been a controversial subject. Among the studies I have found most useful are those of K. Fabricius, *Das Antike Syrakus, Klio* Beiheft XXXII (Leipzig, 1932); H.-P. Drögemüller, *Syrakus*; P. Green, *Armada*, 182-186 and passim; and Dover, *HCT* IV, 466-484. It is not possible to locate Trogilus, and therefore the direction of the wall, with certainty. I have followed Dover (471-475) and most scholars in placing it on the coast, across Epipolae, almost due north of the city. Drögemüller (71-96) places it, not as a point, but as the eastern coastline from just north of the city wall to the inlet Piccolo Seno (see his Map 18, p. 91), so that the new wall, according to him, ran eastward to the water. Green (194-196), who appears not to have seen Drögemüller's work, arrived independently at the same conclusion. The arguments for the former position are made best by Dover. He supports it in his review of Drögemüller (*Phoenix* XXV [1971], 282-285). See also the review by Westlake in *CR* XXI (1971), 97-99, and Dover's review of Green in *Phoenix* XXVI (1972), 297-300.
[36] 6.75.1-2.

learned that the Athenians were trying to bring Camarina over to their side, for Camarina, though a Dorian city, had been allied with Athens and Leontini against Syracuse in the time of Laches in 427.[37] In 415 Camarina was an ally of Syracuse, but the Syracusans had reason to be suspicious of its loyalty, for since the Athenian victory at the Anapus, Camarina had been slow and reluctant in sending assistance to Syracuse. The Syracusans, therefore, sent their ablest diplomat, Hermocrates, to speak to the assembly at Camarina.[38]

Hermocrates used the fullest possible range of arguments to urge resistance to Athens. His first assertion was that the Athenians had not come, as they proclaimed, to restore the Leontines to their land and to aid Segesta against Selinus, but to destroy Syracuse and conquer Sicily. This is interesting evidence that whatever their true intentions, the Athenians were careful to adhere publicly to the officially limited purposes of the expedition. Nor should anyone think, said Hermocrates, that they had come to aid their kinsmen (as Chalcidians, Ionians, and Athenians were thought to be), for they had shown no compunction about enslaving the original Chalcidians on Euboea and all the Ionians in their empire. The Dorian cities of Sicily were not, he pointed out, slavish Ionians, always serving some master, but free men who should join together against the common enemy. Hermocrates knew, of course, that many Sicilians were jealous of Syracusan power and feared his city's domination more than rule by Athens. To counter these fears he emphasized the evil designs of the Athenians and stressed how much more difficult it would be to resist them once Syracuse had been defeated.

The old alliance between Athens and Camarina, apparently still thought to be morally binding, also required attention. Hermocrates implied that it was a purely defensive alliance, effective only when one of the signatories was attacked and therefore not relevant to the Athenian attack on Syracuse. In fact, the treaty was a *symmachia*, a full offensive and defensive alliance. Still, Hermocrates pointed out that even the Rhegians, who like the Leontines were Chalcidians, had refused to honor their *sym-*

[37] 3.86.2.
[38] 6.75.3-4.

machia with Athens. All previous commitments, he implied, had been cancelled by the appearance in Sicily of an Athenian force so large that it could be intended only for the subjugation of the island. If they would only unite, however, the Sicilians had no reason to fear even so great an armament. The Peloponnesians would surely send help, and with it a united Dorian Sicily could defeat the Athenians and win freedom and glory.[39]

The Athenian spokesman at Camarina was neither Nicias nor Lamachus but Euphemus, a man of whom we know nothing. The choice, however, was not a bad one, for he made a case that was as good as possible in the circumstances. Far from avoiding the argument of kinship, he made direct use of it. There was indeed, he conceded, a traditional hostility between Dorians and Ionians. That is why the Athenians had built their empire after the Persian War—to acquire the power to rid themselves of the leadership and domination of the Dorian Spartans. The Athenian Empire, moreover, was justified because the Ionians who were its subjects had fought with the Persians, while the Athenians had provided the material and psychological forces that had defeated the Persians and freed the Ionians from their yoke. But, Euphemus continued, fear and the consequent desire for security were the main motives that had led the Athenians to acquire their empire. Those same motives now required their presence in Sicily. They feared that Syracuse would subjugate its neighbors, dominate Sicily, and use the accumulated power to aid its Dorian kinsmen, the Spartans, in a renewed war against Athens. Euphemus argued that the men of Camarina should have the same fear, for if they supported Syracuse or remained neutral and the Athenians had to leave Sicily without achieving their purpose, Syracuse would surely subjugate Camarina and the other Greek cities of Sicily.

Euphemus was well aware of the various fears and prejudices that the other Greeks felt toward Athens, and he tried to meet these concerns, some patent and some unspoken. To the charge that the disproportionate size of the expedition indicated that Athens had come not to defend its allies but to conquer the island, he responded with the argument Nicias had used back in

[39]6.76-80.

Athens in attempting to prevent the entire undertaking. The Athenians, he said, could not maintain themselves in Sicily without allies such as Camarina, and even if the Athenians should behave badly and conquer Sicily, "they would be unable to hold onto it because of the length of the voyage and their inability to guard large cities equipped with forces appropriate to mainlanders (i.e., hoplites and cavalry)."[40] The Syracusans, because of their proximity, were the real threat, and if the Athenians were allowed to leave the island without reducing Syracuse, Camarina would never again have so good an opportunity to assure its freedom.

Euphemus knew that the enemies of Athens played on the fear that many felt of the Athenian character, of the extraordinary vitality and activity it displayed. The Corinthians had manipulated such fears in trying to persuade the Spartans to fight Athens in 432, claiming that it was the Athenians' nature "neither to enjoy peace themselves nor to allow it to other men."[41] Euphemus responded to this continuing fear that the Athenians were *polypragmones*, busybodies, troublemakers, ceaselessly ambitious, with unappeasable appetites. He did so, moreover, without denying that Athens deserved the title, if not its evil connotations. "We are compelled to involve ourselves in many things (*polla prassein*)[42] because we have many things to protect." He argued that in fact the Athenians had come to Sicily at the request of allies seeking protection. The men of Camarina should neither judge the Athenians nor try to moderate their busy and active character, for the deserved Athenian reputation for widespread interests and activity was a source of protection to the weak and a deterrent to those stronger powers who would take advantage of their weakness. Euphemus asked the Camarinans to avail themselves of the security that the Athenian alliance now offered them and to join in the war against Syracuse, thus ridding themselves of a permanently dangerous enemy.[43]

[40]6.86.3.
[41]1.70.9.
[42]6.87.2. The text reads πολλὰ δ᾽ ἀναγκάζεσθαι πράσσειν. πολλὰ πράσσειν is equivalent to πολυπραγμοσύνη, and Euphemus uses that word in the next sentence.
[43]6.82-87.

Euphemus' speech was, of course, tendentious and suited to the occasion. We should hardly expect him to say anything about conquering Sicily even if that were his intention. Still, what he said was both reasonable and not entirely implausible. The Athenians, after all, had come to Sicily once before at the request of their allies and had returned home without enslaving the island. One might argue that the Athenians' failure to fulfill even the limited goals of helping their allies and checking Syracusan expansion had necessitated the dispatch of much larger forces and that their presence did not by itself prove evil intent. The Camarinans, in fact, were always at odds with Syracuse and were more afraid of the Syracusans, because of their proximity, than of the Athenians. They had sent as little help to Syracuse as possible for the battle at the Anapus, fearing that the Syracusans would win. Thucydides tells us that they felt kindly toward the Athenians, "except in so far as they thought they would enslave Sicily."[44] This was still another occasion when the augmentation of the Athenian expedition brought about by Nicias worked against the original strategy envisioned by Alcibiades. Camarina found it easier to believe the worst about Athenian intentions and chose to follow the path of greatest safety. It would continue to give aid to Syracuse, but as little as possible, so as to avoid offending Athens, for the Athenian victory at the Anapus had impressed the Camarinans. Their formal response was that since they were allied to both states they would give aid to neither for the time being.[45]

Athenian diplomacy now turned to the non-Greek Sicels. Those who lived in the east coastal plains were mostly subjects of Syracuse, and few of them had revolted, but the Sicels who lived in the hill country of the interior were independent, and most of them came over to the Athenians, bringing food and money. As for those who refused, the Athenians sent an army to force them into an alliance, and the Syracusans responded by dispatching garrisons to the threatened Sicel towns. Since Catana was better situated than Naxos for contact with the Sicels, the Athenians

[44]6.88.1.

moved their base back to the former location, rebuilt their camp, and spent the rest of the winter there. From Catana they continued to send messengers to different Sicel tribes, and to Segesta they sent asking for horses. They also gathered materials for the siegeworks that they would build in the spring.[46]

Athenian diplomacy went even further afield. A trireme was sent to Carthage seeking friendship and, if possible, material aid. Another was sent to the Etruscan cities, some of whom volunteered to join the Athenians in the war.[47] The Etruscans were old enemies of Syracuse and had fought a war at sea against it at least as recently as 453; their continued hostility is proved by the fact that they sent ships to help the Athenians against Syracuse in 413.[48] The Athenian request for aid from Carthage is especially interesting. Thucydides tells us that Alcibiades aimed to conquer Carthage, as well as Sicily. Hermocrates told the Syracusans that Carthage lived in fear of an attack from Athens, and Alicibiades himself told the Spartans that the goals of the Athenian expedition to Sicily included the conquest of the Carthaginian empire and Carthage itself.[49] We have seen that such an intention and such goals were never part of the public discussion in Athens, much less part of any of the formal decrees providing the expedition with its orders. If the Carthaginians were afraid of an Athenian attack, it is surprising that the Athenians were either so bold or so naïve as to send a request for help, and we may assume that the talk of Carthaginian fear is the rhetorical invention of Hermocrates. The mission to Carthage may, of course, have been an innovation of Nicias', but since he and Lamachus seem to have been pursuing the strategy of Alcibiades in most other respects, it is likely that he had expected to use his diplomatic talents to enlist help from Carthage as part of his plan. If true, that would contradict the tradition that had

[46]6.88.2.

[46]6.88.3-6.

[47]6.88.6.

[48]For the earlier quarrel see Diod. 11.88.4. For the continuing hostility and the Etruscan assistance see 7.57.11.

[49]Thucydides: 6.15.2; Hermocrates: 6.34.2; Alcibiades: 6.90.2.

Alcibiades aiming at the conquest of Carthage, but we have seen and will see further that there is reason to doubt that tradition.[50]

The Syracusan envoys, meanwhile, made their way along the Italian coast, urging the Greek cities there to resist the Athenians. They reached Corinth and appealed for help to Syracuse's mother city. The Corinthians not only voted help eagerly and immediately but also sent their own ambassadors to support the Syracusans in their request for Spartan assistance. At Sparta they found another advocate of their cause, Alcibiades, who had come over to the Peloponnesus from Italy with his fellow fugitives. He had sailed from Thurii in a merchant ship and landed at Cyllene in Elis.[51] Elis was part of the diplomatic network Alcibiades had woven before the battle of Mantinea; presumably it was still friendly to Alcibiades and hostile to Sparta.[52] He was hesitant to go to Sparta without an invitation, for he expected hostility because of his part in bringing on the battle of Mantinea. But the Spartans sent for him and offered a safe conduct. The Spartan government, i.e., the ephors, the kings and the council of elders, were disposed toward a weak response to the war in Sicily: they would send an embassy to try to prevent Syracuse from yielding to Athens, but they were not inclined to send any aid.[53] The speakers' task was to incite the Spartan

---

[50]Max Treu (*Historia* III [1954/55], 41–57) has argued that there are two conflicting traditions in the Thucydidean account of Alcibiades' plans for Carthage. One, which is dominant, has him aiming at the conquest of Carthage, and the other has him seeking Carthaginian alliance in a vast diplomatic combination. Treu believes the latter is correct. He tries to draw some support from B. D. Meritt's reconstruction of an inscription (*GHI*, #92, 280–281) which Meritt believes mandates "a mission . . . sent from Athens in 406 B.C. to consult with the Carthaginian generals Hannibal and Himilkon in Sicily" (*Athenian Studies Presented to William Scott Ferguson*, HSCP, Suppl. I [Cambridge, Mass., 1940], 247–253). Unfortunately, the inscription is too fragmentary to bear the weight of any interpretation.

[51]6.88.79. I accept Thucydides' version of Alcibiades' itinerary. For discussion of other ancient accounts of his route see Grote, VII, 235, n. 2.; Busolt, GG III:2, 1327, n. 3; and Hatzfeld, *Alcibiade* 207, n. 2.

[52]Dover, *HCT* IV, 360–361.

[53]6.88.10. The words I have rendered as "the Spartan government" are τῶν τε ἐφόρων καὶ τῶν ἐν τέλει ὄντων. Οἱ ἐν τέλει implies different individuals and groups in different states, depending on their constitutions. My list of those involved here is the same as that of Dover (*HCT* IV, 361).

assembly to take stronger action. Perhaps the Spartan invitation to Alcibiades came from those who were eager to renew the war and to send significant assistance to Syracuse. They must have known that he had turned on his native city and was seeking revenge. He could be expected to lend his eloquence to the cause of the struggle against Athens and even to provide valuable information on how to conduct it successfully.

The Syracusan and Corinthian envoys addressed the Spartans, but Thucydides reports only the speech of Alcibiades. The renegade Athenian had several goals as he spoke in the Spartan assembly, but the immediate problem was his own personal security. The Greek world was almost completely divided into two opposed camps, and even neutrals were unlikely for long to harbor fugitives sought by one or another of the leading powers. Alcibiades was vulnerable wherever Athenian power could reach, and if the Spartans proved to be hostile or indifferent, he would have no sanctuary west of the Persian Empire. He needed, therefore, to persuade the Spartans to give him shelter. Plutarch tells us of Alcibiades' remarkable adaptability to Spartan ways. He engaged in vigorous bodily exercise, took cold baths, let his hair grow long in the Spartan manner, and ate the coarse bread and the black porridge of the Spartan mess,[54] but it was inconceivable that he intended to spend his life in Sparta as an ordinary citizen. Had he stayed he would most likely have tried to achieve a high and respected position and to undertake actions equal to his ambition and self-esteem. Therefore, as he addressed the Spartans, Alcibiades must have aimed to impress them with his own talents and capacities. Another purpose was either to avenge himself on the Athenians or to prove himself so dangerous that they might take him back on his own terms. Certainly vindication and a triumphant return to Athens were his ultimate goals, but first he must convince the Spartans to become involved in Sicily and to resume the war in Greece.

The Spartans, however, had many reasons to mistrust and dislike Alcibiades. He had risen to power supported by the democratic mob at Athens and had become the leader of the opposi-

[54]Plut. Alc. 23.3-4.

tion to Sparta's friend Nicias, the author and preserver of peace. He had championed the Peloponnesian policy that brought Athens into alliance with Argos, Mantinea, and Elis, shook Sparta's hold on its homeland, and brought about the battle that had almost destroyed Spartan power. He was also the chief author of the campaign that was currently threatening the peace and the security of Dorian cities on Sicily. Finally, Alcibiades had added to existing doubts about his reliability by turning traitor to his native city.

His speech was calculated to deal with these formidable difficulties and to achieve his goals, and he proceeded with characteristic boldness. For the harm he had done Sparta he blamed the Spartans themselves. He had tried to befriend them after their defeat at Pylos, but they had insulted him by choosing to work through his enemy, Nicias. His role as a democratic leader had come to him as a family inheritance of the Alcmaeonids, and what choice was there in a firmly established democracy but to conform to its ways? Even so, he claimed, he and his family had pursued a moderate policy as compared with the real demagogues, the very men, in fact, who had driven him from Athens. Freed from the restricting circumstances in which he had found himself in Athens, he indicated that he would reject democracy, which he claimed to despise as "recognized foolishness." He even implied that he might have helped to overthrow the democratic constitution had Athens not been engaged in a war against the Spartans.[55]

Next, he sketched his version of the grand design behind the Athenian expedition to Sicily. The first target was the Greek cities of Sicily, then the Greek cities of southern Italy, and finally the Carthaginian empire and Carthage itself. If that part of the scheme succeeded, the Athenians would build an additional fleet of triremes with timber from Italy and hire mercenaries from Iberia and other fierce barbarians. With these and the original Greek forces they would then attack the Peloponnesus, blockading it by sea and invading the land with infantrymen. Money and food would be provided by the conquered cities of

[55] 6.89.

Sicily and would cost the Athenians nothing. Soon they would easily take all the resisting Peloponnesian cities by assault or siege, and "after that they would rule over the entire Hellenic people."[56] Alcibiades said that these plans had been in effect while Alcibiades was with the expedition, and the Spartans were hearing them "from a man who knows most precisely what we had in mind." The Athenian generals who remained, moreover, "will carry out the same plans, if they can, without any change."[57]

Alcibiades stressed that the Spartans must act quickly to prevent such a result. Syracuse was on the point of surrender, and if it fell so would all of Greek Sicily and then Greek Italy, allowing the Athenians to turn their attention back to the mainland. "Let no one, then, believe you are deliberating only about Sicily for the fate of the Peloponnesus is also at stake." The Spartans must immediately send an army to Sicily with the hoplites serving also as rowers on the troopships. Even more important, they must send a Spartiate as commander. He would not only provide the necessary discipline and organization, but his presence would constitute living evidence of Spartan commitment, thereby stabilizing the support of friends and winning over waverers. At the same time the Spartans must resume the war on the mainland to encourage the Syracusans and to distract the Athenians. The best strategy would be to build a permanent fort at Decelea in Attica, the very act the Athenians most feared, for such a fort would deprive them of their crops, the revenues from the silver mines, their flocks, and their slaves. This proof that the Spartans were once again fighting seriously would also deprive Athens of imperial tribute, for her allies would be less likely to honor their obligations.[58]

Alcibiades then turned to the question of his own reliability, the trustworthiness of a traitor. His defense was a series of wily arguments that are better quoted than paraphrased: "I ask that none of you judge me unfavorably because I, who once seemed to be a patriot, now join vigorously with her bitterest enemies in

[56] 6.90.
[57] 6.91.1.
[58] 6.91.

attacking Athens. Nor should you suspect me of using the excessively zealous language of an exile. For I am an exile because of the wickedness of those who expelled me, and not, thereby, prevented from doing you a service. My worst enemies are not you, who only did harm to your enemies, but they, who compelled their friends to be their enemies. As to patriotism—I do not have it when I am treated unjustly, but I had it when I held my rights as a citizen securely. Nor do I believe I am attacking a country that is still my own; instead I am trying to recover one that is no longer mine. The true patriot is not the man who, having lost his own homeland, does not attack it, but the one who tries in every way to recover it because of his passion for it."[59] Finally, Alcibiades offered his services to the Spartans: "If I did you great harm as an enemy I could also do you considerable good as a friend, since I know the plans of the Athenians while I only guessed at yours."[60]

Such was the speech of Alcibiades, a brilliant effort in view of the difficulties he faced. Although most of it might seem plausible if one, being a member of a public assembly, had no time to examine the arguments carefully, it was in fact self-serving, exaggerated, and full of sophistic arguments and deceptions. One assertion in particular cast suspicion on everything else that was said: "The generals who are left will carry out the same plans, if they can, without any change." Alcibiades was referring not to the cautious strategy of diplomatic warfare that he actually had tried to execute, but to the grand design he had sketched for the Spartans. It is inconceivable that Nicias considered such a bold scheme, if, indeed, he had even heard it proposed. The patent falsity of that assertion leads us to ask whether the whole grand design may not have been a fiction created by Alcibiades for the purpose of the moment: to inflate the significance of the Sicilian expedition and thus to frighten Sparta into resuming the war against Athens.

The grand design had never been mentioned before, and Alcibiades' actions in connection with the Sicilian expedition give no evidence that he had such a goal. He had requested only 60

[59]6.92.1-4.
[60]6.92.5.

ships and no army; even once the force had been augmented he rejected Lamachus' plan for a direct attack on Sicily. His own strategy, presented and discussed privately among the three generals, was far from bold, advocating a diplomatic offensive followed by attacks on Selinus and Syracuse only if diplomacy failed. None of this proves that Alcibiades was not keeping more grandiose plans to himself and planning to pursue them if his strategy gained control of Sicily, but we must remember that he claimed that such a plan was the official goal of the Athenians, shared and pursued with equal vigor by Lamachus and Nicias. It seems better to conclude that the grand design was an invention intended to impress the Spartans with the greatness of Alcibiades and his potential value to them, as well as to make them fight Athens again out of fear. Once enunciated, however, the plan was believed and became part of the legend of Alcibiades. Who would believe that anyone could make up so fantastic a story about his own intentions, and who could doubt that a man like Alcibiades was capable of such a grandiose conception?

The evidence suggests that the real Alcibiades was very different from the legend he created about himself. Looked at objectively in the winter of 415/14, Alcibiades was a man of mediocre military attainments whose schemes up to then had failed. He had never commanded an Athenian victory on land or sea. His campaigns were characterized by their low degree of risk, the small number of Athenians involved, their heavy reliance on diplomatic skill, and the ability to persuade others to do the fighting for Athens. Yet his failure to gain consistent, reliable political support at home had undone his work as a diplomat and strategist. His failure to be elected general in 418 helped to defeat his Peloponnesian strategy, for the Athenians at Mantinea, commanded instead by the friends of Nicias, were too few and too late. His plans for the Sicilian campaign were changed when Nicias intervened and caused the assembly to increase the size of the expedition, thereby seriously damaging the diplomatic strategy. In neither case need we believe that his plan would have worked anyway, for nothing in his military career up to then proves that he would have done better than the Athenian generals at Mantinea. His Sicilian strategy had not worked in other hands in 427–424, and it was doing badly under his own leadership in 415. For these very reasons Alcibiades needed to demonstrate his greatness to the Spartans. Although his policy was defeated at Mantinea, he nonetheless boasted to the Athenians about how he had frightened the Spartans and come close to success. Stymied in Sicily, removed from the command, in flight as a condemned criminal with a price on his head, he boasted to the Spartans about the boldest and most ambitious design ever conceived by a Greek. One can only marvel at his boldness, imagination, shrewd psychological understanding, and the size of his bluff.

Thucydides, however, believed that the grand design was real and that Alcibiades, at least, had had it in mind from the first;[61] we must ask why. Thucydides was skeptical and intelligent and an unusually careful historian, but he was in exile, away from Athens during the time at issue. There is every reason to think that he met Alcibiades, perhaps in the Peloponnesus when both were in exile, perhaps in Thrace, where Thucydides had property and Alcibiades built a castle toward the end of the war.[62] If so, it would not be surprising if the exiled historian had seized on the lucky chance to learn as much as he could from a man who was a direct participant in major events and probably as well informed as any man in the world about the history of Greece, particularly events in Athens and the Peloponnesus, in the years since the conclusion of the Peace of Nicias.[63] By universal testimony, Alcibiades was a man of unique personal charm and persuasiveness. As Brunt says, Thucydides "may not always have been able to check from other sources the estimates of his own influence which were implicit in the information that Alcibiades gave him."[64] Nor, we might add, could he check on his reports of the mood and intentions of the Athenian people when they made their decisions. For these reasons Thucydides, however careful he might try to be, was unlikely to be able to reject a

[61]6.15.2.

[62]Thucydides' holdings in Thrace: 4.105; Alcibiades' castle: Plut. *Alc.* 36.2–3.

[63]The case for Alcibiades as a major source for Thucydides is made very well by Peter Brunt (*REG* LXV [1952], 59–96).

[64]Ibid., 95–96.

good deal of what Alcibiades told him, including his retrojection of the grand design to a period before it had in fact been invented.

For similar reasons Thucydides' account tends to inflate the importance of Alcibiades in the course of events, as his treatment of the speech in Sparta shows. The introduction to the speech tells us that Alcibiades "aroused and inflamed the Spartans."[65] At its conclusion Thucydides says: "Even before this the Spartans had it in mind to march out against Athens, but they still hesitated and delayed. They were much encouraged, however, when Alcibiades explained things to them in detail, for they thought they were hearing them from the man who had the most certain knowledge. So now they turned their attention to the fortification of Decelea and to sending some aid to Sicily immediately."[66] The clear implication is that the Spartans, moved by Alcibiades' speech, acted immediately to follow his advice; his speech was the decisive event. But we must ask, with Brunt, "Is it really credible that he was so much more persuasive than the ambassadors of Corinth and Syracuse?"[67] Was his advice either original or effective? The Spartans had long been thinking about a fort in Attica, had used the threat of its establishment to force Athens to accept peace in 421,[68] and had been thinking of resuming the war against Athens for some time. They did not immediately leap into action, as Thucydides implies; not until 413, well over a year after the speech, did the Spartans invade Attica and fortify Decelea, for they waited until an Athenian attack on Laconian territory, a formal breach of the peace, allowed them to attack with right on their side.[69]

To be sure, the Spartans appeared to follow Alcibiades' counsel when they sent a general and a force to Sicily, but even these actions raise questions. The force sent was pitifully small.[70] It consisted at first of only 4 ships, 2 Corinthian and 2 Laconian. It

[65]6.88.10: παρώξυνέ τε τοὺς Λακεδαιμονίους καὶ ἐξώρμησε.
[66]6.93.1-2.
[67]Brunt, REG LXV (1952), 71.
[68]5.17.2.
[69]6.105.
[70]"contemptible naval forces," as Hatzfeld puts it (Alcibiade 212).

is notable that Thucydides says not Lacedaemonian, but Laconian. He is not careless in his choice of such terms, and we may assume that the ships were supplied not by Spartiates but by *perioikoi*, non-Spartan Laconians, and the men were *neodamodeis* and helots.[71] No Spartiate soldiers went to Sicily. Nor did the choice of the general perfectly answer Alcibiades' specification. He insisted on a Spartiate because of the prestige a man of pure Spartan lineage would bring to the task of leading, encouraging, and disciplining the Syracusans. Gylippus was appointed, and technically he must have qualified as a Spartiate. He was, however, the son of Cleandridas, the adviser to King Pleistoanax at the time of his fateful withdrawal from Attica in 445. Cleandridas had been accused of accepting a bribe, fled into exile to the Athenian colony at Thurii rather than face trial, and was condemned to death in absentia.[72] Gylippus' reputation had to endure this burden, but it was also weighted down by the fact that he was a *mothax*, perhaps the son of a helot woman and a Spartan man.[73] Even after his glorious achievements in Sicily he did not act as Spartiates were expected to. After the battle of Aegospotami in 405 he stole some of the money he was carrying to Sparta. Like his father, he was condemned to death and fled into exile.[74] Though such behavior could not be foreseen in 415, it seems to fit a man whose place in Spartan society was insecure better than one whose reputation was solid, as a proper

[71] 7.58.3.

[72] Diod. 13.1-6.10; Plut. *Per.* 22.3.

[73] The evidence for Gylippus' status comes from a late source (Aelian 12.43), but we have no reason to reject it on that account. Busolt, who rejects the same status attributed by Aelian to Lysander (*GG* III:2, 1569, n. 2), seems to reject Gylippus' legitimatized bastardy in the same note, and apparently in his text: "He is said to have been a *mothax*, son of a helot woman, but his appearance was that of a true Spartan" (1330). We have good evidence, however, that the Spartans were giving *mothakes* military opportunities in the latter part of the war (Xen. *Hell.* 5.3.8-9), so we need not be shocked that they chose one for the command in Sicily, especially since he seems to have commanded no Spartans. Detlef Lotze (*Historia* XI [1962], 427-435) has argued that some *mothakes* were not bastards but impoverished Spartiates who had dropped out of the class of *homoioi* because of their poverty and were later adopted as companions for their children by Spartans who were better off. In view of his father's exile, Gylippus could have been one of these.

[74] Diod. 13.106.8-10; Plut. *Lys.* 16-17.

Spartiate's would have been after such a brilliant victory as Gylippus won in Sicily.

The striking thing, then, about the Spartan assistance to Syracuse was not so much its paucity as that all of its components were expendable. Probably the only Spartan on the trip was Gylippus, and his credentials were doubtful. Reasonable Athenian precautions could have prevented the Spartans from ever reaching Sicily,[75] and there was little reason to think that they could accomplish anything of note even if they got there.[76] Alcibiades' impact on Spartan behavior was a great deal smaller than Thucydides believed, but if it had helped persuade the Spartans only to send Gylippus, its ultimate importance was greater than anyone had a right to expect.

[75] 6.104.3.
[76] Thucydides tells us (6.104.1) that even as he was on his way Gylippus no longer hoped to save Sicily but was trying only to save Italy.

11. The Siege of Syracuse

By the spring of 414 the time had come for the Athenians to attack Syracuse. During the winter the generals had sent to Athens to ask for cavalry and money, and the Athenians quickly voted what was requested.[1] The battle at the Anapus proved the superiority of the Athenian phalanx over the inexperienced and ill-organized Syracusan hoplites. The arrival of cavalry would allow the Athenians to invest the city on the land side, and their fleet could close it off by sea. There was little reason to expect any help for Syracuse from the Peloponnesus, and if assistance were sent, the Athenian command of the sea should be able to prevent its arrival. Thereafter, it would be only a matter of time until Syracuse surrendered, or so Nicias and Lamachus might plausibly have reasoned as they waited for the horsemen and money to arrive.

Meanwhile they undertook some minor actions against the Syracusans and their friends. From Catana they marched against the Syracusan fort at Megara Hyblaea, but failed to take it. Withdrawing to the coast, they moved south to the Terias River, ravaged the plain, and destroyed the grain stored in the region.[2] After returning to Catana for supplies they turned their attention to the Sicel towns of the Symaethus valley. They marched to Centoripa, whose position on the heights dominated the upper

[1] 6.93.4.
[2] See Map 9. 6.94.1-2. Dover (*HCT* IV, 368) makes the point that since the grain was not yet ripe, the Athenians must have destroyed stored grain.

Symaethus and the connection with the interior of Sicily,[3] and received its surrender. On the way back they burned the grain they found at Inessa and Hybla, Sicel towns allied to Syracuse. When they returned to Catana they found that 250 horsemen had arrived from Athens, with equipment but without horses, which would therefore have to be acquired in Sicily. The cavalrymen brought with them 30 mounted archers, who would also need horses, and 300 silver talents.[4]

The arrival of the Athenian cavalry changed the entire military situation and moved the Syracusans to action. They decided to place guards at the approaches to Epipolae, the plateau overlooking their city, "for they thought that if the Athenians could not control Epipolae the Syracusans could not easily be walled in, even if they were defeated in battle."[5] They had not taken precautions earlier because there had been no need to fear an Athenian siege so long as there was no cavalry to protect the wall builders. At dawn they moved their entire Syracusan army to the banks of the Anapus for a review. Then they chose 600 men and put them under the command of Diomilus, an exile from Andros. The choice of commander points up the shortage of skilled and experienced officers at Syracuse. His elite corps was to guard Epipolae and to serve as a quick-moving force to meet emergencies.[6]

The Syracusan action came too late. Nicias' intelligence service was apparently still working well, for the night before the Syracusan parade to the Anapus the Athenians had sailed from Catana with their entire force. They landed their army at Leon, not far from the northern cliffs of Epipolae.[7] They anchored their ships at Thapsus and built a stockade across its narrow isthmus to protect them. Before the Syracusans knew what had happened, the Athenian army had moved up to Epipolae at full

[3]Freeman, *History of Sicily* III, 205, and Busolt, *GG* III:2, 1330.
[4]6.94.3-4. The payment is recorded on an inscription (*IG* I², 302 = *GHI*, 77, 11, 73ff.). It probably arrived in late March or early April. See Dover, *HCT* IV, 266.
[5]6.96.1.
[6]96.2-3.
[7]See Map 11. For the location of Leon see Dover, *HCT* IV, 368, and Green, *Armada*, 188, n. 11.

speed by way of the pass at Euryalus.[8] The Syracusans were still engaged in their review by the river when they learned that the Athenians were on the plateau. Diomilus marched his men out as quickly as possible, but they had to cover about three miles over rough country. As Green says, "Euryalus was a good point from which to fight a defensive action, since attackers were forced to fight on a narrow front, after sweating their way up a steep hillside."[9] The Syracusans were also outnumbered and in disorder when they reached the plateau, so they were easily defeated. Diomilus and about 300 of his men were killed; the others retreated to Syracuse. The Athenians held the field and erected a trophy of victory. When they marched to Syracuse the enemy stayed within the walls, not daring to come out against them. The Athenians then built a fort at Labdalum on the northern cliffs of Epipolae to serve as a safe storehouse for their supplies, equipment, and money while they fought any battles necessary and conducted the siege.[10] Only horses for their cavalry were needed before the siege could begin.

Soon the horses arrived, some contributed by Segesta and Catana, others purchased elsewhere. With them came 300 Segestan cavalrymen and another 100 from various allies. Adding the 250 of their own cavalry, the Athenians could put 650 cavalrymen into the field, enough, with their hoplites, to protect the men who would build the siege walls. Wasting no time, they moved forward to a place called Syce, not far from the edge of the plateau, to the northwest of the city (see Map 11).[11] There they built a fort that Thucydides calls "The Circle." This structure need not have been circular, but must have enclosed a reasonable amount of space and been defensible on all sides, for, as Dover says, it "was intended to be [the Athenians'] central fortified position, the base of their main force and their stores, from which they could extend their siege walls."[12]

[8]6.97.1-2. For the location of Euryalus see Dover, HCT IV, 469-471.
[9]Green, Armada, 189.
[10]6.97.3-5. For the site of Labdalum see Dover, HCT IV, 473-474.
[11]For the site of Syce and the fort the Athenians built there see Dover, HCT IV, 473-474, and Map 2, opposite p. 469.
[12]HCT IV, 473.

The Syracusan generals, cowed as they were by their previous defeats, were nonetheless goaded to action by the speed and enterprise of the Athenians. They took their army up to face the enemy, but in the moment before joining combat their generals were dismayed by the disorder of their own troops and withdrew into the city. The Syracusans left part of their cavalry behind to prevent the Athenians from continuing to build their wall, but quickly discovered that the Athenians now had horses. One Athenian tribal division of hoplites supported by the entire newly acquired cavalry was enough to rout the Syracusans and protect the construction.[13] The next day the Athenians began to extend their wall north from "The Circle" toward Trogilus.[14] Unless the Syracusans took action to prevent it, they would soon be shut in by land, but Hermocrates and his fellow generals were unwilling to expose their ill-disciplined troops in another battle. Instead they decided to build a counter-wall that would cut across the line of the projected siegeworks and prevent their completion. They would first erect wooden stockades, which could be put up quickly to protect the wall-builders, and protect these with soldiers. Defended by these wooden palisades and, presumably, by their cavalry, they could hope to repulse Athenian attacks.

The Syracusan wall appears to have run from the newly built city wall around Temenites near the sanctuary of Apollo westward across the firm and gently sloping land above the marsh and below Epipolae to a point just below the cliffs of the plateau.[15] The wall was built of stone and timber, and Apollo's olive trees were cut down to provide it with towers. Instead of challenging this effort, the Athenians ignored it and continued

[13]6.98.2-4.

[14]See Map 11. On the general topographic problem see above, Chap. 10, n. 35. Drögemüller and Green both place Trogilus on the east coast, not far north of the city. The most direct and specific refutation of their arguments is supplied by Dover in his reviews of their books cited in that note.

[15]See Map 11, and Dover's Map 3 (*HCT* IV, opposite p. 477). Thucydides' account is not perfectly in accord with the topographical evidence, and his account of this first counter-wall is one of the passages that raise doubts that he saw Syracuse and its environs. The best account of this topographical problem and its solution is provided by Dover (*HCT* IV, 475-476 with 469-470). It is better understood with Fabricius' map (attached to the end of *Das Antike Syrakus*) at one's elbow.

building the sections of their own wall on the plateau. Thucydides tells us they were unwilling to divide their forces, but perhaps Nicias was also trying to encourage the complacency that soon emerged among the Syracusans. At the Anapus, we should remember, he had also refused battle at first, waiting to take the enemy by surprise. The Athenians confined themselves to destroying the pipes that ran underground into Syracuse, supplying the city with water. Syracuse had springs and wells within its walls, but in summer the reduction of the water supply would at least be annoying.[16] Soon the characteristic Syracusan indiscipline and carelessness showed itself. In the heat of midday most of the Syracusans were taking their siesta in their tents—some had even gone home to the city—and the wall was not being guarded with care by those who remained.

The Athenians had been waiting for such an opportunity and launched a well-planned attack. Speed was essential, so 300 carefully chosen hoplites and a corps of specially selected light-armed soldiers supplied with heavy armor for the occasion acted as shock troops, assaulting the lightly defended wall on the run. Nicias and Lamachus followed with the rest of the army, each leading a wing. One division marched to Syracuse to prevent any attempt at a rescue while the other marched to the end of the wall that joined the city wall around Temenites. The shock troops had an immediate success, driving the guards from their positions at the counter-wall in flight to the wall around Temenites. The pursuers were so quick that they were able to get in through the gate with the fleeing Syracusans, but they were too few to hold their position and were driven out again. So close did the Athenians come to taking the suburb of Temenites by storm. Now the Athenians could take down the counter-wall at their leisure and set up another trophy of victory.[17]

About this time Nicias became ill with the kidney ailment that would trouble him until his death.[18] Though he probably took

[16] 6.100.1.

[17] 6.100.2-3.

[18] Nicias' illness is first mentioned at 6.102.2 and its nature specified at 7.15.1. 6.9.2 may possibly be evidence that he already suffered from it before the expedition, but his actions up to this point suggest that he suffered no acute attacks earlier in the campaign.

part in planning, the execution of the Athenian operations must have been in the hands of Lamachus, and the decisiveness and speed of those actions show his touch. The very day after their victory the Athenians began to build the southern portion of their siege wall, extending from "The Circle" on Epipolae to the Great Harbor south of the city. The completion of that task would accomplish an important part of the encirclement of Syracuse. It would also allow the Athenians to move their fleet from Thapsus, whence they had to haul supplies overland to Epipolae, to a safe anchorage in the Great Harbor, for without the wall, protection of the Athenian fleet on the beach of the Great Harbor would require a dangerous division of Athenian land forces. The first stage of the construction ran south from "The Circle" to the southern cliffs of Epipolae, and the Athenians were able to complete a thousand feet of it before the Syracusans could interfere.[19]

The Syracusans were duly alarmed and began to build another counter-wall, this time across the Lysimeleia marsh, for the extension of the Athenian fortifications made an approach to the edge of Epipolae too dangerous. The Syracusans, therefore, were compelled to construct a stockade and dig a ditch beside it through the middle of the marsh. The Athenians, meanwhile, completed their own wall to the edge of the cliff and prepared for another attack. This time they devised an amphibious movement. They ordered their fleet to move from Thapsus into the Great Harbor, and at dawn they came down from Epipolae. Placing planks and doors on the firmest parts of the marsh, they once again caught the Syracusans by surprise and captured the ditch as well as the stockade. The assault split the Syracusan army in two, the right wing fleeing to the city, the left running to the Anapus. The river is less easily forded near its mouth than further upstream, so the army naturally ran for the bridge, and the 300 Athenian shock troops hurried to cut them off. This tactic proved a mistake, for the Syracusan cavalry was at the river and, with the hoplites, routed the 300 and turned on the right wing of the main Athenian army.[20] The right wing of a

[19]6.101.1; 102.2.
[20]See Dover's Map 4, *HCT* IV, opposite p. 481.

phalanx, of course, is most vulnerable, especially when threatened by a combined attack from infantry and cavalry, and the first tribal regiment on the Athenian right was thrown into panic. The brave and bold Lamachus, though he was on the left wing, learned what was happening and brought help. With a few archers and with the Argive contingent he steadied the line, but his impetuousness led him to be isolated across a ditch with only a few of his soldiers, and killed. The Syracusans took his body with them as they retreated across the river, presumably toward the safety of their fortress at the Olympieum.[21] The Athenian victory in this quarter was gained at a high price, for with Nicias ill, the experience and vigor of Lamachus were more essential than ever.

Back in Syracuse the demoralized army was able to regroup and recover its courage. The Syracusans realized that since the Athenian army was down from the heights, in the plain before the city, its main base at the round fort on Epipolae must have been lightly guarded at best. They therefore sent a part of their army outside the gates, to engage the attention of the Athenians in the plain before the city. At the same time they sent a force to attack "The Circle." The recently built wall running south from the fort was undefended, and the Syracusans captured and demolished it. Within the round fort itself was the ailing Nicias, left behind because of his illness. His ingenuity saved the fort, for he ordered his attendants to set fire to the lumber and siege equipment that was lying about. The fire temporarily drove back the Syracusans, but its main function was to signal to the army down in the plain that the fort was under attack. The Athenains near Syracuse had already driven the enemy off, and they now saw their fleet sailing into the harbor. They were thus able to hurry up to Epipolae and save both the fort and their general. The Syracusans were glad to get back to their city and recover their dead under a truce.[22]

The plight of the Syracusans was now desperate. They had no hope of preventing the Athenians from cutting them off from the

[21]6.101. Plutarch (*Nic.* 18.2) says Lamachus and a Syracusan cavalryman named Callicrates killed each other in single combat.
[22]6.102-103.1.

sea to the south of the city. The Athenians, in fact, wasted no time in beginning the construction of a double wall from the edge of Epipolae down to the harbor. Its completion would provide their besieging army with security from attack from either side and would also allow them to beach their ships with total safety on the coast between the walls. Their navy was in the Great Harbor and could prevent access or egress if it kept close watch. All that would remain was to complete the northern wall from "The Circle" to Trogilus, and Syracuse would be entirely shut in. After that, there was no way to prevent either starvation or surrender. The new situation was widely understood. Sicels who had previously stood aside now joined the Athenian alliance. Supplies came from Italy and the Etruscans sent 3 ships. The Syracusans, too, understood their danger. Thucydides tells us that "the Syracusans no longer thought they could win the war, for no help had come to them from the Peloponnesus." They were already discussing peace terms among themselves, and even with Nicias. They deposed the three generals who had unsuccessfully led the resistance up to then and replaced them with three new ones, Heracleides, Eucles, and Tellias.[23] The air was full of suspicion and there was even talk of treason. Though we have no direct evidence, we may guess that factional divisions emerged in this difficult time. Nicias was well informed about internal deliberations in Syracuse, and he had good reason to hope that the city would soon fall into his hands.

In these happy circumstances Nicias, now sole commander, appears to have become overconfident and careless, utterly ignoring the one distant cloud in the otherwise bright Athenian sky: the few ships coming from the Peloponnesus, one of them carrying the Spartan Gylippus. A great general would have taken a number of steps to guarantee success. He would have hurried to complete the circumvallation of Syracuse, sent a squadron of ships to the straits or to Italy to prevent the arrival of the Peloponnesians, instituted a strict blockade of both the Syracusan harbors to prevent access if even a single ship got past

[23]6.103. This Heracleides is probably the son of Aristogenes. See Dover, *HCT* IV, 376.

his forward interceptors, and guarded or even fortified the approaches to Epipolae, especially Euryalus, in case any of the Peloponnesians got through to Sicily and came to Syracuse by land. A general who was merely prudent would have done some of these things. Nicias did none of them, and the results, contrary to any reasonable expectation at that time, were disastrous for Athens.

Gylippus was still at Leucas where, as we have seen, he received and believed false reports that Syracuse was already completely encircled. At this point he intended only to save the Greek cities of Italy from Athenian control, and he set off with the Corinthian admiral Pythen, each in command of two ships. A second force composed of eight Corinthian ships, two from Leucas and three from Ambracia would sail later.[24] Gylippus and Pythen sped across the Ionian Sea to Taras. From there Gylippus sent an envoy to Thurii where his father had gone into exile and become a leading citizen. He hoped to make use of the connection to win over the Thurians, but the city was always rent by faction, and in light of the recent Athenian successes we should not be surprised that his embassy failed.[25] He was further delayed by a storm off Taras that drove him back to port and damaged his ships. By then Nicias had been informed of his presence in Italy but made no attempt to intercept him, being contemptuous of his tiny fleet and thinking he had come as a piratical nuisance rather than for serious purposes.[26]

As Gylippus and Pythen sailed along the Italian coast toward Sicily important events were taking place back in mainland Greece. The war between Sparta and Argos continued in its fitful way with raids and counter-raids, but no decisive actions. In the spring of 414 the Spartans started out against the Argives, going first to Phlius to gather allied troops.[27] They were advanc-

---

[24]6.104.1-2. See also Dover, HCT IV, 376.

[25]For Cleandridas see Gomme, HCT I, 341. For politics at Thurii see Kagan, Outbreak, 156-166, and Thucydides 7.33.5 and 57.11.

[26]6.104.2-3.

[27]Thucydides (6.95) does not mention Phlius, saying only that the Spartans got so far as Cleonae before turning back. Since Cleonae is to the north and east of Argos, Dover's explanation (HCT IV, 369) is convincing, and I adopt it here. See Map 7.

ing against Argos' ally Cleonae when an earthquake struck and ended the expedition. The Argives retaliated by invading Thyrea and taking away 25 talents' worth of booty.[28] About mid-summer the Spartans tried again, this time moving directly into Argive territory and ravaging the countryside in the traditional manner while the grain was ripening. For some time the Argives had tried to persuade the Athenians to join them on raids in Laconia and had been refused. Athens continued to launch raids into Messenia from Pylos and, in cooperation with the Argives, elsewhere in the Peloponnesus, but never in Laconia. By a very generous interpretation these actions might not be considered violations of the Peace of Nicias, but a direct assault on Laconia must be.[29] In 414 the Athenians responded to the Argive request for help by sending 30 ships under the command of Pythodorus, Laespodias, and Demaratus; their forces landed at a number of places on the Laconian coast and ravaged the territory. The Athenians could hardly have refused to defend their Argive allies vigorously while Argive troops were serving on the Athenian expedition to Sicily. In this way the Sicilian expedition had an important effect on the war as a whole for, as Thucydides points out, these actions "violated the treaty with the Spartans in the most flagrant way."[30] This had an important psychological effect, for it provided the Spartans with a legitimate reason for making war against the Athenians not only in Sicily but even, when the time came, in Attica.[31]

When Gylippus and Pythen reached Locri they received the accurate information that Syracuse was not yet completely shut off and that an army could still get to it by way of Epipolae. They determined to try to save the city, and now the question was whether they should risk sailing directly into one of the Syracusan harbors or go first to friendly Himera, gather forces there, and march overland to Syracuse. They prudently decided to sail for Himera, for the Athenian fleet could be expected to be guarding both Syracusan harbors. One ship might hope to slip

[28] 6.95.1.
[29] See Dover, *HCT* IV, 377-378.
[30] 6.105.1.
[31] 6.105.2; 7.18.

through the blockade at night but four could not. Nicias had learned of their arrival at Locri and was by that time persuaded to send 4 Athenian ships to intercept them. They set out far too late and must have been hampered by the fact that both Messina and Rhegium were hostile, so the Peloponnesians easily got through to Himera. There, fortune continued to smile on them. The men of Himera agreed to join their expedition and to provide arms for the members of the Peloponnesian crew who had none. More help came from Selinus and Gela and from the Sicels, now inclined toward the enemies of Athens because of the death of the pro-Athenian King Archonidas and, like the Sicilian Greeks, by the fervor of Gylippus. When he started on his march to Syracuse he had with him about 3,000 foot soldiers, most of them hoplites, and about 200 cavalry.[32]

Some time after Gylippus and Pythen had taken their tiny squadron to Italy and Sicily, the remaining 11 triremes from Corinth and its allies followed from Leucas. The last of these to sail, under the command of the Corinthian general Gongylus, must have taken the more dangerous route directly across the Ionian Sea to Syracuse, for it slipped through the blockade and reached the city even before Gylippus. The risks he had taken were amply justified, for he found the Syracusans on the point of holding an assembly to discuss giving up the war. He intervened with the authorities to prevent the meeting and told the Syracusans that more ships were on the way and that the Spartan Gylippus had come to take command. The Syracusans took heart and sent their entire army out to meet Gylippus when they learned he was approaching the city. The tide which up to then had flowed in favor of Athens was about to turn.[33]

Gylippus came onto Epipolae from the west, through the Euryalus Pass, just as the Athenians had done, apparently without resistance. It is impossible to defend and difficult to understand the Athenian failure to guard, perhaps even to fortify, the

[32] 7.1; Diod. 13.7.7.

[33] 7.2.1-3. Dover's comment on this point deserves quotation: "This is the turning point of the campaign. Since the loss of their second counter-wall the Syracusans had turned their minds to making peace, but from the moment of the arrival of Gongylus with his heartening news all goes ill for the Athenians" (HCT IV, 380).

pass through which they themselves had come and which was one of the likeliest points of access to their position on Epipolae. Nicias must have known of Gylippus' arrival in Sicily, if from no one else at least from the Athenian ships that had vainly tried to cut him off. He must also have known that he had sailed to the western part of Sicily, since the Athenians dominated the east. There was every reason to take precautions against an assault from the west, but none were taken. Thucydides underscores the significance of Gylippus' arrival on Epipolae: "He happened to come at the critical moment when the Athenians had completed their double wall of seven or eight stadia down to the Great Harbor, except for a short section near the sea which they were still building. For the rest of the wall toward Trogilus and the other sea stones had already been laid out for the greater part of the distance, and some parts were left half-finished while others had been completed. That is how close Syracuse had come to danger."[34]

Gylippus joined forces with the Syracusans and moved forward immediately to challenge the Athenians at their siege wall. Although they were thrown into an uproar by this unexpected attack, their discipline held, and they formed in battle array. Gylippus now tried a bit of psychological warfare, sending a herald to offer the Athenians a truce if they would take their belongings and leave Sicily within five days. The offer was greeted with contemptuous silence by the Athenians, but in fact the gesture must have been intended for the Syracusans. Here was Gylippus, newly arrived with a motley and untested army, joined by a Syracusan force repeatedly defeated in battle and almost ready to capitulate, arrogantly offering safe conduct to the all-victorious Athenians. This was an action meant to inspirit his own forces, and it seems to have had an effect. But however high their spirits, his troops were still weak in training and discipline. When the two armies drew up for battle, probably in the area between the Syracusan winter wall and a completed part of the Athenian siege wall, Gylippus saw that his men were con-

---

[34]7.2.4-5. With Dover (*HCT* IV, 473-474) I delete τοῦ κύκλου from τῷ δὲ ἄλλῳ τοῦ κύκλου πρὸς τὸν Τρώγιλον at the beginning of 7.2.5 to get the translation, "for the rest of the wall."

fused and not in proper order. This was the moment for an alert and daring Athenian leader to strike, before the enemy was ready, before Gylippus could instill discipline, and before his arrival could take full effect in Syracuse and the rest of Sicily. The tactical advantage was only a part of the great opportunity that lay before the Athenians. Even more important was their chance for a great strategic success; if they could inflict a defeat in open combat between hoplite phalanxes on the newly arrived Spartan general, it would certainly dispirit the enemy and possibly end its resistance. Such an opportunity was worth considerable risk, but Nicias let it escape. As Gylippus moved his men away from the walls toward more open country, Nicias did not pursue, "but kept quiet near his own wall."[35] Seeing that he would not be attacked, Gylippus was able to take his army down to Temenites for the night and to lay plans for his next step. Overnight, under his command, the Syracusans could shift from a desperate defense to the offensive.

The next day Gylippus marched the main part of his army to the Athenian wall again, but this was only a diversionary action meant to pin down the Athenian force. While the Athenians were concentrating on the defense of their wall, probably on the southern part of Epipolae, Gylippus sent a force, probably through a gate at the northern end of the Syracusan wall at Trogilus where the Athenians had not yet completed their wall, against the Athenian fort at Labdalum, which the heights in the middle of the plateau blocked from the Athenian view. He appears to have met little resistance, for he took the fort and all its contents, and killed the Athenians in it. Nicias' laxity in leaving his fort, supply depot, and treasury inadequately defended is once again remarkable.[36]

Now Gylippus took advantage of still another Athenian error. Nicias should have given the completion of the circumvallation of Syracuse the highest priority. If the Athenians could not shut

---

[35] 7.3.3.

[36] 7.3.4. As though to emphasize the new contrast between the Athenians and the Syracusans, the laxity of the former and the growing boldness of the latter, Thucydides reports that an Athenian trireme guarding the mouth of the Great Harbor was captured by the Syracusans on the same day (7.3.4-5).

off the Syracusans by land they might as well go home, for a naval blockade would not be sufficient. The arrival of Gylippus and the new spirit he had created in Syracuse made it all the more necessary to move quickly to complete the circuit, yet the Athenians completed the *double* wall to the sea before turning to the northern section on Epipolae from the round fort to Trogilus. The time and manpower used on the second wall to the south were luxuries the Athenians could not afford so long as the northern sector was incomplete.[37] Gylippus moved swiftly to build a counter-wall, the third attempted by the Syracusans to cut across the path of the Athenian wall as it moved north toward Trogilus.[38] The Athenians, after completing the double wall to the sea, came up to Epipolae and were content for the moment to fight off an attack on a weak point in their wall and establish a closer guard on it.

The obvious next step for the Athenians was to complete the northern wall to Trogilus as quickly as possible and to prevent Gylippus from building his counter-wall. That would be in line with the offensive strategy that the Athenians, even under Nicias, had employed late in the summer of 415. But Nicias, now in sole command, was ill, in pain, and unnerved by the sudden turn of events caused by the arrival of the fiery, daring Spartan. His actions reveal that he was no longer thinking offensively, but of defense, escape, and safety for his forces. As Thucydides puts it, "By this time he was inclined to pay more attention to the war at sea, seeing that the situation on land had become quite unfavorable since Gylippus had come."[39] Such an inclination is the best explanation for Nicias' decision to fortify the cape called Plemmyrium on the south of the entrance to the Great Harbor. He meant to make it his new naval base and the storehouse to replace Labdalum, and he built three forts there for that purpose. The disadvantages of this action were many and serious. The little water and firewood in the neighborhood were a considerable distance away. The parties of Athenian sailors who went out to bring water and gather wood were easy prey for

[37]The point is made by Busolt, *GG* III:2, 1340 and n. 3.
[38]See Map 11 and Dover's Map 2, *HCT* IV, opp. p. 469.
[39]7.4.4.

the Syracusan cavalry, who had set up a base near the Olympieum from which they could sortie at will. "For these reasons,
especially, the crews began to deteriorate at that time."[40] The
Athenian fleet and supplies, moreover, were now at some distance from the main Athenian army on Epipolae; if they were
attacked, Nicias would need to have his fort and walls undefended in order to come to the rescue. He could thus easily be
forced down from Epipolae by diversionary attacks at the pleasure of the enemy. The tactical skill he had so often shown in the
past, and which had always prevented him from dividing his
forces, appears to have deserted him.

The reasons that Nicias gave for his actions seem inadequate;
the new forts would make it easier to bring in supplies, allowing
the Athenians to keep closer watch on the harbor, and not be
obliged to come out from deep inside the harbor to meet any
action by the Syracusan fleet.[41] But nothing in the record indicates that the Athenians were having any problems with such
matters, and any advantages gained by the movement were triv-
ial compared to its disadvantages. The likeliest explanation for
these actions appears to be the unspoken and, perhaps, unwitting
motive of Nicias. He was no longer thinking of a siege or an
attack or a blockade; he was thinking of escape, and if he brought
his army down from Epipolae, a base at Plemmyrium would be
the safest place from which to escape now that the fall of Labdalum had severed the route to the north. With naval matters
utmost in his mind, Nicias learned of the approach of the
Corinthian fleet and sent 20 ships north toward Italy to intercept
it before it could reach Sicily.[42]

Gylippus, meanwhile, continued to force the issue on
Epipolae. He worked on the counter-wall using the very stones
the Athenians had laid out for their own use. He continued to
challenge the Athenians by drawing up his army before them.
The Athenians always formed their own army opposite him, but
made no move to attack. We may guess that Gylippus had a
double purpose. He knew, of course, that the issue would be

[40] 7.4.6.
[41] 7.4.4.
[42] 7.4.7.

decided not by a wall-building contest but by a clash of arms, and he was ready to bring it on at any time. On the other hand, he must have sensed Nicias' reluctance to fight, and the Athenians' repeated refusal to give battle could only sap the morale of their soldiers as it increased the confidence of the men under Gylippus. Finally, when he was convinced that the right moment had come, Gylippus led the charge against the Athenians, but he happened to choose a site that was confined by the walls in such a way that the superior cavalry of the Syracusans could play no part, and he suffered a defeat.

This was a dangerous moment for Gylippus and his cause; if the Athenian victory were not quickly undone the confidence of the Syracusans and the prestige of their Spartan commander would be dissipated, and all that had been gained swiftly lost. At this point Gylippus displayed great qualities of leadership. He knew that the chief threat lay in loss of self-confidence by his men, especially the Syracusans, for whom this would be merely one more in a series of defeats at the hands of the apparently invincible Athenians. He therefore took responsibility for the defeat squarely and uniquely upon his own shoulders. The error had been his, he said, not theirs, for he had made them fight in close quarters where they could not use their cavalry and javelin throwers. He told them that they were in no way inferior to the enemy and promised to lead them out to battle again. It was unendurable, he concluded, that Dorians and Peloponnesians like themselves should not defeat and drive from Sicily an enemy composed of "Ionians, islanders, and a mixed mob."[43]

At the next opportunity Gylippus kept his word. This time even Nicias knew he must fight, for the Syracusan counter-wall had almost reached the line taken by the Athenian northern wall and, unless checked, would shortly end all possibility of taking Syracuse by siege. When Gylippus offered battle, therefore, Nicias took his army out against him even though the enemy was now in an open area, away from the walls, where their cavalry and javelin throwers gave them the advantage. The cavalry, in fact, decided the battle, for it routed the Athenian left wing and

[43] 7.5.4.

brought about a general flight. The Athenians saved themselves only by running to the safety of their fortifications, presumably the round fort. By the next night the Syracusans were able to carry their counter-wall beyond the line of the Athenian siege wall. Distracted by the battle on Epipolae, the Athenians allowed the Corinthian squadron commanded by Erasinides that had come from Leucas by way of Italy to sail into Syracuse harbor unharmed in spite of the new Athenian base at Plemmyrium.[44] The crews of these ships supplied Gylippus with well over 2,000 men to help complete the counter-wall and probably to carry it all the way across Epipolae, possibly to the fort at Labdalum, thus cutting Athens off from the plain and the sea to its north.[45] All hope of enclosing Syracuse and starving it into surrender with their present forces was gone, and the besiegers had become the besieged.[46]

Gylippus acted with characteristic zeal to secure his gains and to exploit them fully. Avoiding the errors of Nicias and the Syracusans before him, he began to fortify Epipolae against attack. At Euryalus he built a fort and posted 600 Syracusans nearby to guard it. Elsewhere on the plateau he placed three camps, one manned by the Syracusans, another by the Sicilian Greeks, and the third by the other allies.[47] Knowing that the Athenians were still a formidable enemy and were sure to seek reinforcements from home, Gylippus turned his attention to increasing his own forces. He went about Sicily to seek help both

[44]Thucydides says at 7.7.1 that there were only 12 ships, but at 6.104.1 he says there were 8 Corinthian ships, 2 from Leucas and 3 from Ambracia. Perhaps, for some reason not given, one of the original 13 did not sail from Leucas or stopped along the way. Diodorus (13.8.2) gives the number of ships that made it to Syracuse as 13.

[45]Green (Armada, 233) suggests Labdalum as the terminus for the wall built by Gylippus. Diodorus (13.8.2) reports another battle in which Gylippus attacked the Athenian camp and caused many casualties, afterward destroying the entire Athenian wall on Epipolae and driving the Athenians from the plateau altogether. Thucydides does not mention any of this, and there is little reason to believe it, except for the destruction of the Athenian wall, whose ruins could provide materials to build the Syracusan counter-wall. The Athenians, moreover, continued to have access to Epipolae from the south (7.43.1).

[46]7.6.4 and 7.11.4.

[47]7.43.4-5. For their possible location, not given in the ancient sources, see the suggestions of Green (Armada, 233).

from cautious allies and from cities that had up to then been neutral. Further afield, he also sent embassies to Sparta and Corinth, asking them to send more troops in any available craft. The Athenian navy remained an obstacle to victory, and the Syracusans had been paralyzed into inactivity at sea from fear of it. Now, for the first time, they began to take heart, to fit their ships out for battle, to train their crews with an eye toward contesting the Athenians at sea, as well.[48]

As the summer came to an end Nicias was forced to a decision. Thoroughly disheartened by the growth of the enemy's strength and by his own problems, he concluded that the Athenians in Sicily were in such great danger that they must either give up the expedition or receive reinforcements on a large scale.[49] Everything in his character, previous attitude toward the expedition, and conduct of the campaign indicates that he would have much preferred to abandon Sicily entirely. Technically, he had the power to order the retreat to Athens, for he, Alcibiades, and Lamachus were *autokratores*, generals with "full powers," and since the departure of one and the death of the other he was free to act without consulting anyone else in Sicily. "Full powers" meant that he could act to carry out the charge he had been given without consulting the Athenian assembly in detail, and those powers must surely have included the right to withdraw the army if its existence were threatened. Nor was there any physical hindrance to the retreat, for the Athenians still commanded the sea, and their army was fully capable of protecting a departure.

Several considerations, however, prevented Nicias from simply ordering the abandonment of Sicily. Generals, after all, are accountable for their actions, especially in the Athenian democracy. In the second year of the Peloponnesian War three Athenian generals had been brought to trial even though they had captured Potidaea after a long and costly siege. They were charged with making peace without the approval of the assembly. Although they had been acquitted, the precedent was omi-

[48]7.7.204.
[49]7.8.1.

nous.[50] Still more threatening were the prosecutions of 424. In that year Sophocles, Pythodorus, and Eurymedon were tried and convicted after signing the Peace of Gela, which excluded Athenian influence from Sicily. Officially they were charged with accepting bribes, but Thucydides tells us that they were punished for frustrating the unreasonably great expectations of the Athenian assembly. The first two were exiled, while Eurymedon got off with a fine.[51] In the same year Thucydides himself was exiled for his part in the loss of Amphipolis.[52] Nicias, to be sure, had been sending back reports of his problems as they arose, but such reports must have been a recent development and they followed many that had announced the successes that had led both Nicias and the Syracusans to consider a Syracusan capitulation likely before the arrival of Gylippus. Nor could Nicias fall back on his opposition to the original expedition, for the Athenians had supplied him with everything he asked to guarantee its safety and success.

There was yet another problem. Nicias might honestly believe that the Athenian forces were in danger unless reinforced or evacuated, but that conclusion was neither obvious nor inevitable. When Demosthenes arrived the next summer, he thought that victory might still be snatched from the situation.[53] More than one disgruntled veteran from Sicily speaking in a debate in the Athenian assembly or in a law court might be expected to point out that the retreat had been undertaken with the fleet unbeaten and in command of the sea and the army essentially intact. Where, they might ask, was the danger that justified the abandonment of so expensive and so promising a campaign? They might also be expected to focus on the errors, delays, and omissions committed by Nicias which had allowed certain victory to slip away. The Athenian people, moreover, were in no mood to abandon the Sicilian expedition, as they demonstrated by electing such aggressive generals as Demosthenes and Eurymedon and by their response to Nicias' request for rein-

[50] 2.70.4; Kagan, *Archidamian War*, 97-99.
[51] 4.65; Kagan, *Archidamian War*, 268-269.
[52] 5.26.5.
[53] 7.42.5.

forcements.[54] Clearly, if Nicias had ordered a withdrawal without permission from the Athenian assembly, he would have seriously endangered both his reputation and his own safety.

He chose, instead, to communicate with the assembly, describing the situation and leaving the decision to them. Since Nicias wanted not merely to report facts but to persuade the Athenians to a course of action, as well as to defend his own conduct of the campaign, he wrote a letter in addition to entrusting the more usual oral reports to messengers. The messengers reached Athens, probably in the autumn of 414. They gave their oral reports and answered questions. Then Nicias' letter was read to the assembly. He reported the reverses that the Athenians had suffered since the arrival of Gylippus without discussing the reasons for them. He made it clear that they had been forced onto the defensive and were no longer building an encircling wall about Syracuse. He reported that Gylippus was gathering reinforcements and was planning an attack on the Athenian defenses not only by land but also by sea. Knowing that his last bit of news would both dismay and astonish the Athenians, he explained that the length of the campaign and the need to keep the fleet constantly at sea had led to the deterioration of both the ships and their crews. The enemy, free from the need to maintain a blockade, could easily dry its ships and give its crews practice, but if the Athenians relaxed at all their supplies could be cut off, since everything had to be brought by sea past Syracuse.

Nicias also complained about problems of manpower and discipline. His sailors' need to seek wood, forage, and water at some distance from their camp led to their destruction by the Syracusan cavalry. The change in Athenian fortunes had led to desertion by slaves, mercenaries, and disappointed volunteers who had come to get rich rather than for extended warfare. Some of these last went into business for themselves as traders and convinced the ship captains to accept slaves as substitute rowers. The ships were now short of skilled and disciplined oarsmen, always a minority of the company, and were compelled to use men without any of these qualities, to the great detriment of

[54] 7.16.

their fighting ability. Nicias also complained that he could not control such abuses, for the character of Athenians was difficult to discipline. The loss of these soldiers and sailors, moreover, could not be made good in Sicily, for Athens, unlike the enemy, had few allies in Sicily, and those could help no further. Nicias feared that if things went on as they were, the places in Italy that supplied the Athenians with food would cease to do so as they saw the war going in favor of Syracuse. With this, the Athenian expedition would be finished.

Insisting that he was telling the truth, however unpleasant, so that the Athenians should know the facts accurately and be able to make an informed decision, he also insisted that neither the generals nor the army were at fault for the unhappy turn of events. Then he told the Athenians the choice that confronted them: "you must either recall the force that is here or reinforce it with another just as large, infantry and a fleet and a great deal of money." He also asked to be relieved from his command because of his kidney ailment. His final words were that whatever the Athenians chose to do they should act quickly before the enemy grew too powerful through the reinforcements it was gathering everywhere.[55]

As an explanation and defense of Nicias' work as commander the letter was incomplete and disingenuous, but as effective as circumstances would permit. He was honest in admitting how bad the situation was, indeed he exaggerated its gloominess. The Syracusan fleet was not yet a match for the Athenians, as their next battle would show. There was still no evidence that the Italians were considering closing their markets to the Athenians, who, in any case, were supplied chiefly from Sicily.[56] Still, the Athenians' situation had deteriorated badly, but Nicias made no mention of how his generalship had contributed to the decline. His lethargy, carelessness, and overconfidence had brought Syracuse from the edge of defeat to its new condition of aggressive security. He had disdained to intercept Gylippus' pitifully

[55]7.11-15. Thucydides' account of Nicias' letter is not, of course, a verbatim report of its contents.

[56]At 7.49.2 Demosthenes spells out how the Athenians could support themselves by living off the land from a base at Thapsus or Catana.

small squadron, allowed Gongylus to slip through his blockade to revive Syracuse's flagging spirits, left the approaches to Epipolae unfortified and unguarded, wasted his time building a double wall to the sea and three forts at Plemmyrium while his northern wall was incomplete, allowed his storehouse and treasury at Labdalum to be taken by surprise, permitted the Corinthian squadron to get to Syracuse, and moved his navy to its untenable position at Plemmyrium.

The deterioration of the navy, like all the other misfortunes, was made to seem inevitable, something over which Nicias had no control, but a reasoned analysis, such as that of Peter Green, shows otherwise: "the condition of the fleet remains something of a puzzle. It was only after it left Catana, that same spring, that it lacked normal docking and refitting facilities. Deterioration would not set in to the extent Nicias suggests after a mere four or five months. Had he omitted to overhaul his triremes while he was still in position to do so? In any case, if he could spare twenty ships to intercept the Corinthians, he could equally well have sent off, say, ten a month to be dried out and serviced in Catana. He had, so far as we know, lost only one vessel through enemy action."[57] The loss of sailors through death and desertion and the consequent loss of fighting skill, moreover, resulted directly from the movement of the fleet to Plemmyrium, a decision taken by Nicias. He did well, it would seem, in avoiding a more detailed report.

But perhaps Nicias' cunning once again went astray. All we know about Nicias leads us to conclude that his true opinion was that Athens should abandon the expedition and withdraw its forces from Sicily. Failing that, he wanted at least to be honorably relieved from the command because of his illness. Had he written a straightforward statement of his belief that the chance of victory in Sicily was gone, if it had ever existed, and that he saw no alternative to withdrawal, the Athenians might have been angry with him, replaced, dishonored, perhaps even punished him. On the other hand they might have seen no alternative to accepting his recommendation. Had he admitted some of his

[57]Green, *Armada*, 238-239.

errors and attributed them to his ill health, they might, at any rate, have recalled him and replaced him with a man better able to deal with the situation. Instead, either from concern for his own reputation and well-being, or because he once again sought to attain his ends indirectly, he offered the Athenians a choice. He probably expected the Athenians to be appalled at the notion of sending out a second expedition as large as the already swollen first one and to choose withdrawal instead.[58]

If so, it was the second time he had made exactly the same mistake, for the Athenians voted to send another fleet and army comprising both Athenians and allies. Furthermore, they refused Nicias' request to be relieved and instead chose Menander and Euthydemus, two men already at Syracuse, to be his colleagues for the time being. As regular generals to lead the reinforcements and join with Nicias in the command they chose Demosthenes, the hero of Sphacteria, and Eurymedon.[59] The latter was the same man who had served in the first campaign in Sicily and been fined on his return in 424; apparently the Athenians had thought better of him since that time. The Athenians, then, were sending two highly qualified men to help Nicias, both their ablest and most energetic general and a man with experience in Sicily.[60]

Both elements in the Athenian response are remarkable. All the earlier doubts about the wisdom of the original expedition must have seemed doubly impressive now that it had fared so badly. The prospects for widespread support from allies in Italy and Sicily, for civil strife in Syracuse, for a quick surrender at the sight of the massive Athenian armada—all had proven illusory. Instead the Athenians had settled down for a difficult and expensive siege; the Peloponnesians had sent effective help and were preparing to send more. The Athenians, their illusions disappointed by reality, should have been skeptical of a further commitment. At best, a hard fight might still bring victory, but the prospect of a defeat far from home with all the attendant risks

[58]Such is the suggestion of Busolt (GG III:2, 1348).
[59]For a discussion of the constitutional question involved in the choice of generals see Dover, HCT IV, 391-393.
[60]7.16.2.

should have been taken seriously. Yet the Athenians, apparently without lengthy debate, quickly voted all the reinforcements that Nicias had requested, sending Eurymedon to Sicily at once with 10 ships, 120 silver talents, and the encouraging news that Demosthenes would follow later with much greater forces.[61]

We cannot know why the Athenians chose this response, for Thucydides does not report the debate or offer an answer of his own. Perhaps he intends us to conclude that they continued to be driven by that same mad rapacity and ignorance of Sicily with which he credits them from the first.[62] But we have reason to expect that the failure to win an easy victory would have dampened Athenian zeal. The Athenian response may, perhaps, be better understood as the not unusual reaction of a great and powerful state unexpectedly thwarted by an opponent that had been despised as weak and easily defeated. Prudent consideration might have led the Athenians to conclude that the game was not worth the candle, but prudence is rare in such circumstances, especially in popular governments in which the passions of a people, once stirred, are difficult to rein in. After the mutilation of the Hermae, the parodies of the mysteries, and the ensuing great terror, the atmosphere in Athens was highly charged. Opposition to the expedition or to its reinforcement might be cited as evidence of hostility to the democracy, and few would have dared speak against the proposal.

More surprising was the Athenian assembly's decision to retain Nicias in his command in spite of his request to be relieved. So strange was this action that it has provoked one modern historian to suggest that Nicias' political enemies sponsored it in order to prevent him from returning to Athens.[63] But it is better to

[61]I accept the reading καὶ ἑκατόν found only in manuscript H. For supporting argument see Dover, *HCT* IV, 393. Thucydides tells us that the letter was read to the assembly, and the decision to send reinforcements and appoint the new generals was voted by that assembly. He tells us nothing, however, about the discussion that must have taken place before the votes. We cannot know, therefore, if there was any disagreement or, if so, what was its nature, who and how many were the nay-sayers. Unless Thucydides deceives us badly here, however, we should assume that the favorable majority was substantial and the opposition slight.

[62]6.1.1, 6.6.1, 6.8.4, 6.19.2 and especially 6.24.

[63]Meyer, *GdA* IV, 533. For a response see Busolt, *GG* III:2, 1355, n. 4.

seek an explanation in the special place that Nicias held in the minds of the Athenian people, and Plutarch provides us with important clues to their relationship.[64] Nicias reached the heights of civic honor and political power by a unique variety of devices, some traditional and some new. He had served as a colleague of Pericles on several occasions, succeeding, in part, to his prestige, especially among the opponents of Cleon. Those Athenians who feared and abhorred everything that Cleon represented must have continued to hold a special regard for the man who had always been his principal antagonist. Nicias tried to conduct himself in the same dignified manner as traditional aristocratic politicians, but he lacked the haughtiness that gained both the respect and dislike of the masses. "His dignity was not the austere, offensive kind but was mixed with a degree of prudence; he won over the masses because he seemed to fear them."[65]

The speeches that Thucydides attributed to Nicias show him to be a polished speaker, perhaps even trained by the sophists,

[64]Some readers will question reliance on so late a source as Plutarch. I have set forth my method in dealing with him in the Preface to my *Outbreak*, but it seems useful to say something more here. That no historian can afford to ignore his work can easily be shown by quoting a passage from his life of Nicias: "Those deeds which Thucydides and Philistus have set forth ... I have run over briefly... ; but those details which have escaped most writers, and which others have mentioned casually, or which are found on ancient votive offerings or in public decrees, these I have tried to collect, not massing together useless material of research, but handing on such as furthers the appreciation of character and temperament" (*Nicias* 1.5, Perrin's translation). Thus, Plutarch's account uses not only Thucydides but also Philistus, a contemporary and a witness to the siege of Syracuse, and preserves physical evidence that would otherwise reach us only as the product of the archaeologist's spade. In other passages he quotes the fourth-century historian Timaeus. Timaeus is a much less reliable source, and Plutarch treats him critically. Plutarch also quotes from contemporary comic poets and is often our only source for the quoted passages, as he is for otherwise lost lines of Euripides. These are but the hard nuggets of evidence, otherwise unavailable to us, that the text reveals. Behind them are great stores of histories, chronicles, treatises, compendia, and poetry lost to the modern scholar. Not all these sources deserve equal respect, and we know that Plutarch did not always use them as we would for, among other things, he was a biographer and a moralist, though a careful and critical one. Still, it seems unwise to reject the evidence of an author so much better informed than we are, especially, as in this case, when he is dealing with the reputation of his subject in his own time and afterwards.

[65]Plut. *Nic.* 2.3.

but, as we have seen, he was not quick in debate; he was easily flustered, forced into mistakes, and overcome by his opponents. Once again Plutarch provides a persuasive analysis of the Athenians' reactions to these failings: "In political life his timidity and the ease with which the professional informers put him into confusion even made him seem a popular, democratic figure, and gave him in no small measure the power that comes from the people, because they fear those who are contemptuous of them and increase the power of those who fear them. For there is no greater honor to the masses than not to be despised by their superiors."[66] Besides benefitting from his style and manner, Nicias actively sought to win the favor of the Athenian people by the calculated expenditure of his vast personal wealth. In this he was treading the same ground as Cimon in an earlier generation, but Nicias augmented the effectiveness of his benefactions with a rare theatrical flair. His striking display at Delos was noteworthy both for the care with which its choral and dramatic elements were prepared and for its overall theatrical effect.[67] Even more directly theatrical were the many times he provided a chorus for the dramatic festivals of Dionysus. He never lost, and when his entries won, he dedicated and placed the tripods in the sacred ground belonging to the temple of Dionysus.

Once he used the occasion of one of his choragic victories to stage a performance of his own. In one of the choruses that he supplied, one of his own domestic servants appeared dressed as the god Dionysus. His youthful good looks captivated the audience, which launched into prolonged applause. Seizing the moment, Nicias arose when the applause subsided and publicly gave the slave his freedom, saying "It is unholy for one who has been proclaimed a god to be a slave."[68] In a less extemporaneous way Nicias worked hard at what we might today call "creating an image." Imitating Pericles' practice, he remained aloof and avoided conviviality, as well as public conversations and occasions. Like his model, he buried himself in his official work, whether he was serving as general or member of the Athenian council, but unlike Pericles, he was both ostentatious and

[66]Plut. *Nic.* 2.4.
[67]Plut. *Nic.* 3.4-6 and above,
[68]Plut. *Nic.* 3.3.

apologetic about his behavior. He placed friends at the locked doors of his house to ask the pardon of those who came on the grounds that "at that very moment Nicias was occupied with important public business."[69] Nicias also employed what might be called today a "public relations expert," a certain Hiero who had been raised and educated in Nicias' household. Plutarch calls him Nicias' "chief fellow-tragedian in these matters and his colleague in placing round him a cloak of dignity and reputation."[70] It was one of Hiero's jobs to circulate stories about what a hard life Nicias was living in order to serve his city. "Even when he is taking his bath and while eating his dinner some kind of public business is bound to engage him. He neglects his private affairs by thinking always of the common good and barely begins to lie down to sleep until the first watch of the night. That is why he is not in good physical condition and is not gentle and kind to his friends, and he has lost friends, as well as money, while serving the city. Others gain friends and enrich themselves while enjoying themselves in the public forum and toying with the public interest."[71]

An important aspect of Nicias' public image was his piety. Almost all his public benefactions and dramatic displays, we must remember, were in connection with some religious activity: the rededication of Delos, the festival of Dionysus, gymnastic exhibitions at other festivals (probably the Panathenaic), the dedication of a gilded statue of Athena on the Acropolis, and countless more. In addition, he was famous for his devotion to seers and soothsayers; this may have earned him contempt among the enlightened, but it enhanced his reputation for religiosity and piety among the many. He further increased that reputation by his behavior on the battlefield after his victory at Corinth in 425. As victor he held the field and could collect and bury his dead. Having done so, he marched off but then learned that two corpses had inadvertently been left unburied. He sent a herald back to the Corinthians asking permission to bury them, thereby abandoning the right to set up a trophy of victory, for victors do

[69]Plut. Nic. 5.2.
[70]Plut. Nic. 5.2: Καὶ ὁ μάλιστα ταῦτα συντραγῳδῶν καὶ συμπεριτιθεὶς ὄγκον αὐτῷ καὶ δόξαν Ἱέρων ἦν, . . .
[71]Plut. Nic. 5.3-4.

not need the permission of the enemy to bury their dead. "Nevertheless," Plutarch says, "he preferred to give up the honor and glory of the victory than to leave two citizens unburied."[72] The anecdote is striking evidence of the close relationship that the ancient Greeks saw between civic duty and religion, and it shows why Nicias held a special place in the hearts of his countrymen.

Most Athenians must have believed that such piety went far to explain why Nicias was Athens' most consistently successful general. During the Archidamian War he had captured Cythera, recovered many towns in Thrace, captured Minoa off Megara and the Megarian port of Nisaea, and defeated the Corinthians in a battle in their territory. Plutarch may have been right in saying that he carefully chose his commands with an eye toward those that were likely to be quick, easy, successful, and safe,[73] but the Athenians knew he never lost, any more than his choruses lost in the dramatic competitions of Dionysus. Such a man was likely to be a good general, but even more surely, he was lucky and a favorite of the gods. Why, even his name was connected to the word meaning victory.[74]

We should not be surprised, therefore, that less than two years after the gods had been insulted by the desecration of the mysteries and the mutilation of the Hermae, the Athenians refused to excuse from service the one man most beloved of the gods, the man who was their talisman of victory. If he were ill, he would recover; in any case, he would be assisted by healthy and vigorous colleagues. If he were gloomy and pessimistic, everyone knew of his proverbial caution and the doubts with which he had entered on the expedition. The arrival of Demosthenes and the reinforcements would cheer and reinvigorate him. Even with his original force he had come within a whisker of taking Syracuse. Surely with reinforcement and able colleagues his skill and good fortune would soon produce victory. Such reasoning must have induced the Athenians to maintain Nicias in his unwelcome command.

[72]Plut. *Nic.* 6.4.
[73]Plut. *Nic.* 6.102.
[74]An omen noticed by Timaeus (Plut., *Nic.* 1.3).

12. *Athens on the Defensive*

News of the Athenians' decision to reinforce their army and navy in Sicily reached Sparta late in the winter, perhaps in February of 413. Thucydides tells us that the Spartans were already preparing for the invasion of Attica that would formally renew the war. In addition to the usual preparations, they sent round to their allies to gather tools and iron for clamps with which they meant to build a permanent fort in Attica. The Corinthians, the Syracusans, and Alcibiades had been urging this course on them for some time, and Thucydides tells us that after Alcibiades' speech the previous winter the Spartans at last turned their attention to the fortification on the hill of Decelea.[1] But he also tells us that even before that speech the Spartans had been inclined to invade Attica, but delayed, and even after the speech and the alleged commitment the Spartans waited more than a year to act. What moved the Spartans to action was not the gradual erosion of Spartan resistance by the persuasive talents of Alcibiades and his colleagues, but two important changes in the overall situation.

At the time of Alcibiades' speech the Athenians seemed to be on the point of taking Syracuse. Prudent calculation suggested that the Athenians would soon be able to bring back to mainland Greece their vast armada and considerable army, probably augmented by newly acquired allies from Sicily. Athenian finances, already considerably restored, would be still further increased by booty and contributions from the great island in the

[1] 6.93.2.

west. Cautious leaders in Sparta would have been reluctant to renew open warfare at such a time. There is even some evidence that the peace faction in Sparta may have used that moment to persuade their fellow citizens to strengthen the peace with Athens by offering to submit all outstanding issues to arbitration in accordance with the Thirty Years' Peace of 445.[2] The Athenian refusal of such a proposal would have discredited the Spartan friends of peace, and this refusal may have been the first step in prodding Sparta into action. The news of Gylippus' success and the reversal of Athenian fortunes in Sicily would surely have bolstered Spartan determination. A year after Alcibiades' speech everything had changed. Athens' Sicilian expedition, which had been a deterrent to resuming the war, now constituted a reason for Spartan optimism. Athens was losing, and in the process she was wasting men, ships, money, and prestige. The news that the Athenians were sending another major force to the west only strengthened the argument for invading Attica: the Athenians would be less able to resist, or the invasion might prevent them from sending the reinforcements.[3]

These were reasons sufficient to explain the Spartan mobilization for a campaign in 413, but Thucydides tells us that there

[2]Thucydides (7.18.3) speaks of Spartan proposals for arbitration which were rejected by the Athenians: καὶ ὁσάκις περί του διαφοραὶ γένοιντο τῶν κατὰ τὰς σπονδὰς ἀμφισβητουμένων, ἐς δίκας προκαλουμένων τῶν Λακεδαιμονίων οὐκ ἤθελον ἐπιτρέπειν. The language seems to suggest repeated offers repeatedly rejected, but this is the first mention Thucydides makes of them, and if they were made earlier and repeatedly the omission would be serious enough to amount to distortion. The omission or suppression of these offers and rejections, moreover, would be most surprising, for their inclusion would give strong support to Thucydides' general interpretation that the foolish Athenian *demos*, misled by demagogues and without the guidance of men like Pericles, repeatedly made disastrous errors. The likeliest explanation is that the Spartan offers and Athenian refusals all came in the year before the fortification of Decelea, but even so, Thucydides' failure to be more specific is disquieting. Whenever the offers were made, they were very important, for they were the essential ingredient in obtaining the kind of peace that Pericles had sought and Nicias had not achieved. We should like to know why the Athenians rejected it and how the argument ran. If the offer was sincere it would have provided legitimacy to the principle of dual hegemony in Greece by two equal and cooperating powers; it might even have given the Athenians a free hand in Sicily. The silence of our sources on all this is frustrating.

[3]7.18.1.

was another, no less important element. In all the years since the outbreak of the Peloponnesian War the Spartans had fought with a guilty conscience. They knew that the fighting had begun when their Theban allies had violated a truce with their attack on Plataea. Even more serious, the Spartans recognized that in refusing to submit grievances to arbitration in the years before 431, they had broken their sworn oaths and violated the Thirty Years' Peace. To the pious and superstitious Spartans these transgressions were explanation enough for their sufferings in the war. But here, too, everything had changed in the year since the speech of Alcibiades. It was the Athenians who, by attacking Spartan territory in Laconia, had now broken the oaths that they had taken in the Peace of Nicias; they were now the ones who refused arbitration. The gods could be expected to visit upon the Athenians the kind of retribution hitherto suffered by the Spartans. "At this time, therefore, the Spartans believed that the Athenians had come round to commit the same transgression of which the Spartans had been guilty before and were eager to go to war."[4] Together the changes in the material and moral conditions gave Sparta the confidence to renew the war.

At the beginning of March of 413, earlier than any of their previous invasions, the Spartans and their allies marched into Attica under the command of King Agis. The army began the usual devastation of the countryside and then set to work fortifying Decelea, apportioning the work among the contingents from the several cities. The site was well chosen for its purpose, thanks to the counsel of Alcibiades.[5] Decelea was about fourteen miles to the north-northeast of Athens and about the same distance, along the main route by way of Oropus, from Boeotia. Its hill, on which the Spartans built their fort, was defensible and high enough to dominate the plain for purposes of devastating the country and to keep watch on Athens, which was quite visible from the summit.[6] During this first summer of its exis-

[4] 7.18.3.
[5] For Alcibiades' advice see 6.91.6 and Lysias 14.30. Diodorus (13.9.1) says that Alcibiades came along with Agis, but it seems incredible that Thucydides would omit that detail if it were true. Plutarch (Alc. 23.7) pictures Alcibiades as being in Sparta, engaged in domestic intrigue, while Agis was on campaign.
[6] 7.19.1-2; Dover, HCT IV, 395; Busolt, GG III:2, 1359; see Map 2.

tence the fort at Decelea was occupied by the entire Peloponnesian army, thereafter by garrisons from each of the allied contingents in rotation.[7]

The Spartan occupation of Decelea proved to be a terrible strain on Athenian resources, both material and moral. Even when the Spartans made their annual invasions during the Archidamian War, they had never stayed more than forty days. For the rest of the year the Athenians could use the land in a number of ways and enjoy free access to the country, which was the home of most of them. Now they were permanently deprived of all the territory outside the walled area of the city and the Piraeus. In the first year of the fortification, moreover, more than 20,000 slaves deserted, many of them fleeing from the silver mines, whose revenues would also be denied the Athenians thenceforth. Cattle and pack animals were also lost. The Thebans took special advantage of the opportunities afforded them by their proximity to Attica, as a fourth century historian makes clear: "[Thebes] came to prosper in a much higher degree when the Lacedaemonians fortified Decelea against the Athenians; for they took over the prisoners and all the other spoils of the war at a small price, and, as they inhabited the neighboring country, carried off to their homes all the furnishing material in Attica, beginning with the wood and tiles of the houses. The country of the Athenians at that time had been the most lavishly furnished in Greece, for it had suffered but slight injury from the Lacedaemonians in the former invasion."[8]

The fort at Decelea strained Athenian military resources. As Thucydides puts it, "instead of a city Athens became a garrisoned fortress."[9] Foot soldiers of every age had to do guard duty at the walls or perform military service somewhere else.[10] During the day they took turns, but at night they all had to stand watch against a Spartan attack, and this went on winter and summer for the rest of the war. The cavalry bore even a heavier

---

[7]7.27.3.
[8]*Hellenica Oxyrhynchia* 12.3, translated by B. D. Grenfell and A. S. Hunt in *Oxyrhynchus Papyri* V (London, 1908), 229.
[9]7.28.1.
[10]See Dover, *HCT* IV, 406–407.

burden, for it went out every day to keep the army at Decelea at bay, and the rocky ground lamed the horses, and enemy weapons wounded them.[11] The very fact that Athenian cavalrymen were forced to do service in Attica was a tribute to the success of the fort at Decelea, for they were badly needed in Sicily.

The Peloponnesian occupation of Decelea also imposed a heavy financial burden on Athens, for it barred the road to Oropus and thereby interfered with the import of supplies from Euboea. In 431 the Athenians had moved their major livestock to that island, which became increasingly important to them in the course of the war, both as a pastureland and as a convenient transfer point for imported necessities.[12] The fortification of Decelea compelled the Athenians to abandon the overland route from Euboea which they had formerly used and to replace it with what Thucydides tells us was a more expensive sea passage, around Sunium.[13] The additional cost of imports, the expense of maintaining armed forces in Attica, the loss of revenue from the mines and of capital in the countryside, all at the same time that Athens was expending great sums for the Sicilian campaign, put great pressure on Athenian finances. In an attempt to increase their revenues the Athenians cancelled tribute payments and replaced them with a 5 percent tax on goods imported or exported by sea.[14]

In spite of all these new troubles the Athenians persevered with their Sicilian campaign, and Thucydides conveys a sense of how remarkable their actions were: "The heaviest burden on them was that they had to wage two wars at the same time, and they had reached such a degree of determination as no one would have believed if he heard about it beforehand. For who would believe that they, who were themselves besieged by the Peloponnesians who had built a fortress in their country, would not, even so, abandon Sicily, but would likewise lay siege to Syracuse there, a city no smaller than Athens itself, and that

[11]7.27.5.
[12]2.14.1; 8.96.2; Dover, HCT IV, 406.
[13]7.27.2.
[14]7.28.4.

they should have caused the Greeks to make so great a miscalculation of their power and daring—since at the beginning of the war some thought they could hold out for a year, some two, and some three, but no one for more than three years if the Peloponnesians invaded their country—that in the seventeenth year after the first invasion they should have gone to Sicily, though already thoroughly worn out by the war, and launched another war not smaller than the one they already had against the Peloponnesus."[15]

Athens' financial troubles indirectly led to what was surely the most horrible atrocity in the long and terrible war. During their preparations for sending reinforcements to Sicily the Athenians had hired a special contingent of Thracian peltasts from the Dii tribe. Thirteen hundred of these knife-carrying barbarians arrived in Athens in the spring of 413 after Demosthenes had already sailed, too late to take part in the Sicilian campaign. They might have been useful against the Peloponnesians at Decelea, but the Athenians found it too expensive to pay them in view of the great strain on the treasury at that time. They therefore sent them home under the guidance of Dieitrephes, an Athenian commander. He was ordered to use them to do any damage to the enemy that opportunity offered. As he sailed along the Euripus, he led them in a raid on Tanagra in Boeotia, then quickly retreated across the water to Chalcis in Euboea. From there he crossed the Euripus again by night and landed in Boeotia (see Map 2).

He camped near the little town of Mycalessus and attacked it at daybreak. Surprise was complete, for the town was of no importance, well inland, and never had expected to be involved in the fighting. Its walls were in disrepair, but that did not matter, for the gates were open, so little did the citizens fear attack. What happened next is best described by Thucydides. "The Thracians burst into Mycalessus, sacked the houses and the temples, and butchered the people, sparing neither old nor young, but killing every one they met in whatever order they came upon them, even children and women, and pack animals, too, and anything

[15]7.28.3.

they saw that was alive. For the Thracian race, like the most barbarous peoples, is most murderous when it has nothing to fear. At this time there was much distressed confusion, and every kind of destruction took place. They also attacked a boys' school which was the largest in the town; the children had just come in, and they cut down every one of them. This disaster was greater than any that had befallen a whole city and more unexpected and horrible than any other."[16] When the Thebans learned what had happened, they came as quickly as they could, pursued the barbarians, deprived them of their booty and killed 250 of them before they made their escape. But it was too late for Mycalessus, a good part of whose citizens had been killed.[17]

The Peloponnesians, meanwhile, were not asleep. The good news from Sicily convinced the Corinthians and Spartans that they had been right to help Syracuse and encouraged them to increase their assistance. They planned to send their own and allied hoplites to Sicily in troop carriers and the Corinthians prepared 25 triremes to serve as a convoy for them; they would challenge the Athenian fleet at Naupactus in a naval battle and so allow their troopships to get through to the west.[18] In the spring of 413, while they were building the fort at Decelea, the Spartans picked out 600 of the best helots and *neodamodeis* and placed them under the command of a Spartan officer, Eccritus. The Boeotians selected 300 hoplites under two Thebans and one Thespian commander. Together these two contingents set out at once from Cape Taenarum at the southern tip of Laconia, across the open sea.[19] The Corinthians put together a force of 500 hoplites made up of some Corinthians and some Arcadian mercenaries, while the Sicyonians provided a contingent of 200 hoplites. These troops were able to sail safely through the Corinthian Gulf, past the Athenian fleet at Naupactus, protected by the 25 Corinthian triremes drawn up opposite the Athenians.[20]

[16] 7.27.1; 29.
[17] 7.30.
[18] 7.17.3-4; 18.4.
[19] 7.19.4. I take the words ἐς τὸ πέλαγος ἀφῆκαν to mean that they did not take the usual route along the coast.
[20] 7.19.5.

The Athenians were also busy toward the end of the winter. While Eurymedon was on his way to bring money and encouragement to Nicias and his colleagues at Sicily, Demosthenes was in Athens preparing the major relief expedition. At Athens he gathered ships, money, and hoplites and sent word to the allies to prepare their contingents. He also sent a fleet of 20 ships under the command of Conon to Naupactus to prevent the Corinthians and other Peloponnesians from sending ships to Sicily. Apparently in the years since the Peace of Nicias, Athens had not needed to maintain a fleet there, but the renewal of the war changed that.[21] At the very beginning of spring in 413, at the same time as the Spartan fortification of Decelea, the Athenians sent two fleets off, one under Charicles and the other under Demosthenes. In light of the urgency of Nicias' plea we might expect them to sail to Sicily with all possible speed, but they did not. Charicles, one of the members on the board that had inquired into the mutilation of the Hermae,[22] had orders to take his 30 ships and collect hoplites from Argos and then to attack the Laconian coast. Demosthenes had 60 Athenian and 5 Chian ships, 1,200 Athenian hoplites and an unspecified number from the islands. But he did not sail directly for Sicily, though that was his ultimate destination. Instead he was ordered, along the way, to help Charicles in his attack on Laconia, so he went to Aegina to complete the collection of his forces and to wait until Charicles had picked up the Argives.[23]

When all was ready, he joined Charicles and the Argives, sailed to Epidaurus Limera on the Laconian coast, and ravaged its fields (see Map 4). Then they sailed down the coast to a small cape just opposite the island of Cythera and fortified its isthmus. They intended it to be another Pylos to which helots could escape from the Spartans and from which raids against Laconia could be launched.[24] The idea must have seemed both reasonable and attractive, especially as a countermeasure to the fortifi-

---

[21]7.17.1-2, 4; 31.4; Dover, *HCT* IV, 393.
[22]And. 1.36, where he is also called an extreme democrat. Later on he was a member of the oligarchic Thirty who ruled Athens in 404 (Xen. *Hell.* 2.3.2).
[23]7.20.2-3.
[24]7.26.1-2.

cation of Decelea. Perhaps the Athenians had even higher hopes for it, remembering how their fortification of Pylos had caused the Spartans to evacuate Attica immediately and then to make the mistakes that led to the capture of their men on Sphacteria. If so, they were doomed to disappointment. The new base was not well located to attract helot desertions, for it was far from Messenia, nor do we know of any significant Athenian actions launched from it. The Spartans, moreover, appear not to have responded strongly to its establishment, and the Athenians abandoned it the next winter.[25] The venture turned out not to be worth the effort, and the delay it caused was costly for the Athenian effort in Sicily, but we should not allow the wisdom of hindsight to blind us to its attractions in the spring of 413.

When the fort had been completed, Charicles left a garrison in it and sailed back to Athens, and the Argives went home as well.[26] Meanwhile, Demosthenes sailed along the coast toward Corcyra, on the usual route to the west. At Pheia in Elis he found and destroyed a troop carrier full of Corinthian hoplites bound for Sicily, but the sailors and hoplites got away and were later able to find another ship. Demosthenes sailed on to Zacynthus and Cephallenia, where he recruited more hoplites and sent for others to his friends, the Messenians of Naupactus (see Map 3). From there he sailed to the mainland at Acarnania, the scene of his earlier triumphs, and met Eurymedon on his way back from Sicily. He came to bring Demosthenes the bad news of a serious Athenian reversal near Syracuse. There was need to collect the necessary forces as quickly as possible and hurry to Sicily. Before they could do anything, however, Demosthenes and Eurymedon were joined by Conon from Naupactus. He complained that he had only 18 triremes to combat the 25 Corinthian vessels that prevented interference with Peloponnesian ships in the Corinthian Gulf. Later events would show that Conon was a bold and talented sailor, so it is surprising to find him unwilling to engage the enemy with such odds when we remember the much greater odds Phormio had overcome in

[25]8.4.
[26]7.26.3.

429.[27] Perhaps the crews of his ships were the dregs of the Athenian navy, and the better men were on their way to Sicily. In any case, Demosthenes and Eurymedon sent him "the best 10 ships they had." Then Eurymedon went to Corcyra to collect more hoplites and enough Corcyraean sailors to man 15 ships. Demosthenes gathered slingers and javelin throwers from his old haunts in Acarnania. Soon they both set sail for Italy on the way to Sicily.[28]

The bad news brought by Eurymedon was that Gylippus had captured the Athenian base at Plemmyrium. At the beginning of spring, while the Peloponnesians were at work at Decelea and the Athenians busy in Laconia, Gylippus came back to Syracuse with the soldiers he had recruited throughout Sicily. He had reason to know that all his success could be undone when Demosthenes and Eurymedon arrived with new forces. They would provide bold, vigorous leadership in place of that offered by the discouraged and ailing Nicias. Their appearance and any victory they might achieve could quickly discourage the Syracusans and turn their thoughts once again to peace negotiations. The defense of their city, moreover, was expensive for the Syracusans. None of their allies supplied them with money, and they were supporting perhaps as many as 7,000 foreign soldiers.[29] The Athenian blockade, however imperfect, must have cut off income to private citizens from trade and from the public treasury in import duties. The Syracusans also incurred unusual expenses in building, fitting out, and manning warships for, unlike the Athenians, they neither maintained a fleet in peacetime nor received income from subjects adequate to support one. For all these reasons the Syracusans must have financed their defense in great part with reserve funds, which must have been seriously depleted by 413. For that reason alone, the arrival of the Athenian reinforcements, with their promise of prolonging the war, may have led the Syracusans to consider surrender.

[27] 2.83. Thucydides does not say how the Athenian fleet diminished from 20 to 18.

[28] 7.31.4–5; 33.3.

[29] That is the estimate of Green (*Armada*, 255) whose discussion of Syracuse's financial troubles is enlightening.

Gylippus, therefore, conceived a plan to meet these problems. His practiced military eye discerned the dangerous position in which the Athenians had placed themselves at Plemmyrium. If he could capture the Athenian position there, he could deprive the Athenians of their naval base at the mouth of the harbor, forcing them to move their ships either back to their original base on the shore near Syracuse or out of Syracuse harbor altogether, to Thapsus or Catana. In the first case they would then be exposed to attacks from the land forces of Gylippus and to the diseases coming from the low-lying marshes. In the second, they would find it difficult, if not impossible, to maintain a close blockade of the harbors of Syracuse. A success at Plemmyrium would also bring him the food, naval supplies, and money that were stored in its strongholds, a double gain, at once depriving the enemy and assisting the Syracusans. Finally, a victory of that sort would strengthen Syracusan morale at a crucial moment.

Gylippus' plan required a naval attack to serve as a diversion while his army crept up on the Athenian base from the land side. There was the rub, for the Syracusans had experienced no success against the Athenian fleet and thought it to be invincible. Gylippus' strategy, however, did not require a naval victory, but merely enough of a fight to distract the Athenians from the main action, which would take place on land. Naturally, he could not reveal this aspect of his strategy to the Syracusans, who might drown while creating the necessary diversion, and to persuade them to sail against the Athenians, he relied principally on Hermocrates, who, though no longer in office, had not lost his persuasive powers. His main argument was that the Athenians had become great seamen not through heredity but by the experience that had been forced on them in the Persian war and by the daring with which they terrified their victims. If the Syracusans showed similar daring they would take the Athenians by surprise, terrify them in the same way, and so overcome the enemy's advantage in experience. Gylippus and others also endorsed the plan for a battle at sea, and the Syracusans, enthusiastically persuaded, manned the ships.[30]

[30] 7.21.

Protected by darkness, Gylippus took his army on a night march toward Plemmyrium. Simultaneously, 35 Syracusan triremes from within the Great Harbor and 45 from the Little Harbor made a rendezvous off Ortygia and together launched an attack from the sea against Plemmyrium at different points. The Athenians, though taken by surprise, managed to put 60 triremes into the water; 25 confronted the smaller Syracusan squadron in the Great Harbor, while the rest sailed out to meet the enemy fleet outside it. The fighting at the mouth of the harbor was fierce, as the Athenians tried to prevent the larger squadron from entering, and for a time neither side had a clear advantage. The Athenian land forces, meanwhile, having no notion of Gylippus' plan, went down to the shore to watch the fighting. At daybreak Gylippus attacked the ill-defended forts, took them by surprise and captured all three, the garrisons of the smaller two fleeing without a fight. The fleeing troops were able to make their way back to the original Athenian base near the Anapus on boats and a merchant ship, the difficulty of their flight varying as the naval battle in the harbor gave the advantage first to one side and then the other. Finally, Syracusan inexperience at sea gave way to Athenian discipline and skill. The squadron outside the harbor forced its way in but then broke formation, and its ships fell foul of one another and "bestowed the victory upon the Athenians." Once the tide had turned, the Athenian fleet not only defeated this disorganized squadron but also the fleet from within the harbor which earlier had held the upper hand. The Athenians sank 11 ships and lost 3 of their own. They set up a trophy on a small island off Plemmyrium to prove their victory and control of the sea and withdrew to their camp near the Anapus.[31]

But the Athenians' triumph at sea was Pyrrhic, at best. They suffered many casualties and many of their garrison troops were taken prisoner. The food, property, and naval supplies (the sails and tackle of 40 triremes were lost, as well as 3 triremes caught on shore) in the forts were captured by Gylippus. The greatest cost of the loss of Plemmyrium, however, was strategic, as

[31]7.22–23.

Thucydides makes clear: "The taking of Plemmyrium did the greatest and most serious harm to the Athenian army. Even entry into the harbor was no longer safe for convoys of supplies, for the Syracusans, looking out for them there with ships, stood in their way, and from then on supply ships could only enter by fighting their way through. In general the loss of Plemmyrium brought bewilderment and discouragement to the army."[32]

The Syracusans moved swiftly to take advantage of their success, hoping to gather their resources and defeat the Athenians before Demosthenes and Eurymedon could arrive with their reinforcements. They sent a ship to the Peloponnesus to report their victory and urge their allies to press the war against Athens even more vigorously. The Syracusan admiral Agatharchus took 11 triremes to Italy, for information had been received that Athenian supplies were coming that way. They found the supply boats and destroyed most of them, and at Caulonia they burned timber that had been prepared for Athenian ship repairs. At Locri they picked up some Thespian hoplites who had come on a merchant ship. On the way back they were ambushed by 20 Athenian ships, but slipped through to Syracuse with the loss of only one trireme.

In the Great Harbor of Syracuse the two hostile navies engaged in occasional skirmishes and tried various tricks to harm one another, but, for the most part, each stayed at its base. The Syracusans, however, launched a diplomatic offensive in Sicily, sending envoys from Corinth, Ambracia, and Sparta to the several cities to announce the capture of Plemmyrium and to explain away the defeat at sea as a result only of their inexperience. Foreigners were sent, no doubt, because they were thought to be more credible than Syracusans. Their purpose was to get more help, both on land and sea, and they argued that if the Sicilians could defeat the Athenians before their reinforcements arrived they could drive them from Sicily and end the war there.[33] They met with considerable success, for Camarina sent 500 hoplites, 300 javelin throwers, and 300 archers. Gela sent 5 ships, 400 javelin throwers, and 200 cavalry. Except for Catana and Naxos,

[32] 7.24.
[33] 7.25.

who were allied to Athens, and Acragas, which remained neutral, "almost all of Sicily . . . the others who previously stood by and watched, now joined with and came to the aid of the Syracusans against the Athenians."[34]

While the Syracusans' representatives were doing their work, however, Nicias took steps to check them. He sent word to his Sicel allies at Centoripa, Halicyae, and other places in the interior of the island. His intelligence network was as good as usual, and he had learned that Acragas would not let the newly recruited army pass through its territory on the way to Syracuse. Many of the new troops must have come from the region around Selinus. Since they could not go along the coast past Acragas, they must strike north through the territory of Halicyae (see Map 9). Nicias urged the friendly Sicels to concert their plans and bar the way. They did as he asked and waited in ambush for the enemy army. They took them quite by surprise, killing 800 troops and all but one of the envoys who had collected them. The Corinthian envoy escaped and led the 1,500 soldiers who escaped the ambush to Syracuse, but the surprise assault ended all hopes of attacking Nicias on land before his reinforcements could arrive.[35]

If the Syracusans were to strike a blow before that, they must try their luck at sea again, and since their recent defeat in the Great Harbor something had happened in the Corinthian Gulf, far from Sicily, to increase their chances considerably. Since Demosthenes and Eurymedon had granted Conon's request for help, the Athenians had sent more reinforcements to Naupactus under Diphilus, who replaced Conon as commander of the squadron, that now numbered 33 triremes. The Peloponnesian force, under the Corinthian commander Polyanthes, consisted of about 30 ships.[36] Probably the ease with which Peloponnesian ships were getting out of the gulf led the Athenians to strengthen their force at Naupactus and try to cut off the traffic. The Peloponnesians likewise increased their commitment to keep the

[34] 7.33.1–2.

[35] 7.32.

[36] Thucydides (7.34.1) says that the Peloponnesian fleet was slightly smaller—ὀλίγῳ ἐλάσσους—than the Athenian.

sea lanes free. The Athenians appear to have forced the battle, for it took place off Erineus in Achaea, on the Peloponnesian shore.[37] The Peloponnesians put their ships in line across the mouth of a crescent-shaped cove, placing hoplites on the headlands at each end. This was a typically defensive posture such as the Peloponnesians had been taking at sea since the war began. As Diphilus sailed from Naupactus, he probably considered his greatest problem to be to get the enemy to accept battle, but the Athenians were taken by surprise.

The offensive weapon of the Greek trireme was a bronze ram at the bow. The trireme was like a torpedo which, when its ram struck the hull of the enemy at a good speed, would pierce it and sink the ship. The victory in normal circumstances went to the ships with the greatest speed and maneuverability, for they could break through the enemy line or circle round it, and thus take the enemy on the flank or in the rear. The timing and cohesion needed to achieve such maneuvers required long training and considerable expense. Only the Athenians had been able to provide these, so their crews were normally superior and their ships victorious. To overcome this advantage, Polyanthes made a small but important alteration in the design of his triremes, which permitted him to use a new tactic. At the bow of each trireme there was an *epotis,* "an earlike plank projecting from each side of the ship,"[38] like a cathead on a modern sailing ship from which an anchor can be slung. On the trireme the *epotis* was the terminal of the *parexeiresia,* or outrigger, which was attached to the gunwale on each side of the ship and on which were fixed the oar pins of the thranites, the top-level rowers of the trireme. Normal tactics dictated that the triremes avoid ramming each other head on, for that would damage both ships in a way that would not necessarily bring the advantage to either.

As Diphilus approached the Peloponnesians, they remained quiet, apparently in the old, timid way, but then Polyanthes gave the signal to attack. As the rams passed each other, his strengthened catheads struck the more fragile Athenian ones,

[37]For the location see Dover, *HCT* IV, 414. See Map 5b.

[38]J. S. Morrison and R. T. Williams, *Greek Oared Ships 900–322 B.C.* (Cambridge, 1968), 338. My discussion of the trireme is based on their account.

forcing them to give way, taking the attached outriggers with them and thus crippling, but not sinking, the Athenian ships. Three Corinthian ships were sunk in the battle and no Athenian, but 7 Athenian ships were totally disabled by Polyanthes' maneuver. The results were indecisive, for both sides set up victory trophies, but the strategic victory went to the Peloponnesians. The Athenians, after all, had sought them out to destroy their fleet and its ability to protect merchant ships and troop carriers, and they had failed to do so. For the first time a Peloponnesian fleet had fought a numerically superior Athenian fleet to a standstill. Morally, as well as strategically, this was a great victory for the Peloponnesians. They finally had developed a tactic that, for the moment at least, negated the usual Athenian tactical superiority. In an open sea, against an enemy who was prepared for them, such tactics could be overcome, but in restricted waters, against an unprepared enemy, they could be most effective.[39]

In Sicily the Syracusans, hearing of the imminent arrival of Demosthenes and Eurymedon, decided to try once more to injure the Athenians before the reinforcements could arrive. This time the Syracusans meant to test their luck at sea, and it is clear that the news from the Corinthian Gulf had encouraged them to do so. They devised a complex but clever plan of battle. The inventor seems to have been Ariston of Corinth, who adopted the techniques discovered by Polyanthes and added a few elements of his own.[40] The plan made full use of every advantage circumstances offered. The Syracusan ships employed thickened catheads, buttressed by fixed stay-beams, both inside and outside the ship.[41] In the narrow space of Syracuse harbor, where it would be difficult or impossible for the Athenians to break through the line (*diekplous*) or to circle around (*periplous*), the

---

[39]7.34; Morrison and Williams, *Greek Oared Ships*, 280–281.

[40]On Ariston see 7.39.2; Plut., *Nic.* 25.4; Diod. 13.10.2.

[41]7.36.2. It is not perfectly clear how these stays worked. Morrison (*Greek Oared Ships*, 282) says "The word translated 'fixed' is the geometrical term which makes the English word 'hypotenuse.' The stays were the hypotenuses of right-angles formed by the beams of the *epotides* and the ship's side, both inside and outside." His Figure 9 on the same page illustrates his version. For a different version see Dover, *HCT* IV, 416.

tactic of precipitating head-on collisions with Athenian ships whose prows were not reinforced promised to bring success. The magnitude of a Syracusan victory could be enhanced by the fact that the Syracusans controlled all the land surrounding the harbor, except for the small coastline between the Athenians' walls, where the Athenian fleet was beached and to which alone it could safely return. Since the Syracusans controlled both Ortygia and Plemmyrium, and thus access to the Great Harbor, an Athenian defeat could turn into a disaster, for ships falling out of line could neither flee the harbor nor escape to the land. They would be forced together at a very small point before the area enclosed by the walls, where they could not maneuver and would fall foul of one another.[42]

The Athenians, of course, could do nothing about the restricted land area available to them or the Syracusan command of the entrance to the harbor, but they might have responded to the new tactics used in the Corinthian Gulf by redesigning their own triremes. The Athenians, however, though they knew what had happened to the fleet of Diphilus, learned no lesson from it. They did not know that the head-on collision was a deliberate enemy tactic but instead attributed such crashes to the ignorance of the Peloponnesian helmsmen.[43] That is the kind of arrogance to be expected from a navy made cocky by a long string of victories, and it was to prove costly. It was not, however, the only surprise that Ariston and the Syracusans had in store. Full of renewed confidence, they launched another combined attack on land and sea. Gylippus marched an army to the Athenian wall facing the city; at the same time Syracusan forces from the garrison at the Olympieum, hoplites, cavalry, and light-armed soldiers, came up to the Athenian wall on the other side. This drew full Athenian attention to defending the walls, and when the Syracusan fleet came sailing down on them, the Athenians were thrown temporarily into confusion, some running to one wall, some to the other and, finally, some running to man the fleet. The surprise was not crippling, however. The Athenians were able to put 75 ships to sea against the 80 enemy vessels facing

[42]7.36.
[43]7.36.5.

them. The day was spent in indecisive skirmishing, and after a time both land and naval forces were withdrawn.[44]

The next day the Syracusans took no action, leaving Nicias free to repair such damage as had been done to his ships and to strengthen his naval base in expectation of another attack. The beach on which the Athenians drew up their ships was already protected by a palisade sunk into the sand beneath the water, some distance offshore. It was intended in part, no doubt, as a breakwater to shelter the ships from the strong east wind that often churned up the bay,[45] but it also could protect the Athenian ships against a pursuing enemy. If they needed to escape from battle they could sail to safety through the entrances in it. To increase the opportunities for safe withdrawal from battle Nicias now placed merchantmen in front of the palisade, one before each entrance, the entrances being located about two hundred feet apart. Each merchant ship was equipped with a crane whose beams carried heavy metal weights in the shape of a dolphin. When an enemy ship approached, the "dolphin" could be swung over the side and dropped from on high onto the enemy ship; with good luck it might crash through the ship's hull and sink it.[46]

Although the Syracusans allowed Nicias to proceed undisturbed with these measures, they did not waste the time. Ariston's first stratagem had failed to take the Athenians sufficiently by surprise, so he devised another. On the third day he began his attack at an earlier hour, but he carried out the same operations as on the first day. Again a good part of the day was spent in skirmishing, but then Ariston had the Syracusan admirals order a withdrawal for rest and dinner. The fleet backed water, and the sailors disembarked on the beach, where merchants had been ordered to set up a food market. The Athenian commanders assumed that the Syracusans had once again been overawed by the Athenian fleet. They too withdrew to the shore, they and

---

[44] 7.37-38.1.

[45] The wind and the heavy surf it creates are mentioned by Ferguson (*CAH* V, 301) and confirmed by Green (*Armada*, 259, n. 4).

[46] 7.38.2-3; 41.1-2. These passages are interpreted and discussed by Dover (*HCT* IV, 417-418) and Green (*Armada*, 277-278).

their men dawdling over dinner and other matters, for they thought there would be no more fighting that day. Then the Syracusans leaped to the attack, catching the Athenians not only unprepared but tired and hungry. It was with considerable difficulty that the Athenians manned their ships again.

The two navies faced each other in much the same way as before. Soon the Athenian commanders saw that the strain of continuing at sea in this way would wear down their men and leave them vulnerable to attack by the rested Syracusans, so they ordered an immediate attack. They might, of course, have tried to retreat to their protected base and avoid fighting that day, but retreat before an enemy facing one in line in restricted waters is neither easy nor safe. Besides, for an Athenian fleet to refuse battle to an enemy of almost equal numbers was unheard of.[47] The Syracusans met the Athenian onslaught with the head-on charge they had so carefully prepared, as well as a few new tricks. Since they planned no complicated maneuvers that would require balance and maneuverability, the Syracusans were able to load their decks with javelin throwers whose missiles disabled many Athenian rowers. Even more harm was done by small boats containing more javelin throwers; these boats rowed in under the oar banks of the Athenian triremes, allowing their passengers to kill rowers in all the banks.

These unorthodox tactics, and the disparity in the physical condition of the sailors in the two fleets, resulted in a Syracusan victory. The Athenians escaped disaster by fleeing to safety behind the merchantmen and the palisade. Two reckless Syracusan ships that pursued too hotly were destroyed by "dolphins." Seven Athenian ships were sunk and many were damaged; many Athenian sailors were killed and many taken prisoner. The Syracusans dominated the Great Harbor and set up a trophy of

---

[47]Plutarch (*Nic.* 20.4-5) says Nicias did not want to fight at all until Demosthenes and Eurymedon arrived and that the issue was forced by the other generals who were ambitious and who said that the city's reputation would be ruined if they did not fight at once. Diodorus (13.10.4) says the battle broke out when some of the trierarchs could no longer bear the insults hurled at them by the Syracusans. Thucydides' account indicates that the Athenians had little choice but to fight, as Nicias would have seen.

victory. Their confidence was at its peak; they believed they were superior to the Athenians at sea and would soon defeat them on land, and they made preparations to attack again on both.[48]

[48]7.39-41.

13. Defeat on Land and Sea

Even as the Syracusans rejoiced in their victory and planned to exploit it further, the Athenian reinforcements under Demosthenes and Eurymedon arrived. After the fall of Plemmyrium, at about the time of the ambush of the Sicilian reinforcements by the Sicels, Demosthenes and Eurymedon had sailed from Corcyra to Italy. In Iapygia they enlisted 150 javelin throwers, and at Metapontum 300 more, as well as 2 triremes. From there they moved on to Thurii, where the anti-Athenian faction had recently been driven out, making it easy to recruit 700 hoplites and 300 javelin throwers who might be expected to fight with spirit. The Athenian commanders could not have anticipated a friendly reception during the rest of their trip along the Italian coast, for they were excluded from the cities of Croton, Locri, and Rhegium. Crossing to Sicily, they presumably stopped at Naxos or Catana to prepare for the final leg of their voyage.[1]

The Athenian generals made their appearance in the most impressive manner possible. The armada "was decked out theatrically so that the decorations of the weapons and the ensigns of the triremes and the multitude of coxswains and pipers might strike fear into the enemy."[2] The force consisted of 73 ships, almost 5,000 hoplites, many javelin throwers, slingers, and

---

[1]7.33.3–6; 35. Thucydides does not mention a stop in Sicily before Syracuse, but it would seem to have been necessary.
[2]Plut. *Nic.* 21.1.

bowmen, and a commensurate supply of equipment. Their arrival abruptly dampened the Syracusans' high spirits; they marveled at the Athenians' ability to dispatch another powerful force despite the Spartan fort at Decelea and wondered if there would ever be an end to Syracuse's danger. The Athenians at Syracuse, on the other hand, were naturally encouraged by the new turn of events.[3]

Demosthenes quickly evaluated the situation. As usual, he gave prominence to its psychological elements. Studying the campaign before his arrival, he had been highly critical of Nicias' delay in beginning the siege of Syracuse. He thought that a quick assault and siege would have discouraged the Syracusans and made them surrender without sending for help to the Peloponnesus.[4] He thought that his arrival, likewise, would have its greatest psychological effect if he attacked immediately. He understood at once that the key to everything was the Syracusan counter-wall on Epipolae which had prevented the siege of Syracuse. If that were taken, the Athenians could close off Syracuse by land. Demosthenes appears to have been sure that the arrival of his fleet would allow the Athenians to regain control of the sea and complete the blockade from that side. There can be no doubt that this plan of action was superior to what the Athenians had been doing under Nicias, staying within their double wall and making no attempt to enclose the enemy's city. On the other hand, gaining control of an ascent to Epipolae and defeating Gylippus' forces on it would be both difficult and dangerous, which, in part, is why Nicias had not attempted it. Demosthenes recognized the difficulty and the danger and did not assume success. He was prepared to accept defeat, if necessary, for he believed that defeat was preferable to a long and pointless stay in Sicily, which would waste Athenian resources and risk the safety of its forces. If he attacked Epipolae he might succeed in conquering Sicily; if he failed he would abandon the campaign and take the expedition home to fight again another day. In either case the war in Sicily would be brought to a long overdue end.[5]

[3] 7.42.1-2.
[4] 7.42.3; for a discussion of this judgment see above, pp. 237-238.
[5] 7.42.3-5.

Demosthenes first undertook some preliminary maneuvers, probably to test the mettle of his and the enemy's troops, to give his own men some practice under his command, and to distract and confuse the enemy about his true purposes. He led an army from within the walls to ravage the country about the Anapus River and embarked the fleet to accompany them and defend them from enemy attack by sea. The Syracusan fleet stayed on the beach, and of the army only some cavalry and javelin throwers came down from the garrison on the Olympieum to offer token resistance. From the point of view of morale and general attitude, this was a sign that the initiative had passed once again to the Athenians. Next, Demosthenes launched a direct attack on the Syracusan counter-wall on Epipolae, presumably using "The Circle" as his point of departure. He attacked at several points, using soldiers and siege machinery, but the Syracusans set fire to the machines and drove off the soldiers.[6]

The problems connected with Demosthenes' real plan were serious enough to encourage attempts to succeed otherwise, and it probably appeared unwise not to try an attack on the wall before undertaking more dangerous schemes. In any case, he probably had to exhaust all other devices before he could convince Nicias to permit the riskier strategy.[7] It was immediately obvious that an attack on Epipolae by daylight would not succeed, for the points of access were all difficult and could easily be defended by an enemy who was prepared. Demosthenes, therefore, planned a daring assault by night. In the first week of August he took his entire land army, perhaps as many as 10,000 hoplites and the same number of light-armed troops, through the darkness before the rising of the moon to the pass at Euryalus. The ailing Nicias was left behind within the double walls.[8] The approach must have been remarkably skillful, for although the Athenians came through the pass that both they and Gylippus had earlier used, and although the Syracusans had stationed a

[6]7.42.6–43.1.
[7]Thucydides (7.43.1) tells us that only after persuading Nicias and the other commanders was he allowed to carry out his plan. See also Plut. *Nic.* 21.2–4.
[8]7.43.2. For the date see Busolt, *GG* III:2, 1372 and n. 4. For the numbers see Diod. 13.11.3, and Dover, *HCT* IV, 422. See Map 11.

garrison at the fort that guarded it, the Athenians managed to achieve a surprise. They took the fort and killed some of its garrison, but the others escaped and spread word of the attack.

The first response came from the elite 600 Syracusans whom Hermocrates selected the previous year for special duty. They had been treated roughly in their first encounter with the Athenians, and they fared no better this time.[9] Although the Syracusan elite fought with spirit, the Athenians again routed them and pushed forward to seek out the enemy and complete the victory. This first Athenian corps served as shock troops to clear the way and draw the main attention of the enemy. Another force, right on its heels, headed immediately for the counter-wall as its first assignment.[10] As expected, the Syracusans guarding the wall were taken utterly by surprise and fled without resistance, allowing the Athenians to capture and tear down parts of the wall.

Gylippus had built outworks projecting from the southern side of his wall to protect it. From these, he and his men, still dazed by this daring and unexpected night attack, came out to repel the Athenians, but the Athenians were able to force them back and continue their advance eastward on Epipolae. Their success made them eager to take full advantage of the enemy's surprise and unprepared condition, but in their eagerness to engage the rest of the enemy forces before they could rally the Athenians themselves fell into some disorder, which soon proved costly. As they rushed forward the Athenians encountered a regiment of Boeotian hoplites which, keeping its order and composure, charged the Athenians and put them to rout.[11]

Thucydides tells us how difficult it was to discover what took place in this battle, even though he had access to witnesses from both sides. Even in a battle by day it is hard for participants to

[9] For the 600 select Syracusans see 6.96.3 and 97.4.

[10] 7.43.5. Such is my interpretation of ἄλλοι δὲ ἀπὸ τῆς πρώτης τὸ παρατείχισμα . . . ᾖρουν, and I believe this second force came onto Epipolae by way of Euryalus, right behind Demosthenes. Green (*Armada*, 286, and n. 5) believes that this second force came from the round fort, but nothing in Thucydides requires that, and his account is in accord with the interpretation offered here.

[11] 7.43.6–7; Plut. *Nic.* 21.5. These Boeotians were apparently Thespians. See Busolt, *GG* III:2, 1374, n. 2.

know what is happening anywhere but in their own immediate vicinity. At night, even with the bright moon that had risen by this time, it was harder still, for with large armies engaged and men running in every direction it was difficult to tell friend from foe.[12] Still, Thucydides' account makes it plain that the turning point was the Boeotian check of the Athenian advance. Until that moment the Athenian forces had been advancing smoothly in a generally eastward direction across the plateau, each detachment moving towards its assigned task as it came up onto the heights through the Euryalus Pass. But when one Athenian force was routed and ran back toward the west, confusion set in. In the light of the moon the advancing Athenians could not easily tell whether the men running toward them were friends or foes. There was confusion, too, at the point of ascent. The generals appear not to have placed anyone at the pass to direct the different companies as they came onto the plateau. These newly arrived men found some Athenian forces advancing unchecked, others running toward Euryalus in retreat, and others who had just come up through the pass and were not yet in motion. The new men, as they came onto Epipolae, were therefore unsure as to which group they should join.

The disorder and confusion increased with the passage of time. The Syracusans and their allies, as they rallied and turned back the Athenians, filled the air with cheers and shouts, thereby intensifying the problems of the Athenians, who found it increasingly difficult to distinguish their own retreating men from

---

[12]Plutarch (*Nic.* 21.7-8) says that the moon was setting during the confusion after the Athenian defeat by the Boeotians and so coming from behind the Athenians casting shadows that helped the Syracusans and harmed the Athenians. Busolt (*GG* III:2, 1372, n. 4) points out that the moon rose no more than forty-five minutes before or after 10:00 P.M. on August 3, 4, and 5 of 413. Since the Athenians reached Epipolae without being observed, they must have reached the Euryalus Pass before the rising of the moon, plus or minus 10:00 P.M. Since the moon reached its height between 3:20 and 5:00 A.M. on those three nights, the fighting would have lasted not less than six hours, and probably more, but Thucydides' description and all reasonable judgment make that impossible. Busolt attributes the story of the effect of the fading moonlight to the contemporary Sicilian historian Philistus, and we must agree with his conclusions: "Obviously it is a matter of a fantastic embellishment of the night battle."

the advancing enemy. They repeatedly called out to demand the password from the men approaching them, but soon the Syracusans caught on to the Athenian watchword, and used it to escape whenever they were at a disadvantage. The Syracusans, on the other hand, had rallied their forces and were pressing forward. They had no need to use their password and thus did not reveal it to the enemy, leaving the Athenians without a means to extract themselves from unfavorable positions. The Dorian custom of singing a paean, a war cry or signal for battle, created still greater difficulties for the Athenians. The Syracusans and their allies were chiefly Dorians, and the sound of their paean, revealing that the enemy was suddenly at hand, terrified the Athenians. But the Athenian force, though mainly Ionian, included such Dorian contingents as the Argives and Corcyraeans. They too sang out paeans, which were indistinguishable from the enemy's, thereby adding to the Athenians' terror and complicating the task of distinguishing enemy from ally. "Finally, when they had once been thrown into confusion, they attacked one another in many different parts of the battlefield, friends against friends and citizens against fellow citizens; not only did they fall into a panic but they even came to blows and were separated only with difficulty."[13]

Their unfamiliarity with the terrain, a very serious handicap at night, compounded the Athenians' problems. None of them knew Epipolae as well as the Syracusans, and many of the men who had just arrived in Sicily with Demosthenes and Eurymedon had never seen it before that night.[14] This disadvantage, serious enough during the confused fighting, became disastrous when victory turned to defeat, advance to retreat, and retreat to rout. In their attempt to escape, many Athenian soldiers jumped down the side of the cliffs to their deaths, and many must have fallen to the same fate by accident. Not even all those who got down to the plain were saved. The experienced men from Nicias' army had no trouble finding their way back to camp and safety, but the new men from the reinforcing expedition lost their way

<hr/>

[13] 7.44.7–8.
[14] The point is made by Green, *Armada*, 284.

and wandered about until daybreak, when the Syracusan cavalry hunted them down and killed them. The result was the greatest disaster yet suffered by the Athenians. Between 2,000 and 2,500 men were killed, and all hope of a quick victory at Syracuse was gone.[15] The Syracusans set up victory trophies and, with restored confidence, sent their general Sicanus with 15 ships to Acragas to try to win it over, for a revolution was in process there. At the same time Gylippus went by land on another recruiting expedition into Sicily. He now thought that if he could get enough help, he might be able to capture the Athenian walls by assault.[16]

Syracusan elation and optimism were matched by Athenian discouragement. With the hope of a quick victory gone, the generals met to determine the next step. The defeat had badly damaged the army's morale, which had already been weakened by another source of distress. The Athenian camp was located on marshy ground, and the late summer was a most insalubrious time to be there. The men were coming down with disease, probably malaria and surely dysentery. "The situation appeared to them to be as hopeless as it could be."[17] Demosthenes spoke with his usual decisiveness and voted to abandon the campaign immediately and sail for home while Athens still had naval superiority. "He said it would be of more use to Athens to fight the war against an enemy who was building a fort against it in its own country than against Syracuse, which it was no longer easy to subdue, nor was it right, besides, to expend a great deal of money to no purpose by continuing the siege."[18]

The simple common sense and wisdom of Demosthenes' opinion seems obvious. Attempts to take the Syracusan counter-wall by attacking from the round fort could not succeed. A daylight ascent onto Epipolae from another direction was impossible, and Gylippus would never again allow himself to be surprised by a night attack. Without taking the counter-wall the Athenians

---

[15]Plutarch (*Nic.* 21.9) gives the figure of 2,000, and Diodorus (13.11.5) gives 2,500.

[16]7.45–46.

[17]7.47.2.

[18]7.47.4.

could not besiege Syracuse. They might linger in their present position in the hope that something else would turn up, but, as Demosthenes had pointed out, every day they spent in Sicily exacted a cost from Athens in money, men, and ships she needed to fight Sparta at home. The low morale of the men and the continuing ravages of disease were further reasons for abandoning the campaign, especially since there would be no more reinforcements to supplement and encourage them.

Since Nicias had opposed the expedition from the first, had already asked the Athenians to withdraw it and, if not, at least to relieve him of the command, we may be surprised that he resisted Demosthenes' advice. Thucydides tells us that Nicias knew that the Athenians were in a dangerous situation but did not, in any case, want a vote to be taken in favor of retreat lest word of the decision reach the enemy. He feared that such information would alert the Syracusans to Athenian weakness and encourage them to cut off retreat if and when it was decided upon. Besides, Thucydides continues, Nicias learned from his private sources that the enemy might be in even worse condition than themselves. With their superior fleet the Athenians could still prevent supplies from reaching Syracuse by sea. But his main hope stemmed from his knowledge that there continued to be a group in Syracuse which wanted to surrender to Athens. Nicias was in touch with representatives of this element, and they continued to urge him to hold his ground. Thucydides tells us that with these things in mind, Nicias was still privately undecided whether to stay or to depart.[19]

If the reasons that Thucydides advances were the only arguments Nicias could muster on behalf of staying, however, he should not have hesitated to order his forces' departure, for neither reason was compelling in the least.[20] To think of cutting off Syracusan supplies without controlling access by land was

[19] 7.48.1–3.
[20] It is difficult to understand how Thucydides knew what was in the mind of Nicias on this occasion. Nicias himself cannot have been the source, for he died in Sicily soon after. Perhaps before he died he unburdened himself to a friend who later related the information to Thucydides. The problem is analogous to that posed by Thucydides' claim to knowledge of Cleon's thoughts at the battle of Amphipolis (see Kagan, *Archidamian War*, 325).

nonsense; supplies could be shipped overland from the west, and the Athenians would not be able to prevent their delivery. As for hopes of treason from within the city, they were blatantly vain. We do not know who Nicias' correspondents were; perhaps they were Leontine aristocrats who had moved to Syracuse and now wanted to restore their city.[21] Possibly they were members of a faction that wanted to make the Syracusan constitution more democratic and move the city in the direction that Ephialtes and Pericles had taken Athens in 462/61.[22] They may even have been wealthy Syracusans who were bearing the financial burden of the war and were ready to surrender to save their fortunes. Perhaps the potential traitors came from several or all these groups; it made no difference, for they clearly had little support and were not likely to gain more. Their only chance to surrender the city had been before the arrival of Gongylus and Gylippus. After that, support from the outside and repeated success guaranteed that the Syracusans would hold out to the end. After defeating the Athenians on sea and land and inflicting unheard of casualties, the Syracusans would need to suffer major reversals in the field before they would consider negotiating, and Nicias had in mind no plan that would lead to such defeats.

In his public speech in the debate Nicias suppressed his pri-

[21]Diod. 13.18.5; Dover, HCT IV, 425.

[22]A few years after Athens' Sicilian expedition, Syracuse experienced a constitutional change. Aristotle (Pol. 1304a 27) says "In Syracuse the demos made a change from politeia to democracy." By politeia Aristotle means a mixed form of government closer to moderate democracy than to anything else. Diodorus confirms this account by telling us that after the Sicilian expedition a demagogue named Diocles changed the constitution and introduced the democratic device of electing magistrates by lot. Presumably Diocles and his supporters were in Syracuse in 413 and may have been among those negotiating with Nicias.

This may be the place to mention the story of an alleged abortive slave rebellion in Syracuse at this time. Polyaenus (1.43.1), a late and not especially reliable source, tells the tale. Hermocrates is its hero who contrives to suppress the rebellion and return most of the slaves to their masters except for 300 who desert to the Athenians. Busolt (GG III:2, 756, n. 1, and 1337) thinks Philistus is the ultimate source and therefore takes the story seriously. Freeman (History of Sicily III, 673–674) is more skeptical. The story as it appears in Polyaenus seems to have been embroidered, at the very least, but even if a slave revolt took place it was easily suppressed. The Athenians could not have counted on gaining a serious advantage from it, even if they knew of its existence.

vate doubts and argued unambiguously for remaining in Sicily. Although it in part reflected his private notion that the Syracusans were even worse off than the Athenians in Sicily, Nicias' argument was shaped primarily to counter Demosthenes' complaint about the great financial cost of continuing the campaign. Nicias pointed out that the Syracusans were in even greater financial difficulty. Their need to keep patrol vessels at sea, to man a large fleet, and to pay many mercenary soldiers had already cost them 2,000 talents in silver, and they had borrowed still more. They were already short of money and, if the Athenians stayed in place, would soon run out of it, losing their mercenary contingents as a result. "They should stay on, he said, and maintain the siege and not be defeated by money, in which they were far superior to the enemy."[23]

Again, Nicias' information was accurate as far as it went, but no more than in his private considerations were the conclusions he drew from it persuasive. The Syracusans were indeed short of money,[24] but we have reason to believe that they could have raised more by taxation or by borrowing it from their Peloponnesian allies and elsewhere, for the news of their victories would have improved their credit. The ancient Greeks were less accustomed than we to direct taxation, but when freedom and independence were at stake there was little doubt that they were prepared to resort to it. And that, in fact, was the major source of Nicias' miscalculation. The Athenians could choose to stay on in Sicily at great expense or to give up the campaign and spend their money otherwise. The Syracusans had no such choice. They must resist to the end or lose their freedom along with their wealth. Athenian imperial history demonstrated that when the Athenians conquered a place after a siege they sometimes imposed a war indemnity to pay for its cost, and surely Syracuse could expect no better treatment than Samos in this regard.[25] The Syracusans, therefore, would hold on to their mercenaries as long as they could, but even if they lost some or all of them, they could still hold out. Syracuse was a populous city, and it

[23] 7.48.6.
[24] 7.49.1.
[25] 1.117.3.

was supported voluntarily by Selinus and other Sicilian cities, not for money but from self-interest. The Peloponnesians had already sent help and would send more if necessary. Unless Syracuse could be cut off by land and sea it could hold out indefinitely, and Nicias and the Athenians had proven unable to complete the blockade.

All this should have been as obvious to Nicias as it was to Demosthenes and as it is to us, but Nicias revealed his true motives in the other half of the speech he made in the debate with his colleagues. It is a passage so remarkable as to deserve quotation: "He knew well," says Thucydides, "that the Athenians would not accept the decision of the generals to withdraw without a vote of the assembly in Athens. For the Athenians who would vote on their fate would not have witnessed the course of events, as the generals had, rather than hearing about it from the critical remarks of others. Instead they would learn what had happened from the slanderous statements of any clever speaker and be persuaded by them. Many, indeed most of the soldiers here who are now complaining about the terrible situation we are in will, when they get back to Athens, complain of the opposite: that their generals had been bribed to betray them and withdraw. He himself, at any rate, knowing the character of the Athenians, did not wish to be put to death unjustly on a disgraceful charge by the Athenians but preferred, if he must, to take his chances and meet his own death himself at the hands of the enemy."[26]

Here we see a side of Nicias clearly revealed by Thucydides for the first time but one amply supported in the ancient traditions collected by Plutarch. The comic poets rang many changes on the theme of Nicias' public timidity, his fear of informers, his willingness to pay these extortionists to avoid appearing in court.[27] Plutarch tells us that Nicias was acutely conscious of the suspicion and envy with which the Athenian democracy looked upon its outstanding citizens and worked hard to escape it. He chose his military commands carefully, avoiding

[26]7.48.3–4.
[27]Plutarch (*Nic.* 4.3–6) cites verses from Telecleides, Eupolis, Aristophanes, and Phrynichus.

those likely to bring trouble to the general in charge. He was careful to be publicly modest about his victories, attributing them to fortune and the gods because he feared arousing the dangerous envy of the people.[28] But even if Nicias was unusually timid, bolder men had reason to fear the Athenian people's judgment of their unsuccessful generals. In the Peloponnesian War alone, a number of them had been brought to trial and some of them punished. Few men, in fact, had better reason to understand Nicias' fears than two of the generals he was addressing. In 426 Demosthenes had remained in Naupactus rather than return to Athens after his defeat in Aetolia, "fearing the Athenians because of what had happened."[29] In 424 Eurymedon came back to Athens from Sicily after failing to accomplish all that the Athenians had hoped and was charged with accepting bribes, tried, convicted, and fined, though he appears not to have been guilty.[30]

Since Demosthenes and Eurymedon had good reason to be receptive to Nicias' argument, their resistance is all the more interesting.[31] Apparently, they did not fear the Athenian assembly's reaction to an unauthorized withdrawal. Perhaps they reasoned that if three generals so diverse in their views and in their political associations together explained the necessity of the withdrawal to the assembly, it would be accepted. Certainly men of the prestige of Nicias and Demosthenes would carry great weight. Nicias, of course, had more to fear than the others, for the great and fundamental mistakes had been his. The others had been present for only one battle, while we have already recounted the long string of errors and omissions by Nicias which had caused the Athenian failure. Even in its anger the Athenian people could make distinctions, as they had showed by the different punishments they imposed on Sophocles,

[28]Plut. *Nic.* 6.1–2.
[29]3.98.5.
[30]4.65.3–4; Kagan, *Archidamian War*, 268–269.
[31]Thucydides does not tell us directly that Eurymedon agreed with Demosthenes' desire to abandon Sicily entirely. He does not give us Eurymedon's view one way or the other, but Eurymedon's support of Demosthenes' suggestion to withdraw to Thapsus or Catana suggests that he agreed with him generally.

Pythodorus, and Eurymedon in 424, and by the various treatments they accorded to the generals who lost Amphipolis in the same year.[32] Nicias might well think himself in greater danger than his colleagues, but Demosthenes also had reason to fear the judgment of his fellow citizens. Both the idea for the night assault on Epipolae and its execution had been entirely his responsibility, and the result had been a fiasco. With at least 2,000 soldiers lost, the greatest Athenian military defeat up to that time, there would be no shortage of critics to point out how idiotic and hopeless the idea had been and to criticize the incompetence of its execution.

Nevertheless, Demosthenes voted to return and face whatever charges might result while Nicias voted to remain, knowing in his heart that he would thus expose the entire expedition to serious danger. Grote says that "the idea of meeting the free criticisms and scrutiny of his fellow-citizens—even putting aside the chance of judicial trial—must have been insupportably humiliating. To Nikias—a perfectly brave man, suffering withal under an incurable disease—life at Athens had neither charm nor honour left. Hence, as much as for any other reason, he was induced to withhold the order for departure; clinging to the hope that some unforeseen boon of fortune might yet turn up, and yielding to the idlest delusions from correspondents in the interior of Syracuse."[33] He characterizes Nicias' behavior as "guilty fatuity," but we must agree with Dover that such a judgment is too moderate and prefer his own evaluation: "Nikias' pride and consequent cowardice in the face of personal disgrace lead him to put forward as disgraceful a proposition as any general in history: rather than risk execution, he will throw away the fleet and many thousand of other people's lives, and put his country in mortal peril."[34]

Demosthenes was not persuaded by Nicias' arguments and continued to argue for withdrawal, presumably with the support

[32]Kagan, *Archidamian War*, 268–269; 299–301.
[33]Grote VII, 312–313.
[34]*HCT* IV, 426. It is worth pointing out that Nicias' fear of the death penalty was based on no precedent known to us. Up to his time the only penalties we hear of for disgraced generals were fines or exiles.

of Eurymedon,[35] but Nicias continued to resist, and his resistance was decisive. In so serious a matter we cannot imagine that Demosthenes and Eurymedon would have given way unless outvoted, so we must assume that Nicias' lieutenants Menander and Euthydemus voted with him to form a majority. These two men had been chosen not in the regular way, but in special elections held during the previous winter to select men to assist the ailing Nicias.[36] They were plainly inferior in prestige to their colleagues, and it would have taken extraordinary courage for them to oppose the venerable and beloved Nicias, under whom they had been serving for months, and to join with his opponents in supporting a major decision unauthorized by the Athenian assembly.

His lieutenants' support also enabled Nicias to resist the compromise that Demosthenes and Eurymedon offered when they saw that they could not persuade him to leave Sicily. They urged that the Athenians withdraw at least to Thapsus or Catana, thus enabling them to rescue their troops from the unhealthy swamps. Away from the walls of Syracuse and its army, they could raid the Sicilian countryside and live off the land. By getting their fleet out of Syracuse harbor, they could fight in the open sea where their greater skill and experience gave them the advantage and where they would no longer be hampered by an inadequate base. It was imperative, they asserted, that they move to a new base at once.

Again Nicias refused, and again he had his way; the Athenians stayed where they were. Since Thucydides does not tell us his motive for this decision, we can only speculate. This time he had not the excuse of refusing to act without the permission of the Athenian assembly, for as *autokratores* the generals certainly had the power to move about in Sicily as strategy dictated. His fellow commanders thought, however, that Nicias must know something no one else did, for why else would he want to stay? Plutarch tells us that when Demosthenes could not have his way he made the best of it, encouraging the other generals with the thought that Nicias would not have resisted the idea of departure

[35]See above, n. 31.
[36]7.16.1; Dover *HCT* IV, 391–392.

so strongly unless he had received encouraging news from his correspondents in Syracuse.[37] But there is no evidence to support such a supposition, and the activities of unpatriotic elements within Syracuse, if in fact there were any such activities, never served Athenian purposes. No doubt Nicias' Syracusan contacts had urged him to stay, and perhaps "he yielded," as Grote says, "to the idlest delusions" about the prospects for Syracusan surrender, but his refusal to leave was probably based primarily on his suspicion that once the army embarked on its ships and sailed out of Syracuse harbor, it would be impossible to keep the Athenians in Sicily long. Perhaps we may guess that Demosthenes and Eurymedon thought the same when they made their suggestion.

By this time Gylippus and Sicanus had returned from their missions. Sicanus had accomplished nothing at Acragas, for before he could get there the faction hostile to Syracuse won the civil war and expelled its enemies. Gylippus had done much better, collecting a large army of Sicilians and coming upon a windfall in the form of a body of Peloponnesian hoplites. These were the 600 helots and *neodamodeis* who had started out from Laconia in the spring under the Spartan commander Eccritus. Storms had driven them off course to Cyrene in Africa, but with help from the Greek natives they had made their way across the sea to Selinus, where Gylippus encountered and enlisted them.[38] The arrival of all these reinforcements encouraged the Syracusans once again to consider resuming the offensive on land and sea.

In the Athenian camp the change in the balance of forces had the opposite effect. Disease was further reducing the strength and morale of the Athenian army, and in this context the increase in the enemy's strength was a terrible blow. The decision to stay appeared more ill advised than ever, and even Nicias was no longer as opposed to withdrawal as he had been. He asked only that there be no open vote to retreat, but that orders for withdrawal be sent secretly to the officers of the army. Everyone awaited the signal to leave, and it seemed that the great Athenian

[37]Thuc. 7.49.4; Plut. *Nic.* 22.4.
[38]7.19.3; 50.2.

expedition would, in spite of everything, make its escape essentially intact, when fate, the gods, or chance intervened. On the night of 27 August 413, between 9:41 and 10:30 P.M., the moon was totally eclipsed.

Fear overcame the superstitious Athenian army. The men interpreted the eclipse as a sign of divine disfavor and a warning against sailing immediately. The soothsayers whom Nicias consulted took the same view and recommended that the Athenians wait "thrice nine days" before departing.[39] This interpretation by both layman and expert need not surprise us, for all the Athenians had seen what they believed to be another omen in the summer of 415, the mutilation of the Hermae. On that occasion they had treated it as a human and political act rather than as a supernatural warning. In light of the unfortunate outcome of the Sicilian expedition they might well have thought that they had been wrong to ignore the earlier omen and that they should not make the same mistake again by undertaking a voyage after a divine warning.[40]

The interpretation given by Nicias' soothsayers and accepted by the army was not, however, the only one possible. Philochorus, a historian who lived in the third century B.C. and who was himself a seer, gave the opposite exegesis: "the sign was not unfavorable to men who were fleeing but, on the contrary, very favorable; for deeds of fear require concealment, while light is an enemy to them."[41] Philochorus, of course, had the benefit of hindsight, and he may have been trying to save the good name of seers by explaining away one of their most famous and disastrous errors,[42] but it was not so difficult and remote an interpretation that a clever commander might not have thought of it and used it to good effect. In the Persian War Themistocles had turned an oracle widely perceived as unfavorable to Athenian

[39]7.50.4. Plutarch (*Nic.* 23.6) and Diodorus (13.12.6) say that the customary period of delay after an eclipse of the moon was three days, but there is no reason to prefer them to Thucydides here.

[40]For a recent discussion of the role of religion and superstition in Athens at this time see C. A. Powell, *Historia* XXVIII (1979), 15–31.

[41]Plut. *Nic.* 23.5.

[42]Such is the suggestion of Powell, *Historia* XXVIII (1979), 27.

chances in a naval battle at Salamis into a sign that promised victory in just such an encounter.[43] Plutarch relates an anecdote in which Pericles was in command of a trireme during an eclipse of the sun. His men were paralyzed with fear until the Athenian leader conducted a simple experiment that illustrated the natural origin of the phenomenon.[44]

Pericles had been a man of the Greek enlightenment, a friend of the natural philosopher Anaxagoras who was the first to write scientifically about the phases of the moon,[45] whereas Nicias "was rather too much inclined toward divination and such things."[46] It would have been unreasonable to expect natural explanations from him. He was, moreover, without his best soothsayer, Stilbides, who had died only a short while before. Stilbides "had been his intimate companion and used to set him free from most of his superstitious fears";[47] he might have produced a more favorable interpretation of the omen. In any case, Nicias is unlikely to have accepted any interpretation but the unfavorable one, for it fitted his inclinations perfectly. He had never favored the departure, but his resistance had been overcome by circumstances and the grumbling of the troops. Now the gods had intervened to confirm Nicias' judgment. He seized on the soothsayers' interpretation and "refused to discuss further the question of their departure until they waited thrice nine days, as the soothsayers recommended."[48]

In spite of all precautions, news of the Athenian decision to abandon Sicily and the reasons for the delay in executing it reached the Syracusans through deserters from the Athenian camp.[49] The news was evidence that the Athenians despaired of taking Syracuse from their present base. The reports must also

[43]Hdt. 7.143.
[44]Plut. *Per.* 35.2.
[45]Plut. *Nic.* 22.2.
[46]7.50.4.
[47]Plut. *Nic.* 23.5.
[48]7.50.4.
[49]Diod. 13.13.1. Thucydides does not tell how the Syracusans learned the news. In this and following sections Diodorus seems to have had access to the account of Philistus, as well as to Thucydides. For this reason his narrative offers a number of details which we have no reason to reject.

have mentioned Demosthenes' suggestion that the Athenians set up another base elsewhere in Sicily and continue the campaign from there. It was to prevent this possibility that the Syracusans decided to force another sea battle at once in Syracuse harbor where they had the best chance to win. Since the religious taboo guaranteed that the Athenians would not flee for some time, the Syracusans were able to man their ships and practice naval tactics for the period needed to achieve top efficiency. Then they were ready to attack.

The first assault, however, came by land. The Syracusans made an attack against the Athenian walls and lured a company of Athenian hoplites and cavalry out through a gate to fight. The hoplites were routed, and some of them were cut off before they could get back within the walls. The cavalry also fled, and 70 horses were abandoned by their riders in their hurry to flee to safety through the narrow gate that impeded their mounts.[50] On the next day, probably September third, the Syracusans launched their full attack. An army attacked the Athenian walls, and simultaneously the Syracusan navy sent 76 triremes against the Athenian base. Sicanus commanded the right wing, the Corinthian Pythen the center, and Agatharchus the left. The Athenians went out to meet them with 86 ships; Eurymedon commanded the right wing, to the south, opposite Agatharchus, Menander the center opposite Pythen, and Euthydemus the left wing, on the north, opposite Sicanus.[51] Diodorus sets the Syracusan fleet at 74 ships. Demosthenes is not mentioned and must have been in command of the land forces.[52]

The Athenian numerical superiority allowed Eurymedon's ships on the right wing to extend beyond those of Agatharcus on the Syracusan left. This encouraged the Athenian commander to lead his ships in the circling maneuver, the *periplous*. He started southward, toward the part of the bay off Dascon, but seems to have been too close to the shore to make full speed. Before Eurymedon could complete his maneuver, Pythen broke

[50] 7.51.1–2.
[51] 7.52.1–2; Diod. 13.13.1–2. The date is suggested by Busolt, GG III:2, 1379.
[52] Such is the persuasive suggestion of Freeman, *History of Sicily* III, 328.

through Menander's ships in the Athenian center. Having routed the Athenians, the Corinthian commander made the correct and decisive judgment not to pursue them but to turn south and join with Agatharchus' ships against Eurymedon. The Athenian right wing was forced back toward shore, hemmed in at the recess of the bay near Dascon, and defeated. Eurymedon himself was forced to run to shore where he was killed by one of the enemy; 7 of his ships were destroyed.[53]

Eurymedon's defeat was the turning point in the battle. The entire Athenian fleet was routed and driven toward the shore, many of them finding themselves outside the stockade that had been placed in the sea for their safe escape and away from the area protected by their own walls. Gylippus immediately seized the opportunity to kill the Athenians as they were forced from their ships onto unprotected land and to make it easier for the Syracusans at sea to haul away the abandoned triremes. Clearly expecting no resistance from the Athenian army, he and his men came running in considerable disorder down the seawall between the harbor and the Lysimeleia marsh.[54] To their surprise they came upon a company of Etruscans who had been placed there by the Athenians precisely to guard that approach to their camp. They quickly routed the first Syracusan soldiers to arrive and drove them away from the seawall into the marsh. When Syracusan reinforcements arrived the Athenians came out to help the Etruscans and to protect their ships. The defense was successful; they defeated the enemy, killed some of the hoplites,

[53] 7.52.2; Diod. 13.13.3–4.

[54] Thucydides (7.53.1) says Gylippus and his men came $\grave{\epsilon}\pi\grave{\iota}$ $\tau\grave{\eta}\nu$ $\chi\eta\lambda\acute{\eta}\nu$. The primary meaning of $\chi\eta\lambda\acute{\eta}$ is a horse's hoof, but it is also used, sometimes in the plural, to mean a breakwater or a seawall. In Thuc. 1.63.1 (see scholium and Gomme's note [HCT I, 219]) it clearly means a breakwater. In Diodorus (13.78.6–7) the $\chi\eta\lambda\alpha\acute{\iota}$ may be breakwaters but are probably seawalls. In any case, they are walls constructed of stone, not natural formations. This rules out Dover's interpretation that the quoted words mean "on to the spit" (HCT IV, 484). He, unlike almost all other scholars, places the marsh called Lysimeleia to the southwest of the Athenian walls, just north of the Anapus River and believes that Gylippus launched his attack from the Olympieum. I agree with Freeman (History of Sicily III, 689) and the majority in placing the marsh to the north of the Athenian walls and in believing that Gylippus came from the direction of the city of Syracuse down what Freeman and others call a "causeway," but I think the latter is better designated as a seawall.

and saved most of their ships. Eighteen triremes had been lost, however, and every member of their crews killed in the bloody fighting.

Meanwhile, Sicanus, the commander of the Syracusan fleet in this part of the harbor, conceived of a device to destroy any Athenian ships that escaped to shore. Since the wind was blowing onshore, from the east, toward the Athenians, he set fire to a merchant ship and sent it toward the enemy, but the Athenians found ways to turn it aside and quench the fire, thereby saving their fleet. The Syracusans set up trophies to mark their two victories: one had been placed at the Athenian wall on the previous day and the far more important one was erected at sea.[55]

The Athenians also set up a trophy, as they had a right to do, to mark their rout of Gylippus at the seawall, but it was a pathetic gesture. Athenian morale was once again shattered, this time with little or no hope for its revival. The relief force under Demosthenes and Eurymedon which had sailed so bravely into Syracuse harbor had raised new hopes of victory, but these were now dashed. The augmented Athenian forces had suffered major defeats not only on land, but even at sea. The Athenians, Thucydides tells us, repented the miscalculation that they had made in undertaking the expedition, for they had underestimated the strength of Syracuse in both ships and cavalry. They also had ignored the fact that Syracuse, like Athens, was a democracy and that it was much more difficult to sow the seeds of internal discord and gain control of a hostile city by revolution if it has a democratic rather than an oligarchic constitution.[56]

The first miscalculation can certainly be blamed on the mass of Athenians who voted the vast forces for the expedition and for its reinforcement, though on both occasions they had followed the advice of Nicias. They thought that Syracuse could be conquered by a military force of such strength as they could provide, and events proved them wrong. The second error, however, cannot be blamed on them, for we have no reason to believe that the Athenians counted on internal elements to deliver Syracuse into their hands. That notion belonged to Nicias alone, and

[55] 7.53-54.
[56] 7.55.

in pursuing it long after any reasonable man would have recognized his error, he doomed the Athenians to destruction. If Diocles and his extreme democrats were dissatisfied, they were not so discontented or impatient with the moderate Syracusan democracy as to betray their city to the Athenians. No other faction had the power to do so, but Nicias did not understand or refused to face these facts. The Athenians now understood that they could no longer win either by force or guile. "Even before this they did not know what to do, and when they were defeated even with their fleet, something that they did not think possible, they were much more at a loss than ever."[57] There was no longer any question of victory; the only thought now was of escape.

[57] 7.55.2.

14. Retreat and Destruction

Just as the Syracusan naval victory in the Great Harbor turned Athenian thoughts from victory to escape, so it led the Syracusans to think no longer of saving their city but of destroying the Athenian force. They believed that a total defeat of the Athenians in Sicily would end the war in the rest of Greece, bringing down the Athenian Empire and giving freedom to the Greeks. They thought that they would receive the credit for these achievements, gain honor and fame, and achieve the status of a hegemonal power, along with Sparta and Corinth.[1] Determined to cut off the Athenian retreat by land and sea, they set to closing off the mouth of the harbor by anchoring triremes and other boats across it, bridging them over with boards and connecting them with iron chains. This task was completed in three days.[2]

When the Athenians saw the bridge of boats beginning to stretch across the entrance to the harbor and learned of the increasingly aggressive intentions of the enemy, Nicias, Demosthenes, Menander, and Euthydemus met with the 10 taxiarchs to decide what to do. The situation was desperate, for they were running out of supplies and could expect no more to be shipped from Catana. When planning to leave prior to the eclipse at least ten days earlier, the Athenians had ordered a stop to the import of provisions from Catana, a fact that makes Nicias' decision to stay twenty-seven additional days even more remarkable. Now there could be no question of remaining but only of whether it would be best to try to break out of the harbor on

[1] 7.56.
[2] 7.59.2; Diod. 13.14.1-2.

their ships or to retreat by land to some friendlier quarter of Sicily. Some of the soldiers, as soon as they saw the barrier being built across the harbor entrance, clamored to be permitted to retreat by land. The generals, on the other hand, were naturally reluctant to abandon their navy, which still numbered well over 100 triremes, as well as many other craft. Unlike their soldiers, who were thinking only of immediate escape, the generals may also have wondered how they would get back to Athens without those ships. As a result, they decided to try to break out of the harbor.[3]

The plan was to abandon the upper part of their fortifications, from the round fort on Epipolae to a place as close as possible to the ships, and to build a counter-wall leaving enough space for supplies and the sick; into this limited area they would place a garrison.[4] Every able-bodied man would then be put on board some ship or boat, and the entire armada would try to fight its way out of Syracuse harbor. If they made it through, they would sail to Catana. If they lost, they would burn their ships, get into battle formation, and march in whatever direction seemed most likely to take them to a safe place and a friendly welcome, whether from Greeks or native Sicilians. The stealthy withdrawal from the upper fortifications went smoothly, and the Athenians boarded their ships for battle and, they hoped, escape by sea.

This time the Athenian ships making ready to fight looked quite different from the fleet that had won Athens mastery of the sea. Apart from the usual complement of rowers, marines, and specialists, they were laden with many foot soldiers, in part as a response to the Syracusan tactics in previous battles, in part because they must also serve as troop carriers in the escape. The decks of the 110 triremes carried javelin throwers and bowmen from Acarnania and elsewhere. They also carried hoplites, since the Athenians knew from recent experience that the battle would

---

[3] 7.60.1–2. Plutarch (*Nic.* 25.3) makes Nicias alone unwilling to give up the ships and responsible for the decision, but Thucydides says nothing about any disagreement among the generals. For the number of Athenian ships see Busolt, *GG* III:2, 1381, n. 4.

[4] For this last Athenian camp see Freeman (*History of Sicily* III, 686–689).

contain much hand-to-hand fighting as the ships crowded together and grappled one another. In fact, the Athenians had produced a new device to combat the enemy's tactic of ramming head on with thickened catheads. This was a set of "iron hands," or grappling hooks that would seize the enemy ship and not allow it to back away after ramming the prow of an Athenian ship. So grappled, the Athenians could fight a land battle by sea in which their large contingent of foot soldiers would give them superiority. In the open sea so heavy a burden would overload the ship, destroy its speed and maneuverability and even risk its stability, but in the closed waters of the harbor none of that mattered. Armed with these men, weapons, and tactics, and urged on by a speech from Nicias, the Athenians manned their ships.[5]

Gylippus and the Syracusans were well informed about the Athenian preparations, including their new devices and tactics. Presumably, men continued to desert from the Athenian ranks, and no doubt Gylippus employed spies as well. To counter the "iron hands" the Syracusans stretched hides across the prows and upper portions of their ships. In their speeches to their soldiers and sailors Gylippus and the Syracusan generals said that the Athenians would be inexperienced in the new tactics that they had copied from their enemies. Though the Syracusans had only 74 ships, recent experience had shown that in the confined space of the harbor numerical superiority need not bring victory, especially when the forces of the smaller fleet commanded almost all the coastline along the harbor. The Syracusan generals and Gylippus therefore gave their battle speeches confidently, urging their men on to victory, liberty, and glory.[6]

Just before the Athenians set out, though he had already given a speech to the assembled forces on the beach, Nicias, awestricken by the importance of the coming battle, felt the need to say something more, to be sure nothing had been omitted, though everything had been done. His role in the battle to come was to stay on shore and command the garrison there, but he got on

[5] 7.60–64; Diodorus (13.14.4) gives the number of Athenian triremes as 115.
[6] 7.65–68. Thucydides (7.70.1) says that the Syracusan fleet was about the same size as before (52.1). Diodorus (13.14.4) gives the number of ships as 74.

board a boat and sailed through the Athenian fleet. He stopped at each trireme and, addressing the captain in the old-fashioned way, by his name, his father's name, and his tribe, emphasizing thereby old ancestral and family ties, honors, and responsibilities, he urged each not to dishonor his own reputation or that of his father and his ancestors. In a more Periclean vein he reminded them that their fatherland was the freest in the world and that the style of life it afforded them was the one most full of liberty for all its citizens. Then, in a manner very far from Periclean, he reverted to more banal topics, the sort of thing, Thucydides tells us, that men say in critical times when they are not on their guard against trite statements: "the kind of thing that men call out in much the same language on every occasion, about wives and children and ancestral gods, but which, in the fear of the moment, they think will be useful."[7] Here Thucydides gives us a touching and revealing insight into the kind of man Nicias was. In his words and action we see that special combination of old-fashioned virtue and modern democratic politics that explains his unique popularity with the Athenians. Laden with wealth, full of honors, at the end of a long and distinguished public career, Nicias was without the aristocratic and intellectual haughtiness that prevented Pericles from acquiring the common touch, from making personal appeals and uttering cliches in a banal, if winning, way. Unfortunately, he also lacked Pericles' political and military judgment and his capacity for leadership.[8]

Nicias completed his exhortations and returned to shore. Then he moved his soldiers down to the sea and spread them out along the coast where they could help any sailors driven back to shore and encourage the others still at sea. The Syracusans took up a defensive position dictated by the logic of the situation, but also, if we may believe Plutarch, by divine guidance. When the Athenians abandoned the high ground beneath Epipolae, they also had evacuated the temple of Heracles located there. The Syracusans were now able to worship that god for the first time

[7] 7.69.1-3.
[8] Thucydides (7.69.2) reports Nicias' final remarks. Diodorus (13.15.1) adds the detail that he sailed to each ship by boat. For a defense of Diodorus' credibility here see Freeman (*History of Sicily* III, 694).

since the Athenian occupation of the site, and their priests and generals went there to sacrifice even as the fleet was being made ready. The soothsayers interpreted the outcome of the sacrifices to indicate a great victory for Syracuse if only they fought on the defensive, as the hero Heracles had always done.[9] In light of the Athenian numerical superiority and the strategic situation that required the Athenians to bunch their ships in a narrow and predictable space while trying to break through a barrier, it was good advice.

The Syracusans took up a defensive position guarding the exit from the harbor with one detachment of their ships and spread the others all around the harbor so that, at the right moment, they might attack the Athenian fleet from all directions at once. As before, Sicanus and Agatharcus commanded the wings and Pythen the center. The Syracusan foot soldiers lined the shore of the harbor, and the Athenians likewise arrayed themselves along the small part that they controlled.[10] Within the city of Syracuse the walls on the harbor and every high place were filled with the families of the fighting men, though some of the adolescent boys manned small boats and fought alongside their fathers.[11] Rarely have men fighting at sea had more immediate evidence of the importance of victory or defeat.

At last, Demosthenes, Menander, and Euthydemus led their fleet out toward the barrier at the mouth of the harbor, aiming at the small opening that the Syracusans had left to allow their own ships to pass through. Their numerical superiority over the defending squadron allowed the Athenians to break through to the barrier where they began to cut through the chains holding it together. At this point the other squadrons attacked from all sides, and the intelligence of the Syracusan arrangements made itself felt as the Athenians found themselves threatened on their flanks and in the rear. Even though the battle had now spread out across the harbor, the fighting was fierce and at extremely close quarters, for almost 200 ships fought in an enclosed space. There was practically no opportunity to employ ramming tac-

[9]Plut. *Nic.* 24.5-25.1.
[10]7.70.1.
[11]Diod. 13.14.4.

tics, but there were many accidental collisions in the close fighting. The Athenians shot javelins and arrows at the enemy, but, for men who had never before fought at sea, the difficulty of aiming and delivering accurately from a fast-moving ship in the midst of a tumultuous battle gave the Syracusans an advantage. Instructed by the Corinthian Ariston, who died in the battle, they threw stones, which are easier to aim and more effective in the pell-mell of a sea battle.[12] There was much boarding and hand-to-hand fighting between marines on both sides. Navigation was very difficult, for in the constricted space ships were struck or boarded from one side even as they were in the process of attacking on the other. The shouting of the men was so loud that the rowers could not hear the commands or easily keep the beat of their stroke, and the coxswains themselves grew so excited that they shouted encouragement to their men, which interfered with their recitation of the stroke.[13]

The agony and drama of the battle were witnessed by soldiers from both sides along the shore and Syracusan civilians from the city, all of whom shouted and rejoiced when victory came to their side and groaned in despair when they witnessed defeat. It was a thrilling and fearful spectacle whose outcome was vital to the spectators, and Thucydides' description of it can have no rival. Finally, the Syracusans gained the upper hand and turned the Athenians to flight. Those Athenian ships that had not yet been sunk or captured rowed for shore, where their men abandoned the ships and ran for the Athenian camp. The army on land "broke out in a wailing and groaning at a single impulse, being unable to bear what was happening." Some ran to help their comrades fleeing the ships, others to defend the walls, but the majority now thought only of saving themselves. Defeat was total, and so was the destruction of morale. The Athenians did not even ask for a truce to recover and bury their dead, an almost inconceivable omission. They were prepared to attempt an immediate retreat by night, for they believed that only a miracle could save them.[14]

[12]Plut. *Nic.* 25.2.
[13]7.69.4-70.
[14]7.71-72.2.

Even at this terrible moment Demosthenes did not despair but continued to think like the alert, innovative military man he was. He noticed that after the defeat the Athenians still had 60 seaworthy ships to fewer than 50 for the enemy. He went to Nicias and proposed that they man the fleet and try to force their way out of the harbor at daybreak. It was a daring scheme that might, in theory, have worked. Such a move was probably the last thing the Syracusans would expect, and surprise alone might do the trick for the Athenians. Even without the advantage of surprise, moreover, the reduced number of ships and the resulting increase in open sea would give the Athenians an opportunity to profit from their superior skill and maneuverability. Nicias agreed to Demosthenes' plan, but when the generals asked the men to take to the ships again, they refused. The last defeat at sea had so shattered their confidence that they no longer believed that they could win a naval battle. They all agreed that they must retreat by land.[15]

After the battle the Syracusans gathered their wrecked ships, collected their dead, and sailed back to the city, where they set up a trophy to mark their great victory. Most Syracusans wanted only to rejoice in their deliverance and in the glory of their unbelievably total victory. Some were wounded, and all were tired. Quite appropriately, Syracuse was celebrating a festival and a sacrifice in honor of Heracles. While revelry and drinking ruled everywhere, however, Hermocrates continued to ponder the military situation. He understood that the Athenians, though defeated and demoralized, were still numerous and dangerous. If allowed to escape to some other part of Sicily, they would regroup and become a threat to Syracuse again. He was determined to finish them off, so he went to the generals and other relevant officials with a plan. They should not allow the Athenians to escape but should take the army out at once in full force and barricade the roads and passes that they could use to get away. Plutarch tells us that Gylippus had conceived a similar idea but, seeing the Syracusans abandoned to drunken revelry, gave up all hope of persuading or compelling them to do any-

---

[15]7.72.3–5. Diodorus (13.18.2) wrongly says that Nicias opposed Demosthenes' plan and favored withdrawal by land.

thing useful that night.[16] Events proved him right, for the generals, though they agreed with Hermocrates, thought that the men would not readily answer the call to arms in their current condition. "We expect," they said, "that they would obey any orders from us rather than to take up arms and march out."

Still Hermocrates persisted. He sent some of his friends with a few cavalrymen to the Athenian camp as darkness was falling. Standing off at some distance, they impersonated Nicias' correspondents in Syracuse and called out the names of certain Athenians, asking them to tell Nicias not to take his army away that night. The Syracusans were guarding the roads, they said, and it would be better to leave by daylight. The word got to Nicias, and he believed it, suspecting no trickery. Diodorus argues that if the Athenians had not been taken in by this trick, they would have gotten away safely.[17] But trick or not, the Athenians might well have been unwilling to risk another night maneuver after their experience with night-fighting in enemy territory on Epipolae, and, of course, with or without the false information from Hermocrates, they could not have been sure that the routes of escape would be unguarded. So they decided to stay where they were overnight and fight their way through the enemy, if need be, by daylight. The next morning they still did not hurry on their way, despite the fact that a quick departure would have made it more difficult for the Syracusans to close off all the routes that the Athenians might take in their escape. Instead, the Athenians waited yet another day while the men packed up whatever supplies and equipment they thought most useful. Only on the second day after the battle did the Athenian army finally set out to make its escape to safety.[18]

In the meantime, the Syracusans and Gylippus had wisely and energetically taken advantage of this gift of time. They removed their infantry from the city, much of the cavalry already being stationed at the Olympieum, and positioned it at the roads, river fords, and other places where the Athenians were likely to try to

[16]Plut. *Nic.* 26.1.
[17]13.18.5.
[18]7.74.1; 75.1.

break out and where they might be stopped most easily. They also sent their ships out to haul to Syracuse the abandoned Athenian triremes, for in their confusion and despair the Athenians had not carried out their intention of destroying their own ships, managing to burn only a few.[19]

The Athenians then began their retreat, which was like a terrible nightmare from which there is no waking. About 40,000 men started the march, of whom about half were soldiers and the rest noncombatants of one sort or another, some slave, some free.[20] Rarely have men been more weighted down in mind and spirit than this miserable remnant of the proud and confident forces that had sailed from Athens. They were ashamed when they compared the boasts with which they had undertaken the expedition with their current humiliation. The hoplites and cavalrymen had come like gentlemen warriors, propelled by others on ships, accompanied by servants to carry their baggage and spare weapons. Now they all carried their own food, if they had any, having lost their servants through death or desertion and not trusting those who remained. "They looked like nothing more than a city, and one of considerable size, sneaking away in flight after being reduced by a siege." They were also burdened with guilt, for they had committed the worst of sacrileges by failing to bury their dead. But the guilt that they felt about the living must have been even more painful, for in their flight they had abandoned the sick and the wounded. These poor wretches cried out to the friends and relatives who were leaving them to die, clinging to them as they marched off and following them as far as they could. "And if the energy or physical strength of one or another failed they did not accept their abandonment without further groans and appeals to the gods. As a result the army was plunged so completely into tears and disarray that it could not easily depart, even from a hostile country and although they had already endured suffering beyond tears and feared unknown suf-

[19] 7.74.2.
[20] Thucydides (7.75.5) gives the figure which Busolt (*GG* III:2, 1370, n. 3) thinks too high. It is accepted and explained by Dover (*HCT* IV, 452) and Green (*Armada*, 319 and n. 3).

ferings in the future." So great, indeed, was their fear of what was to come, that even their shame and guilt seemed tolerable in comparison.[21]

In this frightful time Nicias achieved his finest moment. Suffering from his illness and worn with pain and care, he nonetheless went among the men to encourage them as best he could. The speech he made was splendidly suited to raise their spirits and moderate their anxieties. Sensing their shame and guilt, he urged them not to blame themselves, and pointed to himself and his career as an example. Throughout his life he had been well known for piety and virtue, and for the good fortune, both public and private, which the gods had bestowed on him. Yet here he was, suffering at least as much as any of them and in equal danger. Clearly his current misfortune could not be the just recompense for any evil he had done or any impiety he had committed, and he was still confident of divine favor. He implied that his men, like himself, should not imagine that the gods held them in disfavor. Now that they had been brought low and the enemy exalted with success, the gods might be expected to show pity to the wretched Athenians, who might be thought to have been punished enough already and to be jealous of the victorious Syracusans.

Such was Nicias' attempt to deal with the religious fears of his men. From the point of view of logic and reasoned discourse it was no more convincing than most efforts to explain the ways of god to man, but it was probably emotionally effective, for he spoke to desperate and discouraged men, hungry for any words of comfort. Next, Nicias turned to more practical matters. The Athenians, he pointed out, were still good soldiers, and their numbers made them a formidable army. They should not be frightened for, he said, "you should realize that wherever you settle down you are immediately a city and that there is no other city in Sicily that could easily sustain an attack from you or drive you out once you have established yourselves anywhere." In this way Nicias answered the question that must have been haunting his soldiers: even if they escaped safely from Syracuse, what would

[21]7.75.

become of them, since they had no ships with which to return to
Athens? The answer was: they would find a satisfactory place in
Sicily, conquer it, and settle there for as long as it might take
until they could get home permanently. That is why he told his
men to look upon whatever place they chose to fight for as "both
their fatherland and their fortress."

In the days immediately ahead the Athenians planned to make
contact with the Sicels inland, who were still friendly because of
their hostility to the Syracusans, and messages had been sent
ahead requesting them to meet the Athenians at an appointed
place. The Sicels were also asked to bring supplies, for the Athenians were badly short of provisions. Until they were out of
danger, they must march swiftly, day and night, in orderly formation for safety. "Know the whole truth, soldiers," Nicias said.
"You must be brave men, for there is no place near by to which
you can safely escape if you are cowards. And if you get away
from your enemy now you will all some time see again what you
most desire, while those of you who are Athenians will raise up
again the great power of your city, however fallen it may be. For
it is men that make up the city and not walls or ships empty of
men."[22]

Nicias and Demosthenes, who spoke in a similar vein, went
along the ranks to get them in good marching order; then they set
out for Catana.[23] For some time Demosthenes had been pointing

---

[22]7.77.

[23]Diodorus (13.18.6; 19.2) plainly says that the Athenian destination was
Catana until the Syracusans blocked their path and compelled them to turn
back toward the Assinarus River. It is unclear whether Thucydides' words
(7.80.2)—ἦν δὲ ἡ ξύμπασα ὁδὸς αὕτη οὐκ ἐπὶ Κατάνης τῷ στρατεύματι,
ἀλλὰ κατὰ τὸ ἕτερον μέρος τῆς Σικελίας τὸ πρὸς Καμάριναν καὶ Γέλαν—
mean that the Athenians were aiming at Catana first, then veered toward Gela
and Camarina in southwestern Sicily before turning back to the southeastern
coast, as Green (Armada, 323, n. 7) believes or that they never headed for
Catana, as one would expect, but merely sought a rendezvous with the Sicels
near Acrae, which is what Dover (HCT IV, 458) thinks. Dover's reading of
Thucydides seems to me preferable, and if it is, I believe Thucydides was
mistaken and Diodorus, presumably following Philistus, was right. I take this
view because of the compelling topographical arguments of Green (Armada,
321–327). After checking his account against excellent detailed U.S. Army
maps of the area, I accept many of his geographical and topographical suggestions.

out the advantages of withdrawal to Catana, and at this point they must have seemed even greater. It was a considerable city, consistently loyal to Athens. The Athenians could get both a friendly welcome and supplies, and they could use the city as a base for further operations. The most customary route to Catana from the Athenian camp on the Great Harbor led past the southern side of Epipolae, turned around its western end by the modern town of Belvedere, and came into the level ground along the bay between Trogilus and Thapsus (see Map 12). But this way was impossible, for the march would take the Athenians through country heavily guarded by and in full view of the enemy, and it would expose them to attack from the Syracusan cavalry much of the way. So the plan was to march westward along the course of the Anapus, meet friendly Sicels somewhere in the highlands, and turn northward towards Catana at some appropriate place, well to the west of Epipolae and away from the Syracusan forces in the neighborhood.[24]

The Athenian forces were organized into two hollow rectangles with the civilians inside, the first led by Nicias and the second by Demosthenes. The first day's march took them almost directly westward, toward the modern town of Floridia (see Map 12). Almost four miles from Syracuse, near the Capocorso bridge that now crosses the Anapus, they met a force of Syracusans and their allies, but cut their way through, routing the enemy. As they proceeded through the flat country, however, the Syracusan cavalry and light-armed troops kept them company, harrying them with constant attacks and a rain of missiles. Finally, they made camp for the night on a hill beside the road, having covered about five miles that day. The next day they made an early start and marched about two miles to the northwest, down to level ground where they could attend to their pressing needs, food, which they got from the houses in the area, and water, which they could drink and store for the next leg of the journey. Thucydides' description of the land suggests that it was the area

---

[24]Freeman (*History of Sicily* III, 365–368) offers a good discussion of the Athenian plans and agrees that their first destination was Catana.

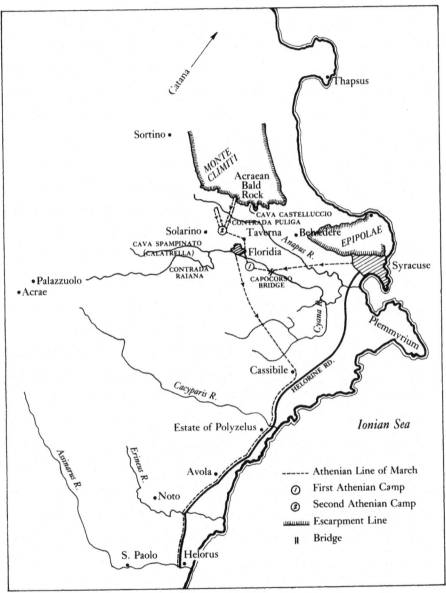

Map 12. Athenian Retreat from Syracuse

north of Floridia and south of the cliffs of Monte Climiti.[25] Here they made camp for the day, since they would be fully occupied requisitioning supplies.

The next day the Athenians planned to attempt their escape through the high barrier that stood before them. "This is the great white limestone massif known as Monte Climiti, a formation not unlike Epipolae in type, but on a far grander and more impressive scale: a vast plateau tapering to a high cliff-face some eight miles northwest of Syracuse. At this southwest corner

---

[25]Green, *Armada*, 321-324. Here Green's account parts company with that of most scholars who wrote before him. Most of them believe that from the beginning the Athenians were aiming for a meeting with their Sicel friends near Acrae, about twenty miles west of Syracuse, and had no further plan (see Map 12). Thus the Athenians would have moved from their first camp near Floridia westward, either through the Cava Spampinato (Calatrella) or the Contrada Raiana. (Most earlier scholars preferred the former. Dover [*HCT* IV, 455-456] introduces the latter into consideration.) Freeman (*History of Sicily*) believed that the Athenians meant to find a roundabout route to Catana after meeting with the Sicels, but he, too, assumes that the Athenians moved west through the Cava Spampinato toward Acrae. All suggestions of a western route encounter serious difficulties, for Thucydides' details are at odds with some aspect of the terrain or another, as Dover admits: "Certain identification is precluded by Thucydides' characteristic lack of precision in his account of the fighting" (idem). The route to the north-northwest suggested by Green, however, seems to fit Thucydides perfectly. There could be, however, one problem with his interpretation. Nicias had already told the Athenians that they could expect to meet with the Sicels on the way (7.77.6). It is possible, of course, that they expected to meet them either before their ascent of Monte Climiti or after it, in any case, in the region north of Floridia. The problem arises over the fact that when the Athenians turned back and reached the seashore south of Syracuse they intended to follow the Cacyparis inland, "for they hoped that the Sicels whom they had sent for would meet them there" (7.80.5). But the course of the Cacyparis (modern Cassibile) is away from Monte Climiti, and its source quite near Acrae and far from Floridia. Since Thucydides says nothing of any further message to the Sicels to change the place of rendezvous, Nicias and the Athenians could hardly expect to find them anywhere near the line of march up the Cacyparis. Green meets this difficulty by inventing an Athenian messenger dispatched when the Athenians knew they must turn back from Monte Climiti toward the sea. "A messenger was sent off across country and under cover of darkness—travelling, probably, by the old road between Solarino and Palazzuolo—to warn the local Sicels of what was happening and to arrange a rendezvous somewhere on the upper reaches of the Cacyparis" (*Armada*, 327). This seems a satisfactory solution, for the sending of a second messenger is the kind of small detail that Thucydides might either miss or take for granted. On balance, then, Green's account seems far the likeliest.

there are two great ravines, the larger and more centrally placed being known as the Cava Castelluccio."[26] Through this ravine the Athenians hoped to make their way over the plateau to Leontini and thence to safety at Catana.

Once again the Syracusans made good use of the time given them. Anticipating the Athenians' destination they built a wall across the ravine to the east of what was then called the Acraean Bald Rock.[27] When the Athenians started forward from their camp on the plain the next morning, moreover, they were attacked once again by the cavalry and javelin throwers of the Syracusans and their allies. The Athenians fought them for a long time but never got so far as the entrance to the ravine before being forced to return to camp. They were also running short of provisions again, for the cavalry kept them from repeating their foraging. Their original plan was foreclosed when the Syracusans got to the pass first and began to fortify it and when the cavalry and javelin throwers arrived on the scene. There was little or no hope of forcing the difficult passage up Monte Climiti against a fortified position and an entrenched enemy and yet there was great danger in remaining on the exposed plain.

Nevertheless, the next day the Athenians again attempted to break through. Starting early, they forced their way through to the ravine as far as the wall that had been built across it. Since the pass was narrow, they found the enemy stacked to considerable depth behind the wall and could make little or no headway. At the same time, they suffered from a rain of spears and arrows hurled down at them from higher up on the sides of the ravine; soon they were forced to draw back and rest. To add to their woes, this was September, the rainy season, and a heavy thunderstorm broke upon them. A sudden torrential rainstorm in a mountain pass can be a dangerous and terrifying thing, and many Athenians took it as a further sign of divine disfavor. Soon, however, they had more reason to fear human than divine dangers, for Gylippus had set to work while they were resting and begun to build a wall behind them. If he were allowed to com-

[26]Green, *Armada*, 323.
[27]7.78.5.

plete it, they would be cut off and destroyed then and there. They therefore sent a force to prevent its completion and quickly moved the entire army back to camp on the level country away from the cliffs.

By now it was clear that there was no possibility of forcing the passage east of the Acraean Bald Rock. The new plan seems to have been to march northwest through the flat land along the Anapus with Monte Climiti on their right. Though it presented difficulties, it probably seemed the least dangerous course, for the Athenians had not abandoned hope of reaching Catana. They must have hoped that the Syracusans had left some ascent to the plateau unguarded and that they could get there before the Syracusans.[28] The next day, the fifth of the retreat, they set out through the flat land today called Contrada Puliga, marching toward the northwest. The Syracusans attacked in full force, using the cavalry and javelin throwers with special effectiveness. They rode and ran in front of the Athenian army, alongside it, and behind it, avoiding close contact with the Athenian hoplites and raining missiles on them from a distance. The cavalry tried to cut off stragglers and ride them down. If the Athenians attacked, the Syracusans retreated; when the Athenians withdrew, the Syracusans charged. They attacked the rear particularly, hoping to cause a panic in the rest of the army. The Athenians fought bravely and with determination, keeping their discipline and marching forward more than half a mile before being forced by the long fighting to make camp and rest.[29]

During the night Nicias and Demosthenes met to consider the situation. They had suffered many losses, many of their men were wounded, and they were still short of supplies. They clearly could not move forward through the exposed flat country against the enemy's cavalry and javelin men. The best alternative was to change the plan of escape, to turn southeast toward the sea, follow one of the rivers that flowed into it to its upland source, and there either seek asylum with friendly Sicels or turn toward Catana by a more roundabout route. The success of this plan depended, in the first instance, on getting away from the

[28]This, in essence, is the plausible suggestion of Green, *Armada*, 326.
[29]7.79.

camp secretly so that the Syracusans could not harass their retreat and block the river valleys leading to escape. To this end
the Athenians lit as many campfires as they could, hoping to
suggest their continued presence, and marched back toward the
sea under cover of darkness. Starting in the plain before Monte
Climiti near the Anapus, their route seems to have taken them
southward, "to Taverna and Floridia, and then more or less
along the existing road as far as the little town of Cassibile."[30] In
the terrifying night they marched through hostile country in two
divisions, Nicias leading the first and Demosthenes following
with half, or a bit more, of the entire army.

They started together but, as was inevitable in such conditions, the march became disorderly and confused. Nicias, since
he had started first and been able to maintain better discipline,
arrived before dawn at the coast, where the road from Syracuse
to Helorus was close to the sea. In spite of its troubles, Demosthenes' division joined its comrades at dawn.[31] From their
meeting place near the sea the Athenians marched southward
along the Helorine road to the Cacyparis River (today, the Cassibile). Their plan was to march inland along its banks to meet
their Sicel friends, to whom they must have sent word of their
change of route.[32] Arriving at the river, however, they found the
Syracusans defending the ford. Gylippus or the Syracusans
must have anticipated this possible escape route and placed a
guard there from the first. They had built a wall on the northern
bank of the river in front of its fordable section, then erected
palisades across the river at each end of the wall. The Athenians,
however, were able to fight their way through the enemy and his

[30]Green, *Armada*, 328.

[31]Green (*Armada*, 328) calculates that the Athenians left their camp about
10:00 P.M., that Nicias could have reached the river by 3:00 A.M. of the next day
and that Demosthenes could have reached the coast about 5:00 A.M. I continue
to follow Green's account of the retreat in most respects. In his review of
Green's *Armada*, Dover speaks respectfully of his account of the retreat in
general and is persuaded by the part under discussion here: "Green's account of
the Athenian movements on and after the fifth day of the retreat is more
convincing to me now than that which I produced (on the basis of the published
material only) in 1970" (297–298).

[32]See above p. 342, n. 25.

defenses, cross the river and continue their march southward toward the next stream in their path, the Erineus.[33]

On the sixth day of the Athenian retreat the Syracusans awoke at their camp near Monte Climiti to find that the Athenians had slipped away during the night. The Syracusans were appalled and blamed Gylippus for knowingly letting them escape.[34] The incident is revealing of the suspicion and dislike with which the Syracusans regarded their savior. Plutarch tells us that "throughout the war they had not borne his harshness and Laconian mode of command easily." He further cites Timaeus, whatever his evidence is worth, to the effect that they also disliked his pettiness and greed.[35] The Syracusans, of course, knew of the friendly relations between Nicias and the Spartans and may have thought Gylippus would extend these sentiments to Nicias' army as well. Finally, now that victory and glory were certain, they may have begrudged the dour Spartan his share of them. In any case, the accusation was nonsense, for in addition to Nicias the Athenian force included Demosthenes, certainly no friend of Sparta's, and something less than 40,000 men who could still pose a serious threat.

---

[33]7.80. My account accepts the story told by Thucydides. Green rejects this account: "A wall-and-stockade complex is clearly intended to be built *across the river*. Such a device is useless in open country, and doubly so at a ford-crossing, which lies at right angles to the stream" (*Armada* 329, n. 13). But if the fordable part of the river was limited, it would make sense to build a wall along the bank of the river in front of the part that could safely be forded and build palisades across the river at either end of the fordable section. Green continues: "The mouth of the Cava Grande [a gorge about two miles upstream—D.K.] is the obvious place to block any anticipated march up-river, and a wall and a stockade the perfect way to do so." Thucydides says nothing of a march up-river and the Syracusans could not know in advance which river, the Cacyparis, the Erineus, or the Assinarus, the Athenians might choose to follow inland, so fortifying in advance an inland gorge on the first stream might be a complete waste of time and effort. Green's final objection is phrased as a question: "having defeated the guard at the ford, why did he not proceed as arranged?" that is, go inland via the Cacyparis. Thucydides provides the answer: "After forcing their way across the river they went forward again toward another river, the Erineus, for their guide told them to go that way" (7.80.6-7). The Athenians, that is, never intended to move inland by way of the Cacyparis but had another river in mind.

[34]7.81.1.

[35]Plut. *Nic.* 28.3-4.

The Athenians' trail was easy to discover, and the Syracusans were swift in their pursuit. Nicias, placing a premium on speed had crossed the Erineus and made camp just beyond it, some fifty stadia or about six miles ahead of Demosthenes.[36] It is always more difficult to keep the rear of an army in good order and moving along at a good pace, and thus Demosthenes' division lagged behind. To compound his difficulties, Syracusan forces, those that the Athenians had forced their way through at the Cacyparis and perhaps others, continued to harass Demosthenes' men. He was forced to slow his retreat even further and when the main Syracusan force from the camp at Monte Climiti, with cavalry and light-armed troops, caught up with Demosthenes' men about mid-day their problems were greatly multiplied. The Syracusans attacked the still disordered and confused band at once, while Demosthenes was still attempting to get his troops into fighting order; the time spent on this task allowed the Syracusans to cut him off not quite a mile south of the Cacyparis.

The Athenians found themselves enclosed in an olive grove surrounded by a wall, with a road on either side, according to Plutarch "the country house of Polyzelus."[37] There the Syracusans could throw and shoot missiles at them from all sides in perfect safety. All through the afternoon the Athenians withstood the hail of spears, stones, and arrows, with great losses and diminishing hopes. At last Gylippus and the Syracusans proclaimed that any islanders in the Athenian force could surrender and be guaranteed their freedom. It was an attempt to divide and conquer, but even in these desperate circumstances it only worked to a degree. The contingents of some states surrendered, says Thucydides, "but not many." After further bloodshed the Syracusans offered terms of surrender to the survivors, and Demosthenes accepted. The Athenians must surrender their arms; in return, "none of them would be killed, either by violence, or

---

[36]7.81.3; 82.3. I accept Green's identification of the Erineus with the modern Fiume de Noto or Falconara (*Armada*, 330 with n. 14).

[37]Plut. *Nic.* 27.1. Polyzelus was the brother of the Syracusan tyrant Gelon, who died in 478/77 (Diod. 11.48.3–6). Green (*Armada*, 331) suggests a site in the Contrada Gallina as "the estate of Polyzelus."

by imprisonment, or by being deprived of the necessities of life."
Of the 20,000 or more men who had begun the retreat under the
command of Demosthenes only 6,000 were left to make their
surrender. They yielded up all the money they had to the
victors, who were able to fill four shields with the loot. The
6,000 prisoners were marched back to Syracuse at once.[38] According to Plutarch, Demosthenes tried to kill himself with his
own sword, but was prevented from accomplishing the suicide
by the enemy.[39]

On the next day, the seventh of the retreat, the Syracusans,
presumably their cavalry, caught up with Nicias, telling him of
the surrender of Demosthenes and ordering him to do the same.
Nicias would not believe what he was told and asked to send a
horseman to Syracuse under truce to check on the report. Learn-
ing that the news was accurate, Nicias sent a herald to inform the
enemy that he was ready to commit Athens to repay to Syracuse
the entire cost of the war. Since that figure would have reached
perhaps as much as 3,000 talents, it was no small promise, and he
offered to leave Athenian soldiers as hostages for the payment,
one soldier for each talent. We cannot know whether the Athenians could or would have honored this commitment or whether
the Syracusans and Gylippus thought that they would. The
latter, in any case, were not interested in bargaining; they now
had it in their power to destroy the enemy totally, and they were
determined to complete their victory. They rejected the offer
and resumed the attack, surrounding the Athenians and pelting
them with missiles, as they had done to the army of Demosthenes. The Athenians were without food and the other
necessities of life, so they tried once again to escape under the
protection of darkness. This time, however, the Syracusans were
alert. When they detected the Athenians taking up their weapons
to move, they sang out the battle paean. Most of the Athenians
were stilled by the dire sound, but 300 determined souls kept
moving and broke through the Syracusan guard into the night.[40]

On the morning of the eighth day Nicias had no choice but to

[38]7.81.4–82.
[39]Plut. *Nic.* 27.2.
[40]7.83.

try to break through the enemy ring and fight his way south to the next river, the Assinarus, some three miles away.[41] There was no longer a plan or any hope of pushing inland to meet the Sicels, just a blind wish to get away from the enemy and an increasingly terrible thirst. They made their way through the same onslaught of missiles, cavalry attacks, and hoplite assaults, and somehow reached the Assinarus. There all discipline collapsed as each man rushed to get across the river first, turning the army into a mob that clogged the passage and made it easier for the enemy to prevent the crossing.[42] Thucydides has described the frightful scene that followed: "Since they were forced to go forward in a close mass they fell on top of and trampled one another; some were killed immediately, impaled on their own spears, while others got tangled in their equipment and with each other and were carried away by the stream. The Syracusans stood along the opposite bank of the river, which was steep, and threw missiles down on the Athenians below, most of them drinking greedily and heaped together in disorder in the hollow bed of the river. The Peloponnesians also came down and butchered them, especially those in the river. And the water immediately became spoiled, but it was drunk, nonetheless, though it was muddy and full of blood, and most of them even fought over it."[43]

The remnant of the great Athenian army that had come to Sicily was destroyed at the Assinarus, most of its men lying in heaps in the riverbed. The few who had gotten across lay on its banks, where they had fallen victim to the cavalry, that same cavalry which from the beginning to the end of the campaign had caused the Athenians so much trouble. Nicias now surrendered

[41] I follow Green in identifying it with the modern Tellaro (*Armada*, 334–335, and n. 2).

[42] Green (*Armada*, 335, n. 3) thinks that again the Athenians found the river blocked by the Syracusans and again turned inland, traveling upstream. He believes that the breach of discipline and attempt to cross occurred at the village of S. Paolo, over four miles inland. Thucydides says nothing about any Syracusan blockage of the Assinarus or any Athenian detour. Here I find Green's arguments from the topography not compelling enough to reject the simpler account of Thucydides.

[43] 7.84.

himself, very carefully not to the Syracusans, but to Gylippus, "trusting him rather than the Syracusans."[44] At this point Gylippus ordered an end to the slaughter, for up to then no quarter had been given. Now he ordered the formal taking of prisoners, but the number taken at the Assinarus on behalf of the state was relatively small, about 1,000.[45] Even before the command Syracusan soldiers had begun to take prisoners secretly, not for the state, but for their own profit. These were the vast majority of all the prisoners, and "all Sicily was filled with them." Many, of course, had been killed at the river and many more during the escape from Syracuse. Finally, many escaped from the Assinarus and others later, after being enslaved, escaped to the same place of asylum, Catana, from which some of them continued the struggle against Syracuse.[46]

At the river the victorious Syracusans collected the public prisoners and their booty to prepare for the march back to the city. They took the armor from fallen Athenians and hung suits of it from the finest and tallest trees along the river; they crowned themselves with wreaths of victory and decorated their own horses festively.[47] After the return to the city the Syracusans held an assembly attended by themselves and their allies who had fought in the war against Athens. One of the popular leaders, probably Diocles, rose and proposed to establish a holiday and a festival called the Assinaria, named after the scene of the great victory, to be celebrated on the day of the capture of Nicias.[48] Diocles then moved that the servants of the Athenians

[44]7.85.1. Plutarch (*Nic.* 27.4-5) reports a speech of surrender and supplication by Nicias and attributes to Gylippus the motive for sparing him of increasing his reputation in Sparta by bringing home the captive Athenian generals.

[45]The total number of state prisoners given by Thucydides is 7,000 (7.87.4). Since 6,000 of these were from Demosthenes' division, the Assinarus yielded only 1,000.

[46]Pausanias 7.16.4-5 and Lysias 20.24-25 tell of individual Athenians who escaped to Catana and fought there.

[47]Plut. *Nic.* 27.6.

[48]Plut. *Nic.* 28.1. Plutarch, who alone mentions this proposal, attributes it to a certain Eurycles, of whom we know nothing. He may, indeed, have made this proposal, but Plutarch also attributes a second proposal to him (see below) which Diodorus (13.19.4) attaches to Diocles, a better known Syracusan demagogue. Plutarch, therefore, may simply be mistaken, and Diocles may have made both motions.

and their imperial allies should be sold into slavery, Athenian citizens and their Sicilian Greek allies should be put into the city's stone quarries for safekeeping, and the generals should be put to death.[49]

The first two proposals were adopted easily, but the proposal to execute the generals provoked debate. Hermocrates objected, employing a phrase that was to be remembered: "better than victory is to use victory nobly."[50] Apart from any magnanimity that he may have felt, Hermocrates may also have been moved by his old vision of Syracusan leadership in Sicily and perhaps beyond, and wanted to avoid any stain on the Syracusan reputation. He was, in any case, shouted down by the assembly. Then Gylippus rose to protest. He wanted the honor and glory of bringing them home to his own city, and so he claimed the two generals for himself and Sparta: Demosthenes, whom the Spartans considered their bitterest enemy because of his victories at Pylos and Sphacteria, Nicias, whom they thought to be a good friend to them because of his argument in favor of releasing the prisoners taken there and his support of peace with the Spartans. But the Syracusans, as we have seen, resented and disliked Gylippus and did not wish to gratify him. Others at the assembly had reasons for wanting to see Nicias, especially, dead. The party in Syracuse which had planned surrender and had been in communication with Nicias was afraid that he might implicate them under torture. The Corinthians had great respect for his abilities and feared that he might use his great wealth to bribe someone, escape, and return to give them new trouble.[51]

The assembly, therefore, put both Athenian generals to death. Thucydides says nothing of Demosthenes, but offers a brief, epigrammatic, and memorable eulogy of Nicias: "For this reason, or for one very much like it, he was killed; of all the Greeks, in my time, at any rate, he least deserved to meet with such extreme misfortune because he had led his entire life in accor-

---

[49]Plut. *Nic.* 28.2; Diodorus (13.19.4) gives slightly different details.

[50]Plut. *Nic.* 28.2. Diodorus (13.19.5) gives a slightly different version: "A finer thing than victory is to bear victory with humanity."

[51]7.86.1–4; Plut. *Nic.* 28. For a discussion of other ancient traditions see Dover, *HCT* IV, 461.

dance with virtue."[52] The judgment of the Athenians was different. The antiquarian Pausanias tells us that he saw a stele in the public cemetery of Athens on which were engraved the names of the generals who died fighting in Sicily, all except that of Nicias. The reason for the omission he learned from Philistus: "Demosthenes made a truce for the rest of his men, excluding himself and was captured while trying to commit suicide, but Nicias surrendered himself voluntarily. For this reason Nicias' name was not written on the stele: he was condemned as a voluntary prisoner and as an unworthy soldier."[53] Even in death Nicias could not escape the very condemnation by his countrymen that he had feared.

The rest of the prisoners, more than 7,000 of them, were not as fortunate as their generals. They were put into the stone quarries of Syracuse where they were crowded together in inhuman condition, burned by the sun during the day and chilled by the autumn cold at night. They were given about a half-pint of water and a pint of food each day, much less than what the Spartans had been permitted to send to the slaves on Sphacteria, and they suffered terribly from hunger and thirst. Men died from their wounds, from illness and exposure, and the dead bodies were thrown on top of one another, creating an unbearable stench. After seventy days all the survivors, except the Athenians and the Sicilian and Italian Greeks, were taken out and sold into slavery. Some of these later escaped or were freed.

---

[52]7.86.5: καὶ ὁ μὲν τοιαύτῃ ἢ ὅτι ἐγγύτατα τούτων αἰτίᾳ ἐτεθνήκει, ἥκιστα δὴ ἄξιος ὢν τῶν γε ἐπ᾽ ἐμοῦ Ἑλλήνων ἐς τοῦτο δυστυχίας ἀφικέσθαι διὰ τὴν πᾶσαν ἐς ἀρετὴν νενομισμένην ἐπιτήδευσιν. There is considerable debate about the meaning of this passage centering chiefly on the word νενομισμένην; some think it modifies ἀρετὴν, others ἐπιτήδευσιν, still others both. I agree with the second group, as do the translations of C. Forster Smith, Crawley, and Rex Warner, among others. The first group includes L. Bodin and J. de Romilly in their Budé translation and Benjamin Jowett. P. Huart (*Le vocabulaire de l'analyse psychologique dans l'oeuvre de Thucydide* [Paris, 1968], 451, n. 1) seems to be alone in holding the third view. For good discussions of the problems see Dover, *HCT* IV, 461-464 and A. W. H. Adkins, *GRBS* XVI (1975), 379-392.

[53]Paus. 1.29.11-12. The last clause reads: καταγνωσθεὶς αἰχμάλωτος ἐθελοντὴς εἶναι καὶ οὐκ ἀνὴρ πολέμῳ πρέπων. There is no good reason to doubt the accuracy either of Pausanias' report of what he saw and did not see or of Philistus' explanation. See Dover, *HCT* IV, 463.

Plutarch tells the tale of slaves freed for their ability to recite the verses of Euripides, for the Sicilians were mad for his poetry. Some Athenians, not, of course, those from the quarries, escaped in the same way and returned to Athens to give thanks to the poet responsible for their salvation.[54] Neither poetry nor anything else could help the men in the quarries. They were left there for eight months; presumably no one survived there any longer.[55]

Thucydides calls the Sicilian expedition "the greatest action of all those that took place during the war and, so it seems to me, at least, the greatest of any which we know to have happened to any of the Greeks; it was the most glorious for those who won and the most disastrous for those who were defeated. For the losers were beaten in every way and completely; what they suffered was great in every respect, for they met with total destruction, as the saying goes—their army, their ships, and everything were destroyed—and only a few of many came back home."[56] But the defeat, total, unprecedented, and terrible as it was, did not end the war. Unlike any other Greek state, Athens had the resources to continue fighting after such a disaster. It now remained to be seen whether the Athenians had the resolve, the wisdom, and the leadership to survive.

[54] Plut. *Nic.* 29.
[55] 7.87.1–4. It is barely possible that a few lived on to be sold into slavery, some of whom may have escaped, too.
[56] 7.87.5–6.

Conclusions

The Peace of Nicias was a failure in its own terms. It had promised peace for fifty years but was formally broken in the eighth year of its existence; in fact it had already become little more than a formality by the summer of 420, when Athens joined the Argive League. It failed in the modest aim of bringing an end to the Peloponnesian War and in the more ambitious one of establishing the basis for a new relationship of peaceful tolerance, if not friendship, between Athens and Sparta. This failure is not surprising, for from the start the peace had been incompatible with reality. Its terms had always proven unacceptable to Corinth, Thebes, and Megara, all major states in the Spartan alliance, and to an important and powerful faction within Sparta itself. It excluded Argos, which was then free to act as a magnet that attracted Elis and Mantinea. The new alliance so created conquered Orchomenus, threatened Epidaurus, and almost won over Tegea by treason. Intended to restore order and stability, the Peace of Nicias almost immediately created defection, disorder, and war. The alliance between Athens and Sparta, quickly invented to halt this process, only quickened it, as the states not controlled by the two great powers came to fear their intentions.

The futility of the peace should have been immediately apparent, for the Spartans never sincerely intended to execute a provision that the Athenians regarded as essential, the restoration of Amphipolis. That city was important enough for the Athenians to exile Thucydides for his role in losing it; Cleon died trying to recover it; and the Athenians did not give up their claim on it or

354

their hopes of getting it back until their conflict with Philip of Macedon in the fourth century. No peace could have been made in 421 without the promise of Amphipolis' restoration, and no peace based on such a promise could last if it were not redeemed. Once it became apparent that Sparta would not restore Amphipolis to Athens, the peace was sure to unravel. No Athenian politician, not even one with the unique political power of Pericles at his strongest, could have compelled the Athenians to restore Pylos to Sparta until Amphipolis was in Athenian hands. Even less could Nicias, who had neither Pericles' power nor his ability, deliver it. With both Amphipolis and Pylos in the wrong hands, it was only a matter of time until distrust and latent hostility turned into open confrontation.

Even though the peace did not achieve its ostensible purpose, events nonetheless vindicated the Spartans in their original decision to make it. They had been driven to seek peace by their desire to recover their fellow citizens captured at Sphacteria and by their fear of continuing to fight a war in which Argos would be added to the forces of the enemy. The peace brought them the return of the prisoners and required no *quid pro quo*. It allowed them to face the threat from Argos while free from war with Athens. Even when the Athenians joined with Argos, their state was so divided and the forces favoring peace so influential, that they made no important contribution to the campaign in which the very existence of Sparta as a great power was threatened. When the peace finally broke down, Sparta had been given eight years of respite, the threat from Argos had subsided almost entirely, and the Peloponnesus, which had been on the verge of explosion, was once again calm and safe under Spartan control. Athens, moreover, had become engaged in a diversionary campaign that in two years drained her of men, money, and morale comparable to the losses she had suffered from the plague and ten years of fighting in the Archidamian War. The resumption of the war in 413 was far more advantageous to Sparta than its continuation in 421 would have been, and she had reason to be thankful to the conditions and men that had made the peace possible.

For the Athenians, of course, the opposite was true. Whatever the attractions of peace, and in 421 they had been great, it was not at that time available on acceptable terms. Competent statesmanship would have anticipated that the Spartans would neither restore Amphipolis nor force the Boeotians to deliver Panactum intact to the Athenians, and it would have realized that the failure to carry out these obligations would destroy the possibility of peace. No doubt the desire for peace had been great and with it went an eagerness to extend the Spartans every courtesy and accommodation necessary to achieve it. But common prudence would have dictated that the performance of obligations be mutual and that the continuation of the peace be conditional on that performance. It was reckless imprudence on the part of Nicias and the Athenians to restore the prisoners and make an alliance with the Spartans even though Sparta, having been chosen by lot to make the first restoration, failed to deliver Amphipolis. Those Athenian actions not only removed much of the pressure on the Spartans to fulfill the terms of the treaty, but also encouraged them to ignore the provision about Panactum, for if the Spartans would not coerce the weak Amphipolitans, they would hardly take action against the powerful Boeotians. Failure to restore Amphipolis also guaranteed a reaction against the peace in Athens, a refusal to restore Pylos, and more friendly consideration of an alliance with Argos.

In pursuing a policy of appeasement, Nicias enhanced the prospects for war. If he had taken a tougher line in his negotiations and insisted on precise compliance with the treaty, the Spartans might have been compelled, entirely against their wishes, to make the effort to return Amphipolis to Athens. Had they been able to do so Athens would have restored Pylos. In those circumstances Thebes might not have dared to destroy Panactum before evacuating it. The mutual fulfillment of the treaty's terms might have strengthened the forces of peace in both Athens and Sparta and given both cities time to grow accustomed to the new circumstances and relationships. By facing reality courageously and making the Spartans face it as well, Nicias and his colleagues might possibly have salvaged the peace.

Even if there were no way to save the peace, a policy that recognized that fact and revealed it plainly to the public would have served Athens better than the one that was followed. Such an approach would have allowed the Athenians to understand that the war was not over and that the peace was only a breathing space. It would have permitted them to recover their strength and to devise and pursue a policy more commensurate with the facts. If lasting peace with Sparta were impossible, the Athenians might choose to take advantage of the opportunity offered by Argive independence and Peloponnesian disarray to form a new and powerful coalition to destroy Spartan power once and for all. If the idea of renewing the war so soon after ten bitter years of suffering were unacceptable, they could at least take up a posture of benevolent neutrality toward the anti-Spartan forces without running any risks of their own. A reasonable and moderate policy would have been not to abrogate the Peace of Nicias, but to refuse an alliance with Sparta, leaving Sparta to deal with Argos and its own rebellious allies. With good luck Spartan power might have been curbed at no cost to Athens; with any luck at all Sparta would have been immobilized and posed no threat to Athens for many years. The one course that offered no advantage was to bolster a fraudulent peace with an insincere alliance; such a policy gave pause to Athens' potential friends and courage to her enemies without bringing anything of value to the Athenians themselves. It only delayed the moment of truth when the duplicity of the Spartans would be revealed and guaranteed a stronger reaction against the peace. This course, however, was precisely the one that Nicias urged and that the Athenians followed.

When at last they turned against Nicias' policy, the Athenians chose the more extreme rather than the more moderate policy, joining in the Argive alliance. That may or may not have been the best course to pursue, but reasonable statesmen should have understood that it was too late to return to a policy of peaceful cooperation with Sparta. The alliance with Argos made war with Sparta, at some time or another, likely, and it was the job of an Athenian patriot from that time forward to abandon political differences and seek to meet that contingency in circumstances likely to bring victory to Athens and her allies. Instead Nicias and his colleagues dragged their feet, and when presented with the great opportunity to destroy Spartan power at Mantinea, Athens made only a grudging, token contribution. As a result, the Spartans won a close victory that allowed them to restore their base of power and ultimately cost Athens the war, its empire, and, for a time, its independence.

Thucydides offers no direct judgment of Nicias' policy of peace and appeasement or of the more militant one favored by Alcibiades, merely pointing out that each acted, at least in part, from personal motives. This view encourages the reader to think back to the historian's portentous remarks about the importance of the removal of Pericles, that great man who, for Thucydides, had both defined and embodied the qualities essential to the statesman: "to know what must be done and to be able to explain it; to love one's country and to be incorruptible."[1] Neither Nicias nor Alcibiades, whichever of them had the better grasp of "what must be done," had the ability to explain it with enough success as to have his policy followed consistently. Both were above corruption by bribery, but each to some extent placed his own concerns, Nicias, the desire to retain his perfect record of success and his public reputation,[2] Alcibiades, his resentment at neglect by the Spartans,[3] before the country's welfare. Their behavior leads us to recall Thucydides' assessment of the successors of Pericles. The historian had written that, "being more equal with one another, and, as each strove to be first, they [Pericles' successors] turned themselves to please the masses and even turned the conduct of affairs over to them";[4] surely he meant us to ponder this statement as we consider the careers of Nicias and Alcibiades.

Thucydides' interpretation suggests that the choice of policy is less important than the tremendous decline in the quality of leadership and the rise in the power of the mindless mob. Thucydides had written that Pericles "restrained the masses, though in a liberal manner, and he was not led by them, but they

[1] 2.60.5.
[2] 5.16.1.
[3] 5.43.
[4] 2.65.10.

by him, for since he did not get his power by improper means by saying what was pleasing to the multitude but held it because of his excellent reputation, he could oppose them even to the point of anger."[5] In his time, "what was in name a democracy was becoming the rule of the first citizen in fact."[6] Thus, Thucydides seems to argue that in addition to the decline in leadership, the growth of true, unrestrained democracy also helps explain Athens' errors during the Peace of Nicias, for some of those errors must certainly be among "the many great blunders" that Thucydides says resulted from these changes in the Athenian government.

If this is a correct reading of Thucydides' message, we can surely agree both with his evaluation of the change of leadership and with his view that the democratic Athenian constitution was a significant element in some of the city's errors. The absence of a strong executive with an extended term of office in which to devise and conduct a consistent policy surely helps to explain Athens' failure to exploit the opportunities presented by this period in history. It is, for example, almost unbelievable that the climax of Alcibiades' foreign policy, the battle of Mantinea, occurred in a year when he was not in office, and that his policy was executed by his enemies, who did not agree with it. Athens paid a heavy price for its inconsistency, but such problems are not unique to Athens or to democracies. Sparta, too, as we have seen, suffered from serious inconsistency in her policy and was fortunate to survive in spite of it. Nor are modern governments, elected for stated terms and having infinitely more freedom from popular interference, always well supplied with foresighted and courageous leadership or even with consistent foreign policies. No system guarantees good leadership, but the Athenian record from the time of Cleisthenes showed that democracy was at least as capable of producing it as any other. It was Athens' misfortune that the leader who held the greatest influence in 421 and the years following was Nicias, a man whose political judgments were timid and shortsighted and whose character made reconsid-

[5] 2.65.8.
[6] 2.65.9.

eration of those judgments in the light of new facts unlikely, if not impossible.

Nicias' role in the Sicilian expedition was no less central. Thucydides, however, emphasizes other reasons for the campaign's failure, and his own direct judgments place no blame whatever on Nicias for the disaster in Sicily. Thucydides, moreover, seems to have had several views of the expedition. He clearly regarded it as a mistake, one of the many errors resulting from the decline in leadership and the growth of democracy that followed Pericles' death.[7] On the other hand, he agrees with Demosthenes' estimate that Syracuse would have fallen if Nicias had followed Lamachus' plan and attacked Syracuse immediately upon his arrival[8]—a view that suggests that the mistake lay in the execution of the campaign, not in the concept itself. When Thucydides specifically designates the mistake he had in mind, however, it is not the tactical error of the general he blames, but the Athenian people and their demagogic leaders: "It [the campaign] failed not so much because of an error in judgment about the people they were attacking, as because those who sent it out failed to take additional measures to support those who went on the expedition, and instead occupied themselves with private intrigues to gain leadership of the people and so carried on the military campaign less keenly and also shook the city with civil discord for the first time."[9]

If Thucydides means what his language most literally says, his interpretation contradicts his own narrative, for the latter points out that the Athenians at home backed the expedition fully, without delay and with enthusiasm.[10] Employing considerable effort and ingenuity, some scholars interpret Thucydides as arguing that the recall of Alcibiades caused the failure of the expe-

[7] 2.65.11
[8] 7.42.3
[9] 2.65.11
[10] Among the scholars who have observed and commented on the contradiction, those who have contributed most to my understanding are: A. W. Gomme, *JHS* LXXI (1951), 72ff. = *More Essays*, 92-111; H. D. Westlake *CQ* VIII (1958), 106ff. = *Essays*, 161-173; P. A. Brunt, *REG* LXV (1952), 59-96; and Dover, *HCT* IV, 242-245.

dition.[11] Even if they are right, Thucydides' narrative also contradicts that interpretation. Nothing in the *History* supports the idea that Alcibiades had proven himself an outstanding commander before his exile in 415.[12] He opposed the strategy of Lamachus, and his own strategy was already a failure at the time of his flight into exile. Whatever its prospects in its original form as a strategy of limited commitment and risk, based chiefly on diplomacy, it was hopeless once Nicias had converted the expedition into a massive amphibious force whose size was sure to alarm the Sicilians and make diplomacy unavailing. Alcibiades did not recognize and adjust to the changed situation, but merely went ahead with his plan without any prospect of success. Thucydides' endorsement of Lamachus' plan shows that he recognized that Alcibiades' strategy was doomed to fail.

Some scholars, embarrassed for Thucydides because of the contradiction, try to defend him by denying its existence. Thus Gomme points out that what Thucydides says in 2.65.11 "is hardly consistent with the opening words of Book VI... for it was this multitude, $οἱ πολλοί$, who voted the adequate forces for the expedition." He also sees that "Thucydides believed that the expedition might well have succeeded, and we, as we read his narrative, cannot but agree with him, *but not for the reasons which he gives in II. 65.11;* they are not borne out by his narrative."[13] Nevertheless, he apologizes on the next page: "This is not to say that Thucydides' judgement in II. 65.11 *contradicts* his narrative in VI–VII (it may only supplement it), still less that it is wrong." But the apology is inadequate, as Gomme reveals in concluding his sentence: "only that judgement and narrative were not written at the same time, in the same breath, as it were, both in the mind of the writer at the same time. The judgement is late; and the narrative presumably earlier."

Theories of different levels of composition in the *History*,

[11]The authors cited in the previous note all hold this view.

[12]Thucydides' praise in 6.15.4, "he managed the affairs of war most excellently," either refers to his actions between 411 and 407 (see Westlake, *Essays*, 171, n. 36, and Dover, *HCT* IV, 242–245), in which case it is debatable, or is without adequate basis.

[13]Gomme, *More Essays*, 96; Gomme's italics.

though well over a century has gone by since the first was proposed, and many have appeared in that time, are notoriously
subjective, even arbitrary, and none has gained general support.[14] Yet this resort to the time-honored technique of trying to
solve Thucydidean problems by devising convenient theories of
his *History*'s composition is a clue that we are dealing with a real
and interesting difficulty, for scholars usually resort to this device when they see a conflict between Thucydides' narrative and
his interpretation, his theory, so to speak, and his practice.
When scholars found that Thucydides' account of the origins of
the Peloponnesian War did not appear to agree with his explanation of it, some suggested that the two elements were composed
at different times and that Thucydides died before he could
reconcile the contradictions.[15] The implication in that case and
in the one before us is that differences of this kind are evidence of
incomplete thought, and that the discrepancies would have been
ironed out or removed in a final draft. But how would
Thucydides have done that? The interpretation in each case is
clearly his later thought and would, presumably, have been retained. To smooth out the discrepancies the historian would
have had to alter the narrative to conform with them. We must
conclude, therefore, that an alteration of the narrative to fit the
later interpretation would not have been a step in the direction of
greater historical accuracy, yet everything we know of
Thucydides indicates his commitment to precision and accuracy.

   To understand Thucydides' procedure and purposes we must
find a different path, and we might begin by presenting a brief
recapitulation of Thucydides' interpretation of the Sicilian expedition, then setting forth the different view that seems to

---

[14]See Kagan, *Outbreak*, 360. Nothing has happened in the last forty years to
invalidate John Finley's observations that "The recent revival of the old controversy on when Thucydides composed the various parts of his *History*, although designed to prove the existence of many early parts in the work which
we have, has apparently tended to prove the opposite. The reason is that each
new participant in the controversy, while advancing his own views, under-
mined those of his predecessors and hence diminished, rather than increased,
the number of passages still capable of being regarded as early" (*HSCP*, Suppl.
I, 1940, 255).
[15]See Kagan, *Outbreak*, 359-360.

emerge from his narrative and attempting to account for the differences. The historian tells us that the Athenians undertook the expedition in ignorance both of Sicily's size and population and of the scope of the war they were undertaking. They meant from the first to employ a larger force than the one they had used in their previous Sicilian campaign and to conquer the island with it. As in his account of the origins of the entire war, and almost in the same language, Thucydides tells us that the Athenians' official explanation for the campaign was their desire to defend their Sicilian kinsmen and allies, but that "the truest explanation" was their desire to add Sicily to the empire. Nicias tried to prevent the expedition but was defeated in the assembly at Athens. He reopened the question at a second assembly, this time trying to deter the Athenians from their purpose by the device of magnifying the forces that would be needed for success and even safety. The people, however, misunderstood his message; instead of being deterred, they were encouraged to pursue their original purpose with even greater enthusiasm. Alcibiades and perhaps others had grand schemes of conquering first Sicily and Italy, then Carthage, then hiring Spanish and other mercenaries for a further assault on and conquest of the Peloponnesus. "A passion [eros] for the voyage fell upon all of them," each for different, if similar reasons, but the great mass were moved simply by greed. Though he was opposed to the expedition and reluctant to serve, the people elected Nicias as one of the generals.

They also chose Alcibiades, the originator and champion of the expedition. But the affairs of the Hermae and the mysteries roused the masses' religiosity and superstition. Demagogues played on their ill-formed fears of tyrannical and oligarchic plots, their suspicion and envy of aristocrats and outstanding men, for their own political purposes. They launched a reign of terror that brought death and exile to many innocent people, and finally brought about the recall of Alcibiades, whose shocking private life made him a greater object of suspicion than anyone else. The removal of Alcibiades was a terrible blow to Athens. He was the author of the expedition and a very talented commander, though his strategy was not as promising as that of Lamachus. Alcibiades' recall, combined with the death of Lamachus, left the expedition in the sole command of a Nicias who was weakened by disease and unenthusiastic about the campaign. The recall also drove Alcibiades to the enemy, where his services were even more damaging to Athens, for he played an important role in persuading the Spartans to renew the war and place a fort in Attica, even advising them as to the best site.

After the departure of Alcibiades, according to Thucydides, Nicias prosecuted the campaign at first with skill, but with undue caution. Had he attacked at once, the Syracusans could not even have sent for help to the Peloponnesus until it was too late. After that, even if reinforcements had come they could not have helped, and Syracuse would have fallen. Nicias, however, delayed, but even so, at one critical moment in the summer of 414 the Athenians were close to completing their walls, and the Syracusans had despaired of getting aid and were discussing terms of surrender. At this point Gylippus and the Corinthians arrived to undo what seemed a certain Athenian success. Soon the situation was reversed by the great skill and daring of the Spartan commander, and the besiegers had become the besieged. At that point Nicias wrote to the Athenians describing the bad situation he was in and asking them either to recall the expedition or to send out reinforcements of great size. In any case, he asked to be allowed to leave his post because of illness. The Athenians chose to send reinforcements under Demosthenes and Eurymedon, but to keep Nicias at his command, promoting two officers on the scene to assist him.

By the time the second expedition arrived the situation had deteriorated utterly. Demosthenes could do no better than try a dangerous night attack that failed. After that, the only thing to do was to withdraw from Sicily, or at least move to a new, healthier, and safer base. Nicias, though he saw the arguments in favor of retreat, nonetheless refused to permit it. He was afraid of giving up the campaign without the express consent of the Athenian assembly, for he feared that in their passion and ignorance the Athenians would be persuaded by clever speakers and unscrupulous politicians and bring false charges against the generals which might even result in their death. Finally, even Nicias agreed to leave, but then a lunar eclipse occurred and, at the behest of the soothsayers and the majority of the superstitious Athenian soldiers, Nicias again delayed his departure. In the disasters that followed Nicias behaved with heroic concern for his men. His death at the hands of the Syracusans and the ignominious failure to which it put an end were deserved less by Nicias than by any man in Thucydides' time, because he had lived his entire life in accordance with virtue.

Such an account may pass for a reasonably accurate summary of Thucydides' interpretation as perceived by an ordinary reader without any particular point of view. It is not, however, the only interpretation possible. Quite a different one emerges from Thucydides' narrative. It might begin by arguing that the original decision to go to Sicily really did arise because of the invitation from Segesta and Leontini. Such an invitation would have appealed to the Athenians for three reasons: they had largely recovered from the Archidamian War and were ready for a new venture; they wanted to prevent Syracuse from dominating Sicily and the Athenian allies on the island and then, perhaps, lending aid to the Peloponnesians in a renewal of the war; and they nurtured a vague hope of extending their empire to the west. The size and character of the expedition that the Athenians voted, however, was not greater than their previous commitment in 424. Since the expedition could not have conquered Sicily, or even Syracuse, by force of arms, the plan must have been to rely primarily on diplomacy for success. Such a venture might not succeed, but it was not a mad scheme, and it could not have led to a serious disaster for Athens. The Athenians could hardly have been grossly ignorant of the size and population of Sicily, for thousands of those who had walked its roads and sailed its waters in 427–424 and 422 were still alive. Nor had the Athenians, at this point, been overcome by the greed that would cause them to act with blind recklessness. Instead they proceeded cautiously, sending an embassy to Sicily to investigate the situation, and only then did they vote the modest expedition that was originally intended, choosing the moderate and cautious Nicias as one of its three commanders.

The plan adopted was surely that of Alcibiades, who was its

chief advocate. He certainly intended to use the opportunity to enhance his prestige and to help him in his political struggle against Nicias. No doubt he hoped, at first, to gain sole command of the expedition and return to Athens with the glorious fruits of his diplomatic and, perhaps, military talents. Even when Nicias and Lamachus were added to the command he did not abandon hope of dominating the expedition, imposing his strategy, and achieving the same results. At no time, however, do we have persuasive evidence that he seriously harbored ambitions to conquer Sicily and Carthage and to accomplish the grand design that he later described in Sparta. Even more certainly, the instructions given the generals by the assembly spoke only of the modest goals described above, not even mentioning the conquest of Syracuse.

At the second assembly, Nicias' ill-conceived rhetorical trick converted a modest undertaking that presented few risks into a massive campaign that made the conquest of Sicily seem not only possible but likely. The fact that Nicias himself agreed to serve, however unwillingly (though Plutarch tells us that it had been common for Nicias to try to avoid such unwelcome assignments),[16] that he had specified the kind of expedition that would guarantee safety, and that the people voted it in every detail, inflamed the popular spirit in favor of the expedition. Nicias' estimate of the military situation, and therefore his judgment of what forces were necessary, was wrong in at least one crucial way: though he appears to have had at least some understanding of the significance of cavalry and of the Syracusan advantage in that arm of warfare, he did not list it among the requirements for the campaign, either at the assembly or in the weeks before the expedition's departure. The absence of that cavalry prevented him from making use of his victory at Syracuse late in the summer of 415; had he done so Athens would have conquered Syracuse before Gylippus and the Corinthians could have intervened.

The hysteria caused by the affairs of the Hermae and the mysteries did considerable damage to Athens by intensifying political divisions and by placing a cloud of religious disfavor

[16]Plut. *Nic.* 6.2.

over the expedition. It also resulted in the recall, condemnation, and exile of Alcibiades, but the harm done to Athens in this way has been much exaggerated. The larger expedition caused by Nicias' intervention vitiated the original strategy of Alcibiades, yet he clung to it and had his way. His expectations of winning over allies were disappointed from the first, and there is no reason to think he would have been successful had he stayed on. To say that things would have gone better had he remained instead of leaving everything in the hands of Nicias is not to say much, for such would also have been the case had the campaign been entrusted to Lamachus, Demosthenes, Eurymedon, or any competent general other than Nicias. Nor does Alcibiades' role in bringing Sparta back into the war and getting the Spartans to build a fort at Decelea appear to have been crucial. The Spartans were pressed equally hard by the Syracusans and Corinthians, but took no action until the Athenians were in trouble in Sicily and until their attack on Laconia formally broke the treaty and gave the Spartans a morally and religiously acceptable reason for renewing the fight, long after Alcibiades and the others had urged them to do so. The choice of Decelea as the best place to fortify did not require the advice of Alcibiades; the Boeotians could have given the Spartans the same advice and may well have done so. The failure of the Sicilian expedition and the Spartan renewal of the war cannot reasonably be attributed to the recall of Alcibiades.

An interpretation based on Thucydides' narrative could argue that even after the opportunity to take Syracuse was lost, the Athenians could have succeeded were it not for Nicias' errors of omission and commission. After a good start in 414 the Athenians could have completed the siege of Syracuse and guaranteed victory, but Nicias did not move swiftly to complete a single circuit of walls. Instead he wasted time building a double wall near Syracuse while the wall across Epipolae was still incomplete. A general with only ordinary judgment and skill would have completed the wall immediately and taken precautions against the arrival of help from overseas. Instead, expecting victory by surrender without an unpleasant siege, Nicias dawdled and talked to Syracusan factions. He did not complete the circuit of walls, he did not send a squadron to cut off Gylippus' arrival in Sicily, he did not mount a competent blockade to prevent Gongylus and the Corinthian ships from reaching Syracuse by sea, he did not fortify and guard Epipolae to prevent a surprise attack. He thereby allowed the enemy to revive and drive the Athenians from their dominant position. He then moved the Athenian navy, the supply depot and the treasury to an untenable position at Plemmyrium, where the morale and quality of the fleet deteriorated and from which Gylippus was able to drive them, capturing the money and supplies.

By the end of the summer of 414 everything pointed to the abandonment of the campaign before more money and lives were wasted, but Nicias refused to withdraw out of fear for his reputation and safety at the hands of the Athenian assembly and law courts. Instead he wrote a letter to the Athenians in which he did not even make an unequivocal argument for withdrawal. Once again he gave the assembly a choice, this time between withdrawal and sending a new force as large as the first. Once again the assembly made the wrong decision, voting a huge reinforcement and refusing Nicias' request to be relieved of his command. Had he been more frank about his mishandling of the situation and bolder and more honest in his advice, the Athenians might have acted otherwise.

After the failure of Demosthenes' assault on Epipolae there was no acceptable choice for the Athenians but to give up the campaign or, at least, withdraw to Thapsus and Catana. Nicias' refusal to move is inexcusable. He deceived himself with groundless hopes of an imminent Syracusan financial collapse that would still give the Athenians victory because he was afraid to face the Athenian assembly and explain his failure. He preferred to risk the lives of his troops and the security of Athens rather than take the chance of condemnation by his fellow citizens. To save his reputation and escape punishment he took an action which, more than any other, caused the destruction of the expedition and the loss of the war. When he seized on the lunar eclipse as a last chance to escape the inevitable, he destroyed the Athenians' final opportunity to escape. His admirable behavior during the retreat cannot begin to compensate for his indefensible behavior up to then. In that light Thucydides' decision to single him out in a eulogy as the man in his time least deserving such a fate is more than a little puzzling.

These summaries reveal that Thucydides' own interpretation stands at odds with the judgment that arises most readily from his narrative—a judgment much the same as that made by those contemporaries who deliberately omitted Nicias' name from the memorial to those who died in Sicily, and similar to the one found in Plutarch's *Life of Nicias*. When difficulties of interpretation of such importance occur in the *History*, as they do in the question of the cause of the Peloponnesian War, they sometimes arise because Thucydides was attempting to combat a current understanding that he thought incorrect and misleading. Thus, the common opinion that the war was brought about by Pericles and that the Megarian Decree was its chief cause led him to organize his work and to provide an interpretation to show that these opinions were wrong, for he wanted to be sure that the reader would learn the correct lessons from the events he described. The same purpose and similar techniques seem to be at work in Thucydides' account and interpretation of the Sicilian expedition.

We may approach the problem in a useful way by examining Thucydides' remarkable eulogy of Nicias in 7.86.5. This passage, too, has caused scholars much trouble. Part of the problem is how to understand the word *arete*, which we translate "virtue." Some want to modify it with another word in the sentence to produce a translation like Jowett's: "No one of the Hellenes in my time was less deserving of so miserable an end; for he lived in the practice of every *customary* virtue."[17] That would make it possible to believe that Thucydides is being ironical, at least, and possibly even cynical, "that in his final judgment on Nicias, [he] is taking an opportunity to sneer at piety."[18] The best readers of Thucydides, however, do not find that the text permits such translation,[19] but even if it did there is no reason to

[17]See above, Chap. 14, n. 52.

[18]These are the words of H. A. Murray (*BICS* VIII [1961], 42), who uses them to describe a point of view with which he does not agree.

[19]See the arguments of Dover, *HCT* IV, 463.

read irony into it. Some scholars who do not see irony nevertheless explain the passage as being altogether unpolitical, as merely
an expression of pity. "No defence of Nicias' conduct of the
campaign is expressed or implied: readers are left to form their
verdict on this from the preceding narrative. The words merely
contrast the blamelessness of his private life with his miserable
death."[20] But there is no reason to reduce the strong, worldly,
and various Greek idea of *arete* to an almost Christian ideal of
personal inoffensiveness. A recent investigation, moreover,
demonstrates that in the passage at hand Nicias "is evaluated
primarily in terms of traditional criteria of excellence... and
there was no necessity for the Greeks of Thucydides' day to
regard the judgement that Nicias was unworthy of misfortune in
virtue of the possession of traditional ἀρετή as either ironic or
bizarre."[21]

But whatever the meaning of *arete*, we would still be struck by
the force of this tribute, for Thucydides calls Nicias not only a
man who did not deserve his terrible fate, but the man in his time
least worthy of it, thereby, in some way, placing Nicias above all
his contemporaries, even Pericles. That emphasis is what catches
our attention and makes us ask why he chose to write one of his
rare eulogies and why he cast it in the form he did. His readers
could be expected to regard the praise as a general commendation
of Nicias' qualities yet, as a keen modern reader has observed:
"No one who has read this history up to the present point is
likely to have formed a favourable view of Nikias."[22] But this
unfavorable view is precisely what made it necessary for
Thucydides to write his eulogy of Nicias; that few readers come
away from the *History* with the unfavorable opinion described
above is evidence of the eulogy's effectiveness.

If we had Thucydides' account of Nicias' career without the
final evaluation we might come to the conclusion that Nicias'
contemporaries seem to have reached and which is reflected in
Plutarch's *Life:* that a major reason for the Sicilian disaster was
the incompetent statesmanship and generalship of Nicias.

[20]H. D. Westlake, *CQ* XXXV (1941), 59.
[21]A. W. H. Adkins, *GRBS*, 388–389.
[22]Dover, *HCT* IV, 461.

Thucydides, it seems clear, would not deny that this was a contributing cause, but it is neither a sufficient explanation nor the main one. Thucydides wants his reader to understand that the main cause of the disaster was the post-Periclean democracy, unchecked by the wise restraining leadership of a powerful and intelligent statesman, misled by thoughtless and ambitious demagogues, abandoned therefore to its own ignorance, greed, superstition, and fear. The mob decided to attack Sicily and add it to the Athenian Empire so that the people could profit from it. The mob was seduced by the ambitious selfishness of Alcibiades, yet it yielded to its superstitious fear and chose Nicias as one of the generals in spite of his opposition to the venture and refused to excuse him from his command even when he was sick and no longer in full possession of his talents. The mob continued to throw money, equipment, and men into the bottomless pit of Sicily long after prudence dictated an end to the campaign. The mob was panicked into a reign of terror by the religious scandals of 415 and manipulated by demagogues into driving away the originator of the very expedition they were undertaking, probably the cleverest man among them, and forcing him into the camp of the enemy where he did great damage to his native land. That is the way of democracies that have degenerated into mob rule, and Thucydides is determined that his reader understand this important lesson.

The eulogy of Nicias points the reader in the right direction, for it calls his attention to the other and greater eulogy in the history, the panegyric of Pericles in 2.65. There he is reminded that after Pericles, Athens, which had really been under the rule of an outstanding statesman, became a true democracy and that the politicians who succeeded him were a lesser breed, each of whom lacked at least some of his qualities. Nicias, though a good man of considerable talents, did not have in sufficient degree the intellectual qualities of intelligence (*xynesis*), foresight (*pronoia*), and good judgment (*gnome*). He was chosen for leadership because of his public reputation for piety and for the success (*eutychia*) that the mob believes to be the fruit of such piety. But Thucydides would have us understand that the mob is wrong, for *eutychia*, in so far as man and not chance contributes to it, comes not from piety and the favor of the gods but from the intellectual qualities of a Pericles. Thucydides was not, we may believe, unconscious of the irony in the fact that the Athenians saw their hopes ruined by their faith in a man who, like themselves, believed that piety and faith in the gods were superior to worldly human wisdom; it was this very faith that brought Nicias from *eutychia* to the most terrible disaster (*dystychia*)—a disaster that he, least of all men, deserved.

In writing that eulogy Thucydides was not interested chiefly in defending the reputation of Nicias, although there is reason to believe he would have been glad to do so. Both men appear to have been admirers of Pericles, both hated Cleon and opposed his policies. Is it too much to believe that when Thucydides was prosecuted for his failure at Amphipolis, probably by Cleon and at least with his support, he was defended or at least comforted by Nicias? The two men had much in common,[23] and Thucydides could easily have seen Nicias as an undeserving victim of the irrational *demos*, much like himself, and written a rather generous obituary. His main purpose, however, was to prevent what he judged to be a misinterpretation, or at least an oversimplification, of the disaster in Sicily which fixed the blame solely on the faults of Nicias. No fair-minded reader can deny that he was right to resist so simple an understanding or fail to appreciate his broader and deeper explanation. But no one should regret that he did not alter his account to conceal the evidence that permits a different emphasis. A modern reader with a lesser knowledge and shallower understanding of the events than the great Athenian historian but, perhaps, with a greater distance from them, may be grateful for the valuable lessons in the behavior of unchecked direct democracies and yet, at the same time, observe that chance put the fate of the Athenians into the hands of the one man who was able to turn a mistake into a disaster.

[23]See Adkins, *GRBS*, 389-392.

Bibliography

Accame, S. "Le archeresia degli strateghi ateniesi nel V secolo," *Riv. Fil.* LXIII (1935), 341–355.

Adcock, F. E. "The Archidamian War, 431–421 B.C.," *AH* V (1940), 193–253.

Adkins, A. W. H. "The *Arete* of Nicias: Thucydides 7.86," *GRBS* XVI (1975), 379–392.

Amit, M. "The Melian Dialogue and History," *Athenaeum* XLVI (1968), 216–235.

Amyx, D. A. "Attic Stelai, Part III," *Hesperia* XXVII (1958), 113–310.

Anderson, J. K. "A Topographical and Historical Study of Achaea," *BSA* XLIX (1954), 72–92.

Andrewes, A. "The Melian Dialogue and Pericles' Last Speech," *PCPhS* n.s. VI (1960), 1–10.

Aurenche, O. *Les groupes d'Alcibiade, de Léogoras et de Teucros.* Paris, 1974.

Badian, E., ed. *Ancient Societies and Institutions: Studies Presented to Victor Ehrenberg on His 75th Birthday.* Oxford, 1966.

Beloch, K. J. *Die Attische Politik seit Perikles.* Leipzig, 1884.

——. *Griechische Geschichte.* 2d ed. Strassburg, Berlin, and Leipzig, 1912–1927.

Bodin, L., and J. de Romilly. *Thucydide Livres VI et VII.* Paris, 1955.

Bradeen, D. W. and M. F. McGregor. *Studies in Fifth-Century Attic Epigraphy.* Norman, 1973.

Bruce, I. A. F. *An Historical Commentary on the Hellenica Oxyrhynchia.* Cambridge, 1967.

Brunt, P. A. "Thucydides and Alcibiades," *REG* LXV (1952), 59–96.

——. "Review of H. Wentker, *Sizilien und Athen*," in *CR* VII (1957), 243–245.

Busolt, G. *Forschungen zur Griechischen Geschichte.* Breslau, 1880.

——. *Griechische Geschichte.* 3 vols. Gotha, 1893–1904.

—— and Heinrich Swoboda. *Griechische Staatskunde*, in Müller's *Handbuch der Allertumswissenschaft.* 2 vols. Munich, 1920–1926.

Calhoun, G. M. *Athenian Clubs in Politics and Litigation.* Austin, 1913.

Camon, F. "Figura e ambiente di Iperbole," *RSC* IV (1961), 182–197.

Carcopino, J. *L'ostracisme athénien.* 2d ed. Paris, 1935.

Cole, J. W. "Perdiccas and Athens," *Phoenix* XXVIII (1974), 55–72.

Connor, W. R. *The New Politicians of Fifth-Century Athens.* Princeton, 1971.

Courby, F. "Le sanctuaire d'Apollon Délien," *BCH* XLV (1921), 174–241.

Curtius, E. *Peloponnesos.* 2 vols. Gotha, 1851.

Davies, J. K. *Athenian Propertied Families.* Oxford, 1971.

De Sanctis, G. "I precedenti della grande spedizione ateniese in Sicilia," *Riv. Fil.* n.s. VII (1929), 433–456.

———. *Problemi di storia antica.* Bari, 1932.

Dickie, M. W. "Thucydides, not Philistus," *GRBS* XVII (1976), 217–219.

Donini, G. "Thuc. 7.42.3: Does Thucydides Agree with Demosthenes' View?" *Hermes* XCII (1964), 116–119.

Dover, K. J. "Anapsephisis in Fifth-Century Athens," *JHS* LXXV (1955), 17–20.

———. "Review of H.-P. Drögemüller, *Syrakus,*" in *Phoenix* XXV (1971), 282–285.

———. "Review of P. Green, *Armada from Athens,*" in *Phoenix* XXVI (1972), 297–300.

Drögemüller, H.-P. *Syrakus, Gymnasium.* Beiheft VI. Heidelberg, 1969.

Fabricius, K. *Das Antike Syrakus, Klio.* Beiheft XXXII. Leipzig, 1932.

Ferguson, W. S. "Sparta and the Peloponnese," *CAH* V (1940), 254–281.

———. "The Athenian Expedition to Sicily," *CAH* V (1940), 282–311.

Finley, J. H. "The Unity of Thucydides' History," *HSCP,* Suppl. I, 1940, 255ff.

———. *Thucydides.* Cambridge, Mass., 1942.

Fornara, C. *The Athenian Board of Generals.* Wiesbaden, 1971.

Forrest, W. G. *A History of Sparta, 950–192 B.C.* London, 1968.

Fougères, G. *Mantinée et l'arcadie orientale.* Paris, 1895.

Freeman, E. A. *A History of Sicily.* 4 vols. Oxford, 1891–1894.

Fuqua, C. "Possible Implications of the Ostracism of Hyperbolus," *TAPA* XCVI (1965), 165–179.

Gilbert, G. *Handbuch der Griechischen Staatsalterthümer.* Leipzig, 1865.

———. *Beiträge zur innern geschichte Athens im zeitalter des peloponnesischen Krieges.* Leipzig, 1877.

Gillis, D. "Collusion at Mantineia," *RIL* XCVII (1963), 199–226.

Gomme, A. W. *Essays in Greek History and Literature.* Oxford, 1937.

———. *A Historical Commentary on Thucydides.* I–III. Oxford, 1950–1956.

———. "Four Passages in Thucydides," *JHS* LXXI (1951), 70–80.

_____. *More Essays in Greek History and Literature*. Oxford, 1962.

_____, A. Andrewes, and K. J. Dover. *A Historical Commentary on Thucydides*. IV. Oxford, 1970.

Green, P. *Armada from Athens*. New York, 1970.

Greenidge, A. H. *A Handbook of Greek Constitutional History*. London, 1896.

Grenfell, B. D. and A. S. Hunt, eds. *Oxyrhynchus Papyri*. V. London, 1908.

Griffith, G. T. "The Union of Corinth and Argos (392–386 B.C.)," *Historia* I (1950), 236–256.

Grote, G. *A History of Greece*. 12 vols. New York, 1855.

Hamilton, C. D. "The Politics of Revolution in Corinth, 395–386 B.C.," *Historia* XXI (1972), 21–37.

Hatzfeld, J. *Alcibiade: Etude sur l'histoire d'Athènes à la fin du Ve siècle*. 2d ed. Paris, 1951.

Henderson, B. W. *The Great War between Athens and Sparta*. London, 1927.

Hignett, C. *A History of the Athenian Constitution*. Oxford, 1952.

Hiller von Gaertringen, F. *Inscriptiones Graecae*. I, *editio minor, Inscriptiones Atticae Euclidis anno anteriores*. Berlin, 1924.

Holm, A. *Geschichte Siziliens im Altherthum*. 3 vols. Leipzig, 1870–1898.

Huart, P. *Le vocabulaire de l'analyse psychologique dans l'oeuvre de Thucydide*. Paris, 1968.

Jacoby, F. *Die Fragmente der griechischen Historiker*. 3 vols.: I–II, Berlin, 1923–1930; III, Leyden, 1940.

Kagan, D. "Corinthian Diplomacy after the Peace of Nicias," *AJP* LXXXI (1960), 291–310.

_____. "The Economic Origins of the Corinthian War (395–387 B.C.)," *Parola del Passato* LXXX (1961), 333–339.

_____. "Argive Politics and Policy after the Peace of Nicias," *CP* LVII (1962), 209–218.

_____. "Corinthian Politics and the Revolution of 392 B.C.," *Historia* XI (1962), 447–457.

_____. *The Outbreak of the Peloponnesian War*. Ithaca, 1969.

_____. *The Archidamian War*. Ithaca, 1974.

Kebric, R. C. "Implications of Alcibiades' Relationship with Endius," *Mnemosyne* XXIX (1976), 72–78.

Kelly, T. "The Traditional Enmity between Sparta and Argos: The Birth and Development of a Myth," *AHR* LXXV (1970), 971–1003.

_____. "Cleobulus, Xenares, and Thucydides' Account of the Demolition of Panactum," *Historia* XXI (1972), 159–169.

_____. "Argive Foreign Policy in the Fifth Century B.C.," *CP* LXIX (1974), 81–99.

Kopff, E. C. "Thucydides 7.42.3: An Unrecognized Fragment of Philistus," *GRBS* XVII (1976), 23–30.

_____. "Philistus Still," *GRBS* XVII (1976), 220–221.

Kromayer, J. *Antike Schlachtfelder in Griechenland.* I. Berlin, 1903.
—— and G. Veith. *Antike Schlachtfelder.* IV. Berlin, 1926.
Laffi, U. "La spedizione ateniese in Sicilia del 415 a.C.," *Rivista Storica Italiana* LXXXII (1970), 277–307.
Larsen, J. A. O. *Greek Federal States.* Oxford, 1968.
Lewis, D. M. "After the Profanation of the Mysteries," *ASI*, 177–191.
Liebeschütz, W. "Thucydides and the Sicilian Expedition," *Historia* XVII (1968), 289–306.
Loring, W. "Some Ancient Routes in the Peloponnese," *JHS* XV (1895), 25–89.
Lotze, D. "Mothakes," *Historia* XI (1962), 427–435.
MacDowell, D. *Andokides on the Mysteries.* Oxford, 1962.
Marr, J. L. "Andocides' Part in the Mysteries and Hermae Affairs, 415 B.C.," *CQ* n.s. XXI (1971), 326–338.
Mattingly, H. B. "The Growth of Athenian Imperialism," *Historia* XII (1963), 257–273.
——. "Athenian Finance in the Peloponnesian War," *BCH* XCII (1968), 460–485.
McGregor, M. F. "The Genius of Alcibiades," *Phoenix* XIX (1965), 27–46.
Meiggs, R. *The Athenian Empire.* Oxford, 1972.
—— and D. Lewis. *A Selection of Greek Historical Inscriptions to the End of the Fifth Century B.C.* Oxford, 1964.
Meritt, B. D. "Athens and Carthage," *Athenian Studies Presented to William Scott Ferguson.* HSCP, Suppl. I. Cambridge, Mass., 1940, 247–253.
——. "The Alliance between Athens and Egesta," *BCH* LXXXVIII (1964), 413–415.
——, H. T. Wade-Gery, and M. F. McGregor. *The Athenian Tribute Lists.* 4 vols.: I, Cambridge, Mass., 1939; II–IV, Princeton, 1949–1953.
Meyer, Eduard. *Forschungen zur alten Geschichte.* II. Halle, 1899.
——. *Geschichte des Altertums.* 5th ed., reprinted in 1954 and 1956, Basel.
Meyer, Ernst. "Methydrion," *PW* XV (1932), 1287–1391.
——. "Oresthasion," *PW* XVIII (1939), 1014–1016.
Momigliano, A. "Le cause della spedizione in Sicilia," *Riv. Fil.* n.s. VII (1929), 371–377.
Morrison, J. S. and R. T. Williams. *Greek Oared Ships 900–322 B.C.* Cambridge, 1968.
Murray, H. A. "Two Notes on the Evaluation of Nicias in Thucydides," *BICS* VIII (1961), 33–46.
Pippin, A. "The *Demioprata* of Pollux, Attic Stelai, Part II," *Hesperia* XXV (1956), 318–325.
Popp, H. *Die Einwirkung von Vorzeichen, Opfern und Festen auf die Kriegführung der Griechen.* Würzburg, 1957.

Poralla, P. *Prosopographie der Lakedaimonier.* Breslau, 1913.
Powell, C. A. "Religion and the Sicilian Expedition," *Historia* XXVIII (1979), 15-31.
Pritchett, W. K. "Attic Stelai, Part I," *Hesperia* XXII (1953), 225-299.
———. "Dotted Letters in Greek Epigraphy," *AJA* LIX (1955), 55-61.
———. "Attic Stelai, Part II," *Hesperia* XXV (1956), 178-317.
———. "Five New Fragments of the Attic Stelai," *Hesperia* XXX (1961), 23-29.
———. *Studies in Ancient Greek Topography,* 2 vols. Berkeley and Los Angeles, 1965 and 1969.
Rahe, P. A. "The Selection of Ephors at Sparta," *Historia* XXIX (1980), 385-401.
Raubitschek, A. E. "Athens and Halikyai," *TAPA* LXXV (1944), 10-12.
———. "The Case against Alcibiades (Andocides IV)," *TAPA* LXXIX (1948), 191-210.
Reverdin, O. "Remarques sur la vie politique d'Athènes au Vᵉ siècle," *Museum Helveticum* II (1945), 201-212.
Ste. Croix, G. E. M. de. *The Origins of the Peloponnesian War.* London and Ithaca, 1972.
Sartori, F. *Le eterie nella vita politica ateniese del VI e V sec. a.C.* Rome, 1957.
Seager, Robin. "After the Peace of Nicias: Diplomacy and Policy, 421-416 B.C.," *CQ* n.s. LXX (1976), 249-269.
Smart, J. D. "Athens and Egesta," *JHS* XCII (1972), 128-146.
Stahl, H.-P. *Thukydides.* Munich, 1967.
Swoboda, H. "Hyperbolos," *PW* IX (1916), 254-258.
Tod, M. N. *A Selection of Greek Historical Inscriptions to the End of the Fifth Century B.C.* 2d ed. Oxford, 1946.
Treu, M. "Athen und Karthago und die Thukydideische Darstellung," *Historia* III (1954/55), 41-57.
Wentker, H. *Sizilien und Athen.* Heidelberg, 1956.
Westlake, H. D. "Corinth and the Argive Coalition," *AJP* LXI (1940), 413-421.
———. "Nicias in Thucydides," *CQ* XXXV (1941), 58-65.
———. "Thucydides 2.65.11," *CQ* n.s. VIII (1958), 102-110.
———. *Individuals in Thucydides.* Cambridge, 1968.
———. *Essays on the Greek Historians and Greek History.* Manchester, 1969.
———. "Review of H.-P. Drögemüller, *Syrakus,*" in *CR* XXI (1971), 97-99.
Wick, T. E. "Athens' Alliance with Rhegium and Leontini," *Historia* XXV (1976), 288-304.
———. "A Note on the Date of the Athenian-Egestan Alliance," *JHS* XCV (1978), 186-190.
Will, E. *Korinthiaka.* Paris, 1955.

_____. "Review of O. Aurenche, *Les groupes*," in *Revue de Philologie* LI (1977), 92–96.

Woodhead, A. G. "I.G., I², 95 and the Ostracism of Hyperbolus," *Hesperia* XVIII (1949), 78–83.

_____. *Thucydides on the Nature of Power*. Cambridge, Mass., 1972.

Woodhouse, W. J. "The Campaign and Battle of Mantinea in 418 B.C.," *BSA* XXII (1916–1918), 51–84.

_____. *King Agis of Sparta and His Campaign in Arcadia in 418 B.C.* Oxford, 1933.

General Index

Index of Modern Authors

Index of Ancient Authors and Inscriptions

Library of Congress Cataloging in Publication Data

Kagan, Donald.
  The Peace of Nicias and the Sicilian Expedition

  Bibliography: p.
  Includes indexes.
  1. Greece—History—Peloponnesian War, 431-404 B.C. I. Title.
DF229.K33   938'.05   81-3150
                              AACR2

ISBN 0-8014-1367-2

Lightning Source UK Ltd.
Milton Keynes UK
UKOW04f1959121017
310781UK00001B/36/P